MW01205724

INTRODUCTION TO
COMPUTER PROGRAMMING
RPG

PUBLISHING CO.

ANAHEIM PUBLISHING COMPANY

Specialist in Data Processing Textbooks

CERTIFICATE IN DATA PROCESSING REFERENCE MANUAL

  REVIEW MANUAL FOR CERTIFICATE IN DATA PROCESSING, Thomas J. Cashman

COMPUTER PROGRAMMING

  INTRODUCTION TO COMPUTER PROGRAMMING SYSTEM/360 COBOL, Thomas J. Cashman
  IBM SYSTEM/360 COBOL PROBLEM TEXT, Thomas J. Cashman
  IBM SYSTEM/360 COBOL DISK/TAPE ADVANCED CONCEPTS, Shelly & Cashman
  DOS JOB CONTROL FOR COBOL PROGRAMMERS, Shelly & Cashman
  IBM SYSTEM/360 RPG PROGRAMMING, Volume I - INTRODUCTION, Fletcher & Cashman
  IBM SYSTEM/360 RPG PROGRAMMING, Volume II - ADVANCED CONCEPTS, Fletcher & Cashman
  IBM SYSTEM/360 ASSEMBLER LANGUAGE, Cashman & Shelly
  IBM SYSTEM/360 ASSEMBLER LANGUAGE WORKBOOK, Cashman & Shelly
  IBM SYSTEM/360 ASSEMBLER LANGUAGE DISK/TAPE ADVANCED CONCEPTS, Shelly & Cashman
  DOS JOB CONTROL FOR ASSEMBLER LANGUAGE PROGRAMMERS, Shelly & Cashman
  INTRODUCTION TO COMPUTER PROGRAMMING SYSTEM/360 PL/I, Shelly & Cashman
  MATHEMATICS ORIENTED COMPUTER PROGRAMMING WITH BASIC FORTRAN IV, Luter & Johnson
  DOS UTILITIES SORT/MERGE MULTIPROGRAMMING, Shelly & Cashman
  OS JOB CONTROL, Shelly & Cashman
  BASIC LOGIC FOR PROGRAM FLOWCHARTING AND TABLE SEARCH, Jones & Oliver
  INTRODUCTION TO FLOWCHARTING AND COMPUTER PROGRAMMING LOGIC, Shelly & Cashman
  INTRODUCTION TO COMPUTER PROGRAMMING BASIC FORTRAN IV - A PRACTICAL APPROACH,
                                                              Keys & Cashman

  INTRODUCTION TO COMPUTER PROGRAMMING RPG, Shelly & Cashman

INTRODUCTION TO DATA PROCESSING

  BASIC PROJECTS IN DATA PROCESSING, Cashman & Keys
  PRACTICAL PROJECTS IN DATA PROCESSING, Cashman & Keys
  INTRODUCTION TO CONTROL PANEL WIRING - 548 INTERPRETER, Cashman & Keys
  CONTROL PANEL WIRING - 514 REPRODUCER, Cashman & Keys
  CONTROL PANEL WIRING - 85 COLLATOR, Cashman & Keys
  CONTROL PANEL WIRING - 402 ACCOUNTING MACHINE, Cashman & Keys
  CONTROL PANEL WIRING - 407 ACCOUNTING MACHINE, Cashman & Keys

PUBLISHING CO.

INTRODUCTION TO COMPUTER PROGRAMMING RPG

By:

Gary B. Shelly
Educational Consultant
Instructor, Long Beach City College

&

Thomas J. Cashman, CDP, B.A., M.A.
Long Beach City College
Long Beach, California

ANAHEIM PUBLISHING COMPANY
1120 E. ASH
FULLERTON, CALIFORNIA

First Printing
November 1972

ISBN 0 - 88236 - 225 - 9

Library of Congress Catalog Card Number: 72 - 95673

ⓒ *Copyright 1972 Anaheim Publishing Company*

All rights reserved. This book or any part thereof may not be
reproduced without the written permission of the publisher.

PREFACE

Since the introduction of the System/360, the Report Program Generator programming language has played an important part in business application programming. RPG is the most prominent programming language used on small scale computer systems with a number of manufacturers, and an extension of RPG called RPG II is the predominant language on the IBM System/3 computer series. In addition, RPG is widely used in both DOS and OS environments for programming problems not requiring the sophistication of other languages such as COBOL or Assembler Language.

As RPG is basically an application-oriented rather than a procedure-oriented programming language, it is sometimes the first programming language to which beginning students are introduced. This text is oriented toward the beginning student who has not had experience in writing computer programs. The text uses a problem-oriented approach which means that the student is introduced to programming concepts and techniques by means of a series of programs illustrating typical business applications. Only those statements and segments of the language necessary in the solution of the problem are explained. The student, therefore, learns RPG programming in relation to the total problem, and is not burdened with the task of remembering a series of isolated facts concerning the individual segments of the language. Each of the chapters in the text introduces additional programming concepts. Upon completion of the text the student will have been exposed to the most frequently used characteristics of the language and should have the capability of writing a wide variety of RPG programs.

Every effort has been made to simplify the concepts presented in the text through the use of realistic problems, numerous examples and illustrations, and completely documented and fully programmed examples. Each of the programs illustrated has been fully tested and executed on a System/360 Model 30 computer operating under DOS. The programs explained in each of the chapters include the following operations or programming techniques: Basic Input/Output, Addition, Subtraction, Multiplication, Division, Editing, Total Processing, Comparisons, Control Codes, Report Headings, Single and Multi-Level Control Breaks, RPG Fixed Program Logic, Group Indication and Group Printing, Field-Record Relations, Multiple Record Types, Table Look-Up, Matching Records, Magnetic Tape, Sequential Disk Processing, Indexed Sequential Access Method, Record Address Files, and Chaining.

At the conclusion of each chapter except the first there are four types of activities which should be performed by the student and which lead to a more thorough understanding of the information within the chapter. The first activity is a set of Review Questions which require the student to apply the knowledge learned within the chapter to a set of questions. The next activity is a series of short coding problems which require the student to write small portions of a program and test the student's skill in using RPG to perform various functions. The third activity involves actually debugging RPG programs. In each chapter, one problem concerns correcting diagnostics within the program and one problem concerns correcting errors which occur in the execution of the program. Source listings, diagnostics, and output listings are given for the student to correct. The fourth activity involves actually writing RPG programs. Two programming assignments are included for each chapter. The first assignment is relatively close to the program illustrated in the text and requires a basic understanding of the problem and concepts presented in the text. The second programming assignment is an extension of the concepts presented and will challenge the student to broaden the concepts to fit a more complicated problem. For all of the programming assignments, test data and the DOS job control statements required for the program are included.

A comprehensive set of appendices is included for student reference covering such topics as Internal Data Representation, Fixed RPG program logic, and an explanation of the RPG source listing and diagnostics. Including these topics in the appendices offers the instructor flexibility in presenting these topics in the course without disturbing the logical sequence of the presentation of the text material. It is suggested, however, that the contents of the appendices be included as a formal part of the course of study, and that the student using the text be thoroughly familiar with the information presented in each of the appendices upon conclusion of the course in RPG programming.

After the student has completed the study of the material contained in the text, he should have a firm foundation in the concepts of programming in RPG and should be capable of solving a wide variety of business type problems using card, printer, magnetic tape, and direct-access devices, including the sequential access method and the indexed sequential access method. In addition, he will have the ability to write programs using RPG II, which is widely used on the IBM System/3, as RPG II is merely an extension of the RPG programming language taught in this book.

This book may be effectively used in a one semester course in computer programming at the junior colleges, colleges, and private or vocational schools teaching RPG. Professional programmers wishing to learn RPG should find no difficulty in applying known programming concepts to the RPG language, and the beginning student of data processing should find the text simple enough to benefit from "home study".

The authors would like to thank Carole Foth for her patience and the thorough job she did in preparing the finished copy from sometimes very rough drafts.

Gary B. Shelly

Thomas J. Cashman

TABLE OF CONTENTS

CHAPTER 1

INTRODUCTION TO PROGRAMMING

INTRODUCTION

The data processing industry has undergone dramatic changes since it first began in the late 1940's. Much of the drama has centered around the changes and improvements in the computer hardware and the related peripheral equipment such as card readers, magnetic tape units, disk storage devices, and other input/output units which are used with the computer.

As computer hardware has gone through an evolutionary period, so too has the art or science of programming. This includes both the jobs done by programmers and the methods available to the programmer for solving problems. Programming may be broken down into two broad categories: Systems programming and Applications programming. The systems programmer is concerned with writing programs that make it easier to operate and program computers. Systems programmers turn out control programs that operate input/output equipment, test programs that detect errors and malfunctions within the computer, utility programs, such as sorts, which provide for easy manipulation of data, and programming languages and compilers which are available for the applications programmer to use to solve problems.

Applications programming may be broken down into two general areas: Scientific and Engineering programming and Business programming. The scientific applications programmer is normally involved in programs requiring a great deal of complex mathematical work. In many cases, scientific applications programmers are also mathematicians or engineers who are using the computer to solve problems with which they are directly concerned.

The business applications programmer writes programs to solve problems relating to the business transactions of a company. Such applications as payroll, billing, and inventory control are the areas of concern to a business applications programmer. Business programming is normally not performed by a person such as an accountant or a production manager. Rather, in most businesses, the job of programming is assigned to an individual working in the data processing department. The business programmer writes a variety of programs for various business applications within a company.

BASIC PROGRAMMING CONCEPTS

Even though the types of programming may vary to a large extent, the task of the programmer is always the same, that is, write a program, or set of instructions, which direct the computer to process data in a way which will solve the given problem. The usefulness of computers stems from their ability to perform logical and arithmetic operations accurately and at very high speeds. The number and complexity of the basic operations that can be performed by a given machine varies from computer to computer, but all computers must have some type of program which consists of a series of instructions directing the operations of the computer.

An instruction which causes a computer to perform a given function consists of an operation code, which directs the computer to perform a specific operation, and one or more Operands which are normally used to reference where the data to be processed is stored. When the instruction is executed by the computer, the central processing unit interprets the operation code and the operand as a function to be performed. This concept of placing instructions in the storage unit of the computer to direct it to perform a specific operation is called the "Stored Program" concept.

The set of specific basic operations that can be performed by a given computer is called its instruction set. A portion of the instruction set of the System/360 computer is illustrated below.

Instruction	Machine Operation Code
Add Decimal	FA
Compare Decimal	F9
Divide Decimal	FD
Edit	DE
Edit and Mark	DF
Multiply Decimal	FC
Subtract Decimal	FB
Zero and Add	F8

Figure 1-1 Portion of the System/360 Instruction Set

Note from the example in Figure 1-1 that the operation code of the instruction to cause two numbers to be added is FA. Thus, the operation code "FA", when recorded in the storage unit of the computer and analyzed by the controlling electronic circuitry, will cause the computer to perform an addition operation.

As noted, an instruction which causes an operation to be performed normally consists of an Operation Code as illustrated in Figure 1-1 and one or more operands. The operands used with the addition instruction are illustrated below.

Operation Code   First Operand   Second Operand

FA   11 A047   A0B4

Figure 1-2 Example of Machine Language Instruction

Note from the example above that the operation code is "47". The first operand as illustrated in Figure 1-2 consists of the lengths which determine the size of the numbers to be added and the address of the first number to be added. The second operand contains the main storage location of the second number to be used in the add operation.

The instruction illustrated in Figure 1-2 is an example of a "machine-language" instruction, that is, an instruction in a format which the controlling circuitry of the computer can understand and which will cause the computer to perform the desired operation. In the early 1950's, all programming was done in machine language. Although machine language is not a complex language, it is difficult for human beings to work with. Programmers found writing programs in the language awkward, inconvenient, and subject to many errors. Because machine language was difficult to work with, "symbolic programming languages" were developed. These programming languages used symbols to represent machine language instructions. An example of a symbolic programming language is the "Assembler Language" which may be used on the System/360 computer. The assembler language provides for a series of symbolic representations of machine language operation codes. These symbolic representations are often called "Mnemonic operation codes".

The following chart illustrates several of the instructions which are available on the System/360 and the corresponding Mnemonic and Machine Language instructions.

Instruction	Mnemonic Operation Code	Machine Operation Code
Add Decimal	AP	FA
Compare Decimal	CP	F9
Divide Decimal	DP	FD
Edit	ED	DE
Edit and Mark	EDMK	DF
Multiply Decimal	MP	FC
Subtract Decimal	SP	FB
Zero and Add	ZAP	F8

Figure 1-3 Mnemonic and Machine Language Operation Codes

Note from the chart above that the Mnemonic Operation Codes correspond somewhat to the function of the instruction. For example, the Mnemonic Operation code for the add instruction is AP. The corresponding Machine Language operation code is FA.

In order to have the computer solve a problem, the user must give it a set of step-by-step instructions that will result in the solution of the given problem. Such a set of instructions is called a "program". Guided by a program stored in its memory, a computer can solve commercial and scientific problems at very rapid speeds and with remarkable accuracy.

As noted, symbolic programming languages were developed in order to ease the task of programming. An example of a program written in System/360 Assembler Language is illustrated below.

EXAMPLE

```
      LOC  OBJECT CODE     ADDR1 ADDR2  STMT    SOURCE STATEMENT

                                        1       PRINT NOGEN
      000000                            2 PGM1  START 0
                                        3 NAMEFLE DTFCD DEVICE=2501,                    C
                                                        DEVADDR=SYSIPT,                 C
                                                        TYPEFLE=INPUT,                  C
                                                        IOAREA1=CARD,                   C
                                                        EOFADDR=ENDJOB
                                        24 PRINTFL DTFPR DEVICE=1403,                   C
                                                        DEVADDR=SYSLST,                 C
                                                        IOAREA1=LINEOUT,                C
                                                        BLKSIZE=132
      000068 0520                       45 BEGIN BALR  2,0               ESTABLISH BASE REGISTER
      00006A                            46       USING *,2
                                        47       OPEN  NAMEFLE,PRINTFL   OPEN FILES
                                        56 READCARD GET  NAMEFLE         READ A CARD
      00008A 9240 20B6       00120      61       MVI   LINEOUT,X'40'     CLEAR PRINT LINE
      00008E D282 20B7 20B6 00121 00120 62       MVC   LINEOUT+1(131),LINEOUT
      000094 D217 20B6 2067 00120 000D1 63       MVC   NAMEOUT(24),NAME  MOVE NAME TO OUTPUT LINE
      00009A D218 20D3 207F 0013D 000E9 64       MVC   ADRESOUT(25),ADDRESS  MOVE ADDRESS TO OUTPUT LINE
      0000A0 D218 20F1 2098 0015B 00102 65       MVC   CITYOUT(25),CITY  MOVE CITY TO OUTPUT LINE
      0000A6 D204 210F 20B1 00179 0011B 66       MVC   ZIPOUT(5),ZIP     MOVE ZIP TO OUTPUT LINE
                                        67       PUT   PRINTFL           PRINT A LINE
      0000B8 47F0 2014       0007E      72       B     READCARD          BRANCH TO READ ANOTHER CARD
                                        73 ENDJOB CLOSE NAMEFLE,PRINTFL  CLOSE FILES
                                        82       EOJ
      0000D0                            85 CARD  DS    0CL80             DEFINE FORMAT OF CARD
      0000D0                            86       DS    CL1               BLANK
      0000D1                            87 NAME  DS    CL24              NAME FIELD
      0000E9                            88 ADDRESS DS   CL25             ADDRESS FIELD
      000102                            89 CITY  DS    CL25              CITY FIELD
      00011B                            90 ZIP   DS    CL5               ZIP CODE FIELD
      000120                            91 LINEOUT DS   0CL132           DEFINE FORMAT OF PRINT LINE
      000120                            92 NAMEOUT DS   CL24             NAME AREA
      000138                            93       DS    CL5               BLANK
      00013D                            94 ADRESOUT DS  CL25             ADDRESS AREA
      000156                            95       DS    CL5               BLANK
      00015B                            96 CITYOUT DS   CL25             CITY AREA
      000174                            97       DS    CL5               BLANK
      000179                            98 ZIPOUT DS    CL5              ZIP AREA
      00017E                            99       DS    CL38              BLANK
      000068                            100      END   BEGIN
```

Figure 1-4 Example of System/360 Assembler Language Program

From the example above it can be seen that the program consists of a series of machine oriented instructions which cause the computer to process the data.

FORTRAN

Although the use of symbolic programming languages was far superior to the use of machine language programs, it was also recognized that in order to effectively use a computer system as a tool for the solution of scientific and business problems, there was a need for "high-level" programming languages, that is, programming languages which were not machine-oriented.

In 1957, International Business Machines released the specifications for a high-level scientific oriented language called FORTRAN (FORmula TRANslation). This programming language substantially relieved the user from having a detailed knowledge of the internal operation of an electronic data processing system, and allowed the programmer to define the input to be processed, the calculations to be performed, and the output to be produced in a format far removed from the internal operation of the computer. With FORTRAN, the programmer was not required to have a detailed knowledge of internal data representation, storage locations, etc. An example of a FORTRAN program is illustrated below.

EXAMPLE

```
                    DISK OPERATING SYSTEM/360 FORTRAN
      DIMENSION NAME(24),KADRES(25),KCITY(25)
    1 FORMAT (1X,24A1,25A1,25A1,I5)
    2 FORMAT (1X,24A1,5X,25A1,5X,25A1,5X,I5)
    3 READ (1,1) NAME,KADRES,KCITY,KZIP
      IF (KZIP - 99999)4,5,5
    4 WRITE (3,2) NAME,KADRES,KCITY,KZIP
      GO TO 3
    5 STOP
      END
```

Figure 1-5 Example of FORTRAN Program

In the example above it can be seen that the format of the language is much closer to mathematical notation than it is to the machine-oriented language, Assembler Language. It is this way so that the scientific or mathematical programmer is able to express the processing to be performed in a manner similar to the notation he is familiar with.

COBOL

The need for a "high-level" business oriented language was also recognized. On May 28 of 1959, a meeting was called by the Department of Defense, at the suggestion of a small group of computer users, manufacturers, and universities to discuss the problem of of developing a common business language for computers. This original committee meeting was called CODASYL (Conference On DAta SYstems Languages). The purpose of this conference was to consider both the desirability and feasibility of establishing a common language for use by all manufacturers of electronic data processing systems. A short range committee was established and composed of representatives from six manufacturers (Burroughs, IBM, Honeywell, RCA, Remington Rand, and Sylvania Electric Products); two government agencies, the Air Material Command, and the Department of the Navy, in addition to a representative from the Bureau of Standards. The first specifications for the new programming language called COBOL (COmmon Business Oriented Language) were released in April of 1960. Since that time a number of revisions and additions have been made to the original language specifications.

The purpose of COBOL was to provide a common business-oriented language which could be used on a number of different machines manufactured by different computer manufacturers. In addition, a basic objective was that the language was to be natural, where natural was defined as "English-like". COBOL was not designed to permit concise writing; on the contrary, the language is very "wordy". However, the benefit gained from this is the increased readability of the programs and the "built-in" documentation because of the readability of the language. The following is an example of a COBOL program.

EXAMPLE

```
LINE NO.                  SOURCE STATEMENT                           CBD CL3-5 08/13/70

   1        IDENTIFICATION DIVISION.
   2        PROGRAM-ID. 'PROB1'.
   3        AUTHOR. TJC.
   4        INSTALLATION. LONG BEACH.
   5        DATE-WRITTEN. 01/02/71.
   6        DATE-COMPILED. 01/02/71.
   7        SECURITY. UNCLASSIFIED.
   8        REMARKS. PROGRAM READS NAME AND ADDRESS CARDS AND PREPARES
   9           A PRINTED REPORT.
  10        ENVIRONMENT DIVISION.
  11        CONFIGURATION SECTION.
  12        SOURCE-COMPUTER. IBM-360 E30.
  13        OBJECT-COMPUTER. IBM-360 E30.
  14        INPUT-OUTPUT SECTION.
  15        FILE-CONTROL.
  16           SELECT NAME-ADDRESS-FILE ASSIGN TO 'SYS007' UNIT-RECORD
  17           2501 UNIT.
  18           SELECT PRINTER-FILE ASSIGN TO 'SYS008' UNIT-RECORD
  19           1403 UNIT.
  20        DATA DIVISION.
  21        FILE SECTION.
  22        FD  NAME-ADDRESS-FILE,
  23           RECORDING MODE IS F,
  24           LABEL RECORDS ARE OMITTED,
  25           DATA RECORD IS CARD.
  26        01  CARD.
  27           03 FILLER                PICTURE X.
  28           03 NAME                  PICTURE X(24).
  29           03 ADDRESS               PICTURE X(25).
  30           03 CITY                  PICTURE X(25).
  31           03 ZIP                   PICTURE X(5).
  32        FD  PRINTER-FILE,
  33           RECORDING MODE IS F,
  34           LABEL RECORDS ARE OMITTED,
  35           DATA RECORD IS LINEOUT.
  36        01  LINEOUT.
  37           03 FILLER                PICTURE X.
  38           03 NAME-OUT              PICTURE X(24).
  39           03 FILLER                PICTURE X(5).
  40           03 ADDRESS-OUT           PICTURE X(25).
  41           03 FILLER                PICTURE X(5).
  42           03 CITY-OUT              PICTURE X(25).
  43           03 FILLER                PICTURE X(5).
  44           03 ZIP-OUT               PICTURE X(5).
  45           03 FILLER                PICTURE X(38).
  46        PROCEDURE DIVISION.
  47        BEGIN.
  48           OPEN INPUT NAME-ADDRESS-FILE OUTPUT PRINTER-FILE.
  49        READ-CARD.
  50           READ NAME-ADDRESS-FILE AT END GO TO END-JOB.
  51           MOVE SPACES TO LINEOUT.
  52           MOVE NAME TO NAME-OUT.
  53           MOVE ADDRESS TO ADDRESS-OUT.
  54           MOVE CITY TO CITY-OUT.
  55           MOVE ZIP TO ZIP-OUT.
  56           WRITE LINEOUT AFTER ADVANCING 1 LINES.
  57           GO TO READ-CARD.
  58        END-JOB.
  59           CLOSE NAME-ADDRESS-FILE, PRINTER-FILE.
  60           STOP RUN.
```

Figure 1-6 Example of COBOL program

Note from the example above that the language bears no resemblance to the machine-oriented Assembler Language. It does, however, allow the programmer to write the specifications of the program in a manner which is easy to read and which normally produces fewer errors than the same program written in a machine-oriented language.

RPG

In addition to FORTRAN and COBOL, many other "high-level" programming languages have been developed in order to facilitate the writing of programs. One of the most useful when writing programs for business applications is RPG (Report Program Generator). RPG is not a "procedure-oriented" programming language such as Assembler Language or COBOL where the processing is determined by a sequence of instructions specified to process a given procedure. Rather, it is a "problem-oriented" language in which the procedures to be followed are fixed and the programmer merely specifies the processing which is to be accomplished on RPG Specification forms.

RPG offers many of the programming capabilities of machine-oriented and high-level programming languages but, in most cases, is easier and quicker to code. Its primary advantage is that it provides a quick and easy method of writing programs which do not require a great deal of intricate logic and the ability to manipulate data in a complex manner.

When a programmer codes a program in RPG, he writes the program on coding sheets which are designed for the Report Program Generator. The example below illustrates the File Description Sheet, the Input Specification Sheet, and the Output-Format Specification Sheet which are used with RPG.

EXAMPLE

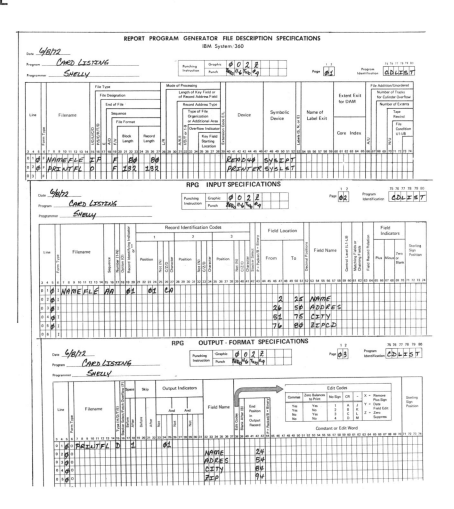

Figure 1-7 Example of RPG Source Program

1.7

Note from the example in Figure 1-7 that the RPG Specification sheets allow the various entries which are required for the program to be written in predetermined columns of the form. Once this "Source Program" has been written on coding sheets, it is normally punched on cards to be processed by the computer. The following is the program after it has been punched on cards.

EXAMPLE

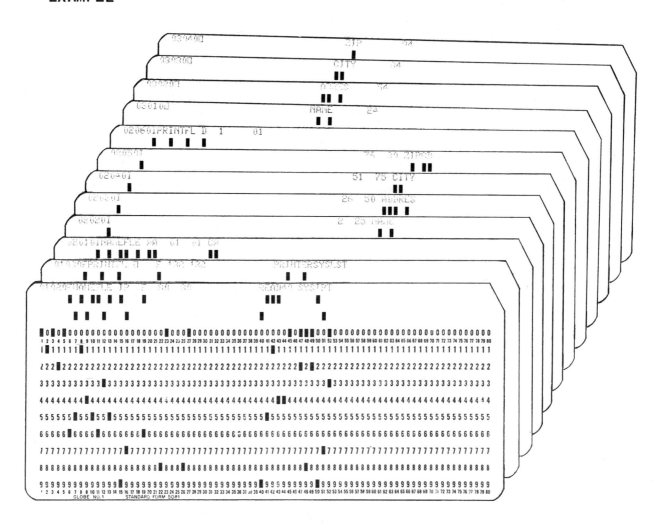

Figure 1-8 Source Deck Punched in Cards

Note from Figure 1-8 that the source program is punched on cards and is in the same format as the entries on the program specification sheets. This source program contains all of the instructions which are required in order to process the program.

It should be noted that the computer can only understand instructions on a machine language level; therefore, the statements written on the Program Specification Sheets must be converted to machine language instructions prior to processing data with the program. For example, an ADD statement in an RPG program must be converted to the machine language operation code FA in order for the computer to "understand" the function to be performed.

Because computers only understand instructions in machine language form, a "translator" program must be used which enables a computer to translate the RPG source statements into machine language instructions. This "translator" program is called a "Compiler". A programming language and its associated "compiler" is called a "programming system".

The following diagram illustrates the basic steps to compile an RPG program.

EXAMPLE

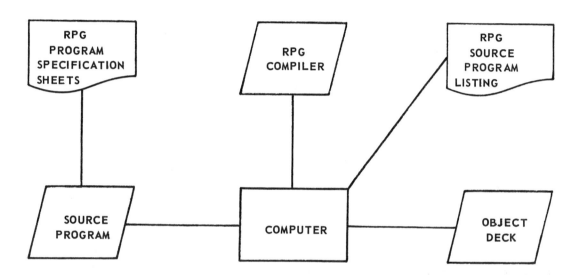

Figure 1-9 Step 2 in Compiling RPG Source Program

To "convert" a program from a symbolic form to machine language, the Compiler is read into the storage unit of the computer followed by the RPG Source program which is normally punched on cards. The compiler then "translates" the symbolic statements of the source program into a machine language form and punches an object program. The Object Program is the machine language instructions generated by the Compiler from the RPG Source statements.

The compiler also provides auxiliary functions that assist the programmer in checking and documenting programs. Some of these functions are:

Source Program Listings: A listing of the source program statements may be produced by the RPG compiler for each source program which is compiled.

Error Indications: As a source program is compiled, it is analyzed for actual or potential errors in the use of the RPG language. Detected errors are indicated in the program listing.

The following is a segment of a listing of an RPG program generated by the compiler and the "diagnostics" or errors detected by the compiler. These errors must be corrected before the computer can execute the object program and process the data.

Source Program Listing

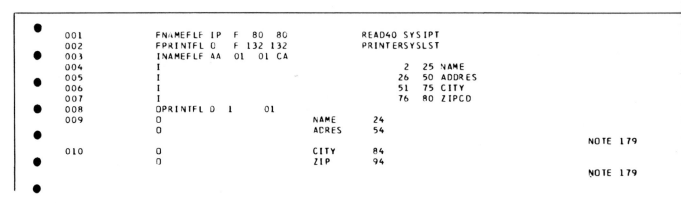

Diagnostics

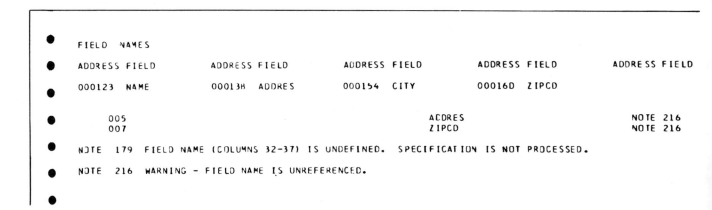

Figure 1-10 RPG Source Listing and Diagnostics

PROGRAMMING STEPS

Whenever a problem is to be solved on the computer, the programmer must write the program which will process the data on the computer. Contrary to popular belief, however, all of a programmer's time is not spent in "writing" the program, that is, coding the program in a programming language. A great deal of the programmer's time is spent in analyzing a problem, determining the solution to the problem, testing the program to ensure that it works properly, and documenting the program. The various duties which are performed by the programmer are explained below.

1. Problem Analysis — The normal sequence of an application which is to be implemented on a computer is for a systems analyst to design the overall system, which is composed of one or more programs. The systems analyst gathers the information which is necessary to comprise the system from the eventual user of the system, from management, and from past experience which would indicate the type of processing which should be included in the system. He then places this information in a form which may be communicated to the programmer. Typically, the manner of presentation will include record formats, that is, the format of the input and output records which are to be processed by the program, printer spacing charts which are used to illustrate the format of a printed report, and some type of written narrative which will describe in detail the processing which is to take place within the system and within each program included in the system. The example in Figure 1-11 illustrates a record layout form and a printer spacing chart for a "typical" application involving the preparation of a sales analysis report.

Card Input

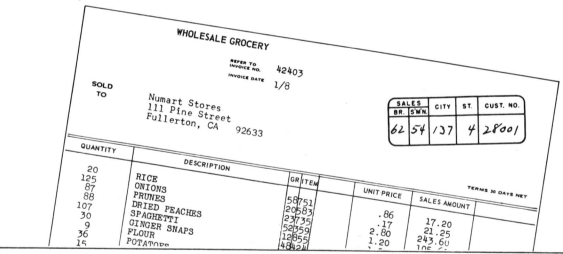

Sales Order and Multiple-Card Layout Form

1.11

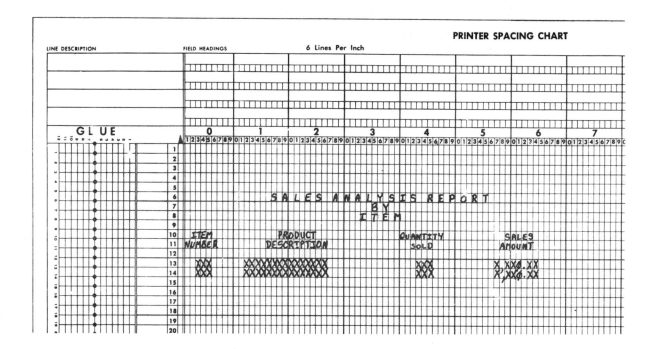

Figure 1 - 11   Example of Printer Spacing Chart and Multiple - Card Layout Form

In the example in Figure 1 - 11 it can be seen that a Multiple - Card Layout form is used to specify the layout of the card which is to be processed, and that the printer spacing chart is used to illustrate the format of the report which is to be produced by the program.

To layout a report on the Printer Spacing Chart the programmer selects the print positions for the headings and fields to be printed on the report and makes a notation in the selected positions.   The numbers across the top of the spacing chart represent the actual print positions used by the computer printer. The numbers down the left are line numbers.   There are six horizontal lines to an inch.   Heading or constant information to be printed is written on the printer spacing chart in the same form as it is to be printed on the report. Variable information is represented by placing an "X" in the appropriate position on the spacing chart. It should be noted that the position in a field where zero suppression ends is indicated by a zero rather than an "X" and punctuation is shown as it would appear in edited amounts.

When the programmer writes the program to process the data to produce the report, the definition of the input and printed output will normally be in the form of a Multiple - Card Layout Form and a Printer Spacing Chart.

An example of the printed report and the actual card which would be used as a result of the layouts presented in Figure 1-11 are illustrated below.

EXAMPLE

Card Input

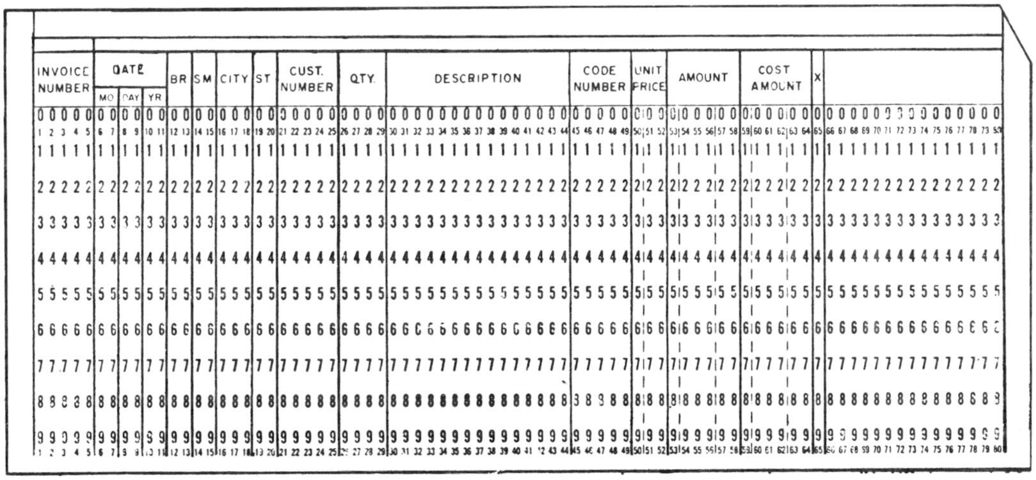

Printed Output

SALES ANALYSIS REPORT
BY
ITEM

ITEM NUMBER	PRODUCT DESCRIPTION	QUANTITY SOLD	SALES AMOUNT
8	AMMONIA	98	78.40
15	ANIMAL CRACKERS	9	8.37
24	APPLE SAUCE	100	50.00
32	APPLES	16	25.60
39	APRICOTS	9	42.30
48	ASPARAGUS	8	29.60
56	BROOMS	60	336.00
135	BUTTER SALT	47	145.70
152	CELERY	360	64.80
161	CEYLON TEA	70	77.00
169	CHICKEN SOUP	10	48.00
192	CHOW CHOW	60	226.80
207	CIDER	29	9.86
216	CLAM BROTH	290	406.00
233	COCOA	60	3.00
257	COFFEE	486	403.38
263	CONDENSED MILK	470	1,353.60
272	CORN	150	390.00
289	CRACKERS	50	120.00
312	DRIED PEACHES	20	62.00
359	FLOUR	183	150.06
383	GELATINE	26	210.60
408	GINGER SNAPS	30	43.50
424	HORSE RADISH	37	129.50
456	LEMON SODA	90	37.80

Figure 1-12 Example of Actual Print-Out and Card Input

As can be seen from the example above, the Sales report which is generated from the program is in the same format as the printer spacing chart in Figure 1-11. The same is true of the input card. Thus, through the use of the record layout forms, the analyst informs the programmer of the formats of the records to be processed by the program.

When the program specifications have been received from the systems analyst, the programmer must very carefully review the specifications so that every aspect of the program which he is to write is fully understood. Too much emphasis cannot be placed on the requirements that the programmer fully understand the processing which is to take place within a program. It is quite obvious that if the programmer does not understand what is required in a program, the program cannot possibly contain the proper coding to process the data. Beyond that basic truism, however, is the fact the a programmer can many times find errors or omissions within the system specifications which must be corrected prior to the programming effort. An extremely detailed perusal of the system specifications must always be undertaken before any coding is performed on the program.

2. Determine Problem Solution – Once the programmer has determined that the problem to be solved is fully understood, he must then determine the method of solving the problem. This task normally involves determining the program logic which must be used in order to get the correct results in a program and is many times the most difficult step in solving a problem on the computer. The techniques which are used to determine the logical processing which is to take place within a program are many and varied. They include flowcharting and decision tables or narrative instructions. Whatever technique is used to graphically illustrate the logic required to process the data within the program, it is necessary that the logic include all of the processing which is to take place in enough detail that the programmer can write the source program from the logic illustrated. With RPG much of the internal program logic is incorporated into the RPG compiler relieving the programmer of the need to flowchart program logic in most problems; nevertheless, it is essential that the programmer thoroughly understand the steps in the solution of the problem.

3. Coding – After the logic which is to be incorporated into a program has been thoroughly understood, the program is coded to reflect the processing which is to occur. The programmer should take great care in preparing the Program Specification Sheets to include all of the steps which are required for the program. Attention to detail and accurary in preparing the RPG program will result in fewer errors when the program is tested and a more reliable program after it is in production.

4. Testing and Debugging: After the RPG source program has been written, it is normally keypunched into cards so that it may be processed on the computer. After it has been key-punched, it is compiled on the computer as illustrated in Figure 1-9. As noted previously, when the compilation process is performed, errors are many times found in the coding due to improperly used statements or keypunching errors. These errors must be corrected by the programmer until the program is compiled with no errors in the source coding.

After a program has been successfully compiled, it must be tested in order to determine that the program is correct and the data is being processed properly. Testing a program involves several important steps which must be followed in order to ensure that a program is debugged completely and that it will operate successfully. These steps are explained below.

a). Desk Checking – After a program has been compiled, it should be "desk-checked" prior to being executed on the computer. Desk-checking refers to the process of the programmer "playing computer", that is, examining each source statement within the program as if the computer were processing the statements. By doing this, the programmer can find errors both in the use of statements and in the logic which will be performed by the program. Desk-checking is a very important part of debugging a program because errors can be found which would otherwise not be found until the program were actually processed on the computer.

b). Preparing Test Data — When a program is to be tested, it should be tested with data which was specifically prepared to test the various routines within the program. It should not be tested with data which will be processed by the program after it has been put into production, that is, after it has been debugged and is ready to be run using actual "live" data. The reason for this is that "live" data, no matter how it is chosen, is not likely to contain all of the situations which may occur in the program. Thus, some occurrences which are programmed for will never be adequately tested. It is these routines which are probably going to fail when the program is in production. Instead, the programmer should design data which can be used to test all aspects of the program so that all routines and processing decisions are tested. The preparation of test data is a difficult and arduous task but a program cannot be adequately tested unless good test data is used.

c). Program Debugging — After the program has been desk-checked and good test data has been prepared, the program may be tested on the computer. The number of test runs which will be required to completely debug a program is normally dependent upon the size and complexity of the program. Regardless of the size and complexity of the program, however, it is important that the program be completely debugged prior to being used in actual production runs. Too often it has been found that programs have not been entirely debugged prior to processing actual data and this leads to many problems both within the data processing department and with the users of the program. Testing a program is a difficult task and only when great care is used in testing will a properly debugged program result.

5. Documentation — Documentation is the process of recording the facts concerning a computer program. Included in the documentation will normally be a program narrative describing the routines and programming techniques used in the program, the source listing, the formats of the data which is processed by the program, and a sample running of the program including control cards which must be used and any reports which are produced by the program.

The documentation of a program is an often neglected job of the applications programmer. This neglect may be caused by data processing management, which desires the programmer to begin writing new programs, or by the programmer himself, who does not enjoy the rather mundane task of preparing narratives of his program and drawing file layouts, etc. It has been found, however, that proper documentation of a program is absolutely vital to the smooth functioning of a data processing department. In many applications, changes must be made to a program once it has been put into production and many times, the programmer making the changes is not the same person who originally wrote the program. Thus, if the "maintenance programmer", that is, the programmer who is making the changes, does not have sufficient documentation to indicate the processing which is occuring in the program and the methods used in the program, it becomes quite difficult to make changes which will work properly. It is, therefore, incumbent upon the programmer who originally writes a program to supply enough documentation to ensure that any programmer assigned to make changes to the program can do so with a minimum of time spent on the job of determining how the program processes the data.

SUMMARY

As was noted previously, the job of a programmer is much more diversified than just coding a program in a programming language. The jobs of testing a program and preparing documentation require a goodly portion of the programmer's time and effort. The task of problem analysis and problem solving also require much time and are quite critical to the solution of problems on the computer.

Regardless of the problem to be solved and the method of solution, however, the program must be written in order for the computer to process the program. As noted, a number of programming languages are available. The one to which the remainder of the text will be devoted, RPG, is a major programming language in business applications and a knowledge of RPG gives the programmer an important tool in business application programming.

REVIEW QUESTIONS

1. Discuss the difference between a machine-oriented instruction as found in Assembler Language and the actual machine language instruction.

2. What are the steps involved in translating a source program to a machine language program?

3. Discuss the importance of problem analysis in the steps of programming.

CHAPTER 2

BASIC INPUT/OUTPUT

INTRODUCTION

After the input for the solution of a problem has been established, the format of the printed report developed, and the approach to the solution of the problem determined, the coding of the RPG program may take place. Programming for basic input/output operations, such as reading a card and preparing a printed report, requires an understanding of the following RPG concepts:

1. Use of the RPG Heading Control Card.

2. Use of the File Description Specifications Form to define the card input file and the printer output file.

3. Use of the Input Specifications Form to define the fields in the card input record.

4. Use of the Output - Format Specifications Form to define the report to be printed on the printer.

To illustrate the basic concepts of programming and the entries required to write an RPG program, a sample program is introduced in this chapter which is to prepare a Name and Address Listing from a file of Name and Address cards. The input, output, and RPG program to produce the listing are illustrated on the following pages.

Input for the sample problem is a Name and Address File which consists of punched cards. These punched cards contain a Name field in card columns 1-25, an Address field in card columns 26-50, and a City/State field in card columns 51-75. The card format is illustrated in Figure 2-1.

Input

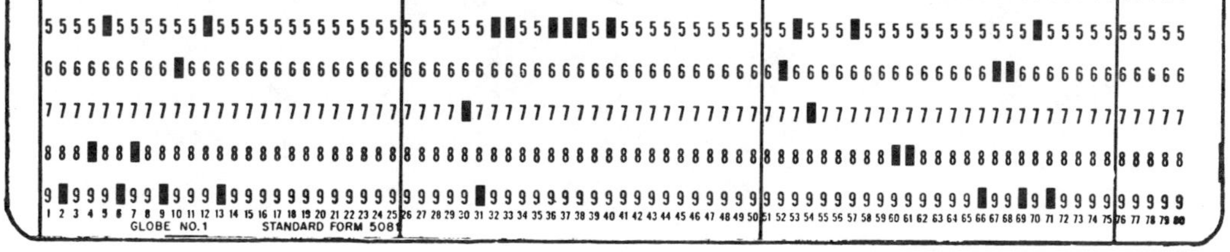

Figure 2-1 Name and Address Card

The output of the sample program is to consist of a printed report listing all of the fields on the cards. A printer spacing chart and the related output are illustrated below.

Output

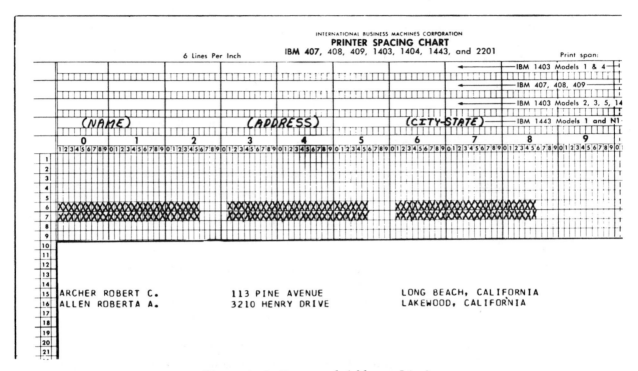

Figure 2-2 Name and Address Listing

It can be seen from the printer spacing chart and the related computer printout that the Name field, the Address field, and the City/State field from the card input are printed on the output listing.

The basic computer system used to process the Name and Address file and all of the programs in subsequent chapters consists of three 2311 Disk Storage Units, a 2540 Card Reader and Punch, a 1403 Printer, four 2415 Tape Units, and an IBM System/360 Model 30 Central Processing Unit with 65,536 bytes of main storage.

In order to process the data, the RPG program must read the input card and write the output report. The following steps take place when the RPG program prepares the printed report from the input cards.

Step 1: A Card containing a Name, Address and City/State is read into an Input Area in Main Storage.

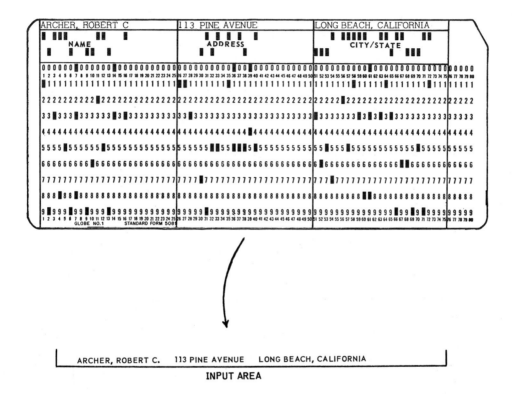

Figure 2-3 Data Card Is Read

Step 2: The data from the input area is moved to "Input Fields" in main storage.

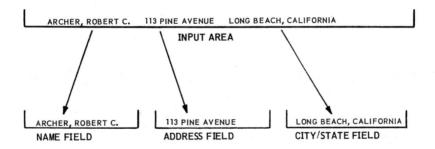

Figure 2-4 Data is Moved to Input Fields

2.3

Step 3: The data is moved from the "Input Fields" to an output area in main storage.

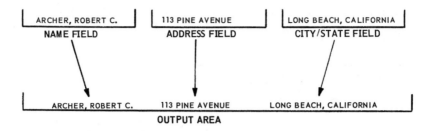

Figure 2-5 Data is Moved to the Output Area

Step 4: The data in the output area is printed on the report.

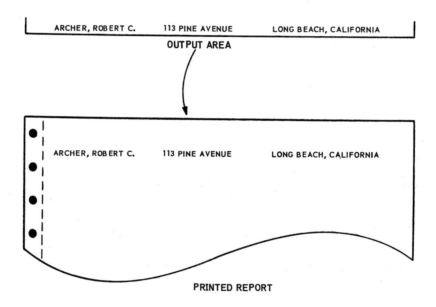

Figure 2-6 Data in the Output Area is Printed

As can be seen from the four steps illustrated in the previous example, the data which is stored on a punched card must be placed in main storage by instructions which are included in the object program which is generated as a result of being processed by the RPG compiler. The input data is then stored in fields which are assigned for each field which is defined in the RPG program for the input data. The data is then moved to an output area from which the line is printed on the report. The actual instructions to read the card into main storage, move the data to and from the input fields and to write the line on the report are contained in the object program which is generated from the compilation processing. The RPG source program, that is, the program which is written by the programmer on the RPG Specification forms and punched on cards for input to the RPG compiler, merely describes the data which is to be processed and the characteristics of the files which are input and output to the program. The RPG source program to accomplish the processing illustrated in Step 1 through Step 4 is illustrated in Figure 2-7.

2.4

RPG Program

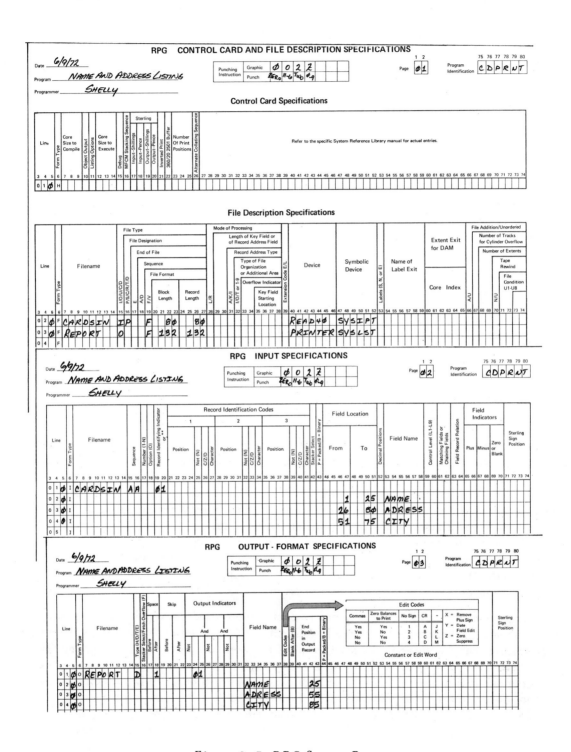

Figure 2-7 RPG Source Program

As can be seen from the program in Figure 2-7, the RPG source program is written on specially-designed forms called the File Description Specifications, the Input Specifications, and the Output-Format Specifications. Each of these forms has certain portions which are common. These common areas on the specification sheets are illustrated in Figure 2-8.

EXAMPLE

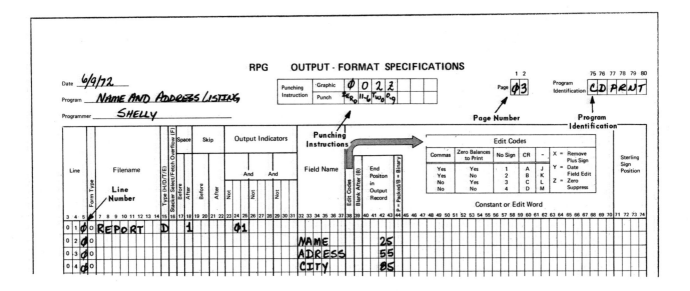

Figure 2-8 Example of Common Entries on RPG Specification Sheets

The common fields which are found on each RPG Specification Sheet are used primarily for identification purposes. Thus, the Date, Program, and Programmer entries on the upper left of the forms are used to specify the identification of the program. The section labeled "Punching Instructions" may be used to give instructions to the keypunch operator concerning certain characters which may cause confusion when read by the operator. Any character which may cause confusion can be assigned a special symbol or "graphic" to identify the card code to be punched by the operator. For example, in the coding sheet illustrated in Figure 2-8, it can be seen that the graphic "O" is punched as an 11-6, thus indicating that "O" is a letter of the alphabet. The graphic "Ø" is to be punched as a zero and is thus a numeric zero when encountered on the coding form.

The page number field is used to identify each page of coding within the program. Note from the example in Figure 2-8 that the page number "03" is entered on the specification form indicating that the sheet illustrated is the third page of coding in the program. The page number is punched in columns 1 and 2 on the cards which comprise the source deck. The program identification, which is punched in column 75 through 80 in the source deck, is used for documentation purposes to identify the program. This area may contain any characters desired by the programmer in order to uniquely identify the program. In the example, the characters "CDPRNT" are used to identify the program as the card-to-print program.

The line number on each coding form is used to identify each line of source coding in the program. As can be seen, these lines are pre-numbered on the form, beginning with the value "01" in columns 3 and 4 of the source card. The value "Ø" is inserted following these numbers. Thus, the first six columns of each source card in the source deck will contain the page and line number. For example, the first card will contain the value "01010", the second card "01020", etc.

2.6

CONTROL CARD AND RPG FILE DESCRIPTION SPECIFICATIONS

The first form normally coded when an RPG program is to be written is the Control Card and File Description Specifications. The form for the sample program to read the Name and Address file and print the report is illustrated below.

EXAMPLE

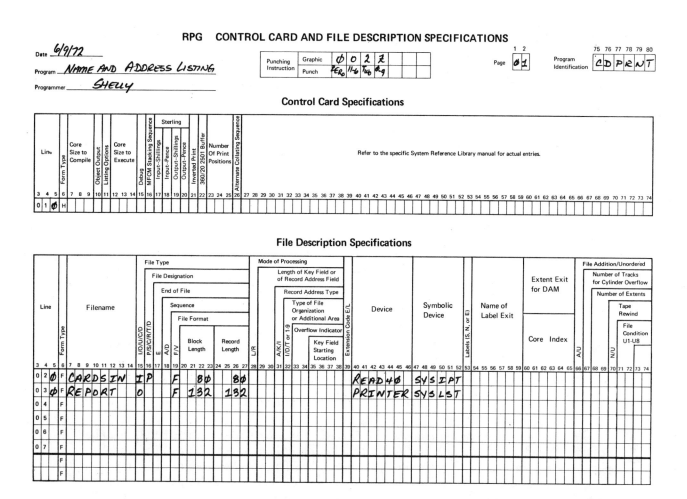

Figure 2-9 Control Card and File Description Specifications

As can be seen from the example above, the Control Card and File Description form is used to define two types of cards which are in the source program – an RPG control card which is used to pass certain parameters to the RPG compiler program and the File Descriptions of the input and output files which are to be processed by the program. In the sample program, the files to be processed are the card input file containing the Name and Address cards and the printer file which is the Name and Address listing.

RPG Control Card

As noted, the control card, which is the first card in the RPG source deck, is used to pass certain information to the RPG compiler concerning the size of core storage, certain options concerning the compilation, etc. In the sample program, the standard compilation is to be performed so there is no need for any special entries on the control card. Thus, the only entries which are required on the control card are the page number in column 1 and column 2, the line number in columns 3, 4, and 5, and the card identification which is punched in column 6. Each different type of card which is input to the RPG compiler, that is, the File Description cards, the Input Specification cards, etc. must contain a unique identifier in column 6 so that the compiler can differentiate the type of cards. For the control card, the value "H" must be punched in column 6 to identify the card as the control card or Heading card. This is illustrated in Figure 2-10.

EXAMPLE

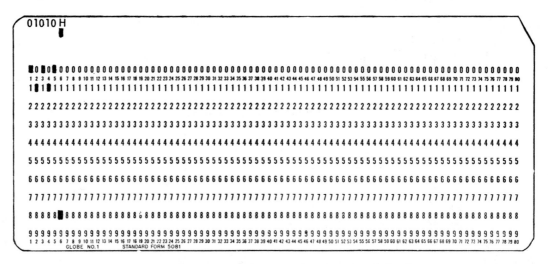

Figure 2-10 Example of Control Card

As can be seen from the example in Figure 2-10, the page number, 01, is punched in columns 1 and 2 and the line number is punched in columns 3-5. The "form type" is punched in column 6 to identify the type of card which is to be processed by the compiler. Note that even though there is no special information which must be passed to the compiler, the Control Card is still required as the first card of the source deck.

RPG File Description Specifications

The next cards to be included in the source deck are the File Description cards. The File Description specification form consists of a number of entries which must be specified in order to define the files which are to be processed within the program.

The first line (line number 020) in the sample program is used to define the card input file, that is, the file of Name and Address cards. The entry to give the file a name is illustrated in Figure 2-11.

EXAMPLE – FILE DESCRIPTION SPECIFICATIONS

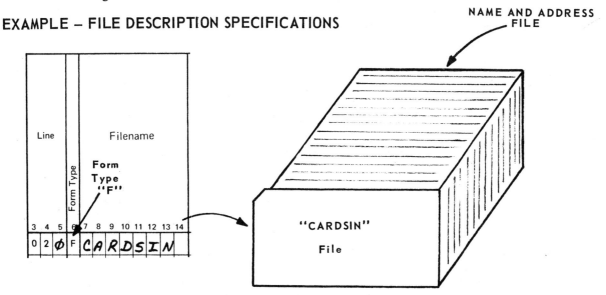

Figure 2-11 Use of FILENAME Entry

Note from Figure 2-11 that the File Description specifications, as do all RPG specifications, contain a Form Type identification value in column 6. For the File Description Specifications, the form type is an "F". The Filename entry is used to give the file which is to be processed a name. In the example, it can be seen that the filename CARDSIN is used to reference the file, or group, of cards which are to be read by the program. This file of cards consists of the Name and Address cards illustrated in Figure 2-1.

As with most names used in an RPG program, the filename used may be any desired by the programmer, but the name must conform to certain rules. The rules for the filenames entered on the File Description sheet are: 1) The name must be 1-7 characters in length; 2) The filename must begin with an alphabetic character (A-Z) or the special characters dollar sign ($), "at" symbol (@), or the pound symbol (#). No other characters may be the first character in the filename; 3) The remainder of the name may consist of alphabetic characters, numeric characters or the three symbols illustrated above. There may not be any other special characters and there may be no embedded blanks within the filename used, that is, a blank between a character used in the filename is not permitted.

From the portion of the File Description Specification illustrated in Figure 2-11 it can be seen that the filename will begin in column 7 of the card and can continue through column 13.

Columns 15 and 16 are used to specify the File Type and the File Designation. This is illustrated in Figure 2-12.

EXAMPLE – FILE DESCRIPTION SPECIFICATIONS

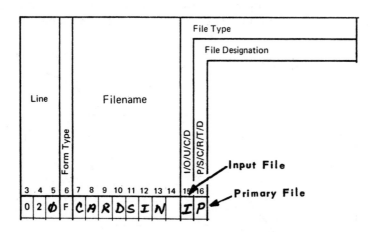

Figure 2-12 Example of File Type and File Designation Entries

Note from the example in Figure 2-12 that the entry in column 15 specifies that the File Type is to be entered. In the sample program, the card file is an input file because it is to be read by the program. Thus, the entry in column 15 is "I", which indicates that the file CARDSIN is an input file. The File Designation field in column 16 contains the value "P", which indicates that the file being described, CARDSIN, is the primary file in the program. In some programs, it is possible to have more than one input file; when this is the case, one file is designated as the primary file and the remaining input files are designated as Secondary files. Since there is only one input file in the program, it is designated as the Primary file. It must be noted that there must be an entry in the File Designation column for each input file which is defined within the program.

Thus far, the card input file has been given a name, CARDSIN, and it has been indicated to the RPG compiler that it is an input file. It remains to specify the attributes of the file, that is, the record format and the size of the records in the file, and also the device from which the records will be read. In order to specify the record formats and sizes, the File Format, Block Length and Record Length entries are used as illustrated in Figure 2-13.

EXAMPLE – FILE DESCRIPTION SPECIFICATIONS

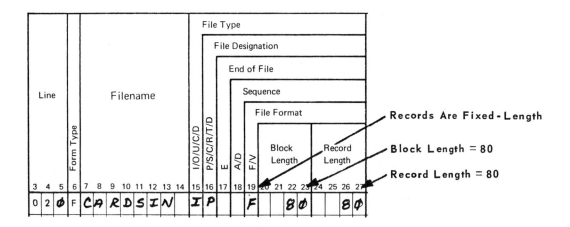

Figure 2-13 Example of File Format, Block Length and Record Length Entries

Note from Figure 2-13 that the value "F" is entered in the File Format column (19). This indicates that the records in the CARDSIN file are Fixed in length, that is, each record contains the same number of characters. All card records which are processed in an RPG program are fixed-length. The entries in the Block Length field (Column 20-23) and the Record Length field (Column 24-27) both contain the value 80. This indicates that the record length is equal to 80 bytes for each record in the file. This, of course, corresponds to the number of columns in a punched card and the value 80 is always used when describing a punched card file. The block length is also 80 which indicates that there is one record per "block" in the card file. When describing tape and disk files, as will be done later in the text, it is possible to have more than one record in a block and the block length, therefore, will be larger than the record size. When a card file is being used, however, the block length and the record length are always 80 bytes.

It should be noted that both the block length and the record length may be a maximum of four digits, that is, the block length is specified in columns 20-23 and the record length is specified in columns 24-27. When all four of the columns are not required in order to specify the block and record lengths, the values specified are "right-justified", that is, they are placed in the right-most columns of the four-column field. In the example of the record length, it can be seen that the value 80 is placed in columns 26-27 and columns 24-25 contain blanks. Thus, this entry follows the rule that the values must be right-justified. Note that leading zeros need not be placed in columns 24-25.

After the characteristics of the file have been described, an entry must be made to specify the type of device from which the file will be read and which device will be used. This is done through the use of the Device field and the Symbolic Device field on the File Specification sheet as illustrated in Figure 2-14.

EXAMPLE – FILE DESCRIPTION SPECIFICATIONS

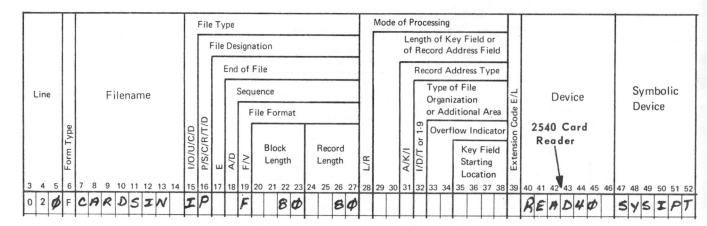

Figure 2-14 Use of Device and Symbolic Device Entries

The entry in the Device field (columns 40-46) indicates the type of device which is is to be used for the file. In the example, the value READ40 is entered. Note that the entry is left-justified, that is, it must always begin in column 40. The entry READ40 indicates that a 2540 Card Read-Punch is to be used to read the punched cards comprising the CARDSIN file. In addition to the value READ40, the following values may be used for card reading devices:

READ01	IBM 2501 Card Reader
READ20	IBM 2520 Card Read-Punch
READ42	IBM 1442 Card Read-Punch

As can be seen, these entries are used to indicate the type of device which is to be used for the file. The entry in the Symbolic Device field (columns 47-52) is used to specify a Symbolic Name which will be assigned to the appropriate device when the program is executed. Note from the example that the value "SYSIPT" is entered in the Symbolic Device field. This means that the symbolic device name SYSIPT will be assigned to an actual device which is connected to the computer when the program is executed.

All of the entries illustrated in Figure 2-14 for the input file CARDSIN are required to define the file. They should be specified as illustrated. In addition to the card file, there is also a printer file in the same program. The entries to define the printer file on the File Description sheet are illustrated in Figure 2-15.

EXAMPLE — FILE DESCRIPTION SPECIFICATIONS

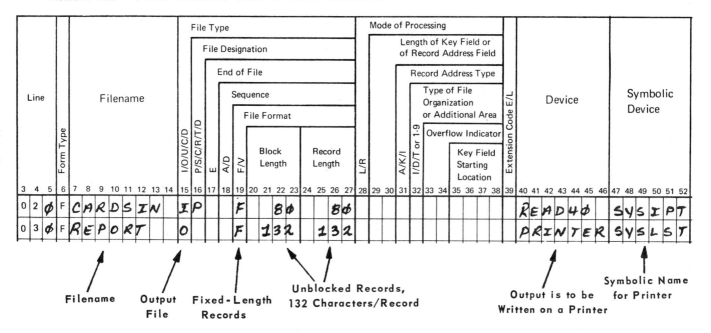

Figure 2-15 Example of Entries for Printer Output File

In the example above, the printer output file is given the filename REPORT. Note that this entry is placed in columns 7-12. The entry REPORT follows the rules governing the names of files as explained previously. The entry in the File Type field, column 15, is the letter of the alphabet O. This indicates that the file is an Output file and is required for all output files. The printer file is considered an output file because the data is written on the printer from the program instead of being read into the program such as when a card is read.

The record format for the printer output file REPORT is fixed in length and each output record is to contain a maximum of 132 characters. The 132 represents the maximum number of print positions available on the printer. Note that the block length and the record length are both specified as 132. It is always true for a file which is to be written on the printer that the block length and record length are the same.

The entry in the Device field for the printed report is the word PRINTER. This value must always be specified in columns 40-46 on the File Description Specification form when the file is to be printed on the printer. The symbolic name used for the file, which is specified in columns 47-52, is SYSLST, which should normally be used for all printer files.

As can be seen from Figure 2-15, both the card input file and the printer output file must be defined on the File Description Specifications form in order to inform the RPG compiler that these files are to be used within the program. The compiler will then generate the appropriate instructions in order to process the files. Note that there are some fields on the File Description Specification sheet which are not used when the card and printer files are defined. These fields are used when more than one input and/or output file are to be processed and when disk and tape files are to be processed, and will be explained in subsequent chapters.

2.13

INPUT SPECIFICATIONS FORM

As has been seen, the File Description Specifications form is used to define each file which is to be processed within the program. Within each file, however, are individual records which are processed. The fields within these records must be defined so that the RPG compiler can generate instructions to process each of the fields. For example, in the sample problem, the Name, Address, and City/State fields within the card records must be defined. These fields are defined through the use of the Input Specifications form. The entries for the file CARDSIN are illustrated below.

EXAMPLE

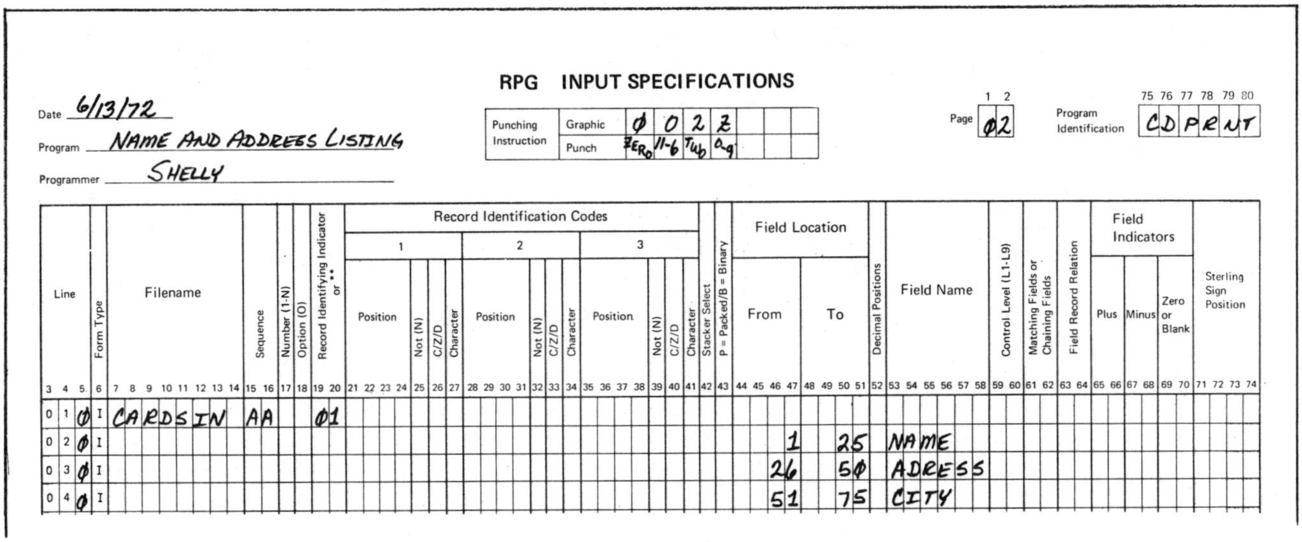
RPG INPUT SPECIFICATIONS

Date 6/13/72
Program NAME AND ADDRESS LISTING
Programmer SHELLY

Punching Instruction — Graphic: Ø O 2 Z; Punch: ZERO, 11-6, TWO, A-9

Page Ø2 Program Identification CDPRNT

Line	Form Type	Filename	Sequence	Number (1-N)	Option (O)	Record Identifying Indicator	Field Location From	Field Location To	Field Name
01Ø	I	CARDSIN	AA			Ø1			
02Ø	I						1	25	NAME
03Ø	I						26	5Ø	ADRESS
04Ø	I						51	75	CITY

Figure 2-16 Example of Input Specifications Form

In the example above, it can be seen that the Input Specifications form has the same common areas as the other forms, that is, the space for the date, the program name, the programmer's name, and the punching instructions. In addition, the page number and program identification can be specified to be punched in the source deck. Note that the page number for the Input Specifications is "02" and the program identification is CDPRNT.

The first entry to be entered by the programmer is the filename of the file in which the records appear. In this example, the filename is CARDSIN because this is the name of the file containing the Name and Address cards. This relationship between the File Description Specifications form which defines the file and the Input Specifications form is illustrated in Figure 2-17.

EXAMPLE

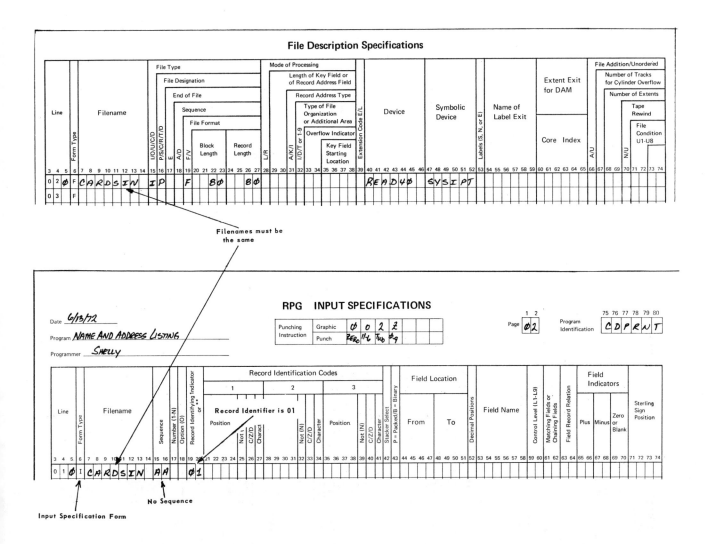

Figure 2-17 Filename Relationship on File Description and Input Specifications

Note from the example above that the entry in the Filename columns on the Input Specifications is the same as the filename for the input file on the File Description Specifications form. These filenames must be the same so that the RPG compiler can relate the file description on the File Description Specifications form with the records which are defined on the Input Specifications form.

Note also in Figure 2-17 that the "form type" column (column 6) contains the value "I", which identifies the form as an Input Specifications form. As was indicated earlier, each card which is part of the RPG source deck must have an identification value in column 6. The entry following the filename entry in the Input Specifications form is the "Sequence" entry. This entry is used if there is a required sequence of the cards in the input file. In the Name and Address file, there is no sequence, so any two alphabetic characters may be entered in columns 15-16. The value entered must not be numeric. In the example the value "AA" is used but any two alphabetic characters could be used to indicate that there is no required sequence of cards in the CARDSIN file.

2.15

The entries in columns 17 and 18 are used in conjunction with the Sequence entry. When an alphabetic value is entered in columns 15 and 16, the Number entry in column 17 and the Option entry in column 18 must be left blank.

The Record Identifying Indicator field in columns 19-20 is used to specify a value which will be associated with the corresponding type of card which is read from the input file. In the example, only one type of card, the Name and Address Card, is to be read from the CARDSIN file. The value "01" is placed in the Record Identifying Indicator field to allow the Name and Address card to be referenced by this number. When a card is read, Record Identifying Indicator 01 goes "ON". When Record Identifying Indicator "01" is on, the card is printed. It should be noted that any value from 01 through 99 could be placed in this field to identify the record. There is nothing unique about the value 01 other than the fact that it is commonly used to identify the first or only type of card which is to be read from the file. Whenever a Name and Address card is read, it will be identified by the Record Identifying Indicator "01" so that other portions of the program will be able to process the data in the card.

As was illustrated in Figure 2-1, the Name and Address cards contain three fields — the Name field, the Address field, and the City/State field. These fields must be defined on the Input Specifications form in order to inform the RPG compiler where on the card they are located. The entries to do this are illustrated below.

EXAMPLE – INPUT SPECIFICATIONS

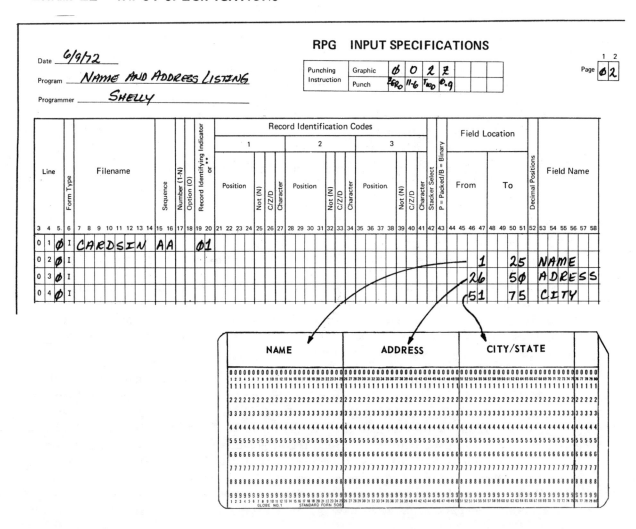

Figure 2-18 Example of Defining Fields on Input Specifications Form

2.16

From Figure 2-18 it can be seen that the fields on the Name and Address card are defined in the RPG program through the use of entries in the Field Location portion of the form (columns 44-51) and the Field Name portion of the form (columns 53-58). The Field Location specification contains two entries — the "From" entry and the "To" entry. The "From" entry is used to specify the column in the card where the field begins. From the example, it can be seen that the value entered for the Name field in the card is "1" because the Name field begins in the first column of the card. Note that the value "1" is right-justified in the "From" columns. The "To" entry is used to note the last column in the card used for the field. Thus, 25 is entered for the Name field because this is the last column used for the Name. Note that the "To" entry is also right-justified. The other "From-To" entries specify the beginning and ending columns in the card for the Address and City/State fields.

The Field Name specification is used to give a symbolic name to each field within the card. The rules for forming the Field Name are similar to those for the file names, that is, they must begin with an alphabetic character and may include either alphabetic or numeric characters in every position except the first position. There may be no embedded blanks within the name. Unlike filenames, however, the maximum length of a field name is six characters, as can be seen from the form where only six positions, in columns 53-58, are alloted for the field name. Note from the example in Figure 2-18 that the value "NAME" is chosen for the Name field, the value "ADRESS" for the address field, and the value "CITY" for the City/State field. When determining the name to be used for a field, it is normally a good practice to make the name as descriptive of the field as possible. Thus, the names chosen reflect the values which are in the fields.

It should also be noted that the definitions of the fields begin on the second coding line, that is, on the line numbered "020", not on the line numbered "010", which is where the name of the file is specified. The field definitions can never be on the same line as is used for the name of the file. They must begin on the next subsequent line.

OUTPUT-FORMAT SPECIFICATIONS FORM

Just as the format of the input records must be defined, so too must the format of any output files which are to be produced from the program be defined. The OUTPUT-FORMAT SPECIFICATIONS form is used to define output files. The example in Figure 2-19 illustrates the entries which are required to define the Name and Address Listing which is to be produced on the printer.

EXAMPLE

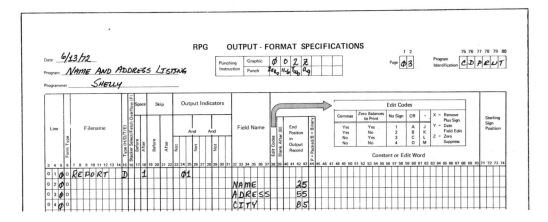

Figure 2-19 Example of OUTPUT-FORMAT SPECIFICATIONS Form

2.17

In the example in Figure 2-19 it can be seen that the Output-Format Specifications form, as do all RPG forms, contains space for the date, program name, programmer's name, punching instructions, page numbers, and program identification. As with the other forms, these portions of the programming form should always be completed to provide as much documentation as possible on the coding sheet.

As can be seen from the example, the first entry on the Output-Format Specifications is the filename, which must be the same as the filename specified on the File Description Specifications. This is illustrated below.

EXAMPLE

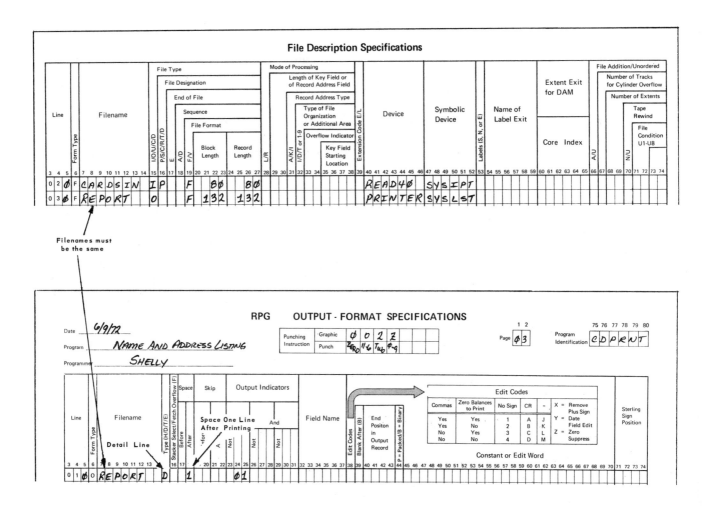

Figure 2-20 Example of Output-Format Specifications Form

From the example above it can be seen that the line number is specified in columns 3-5 as on the other forms. The form type is an alphabetic "0" which signifies that the form is the Output-Format Specifications Form. The filename REPORT is entered in the Filename specification on the form. This filename must be the same as the filename specified on the File Description Specifications form as illustrated above. It is through this filename that the RPG compiler is able to relate the description of the file with the description of the individual records in the file. The filename must be left-justified, that is, begin in column 7 of the Output-Format Specifications form.

The value entered in the "Type" field on the form (columns 15) is "D". This value indicates that the output line to be defined for the REPORT file is to be a Detail line. When an output line is specified as a Detail line, it means that one line is to be printed on the report for each card which is read from the card reader. Each single card which is read from the card reader is considered to be a detail record; thus, when a line is defined as a detail line on the Output Specifications, it specifies that an output record is to be written for each input record which is read.

Whenever a printed report is to be created, it is necessary to consider the spacing of the report, that is, the number of lines which must be spaced between each line which is written on the report. The "Space" specification in column 17 and column 18 is used to specify the number of lines which will be spaced before a line is written (column 17) and after a line is written (column 18). The use of the space specification is illustrated below.

EXAMPLE – OUTPUT SPECIFICATIONS

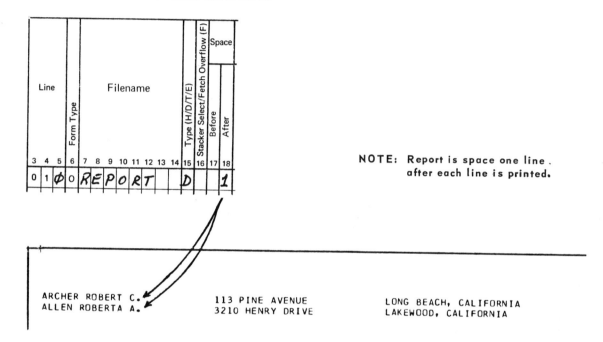

Figure 2-21 Example of Spacing After Printing One Detail Line

Note from the example above that after a line is printed on the report, the printer is spaced one line so that the next line which is printed will not "overprinted" on the line which was previously printed. The values 0, 1, 2, or 3 may be specified to indicate that no spacing is to occur, one line is to be spaced, two lines are to be spaced or three lines are to be spaced. Note that entries may be made to specify spacing both before the line is printed and after the line is printed. In the example, the entry specifies that the spacing should occur after the line is printed on the report and will result in a report which is single-spaced.

The example in Figure 2-20 illustrated also the use of an "Output Indicator". The use of an output indicator is again illustrated below.

EXAMPLE – OUTPUT SPECIFICATIONS

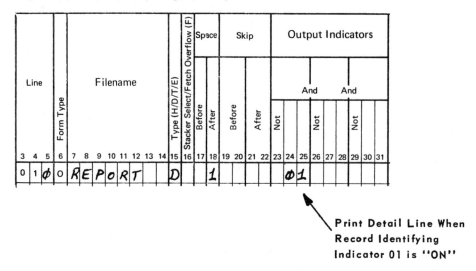

Figure 2-22 Example of Output Indicator

The function of an Output Indicator is to control when an output record is to be written. In the example above, it can be seen that the value "01" is entered in columns 24-25. Thus, this indicator must be "on" before the line will be printed. It will be "on" when a Name and Address card is read because 01 is the Record Identifying Indicator which is set on when a card is read. This is illustrated in Figure 2-23.

EXAMPLE

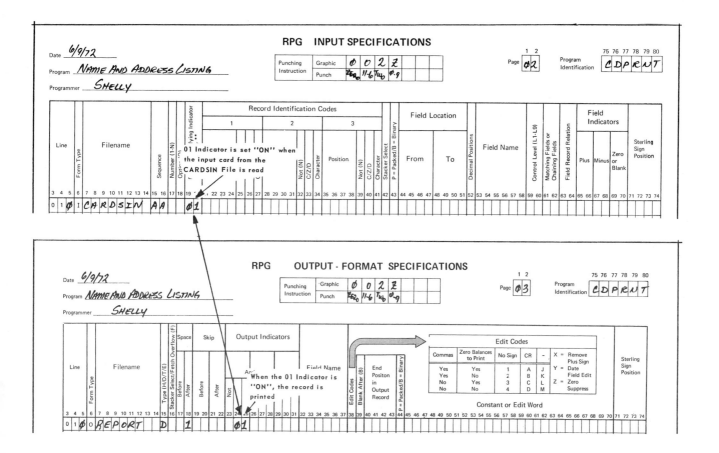

Figure 2-23 Use of Indicators

Note from Figure 2-23 that the value "01" is specified in the Record Identifying Indicator field (column 19-20) on the Input Specifications for the CARDSIN input file. When a record is read from that file, the 01 Indicator is said to be set "on" by the object coding which is generated as a result of the RPG compilation. The action of setting an indicator "on" merely means that a character within the object program is set to a specific value which means the indicator is "on". When the character within the object program does not have the specific value, the indicator is "off". A record identifying indicator is always set "off" immediately before the next input record is read. After the record is read, the indicator is "on". As noted, the indicator will remain "on" until just before the next data card is read. Thus, after the data has been moved to the output area, as illustrated in Figure 2-5, the indicator is still "on". Therefore, the object program can check the status of the indicator just before printing the line of the report to determine if it is "on" or "off". As noted, when it is on, the data line will be printed on the report because the output indicator 01 is specified in column 24 and column 25.

In a previous example it was seen how the Input Specifications are used to specify the fields within the input record. The Output-Format Specifications are used to perform the same function for the output records. This is illustrated in the following example.

EXAMPLE – OUTPUT SPECIFICATIONS

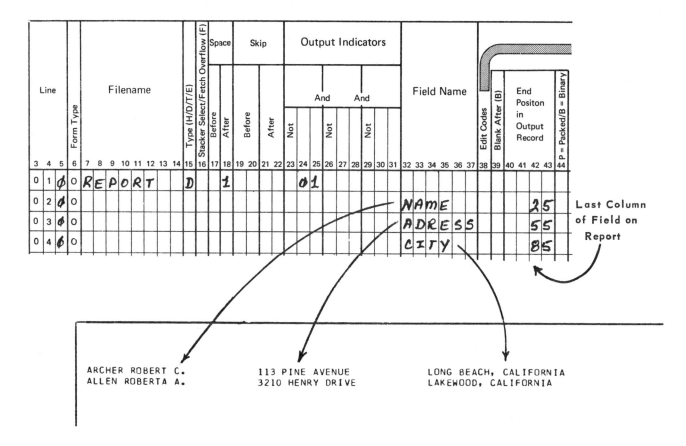

Figure 2-24 Example of Report and Field Definitions

In the example in Figure 2-24, it can be seen that the "Field Name" portion of the Output-Format Specifications form is used to specify the name of the field which is to be printed on the report. The names which are placed in columns 32-37 of the Output-Format Specifications form must have been previously defined within the program. In this example, they were defined on the Input Specifications form (see Figure 2-18). Thus, the Name field (NAME), the Address field (ADRESS), and the City/State field (CITY) will be printed on the report. Note that the field names which are specified must be left-justified in the Field Name portion of the form, that is, the field names must begin in column 32. Columns 40-43 on the Output Specifications form are used to indicate the ending position of the data in each field in the output record or print line. Note that the entry for the NAME field is 25, the entry for the ADRESS field is 55, and the entry for the CITY field is 85. Thus, the ending column on the printed report for the NAME field will be column 25. This means that the Name will be printed in column 1 through column 25 of the report, since the Name field is 25 characters in length as defined on the Input Specifications form. The address will be printed in columns 31-55 of the report because the Address field is 25 characters in length (cols 26-50 on the Name and Address card) and column 55 is specified as the right-most column for the Address field on the Output-Format Specifications form. The City/State field will be printed in columns 61-85 of the report because it is 25 characters in length and is specified to end in column 85 of the report.

Note also from the example in Figure 2-24 that the entries describing the fields within the report cannot begin on the same line as the entries specifying the Filename, the Type of record to be printed, the Spacing of the report, and the Output Indicator, which are all on line 010 of the form. The entry for the first field in the output record must begin on the next subsequent line, which, in the example, is line 020.

As can be seen from the previous examples, the File Description Specifications Form, the Input Specifications Form and the Output-Format Specifications Form are used in order to define the files and records within the files which are to be processed by the RPG program. The source deck will be punched from the entries made on these forms and then will be input to the RPG compiler as was illustrated in Chapter 1. The resultant object deck will process the Name and Address listing.

SAMPLE PROBLEM

As noted, the sample problem in this chapter involves the preparation of a Name and Address Listing from a file of Name and Address Cards. The format of the input cards and the format of the printed report are again illustrated below.

Input

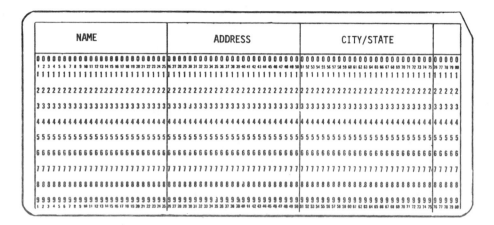

Figure 2-25   Card Input

Output

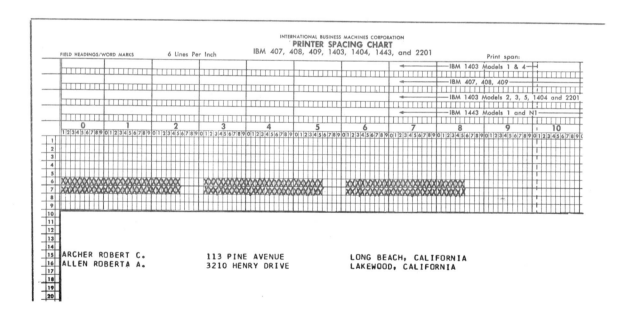

Figure 2-26   Printer Output

RPG Coding

The entries required for the RPG Specifications to produce the Name and Address Listing are again illustrated below.

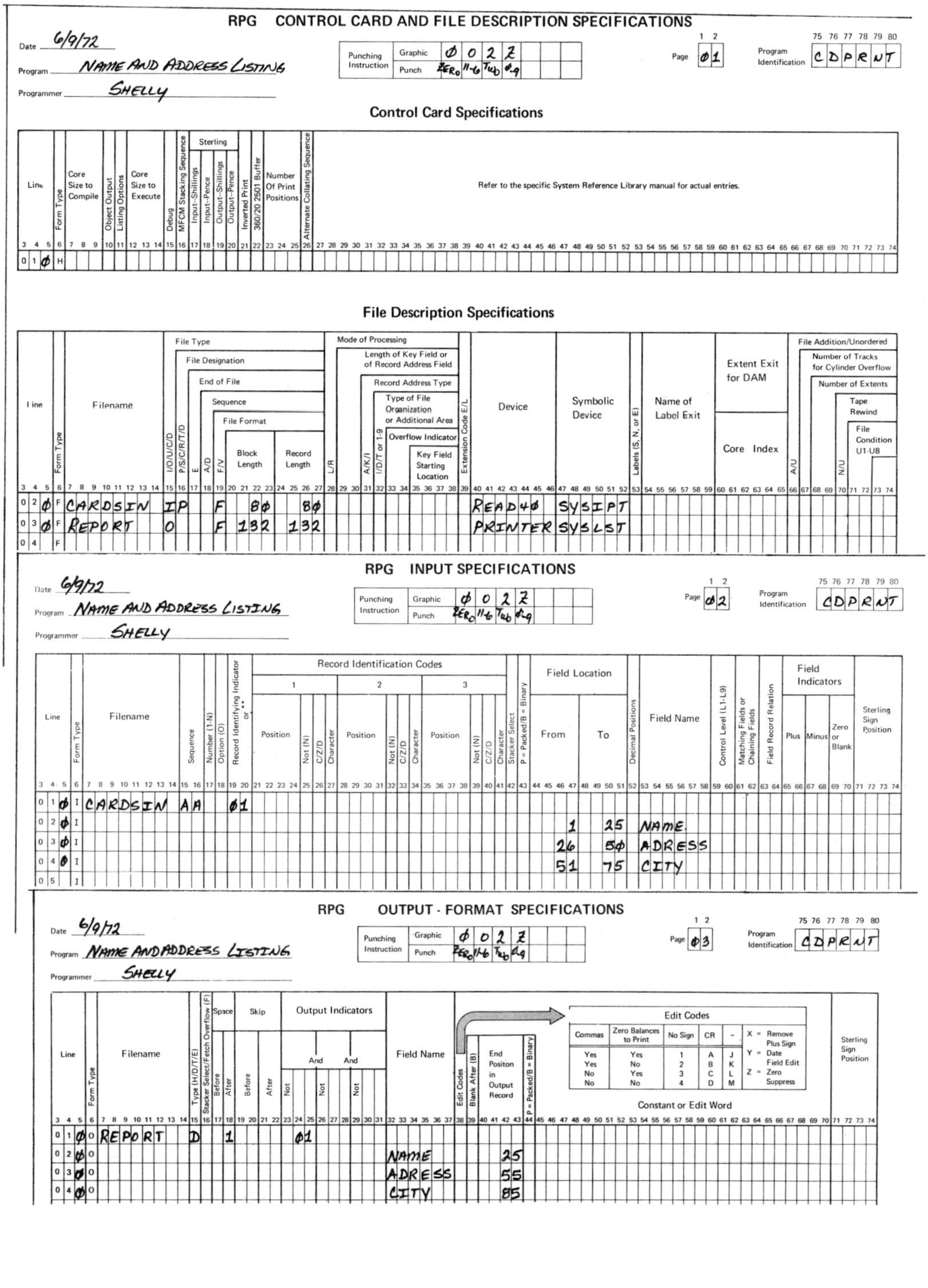

Figure 2-27 RPG Coding

2.25

Program

The program to create the Name and Address Listing is illustrated below. This computer listing is the output of the RPG compiler when the program is compiled.

```
DOS/360*RPG*CL 3-9                    CASHMAN                      09/11/72         PAGE 0001
                01 010 H                                                           CDPRNT
001             01 020 FCARDSIN IP  F  80  80            READ40 SYSIPT             CDPRNT
002             01 030 FREPORT   O   F 132 132           PRINTERSYSLST             CDPRNT
003             02 010 ICARDSIN AA  01                                             CDPRNT
004             02 020 I                                      1  25 NAME           CDPRNT
005             02 030 I                                     26  50 ADRESS         CDPRNT
006             02 040 I                                     51  75 CITY           CDPRNT
007             03 010 OREPORT   D  1      01                                      CDPRNT
008             03 020 O                           NAME      25                    CDPRNT
009             03 030 O                           ADRESS    55                    CDPRNT
010             03 040 O                           CITY      85                    CDPRNT
```

Figure 2 - 28 RPG Computer Listing

1. What information should always be included on the top of the coding form in the area called "Punching Instructions"?

2. In what order must the source deck be placed in order to be compiled properly?

3. Distinguish the difference between the entry in the DEVICE columns and the SYMBOLIC DEVICE columns on the File Description Specifications.

4. Why do you suppose that the beginning and ending columns must be specified on the Input Specifications but only the ending column is specified on the Output Specifications?

STUDENT EXERCISES

1. Record the entries to define a card file which is to be read from a 2501 card reader assigned to SYSIPT. The filename is CARDIN. Also record the entries to define printer output file of 132 print positions, using the 1403 printer assigned to SYSLST. The filename is PRTFLE.

File Description Specifications

Line			Form Type	Filename	I/O/U/C/D	P/S/C/R/T/D	E	A/D	F/V	Block Length	Record Length	L/R	A/K/I	I/D/T or 1-9	Key Field Starting Location	Extension Code E/L	Device	Symbolic Device
3	4	5	6	7 8 9 10 11 12 13 14	15	16	17	18	19	20 21 22 23	24 25 26 27	28	29 30	31 32	33 34	35 36 37 38	39	40 41 42 43 44 45 46	47 48 49 50 51 52
0	2		F															
0	3		F															
0	4		F															
0	5		F															
0	6		F															
0	7		F															
			F															
			F															

2. Record the entries to define the fields within the card input file defined in Question 1 above. The fields are:

Col 1-5:   Employee Number
Col 20-39: Employee Name
Col 65-70: Department Number

The field names are to be determined by the programmer as well as the Record Identifying Indicator to be used.

RPG   INPUT SPECIFICATIONS

Line			Form Type	Filename	Sequence	Number (1-N)	Option (O)	Record Identifying Indicator or **	Position (1)	Not (N)	C/Z/D	Character	Position (2)	Not (N)	C/Z/D	Character	Position (3)	Not (N)	C/Z/D	Character	Stacker Select	P = Packed/B = Binary	From	To	Decimal Positions	Field Name
3	4	5	6	7 8 9 10 11 12 13 14	15 16	17	18	19 20	21 22 23 24	25	26	27	28 29 30 31	32	33	34	35 36 37 38	39	40	41	42	43	44 45 46 47	48 49 50 51	52	53 54 55 56 57 58
0	1		I																							
0	2		I																							
0	3		I																							
0	4		I																							
0	5		I																							

3. Record the Output-Format Specification entries for a printer file which is to be used to print the cards read from the file defined in Questions 1 and 2. The columns on the printed output are to be the same as on the input card. The report is to be double-spaced.

RPG   OUTPUT - FORMAT SPECIFICATIONS

Edit Codes					
Commas	Zero Balances to Print	No Sign	CR	–	X = Remove Plus Sign
Yes	Yes	1	A	J	Y = Date Field Edit
Yes	No	2	B	K	
No	Yes	3	C	L	Z = Zero Suppress
No	No	4	D	M	

Line — Form Type — Filename — Type (H/D/T/E) — Stacker Select/Fetch Overflow (F) — Space Before/After — Skip Before/After — Output Indicators And And (Not) — Field Name — Edit Codes — Blank After (B) — End Position in Output Record — P = Packed/B = Binary — Constant or Edit Word

Line			Form Type	Filename								Type (H/D/T/E)	Stacker Select/Fetch Overflow (F)	Space		Skip		Output Indicators							Field Name						Edit Codes	Blank After (B)	End Positon in Output Record			P = Packed/B = Binary	Constant or Edit Word
3	4	5	6	7 8 9 10 11 12 13 14								15	16	17 18		19 20 21 22		23 24	25 26	27 28	29 30 31			32 33 34 35 36 37						38	39	40 41 42 43			44	45 46 47 48 49 50 51 52 53 54 55 56 57 58 59 60 61 62 63 64 65 66 67 68 69 70
0	1		O																																		
0	2		O																																		
0	3		O																																		
0	4		O																																		
0	5		O																																		
0	6		O																																		
0	7		O																																		
0	8		O																																		
0	9		O																																		
1	0		O																																		
1	1		O																																		
1	2		O																																		
1	3		O																																		
1	4		O																																		

Debugging RPG Programs

Problem 1

Instructions: The following RPG program contains an error or error which have occurred during compilation. Circle each error and record the corrected entries directly on the listing. Explain the error and method of correction in the space provided below.

```
DOS/360*RPG*CL 3-9              CASHMAN                    10/05/72           PAGE 0001

          01 010 H                                                           CDPRNT
001       01 020 FCARDSIN IP  F  80  80          READ40 SYSIPT               CDPRNT
002       01 030 FREPORT   O  F 132 132          PRINTERSYSLST               CDPRNT
003       02 040 ICARDSIN AA  01                                            CDPRNT
004       02 050 I                              1  25 NAME                  CDPRNT
005       02 060 I                             26  50 ADDRES                CDPRNT
006       02 070 I                             51  75 CITY                  CDPRNT
007       03 080 OREPORT   D  1      01                                     CDPRNT
008       03 090 O                      NAME      25                        CDPRNT
          03 100 O                      ADRESS    55                        CDPRNT
                                                                              NOTE 179
009       03 110 O                      CITY      85                        CDPRNT
```

```
DOS/360*RPG*CL 3-9              CASHMAN                    10/05/72           PAGE 0002

                                   SYMBOL   TABLES

RESULTING  INDICATORS

ADDRESS RI         ADDRESS RI         ADDRESS RI         ADDRESS RI         ADDRESS RI         ADDRESS RI         ADDRESS RI

 000014 1P          000015 LR          000016 00          000017 01          00007A L0          000085 H0          000086 H1
 000087 H2          000088 H3          000089 H4          00008A H5          00008B H6          00008C H7          00008D H8
 00008E H9
FIELD  NAMES

ADDRESS FIELD        ADDRESS FIELD        ADDRESS FIELD        ADDRESS FIELD        ADDRESS FIELD

000123 NAME          00013C ADDRES        000155 CITY

   005                                          ADDRES                       NOTE 216

NOTE  179  FIELD NAME (COLUMNS 32-37) IS UNDEFINED.  SPECIFICATION IS NOT PROCESSED.

NOTE  216  WARNING - FIELD NAME IS UNREFERENCED.
```

EXPLANATION_____

_____

_____

_____

Debugging RPG Programs

Problem 2

Instructions: The following RPG program contains an error or errors which occur during execution. Circle each error and record the corrected entries directly on the listing. Explain the error and method of correction in the space provided below.

```
DOS/360*RPG*CL 3-9              CASHMAN                    10/05/72         PAGE 0001

            01 010 H                                                       CDPRNT
    001     01 020 FCARDSIN IP   F  80  80            READ40 SYSIPT        CDPRNT
    002     01 030 FREPORT   O   F 132 132            PRINTERSYSLST        CDPRNT
    003     02 040 ICARDSIN AA   01                                        CDPRNT
    004     02 050 I                               1   25 NAME             CDPRNT
    005     02 060 I                              26   50 ADRESS           CDPRNT
    006     02 070 I                              51   75 CITY             CDPRNT
    007     03 080 OREPORT   D  1      01                                  CDPRNT
    008     03 090 O                      NAME      01                     CDPRNT
    009     03 100 O                      ADRESS    26                     CDPRNT
    010     03 110 O                      CITY      51                     CDPRNT
```

```
DOS/360*RPG*CL 3-9              CASHMAN                    10/05/72         PAGE 0002

                                   SYMBOL   TABLES

RESULTING  INDICATORS

ADDRESS RI        ADDRESS RI        ADDRESS RI        ADDRESS RI        ADDRESS RI        ADDRESS RI        ADDRESS RI

 000014 IP         000015 LR         000016 00         000017 01         00007A L0         000085 H0         000086 H1
 000087 H2         000088 H3         000089 H4         00008A H5         00008B H6         00008C H7         00008D H8
 00008E H9
FIELD  NAMES

ADDRESS FIELD        ADDRESS FIELD        ADDRESS FIELD        ADDRESS FIELD        ADDRESS FIELD

 000123 NAME          00013C ADRESS        000155 CITY

    008                                                                          NOTE 229

NOTE  229   END POSITION IS LESS THAN THE FIELD LENGTH.  FIELD IS NOT PROCESSED.
```

```
   105 HOLLY STREET      LONG BEACH, CALIFORNIA    ◄────NOTE: No Name
   1331 WILLIAMS WAY     LAKEWOOD, CALIFORNIA               on Listing
   4242 YUCCA STREET     LOS ANGELES, CALIFRONIA
   1417 MEDOW AVENUE     LONG BEACH, CALIFORNIA
   3333 WAYNE STREET     LOS ALAMITOS, CALIFORNIA
```

EXPLANATION _____

_____

_____

_____

PROGRAMMING ASSIGNMENT 1

INSTRUCTIONS

A listing of the employees of a company is to be prepared. Write the RPG program to prepare this listing.

INPUT

Input is to consist of Employee Name Cards that contain the Employee Number, Employee Name, and the Department Number to which the employee is assigned. The format of the Employee Name Cards is illustrated below.

OUTPUT

Output is to consist of a listing of the employees and is to contain the Department Number, the Employee Number, and the Employee Name. A printer spacing chart and a segment of the report is illustrated below. Note that the Department Number appears first on the report.

```
10    15433    ACHER, WILLIAM
10    23749    BROWNE, EDGAR
20    54801    EVANS, EDWARD
```

TEST DATA — ASSIGNMENT NO. 1

Employee Number (Col 1-5)	Employee Name (Col 6-30)	Department (Col 31-32)
15433	Acher, William	10
23749	Browne, Edgar	10
54801	Evans, Edward	20
44389	Finch, Richard	23
55907	Zelfer, Donald	28

DOS JOB CONTROL

// JOB jobname
// OPTION LINK
// EXEC RPG

  — Student Source Deck —

/*
// EXEC LNKEDT
// EXEC

  — Test Data —

/*
/&

Note: This assumes that the assignments for the card read and printer are standard assignments known to the student.

PROGRAMMING ASSIGNMENT 2

INSTRUCTIONS

A listing of the customers of a company is to be prepared. Since two listings are required, it has been decided to print each of the fields on the card twice on the same line.

INPUT

The input is to consist of Customer Name and Address Cards that contain the Customer Number, Customer Name, and Customer Address. The format of the cards is illustrated below.

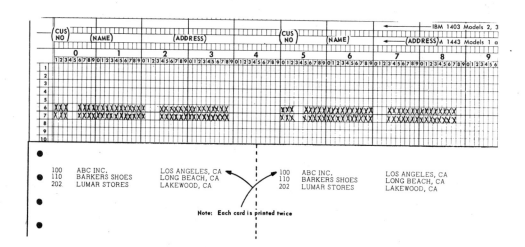

OUTPUT

The output is to consist of the two listings of the card. A printer spacing chart and a segment of the report that is to be prepared is illustrated below.

100	ABC INC.	LOS ANGELES, CA	100	ABC INC.	LOS ANGELES, CA
110	BARKERS SHOES	LONG BEACH, CA	110	BARKERS SHOES	LONG BEACH, CA
202	LUMAR STORES	LAKEWOOD, CA	202	LUMAR STORES	LAKEWOOD, CA

Note: Each card is printed twice

TEST DATA — ASSIGNMENT NO. 2

Customer Number (Col 1-3)	Customer Name (Col 4-20)	Customer Address (Col 21-35)
100	ABC Inc.	Los Angeles, CA
110	Barkers Shoes	Long Beach, CA
202	Lumar Stores	Lakewood, CA
278	Jamieson Furn.	San Pedro, CA
442	Nancy's Clothes	Hollywood, CA
668	Julie's Jewelry	Costa Mesa, CA

DOS JOB CONTROL

```
// JOB jobname
// OPTION LINK
// EXEC RPG

   — Student Source Deck —

/*
// EXEC LNKEDT
// EXEC

   — Test Data —

/*
/&
```

Note: This assumes that the assignments for the card reader and printer are standard assignments known to the student.

CHAPTER 3

ADDITION – SUBTRACTION

EDITING

INTRODUCTION

The arithmetic operations of addition and subtraction are basic to many business applications. When programming using the RPG language, addition is accomplished through the use of the ADD statement and subtraction is accomplished through the use of the SUB statement, both of which appear on the Calculation Specifications.

The sample program developed in this chapter illustrates a basic crossfooting operation in which two fields are added together giving a total. The RPG program is designed to add a Regular Earnings field to an Overtime Earnings Field to determine an Employee's Total Earnings. In addition, a final total of the Employees' total earnings will be taken and a total of the number of employees processed will be printed.

INPUT

The input for the sample program consists of a file containing Employee Earnings Cards. The card format is illustrated below.

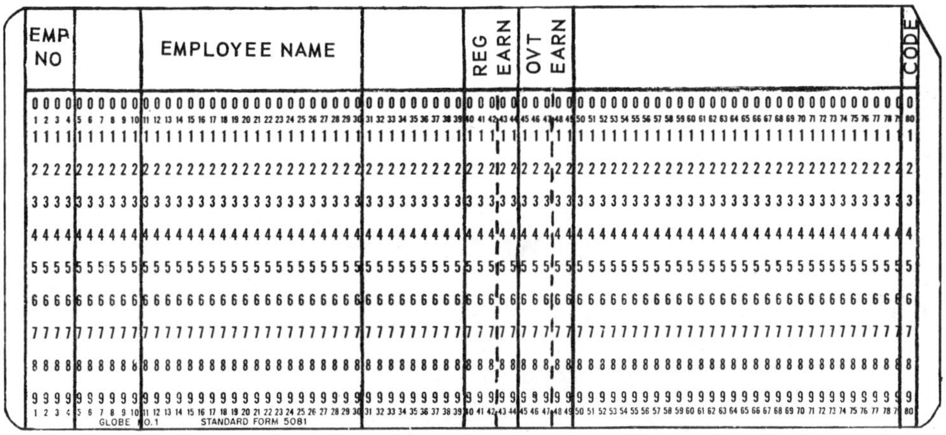

Figure 3-1 Card Format

Note from the illustration above that the input card contains the Employee Number, the Employee Name, the Regular Earnings, the Overtime Earnings, and a Code. The Code is used to signify a Pay card and will always contain the value "P" in card column 80.

Output

The output of the program is a printed report which lists the Employee Number, the Employee Name, the Regular Earnings, the Overtime Earnings, and the Total Earnings of the Employee. In addition, a final total is taken for the Earnings of an Employee. A final total is the total of all of the Earnings of all of the employees which are listed on the report. A final total of the number of employees processed is also included. The format of the report is illustrated below.

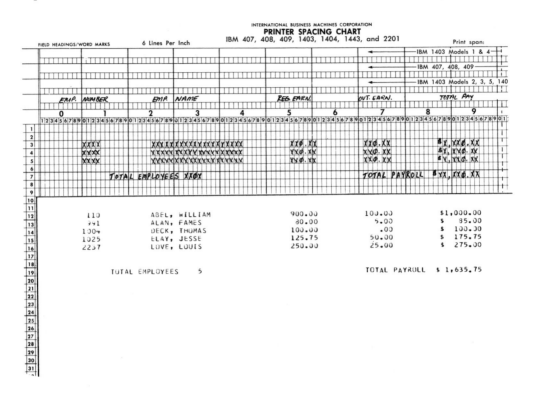

Figure 3-2 Output Report Format

Note in the segment of the sample report shown above that the Employee Number field is "zero-suppressed" and the Regular Earnings field, the Overtime Earnings field, the Total Earnings field and the Final Total are "zero-suppressed" and "edited". Zero-suppression refers to the process of suppressing the printing of zeros to the left of the first significant digit of a field. For example, a field consisting of the numbers "0010" would be printed as "10" when zero-suppressed. Editing refers to the process of inserting special characters such as the decimal point, comma, and the dollar sign in the fields which are to be printed.

In the sample output in Figure 3-2, it can be seen that the Regular Earnings field and the Overtime Earnings field are zero-suppressed and edited with a decimal point. The Total Earnings field and the Final Total field are zero-suppressed and edited with a dollar sign, comma, and decimal point.

Program

The program to prepare the Pay Report from the Pay cards is illustrated below.

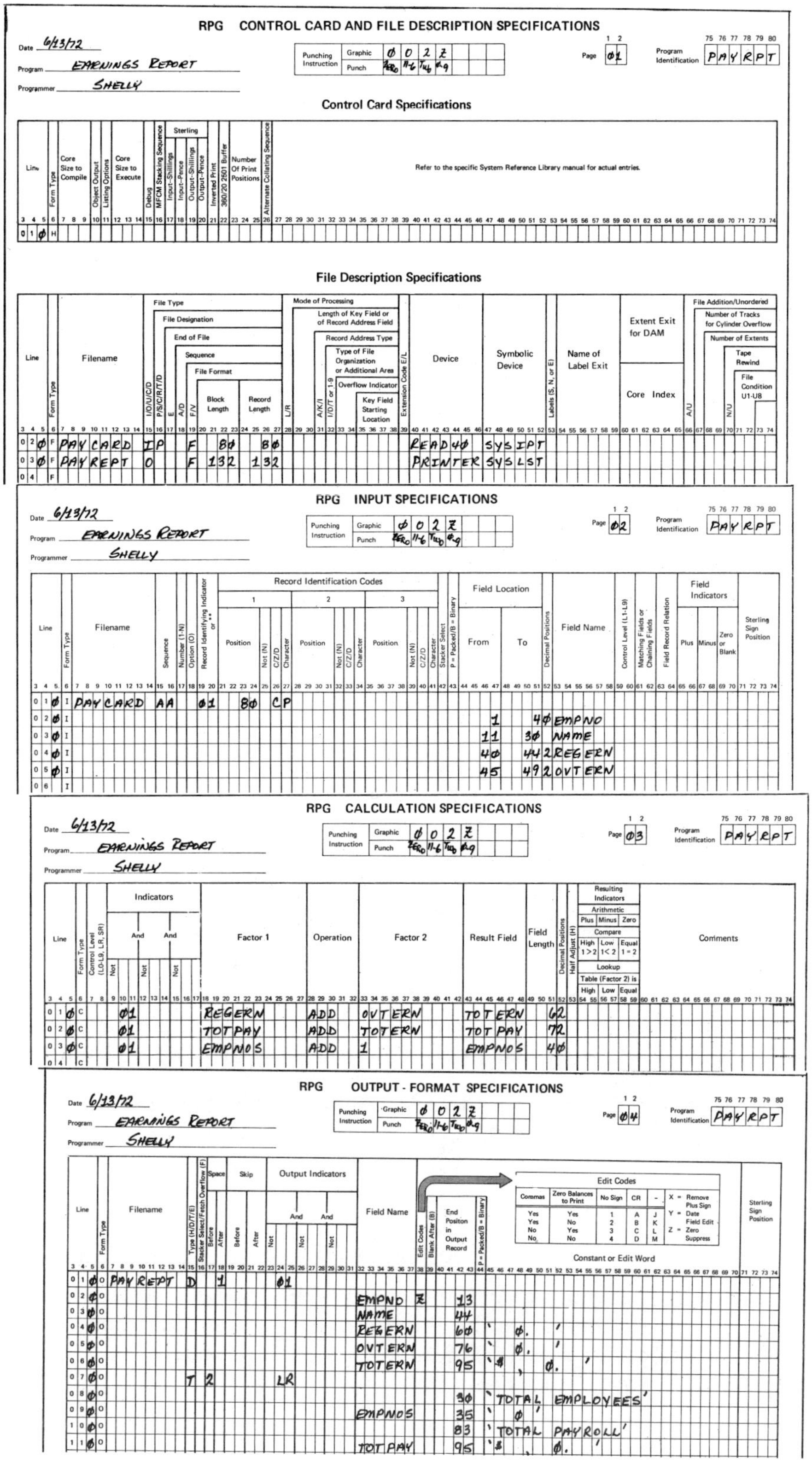

Figure 3-3 RPG Program

FILE DESCRIPTION SPECIFICATIONS FORM

As with the program presented in Chapter 2, the card input file and the printer output file used in this sample program must be defined on the File Description Specifications form. The entries to describe these files are illustrated below.

EXAMPLE

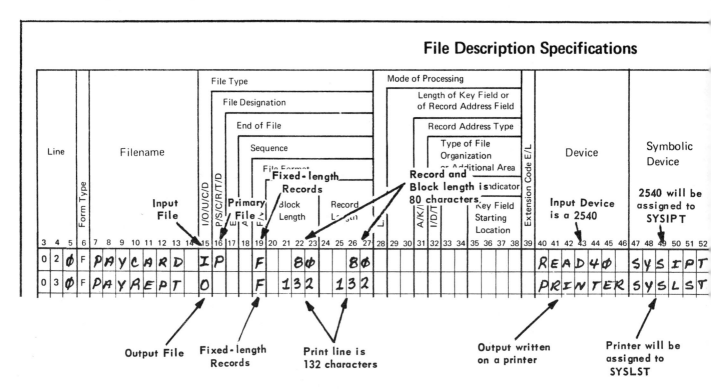

Figure 3-4 File Description Specifications

Note from the File Description Specifications form illustrated above that the entries for the card input file PAYCARD and the printer output file PAYREPT are the same as those used in Chapter 2. The PAYCARD input file is specified as an input file through the use of the "I" in column 15 and as the primary file with the "P" entry in column 16. The card input records are fixed-length containing 80 characters in each record. The file is to be read from a 2540 Card Reader assigned to the symbolic-device name SYSIPT.

The PAYREPT output file contains fixed-length records each 132 characters in length. The report will be written on the printer assigned to the symbolic-device name SYSLST.

INPUT SPECIFICATIONS FORM

After the files have been defined on the File Description Specifications sheet, each record within the input file must be described on the Input Specifications form. In the sample program, the input records are the Pay Cards which are contained in the PAYCARD file. The Input Specifications form in Figure 3-5 is used to specify the characteristics of each record in the PAYCARD input file.

EXAMPLE

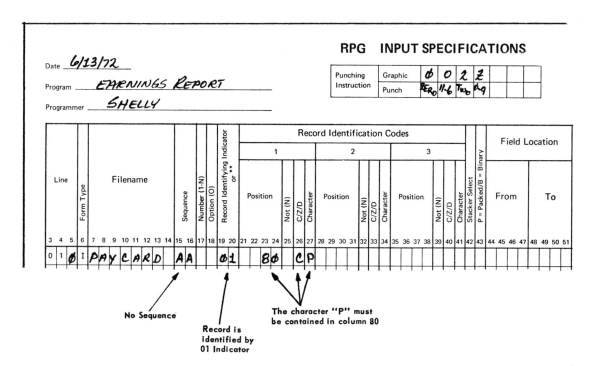

Figure 3-5 Input Specifications Form

In the example above it will be noted that the filename PAYCARD is entered in columns 7-13 and this filename corresponds to the filename used on the File Description Specifications in Figure 3-4. As with the program in Chapter 2, there is no required sequence of cards within the PAYCARD input file, so any alphabetic value may be entered in columns 15-16. In the example, the value "AA" is entered. The Record Identifying Indicator 01 is to be used to identify the input record from the PAYCARD file. As was noted in Chapter 2, when a card is read from this file, the 01 Indicator will be set "on" to indicate that a card has been read and is ready for processing.

Previously it was noted that each card in the PAYCARD file will contain a "code" in column 80 and the code is the letter of the alphabet "P". If the input card does not contain a code value of "P" in column 80, the program is to be cancelled because an invalid card is in the input file. In order to check code values which are to be punched in a single column of an input record, the Record Identification Codes portion of the Input Specifications form is used. As can be seen from Figure 3-5, this area on the form encompasses columns 21 through 41. Within these columns, there is room to specify three different codes which may be placed within an input record for identification purposes. Column 21 through column 27 contain entries for the first code, column 28 through column 34 contain entries for the second code, and column 35 through column 41 contain entries for the third code. In the sample program in this chapter, there is only one code to be tested; therefore, only columns 21 through 27 are utilized.

Columns 21-24 are used to specify the position of the code character within the input record. In the example in Figure 3-5, it can be seen that the value "80" is entered in column 23-24. This entry indicates that the code value to be checked is contained in column 80 of the input card. This, of course, corresponds to the card format as illustrated in Figure 3-1. Note that the "position" entry in columns 21-24 is right-justified and leading zeros need not be included in the entry.

3.5

As well as identifying the position of the code character to be checked, the Record Identification Codes portion of the form is used to specify which character is to be checked, that is, the value which must be contained in the given position within the record. In the example, it can be seen that the value "C" is placed in column 26 and the value "P" is placed in column 27. The "C" is used to specify the type of value which is to be checked, that is, it specifies that the value to be checked is a "character". Two other values may be specified in this column – a "Z" and a "D". The "Z" specifies that the zone portion of the value in the given position of the record is to be checked and the "D" specifies that the digit portion of the value is to be checked.

The "Character" entry on the Input Specifications form is used to specify the value which is to be checked for. In the example in Figure 3-5, it can be seen that the value "P" is entered in column 27. This indicates that the object program which is generated by the RPG compiler should check column 80 in each input card for the value "P". If this value is not found in the input card, the program will normally be cancelled.

The use of the entries in columns 26 and 27 can allow almost any configuration desired to be checked. The following examples illustrate some of the combinations which can be tested.

EXAMPLE 1: Checks for the character "A" in card column 80.

Record Identification Codes												
1				2				3				
Position	Not (N)	C/Z/D	Character	Position	Not (N)	C/Z/D	Character	Position	Not (N)	C/Z/D	Character
21 22 23 24	25	26	27	28 29 30 31	32	33	34	35 36 37 38	39	40	41
8Ø		C	A								

EXAMPLE 2: Checks for the digit "5" in card column 23 — a "5" punch in a card or the letter of the alphabet "E", "N" and "V" would satisfy the test.

Record Identification Codes																				
1							2							3						
Position				Not (N)	C/Z/D	Character	Position				Not (N)	C/Z/D	Character	Position				Not (N)	C/Z/D	Character
21	22	23	24	25	26	27	28	29	30	31	32	33	34	35	36	37	38	39	40	41
		2	3		D	5														

EXAMPLE 3: Checks for a "12 Zone" in card column 42 — checks a "12 zone" because the letter "B" contains a "12 zone".

Record Identification Codes																				
1							2							3						
Position				Not (N)	C/Z/D	Character	Position				Not (N)	C/Z/D	Character	Position				Not (N)	C/Z/D	Character
21	22	23	24	25	26	27	28	29	30	31	32	33	34	35	36	37	38	39	40	41
		4	2		Z	B														

EXAMPLE 4: Checks for a "11 Zone" in column 42 — checks an "11 zone" because the letter "J" contains an "11 zone".

Record Identification Codes																				
1							2							3						
Position				Not (N)	C/Z/D	Character	Position				Not (N)	C/Z/D	Character	Position				Not (N)	C/Z/D	Character
21	22	23	24	25	26	27	28	29	30	31	32	33	34	35	36	37	38	39	40	41
		4	2		Z	J														

EXAMPLE 5: Checks for an "11 Zone" in column 23 — the minus sign (−) always specifies a check for an "11 zone".

Record Identification Codes																				
1							2							3						
Position				Not (N)	C/Z/D	Character	Position				Not (N)	C/Z/D	Character	Position				Not (N)	C/Z/D	Character
21	22	23	24	25	26	27	28	29	30	31	32	33	34	35	36	37	38	39	40	41
		2	3		C	−														

EXAMPLE 6: Checks for a "12 Zone" in column 80 — the ampersand (&) always specifies a check for a "12 zone".

Record Identification Codes																				
1							2							3						
Position				Not (N)	C/Z/D	Character	Position				Not (N)	C/Z/D	Character	Position				Not (N)	C/Z/D	Character
21	22	23	24	25	26	27	28	29	30	31	32	33	34	35	36	37	38	39	40	41
		8	0		C	&														

Note from the previous example that many combinations of zone punches, digit punches, and characters may be tested by placing entries in the Record Identification Codes portion of the Input Specifications form. When the code specified in the Record Identification Codes area is found in an input card, the corresponding Record Identifying indicator is set "on". Thus, from the example in Figure 3-5, it can be seen that if there is a "P" punched in column 80 of the input card, the record identifying indicator "01" will be set "on". If the card read does not contain the character "P" in column 80, the program will be cancelled before the next input record is read.

In addition to specifying the Record Identifying Indicator and the Record Identification Codes, the Input Specifications form is used to define the fields within the input record. The entries to describe the fields in the Pay Cards are illustrated below.

EXAMPLE – INPUT SPECIFICATIONS

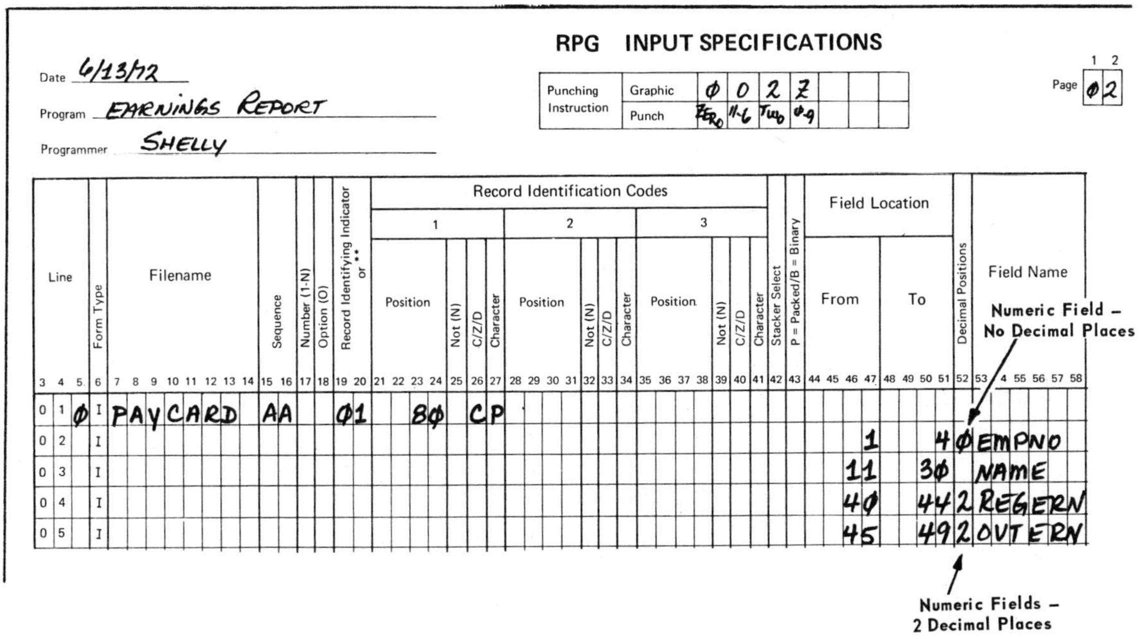

Figure 3-6 Example of Field Definitions

Note from the example in Figure 3-6 that the Field Location and Field Name portions of the form are used in the same manner as was illustrated in Chapter 2. The "From-To" columns are used to specify the beginning and ending columns for each of the fields in the input card. These beginning and ending columns correspond to the format of the card as illustrated in Figure 3-1. The entries in the Field Name portion of the form are used to give symbolic names to the fields within the card.

In addition to these entries, however, it will be noted that entries have been made in the "Decimal Positions" field (column 52). Entries are made in this field when the field in the input record contains numeric data and is to be used either in some type of arithmetic calculation or is to be edited or zero-suppressed. The value entered in column 52 must be a numeric value and is used to specify the number of positions to the right of the decimal point in each number. In the example above it can be seen that the value "0" is entered in column 52 for the EMPNO field. This entry specifies that the Employee Number field contains numeric data and that it is a whole number, that is, there are no values to the right of the implied decimal point.

3.9

For the Regular Earnings field (REGERN) and the Overtime Earnings field (OVTERN), the value "2" is specified in the Decimal Positions field (Column 52). This specifies that there are to be two digits to the right of the decimal point and is the normal situation when the field is to contain dollar values, such as the Regular Earnings of the employee and the Overtime Earnings of the employee. It should be emphasized that the decimal point which is implied by the entry in the "Decimal Positions" column is not in fact punched in the data card. Only the numeric values of the field are punched in the card. The implied decimal position, as specified in Column 52, is used to merely indicate to the RPG compiler where the decimal point should be assumed to be so that proper alignment in calculations and editing will take place. Again, it should be noted that an entry in Column 52 is required to define the field as a numeric field if any calculations are to take place involving the field or if the field is to be edited on a printed report.

CALCULATION SPECIFICATIONS

Addition

As noted at the beginning of the chapter, the values in the Regular Earnings field are to be added to the values in the Overtime Earnings field in order to determine the total earnings of an employee. In addition, a total is to be taken of all of the total earnings for all of the employees to be printed after all of the detail cards have been processed. Whenever calculations are to be performed within an RPG program, the CALCULATION SPECIFICATIONS form is used. The Calculation Specifications form used in this program is illustrated in Figure 3-7.

EXAMPLE

RPG CALCULATION SPECIFICATIONS

Date 6/13/72

Program EARNINGS REPORT

Programmer SHELLY

Punching Instruction — Graphic: Ø O 2 Z; Punch: ZERO, 11-6, Two, 0-9

Page (1 2): Ø3

Program Identification (75–80): PAYRPT

Line (3–5)	Form Type (6)	Control Level (L0-L9, LR, SR) (7–8)	Indicators (9–17)	Factor 1 (18–27)	Operation (28–32)	Factor 2 (33–42)	Result Field (43–48)	Field Length (49–51)	Decimal Positions (52)	Half Adjust (H) (53)	Resulting Indicators (54–59)	Comments (60–74)
01Ø	C		Ø1	REGERN	ADD	OVTERN	TOTERN	6	2			
02Ø	C		Ø1	TOTPAY	ADD	TOTERN	TOTPAY	7	2			
03Ø	C		Ø1	EMPNOS	ADD	1	EMPNOS	4	Ø			

Resulting Indicators: Arithmetic — Plus, Minus, Zero; Compare — High 1>2, Low 1<2, Equal 1=2; Lookup — Table (Factor 2) is High, Low, Equal

Figure 3-7 CALCULATION SPECIFICATIONS Form

From the example above it can be seen that Calculation Specifications form, as do all other RPG forms, contains space for the date, the program name, the programmer's name, the punching instructions, the page number, and the program identification. These portions of the form should always be completed for documentation of the program.

When calculations are to be performed on data which is read as input, the RPG compiler must be informed when the calculations are to be done. This is accomplished through the use of Indicators which may be "on" at the time the calculation is to take place. The use of the Indicators in the sample program is illustrated below.

EXAMPLE

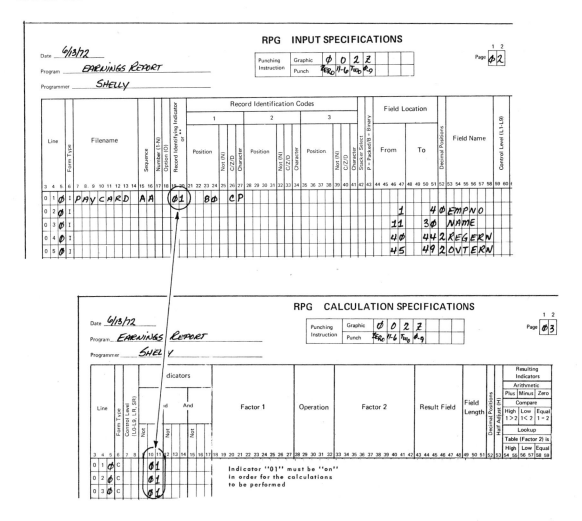

Figure 3-8 Example of the use of Indicators

As was noted previously, when the input card with the character "P" in column 80 is read, the "01" indicator is turned "on" by the object program. The entry in column 10 and column 11 of the Calculation Specifications form of "01" indicates that the calculation on that line is to take place only when the "01" indicator is "on", that is, only when an input card with the value "P" in column 80 is read. The indicators on the Calculation Specifications form specify when a calculation is to take place, not an indicator which is to be set.

3.11

As was noted previously, the Regular Earnings in the input card is to be added to the Overtime Earnings in the input card to give the Total Earnings of the Employee. The ADD operation is performed to add two numbers together. This is illustrated below.

EXAMPLE – CALCULATION SPECIFICATIONS

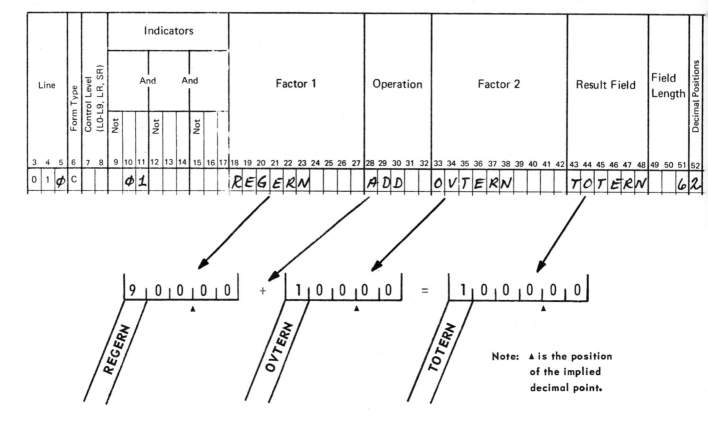

Figure 3-9 Example of ADD Operation

As can be seen, the addition operation will take place only when the "01" indicator is "on" because the value "01" is specified in columns 10-11. When an add operation is to take place, the word "ADD" must be placed in the Operation field (columns 28-32). Note that the word must be left-justified, that is, it must begin in column 28. The fieldname entered in the Factor 1 portion of the form (column 18 through column 27) is the name REGERN, which is the name of the Regular Earnings field in the input card (see Figure 3-6). The fieldname entered in the Factor 2 portion of the form is OVTERN, which is the name of the Overtime Earnings field in the input card. Note that both of these names are left-justified in their respective fields on the form. When the ADD operation takes place, the value stored in the field specified in the Factor 2 specification is added to the value stored in the field specified in the Factor 1 specification and the answer is stored in the field specified in the Result Field portion of the form.

From the example in Figure 3-9 it can be seen that the name of the result field is TOTERN. This field is to be used to store the total earnings of each employee. The field TOTERN has not been previously defined in the Input Specifications because it is not part of the input card. Thus, in addition to specifying the name of the result field, the Calculation Specifications form must be used to define the attributes of the result field. The example below illustrates this definition.

EXAMPLE

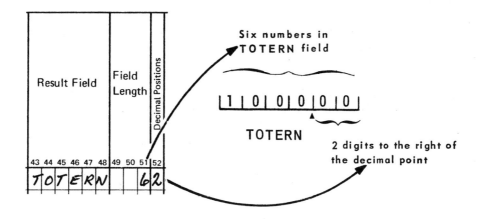

Figure 3-10 Definition of RESULT Field

In the example above, it can be seen that the name TOTERN is used to define the field which is to contain the result of the addition of the values in the REGERN and OVTERN fields. The result field which is defined on the Calculation Specifications must have a name which is six or less characters and which begins with an alphabetic character. Thus, the name of the result field must follow the same rules as those used when defining field names on the Input Specifications form.

The field length entry (Column 49-51) is used to specify the total length of the result field. In the example, it can be seen that the value "6" is specified in column 51, indicating that the field TOTERN is to contain 6 numeric digits. As can be seen, the entry for the length of the field must be right-justified in the Field Length specification and leading zeros need not be included. The maximum length which may be specified for a result field of an arithmetic operation is 15 digits.

The "Decimal Positions" specification (column 52) is used to state the number of positions which are to be assumed to the right of the implied decimal point. This field performs the same function as the "Decimal Positions" field on the Input Specifications form. It must be noted, however, that the decimal positions specified are not in addition to the length specified in the Field Length entry. Thus, as seen above, the field length entry (6) specifies the total number of digits in the field. The "2" in the Decimal Positions field states that within the 6 digits in TOTERN, two of them are to the right of the decimal point. Thus, from the definition in Figure 3-10, there will be 4 positions to the left of the decimal place and two digits to the right of the decimal place in the TOTERN field.

Thus, from the ADD operation specified in Figure 3-9, the value in the REGERN field (900.00) will be added to the value in the OVTERN field (100.00) and the answer (1000.00) will be stored in the TOTERN field.

3.13

A second addition operation is also required in the program. The total earnings for each employee, in the field TOTERN, are to be added so that a total of all of the employees' earnings can be printed at the conclusion of processing the input cards. In order for this total to be accumulated, the value in TOTERN must be added to a field which will accumulate these values. This is illustrated below.

EXAMPLE – CALCULATION SPECIFICATIONS

Line	Form Type	Control Level (L0-L9, LR, SR)	Indicators And		And		Factor 1	Operation	Factor 2	Result Field	Field Length	Decimal Positions
			Not		Not		Not						
3 4 5	6	7 8	9 10 11	12 13 14	15 16 17	18 19 20 21 22 23 24 25 26 27	28 29 30 31 32	33 34 35 36 37 38 39 40 41 42	43 44 45 46 47 48	49 50 51	52
0 1 0	C		0 1			REGERN	ADD	OVTERN	TOTERN	6 2	
0 2 0	C		0 1			TOTPAY	ADD	TOTERN	TOTPAY	7 2	

FIRST CARD

Line

010 | 9 | 0 | 0 | 0 | 0 | 0 | + | 1 | 0 | 0 | 0 | 0 | 0 | = | 1 | 0 | 0 | 0 | 0 | 0 | 0 |
  REGERN   OVTERN   TOTERN

020 | 0 | 0 | 0 | 0 | 0 | 0 | 0 | + | 1 | 0 | 0 | 0 | 0 | 0 | = | 0 | 1 | 0 | 0 | 0 | 0 | 0 |
  TOTPAY   TOTERN   TOTPAY

SECOND CARD

010 | 0 | 8 | 0 | 0 | 0 | + | 0 | 0 | 5 | 0 | 0 | = | 0 | 0 | 8 | 5 | 0 | 0 |
  REGERN   OVTERN   TOTERN

020 | 0 | 1 | 0 | 0 | 0 | 0 | 0 | + | 0 | 0 | 8 | 5 | 0 | 0 | = | 0 | 1 | 0 | 8 | 5 | 0 | 0 |
  TOTPAY   TOTERN   TOTPAY

Figure 3-12 Example of Accumulating a Final Total

In the example above it can be seen that the field used to accumulate the final total, TOTPAY, is defined on the Calculation Specifications form as containing seven numeric digits (Columns 49-51) with two positions to the right of the decimal point (column 52).

It should be recalled that with the ADD operation the field referenced in FACTOR 2 is added to the field referenced in FACTOR 1 and the answer that develops is stored in the area referenced by the RESULT FIELD. Thus, in the example above, on line 020, TOTERN will be added to TOTPAY and the answer will be stored in TOTPAY.

3.14

When the first input card is processed, as illustrated in Figure 3-12, the value in the Regular Earnings field (REGERN) is added to the value in the Overtime Earnings field (OVTERN) and the result is stored in the Total Earnings field (TOTERN). The value just calculated in the TOTERN field is then added to the value in the Total Pay Field (TOTPAY). Note that when the first card is processed, the value in TOTPAY is equal to zero. This is because the RPG compiler sets all numeric fields defined on the Calculation Specifications to zero prior to beginning the processing of the program. After the addition takes place, the field TOTPAY contains the value 1000.00, which is the total earnings of the first employee processed.

When the second card is read, the value in the Regular Earnings field is again added to the value in the Overtime Earnings field to determine the total earnings of the second employee. Note that the result is again stored in the TOTERN field, and that the value from the first card is no longer available. Thus, after the addition on line 010 takes place, the TOTERN field will always contain the total earnings of the employee being processed.

The total earnings of the second employee, which is stored in the TOTERN field, is again added to the value stored in the TOTPAY. When the second card is processed, however, the value in TOTPAY is not equal to zero as when the first card was processed. Instead, it contains the total earnings from the first employee. Thus, when the value in TOTERN is added to the value in TOTPAY for the second employee, the field TOTPAY will contain the total of the first employee's pay and second employee's pay. This is the desired result since the contents of the field TOTPAY are to be printed at the conclusion of the processing of the input data and should contain the total pay for all of the employees processed. As can be seen, the field TOTPAY is used to accumulate the pay for all of the employees which are processed.

Literals

In the previous examples of the addition operations, both Factor 1 and Factor 2 have been fields which contained values to be added or subtracted. It is also possible to specify actual numeric values to be used in the arithmetic operations instead of fields. The example in Figure 3-13 illustrates the use of a "Literal" value in an addition operation.

EXAMPLE – CALCULATION SPECIFICATIONS

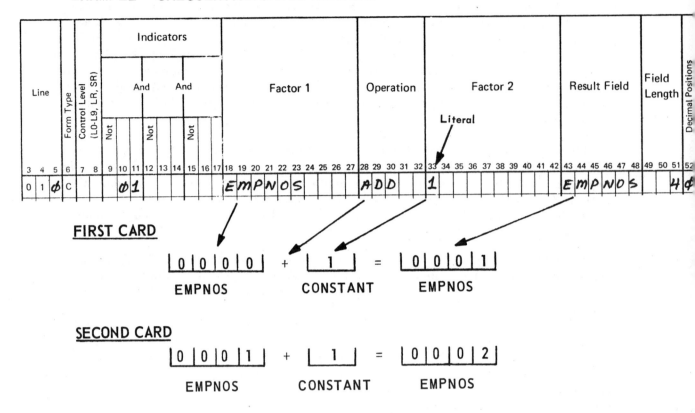

FIRST CARD

SECOND CARD

Figure 3-13 Example of Using a LITERAL Value

Note in the example above that the addition operation will take place only when the 01 Indicator is "on". The field specified in the Factor 1 portion of the form is EMPNOS. This field is to be used to accumulate the number of employees which are processed. The number of employees processed is the same as the number of input cards read. Thus, by adding one to this field each time a card is read, the total number of employees will be accumulated. The operation code, which is always used when an Add operation is to take place, is ADD. The value "1" is specified in column 33 of the Factor 2 field. Note that this value is not the name of a field; rather, it is the actual value which is to be used in the addition operation. The value which is specified in one of the Factor fields instead of a fieldname is called a LITERAL. In this example, the literal is the value "1". A literal used in an arithmetic operation may be 1-10 digits in length and is specified as shown above.

The Result field is the field with the name EMPNOS. Since EMPNOS has not been defined on the input specifications, its length and number of decimal positions must be specified on the Calculation Specifications. Note that the field EMPNOS is defined as 4 digits in length and the zero in column 52 specifies that there are no values to the right of the decimal point. As with the input specifications, if a field contains a value which is to be used in an arithmetic operation or is to be zero-suppressed or edited, it must be defined as a numeric field by specifying a value in the decimal positions field. If there are no decimal values in the field, the number "0" must be placed in the "decimal positions" portion of the form.

REPORT EDITING

Business reports normally require some form of editing, that is, the insertion of special characters such as a dollar sign or period, or the suppression of leading zeros, in order to make the information on the report more meaningful. Editing and zero-suppression are easily accomplished using RPG through the use of special editing characters placed on the Output-Format Specifications form and through special symbols entered on the form. The example below illustrates the Output-Format Specifications form used to edit the detail lines of the payroll report.

EXAMPLE

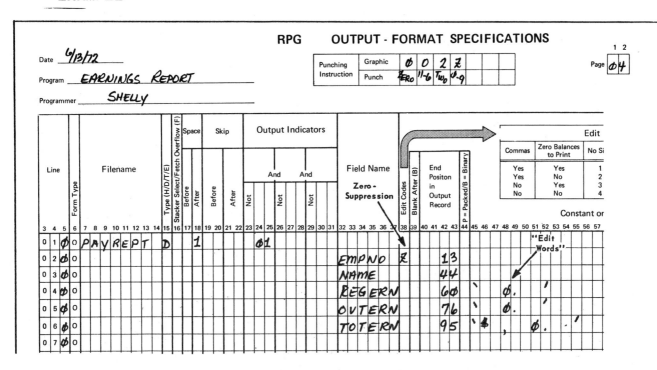

Figure 3-14 Example of Zero-Suppression and Edit Words

Note from the Output-Format Specifications form illustrated above that the entries are specified for the PAYREPT file, which is the payroll report. The line described is a detail line which is to be printed when the "01" indicator is "on". The printer is to be spaced one line after each line is printed on the report.

Zero Suppression

When a field is zero-suppressed on a report, the leading, non-significant zeros in the field are changed to blanks so that the zeros do not appear on the report. In order to zero-suppress a field, the letter of the alphabet "Z" is entered in column 38 of the Output-Format Specifications as illustrated in Figure 3-14. This entry causes a field to be zero-suppressed. The example in Figure 3-15 illustrates the results of zero-suppressing a field.

3.17

DATA IN STORAGE	PRINTED OUTPUT
00001	1
02132	2132
10032	10032
07045	7045
00000	(blank)

Figure 3-15 Examples of Zero-Suppression

As can be seen from the example above, a zero which precedes a significant digit in the field to be edited is changed to a blank in the printed output when a numeric field is zero-suppressed. Significant zeros, that is, zeros which follow the first significant digit in the field, remain in the number.

Editing

When special characters, such as commas, periods, and dollar signs are to be placed in a value which is to be printed, "Edit Words" are used. An "edit word" is a set of characters which are used to indicate the format of the output field. The example in Figure 3-16 illustrates the use of an edit-word in order to edit the Regular Earnings field.

EXAMPLE

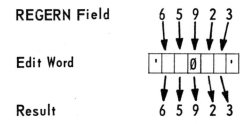

Figure 3-16 Example of the Use of an Edit Word

In the example above, it can be seen that the value 65923, which is stored in the REGERN field, is edited and the result on the printed report will be the 65923. In order to create an edit word, the following rules must be followed:

1. The Edit Word is placed in columns 45-70 on the Output-Format Specifications form.

2. The Edit Word must be enclosed within apostrophes, as illustrated in Figure 3-14 and Figure 3-16.

3. A blank within the Edit Word, that is, within the apostrophes, will be replaced with a character from the corresponding position of the data field which is to be edited. In the example in Figure 3-16, the field to be edited is the REGERN field. As can be seen from the example, the first digit in the REGERN field is "6" and it replaces the first blank in the edit word. The second digit is a "5" and it replaces the second blank in the edit word.

4. A blank within the edit word specifies that a non-significant zero is to be zero-suppressed. This is illustrated in Figure 3-17.

EXAMPLE

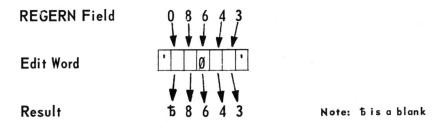

Figure 3-17 Example of Zero-Suppression

Note from the example above that the leading zero in the REGERN field is zero-suppressed because a blank appears in the corresponding position in the Edit word.

5. A zero is entered in the rightmost position of the edit word where zero-suppression is to stop for data edited with an edit word. The zero is replaced with the corresponding character in the field being edited if that position is not zero-suppressed. This is illustrated in Figure 3-18.

EXAMPLE

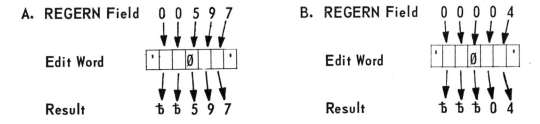

Figure 3-18 Example of Stopping Zero-Suppression

In Example A above, note that a zero is placed in the Edit word in the third position. This indicates that the third position in the field is to be the last position to be zero-suppressed. All digits to the right of the zero in the edit word are to be printed regardless of their value, that is, they will be printed even if they are zero. This is illustrated in Example B, where the value 04 is printed even though the leading zero is non-significant.

6. When punctuation is to be included in the printed output, such as a comma or a decimal point, they are placed in the edit word in the same relative position in which they are to appear in the printed output. This is illustrated below.

EXAMPLE

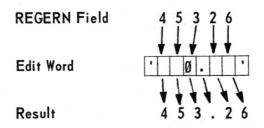

Figure 3-19 Example of Inserting Punctuation in Edited Field

Note in the example above that, since the value in the REGERN field is a "dollar and cents" value, a decimal point is to be inserted in the field between the third and fourth digits in the field. Thus, the decimal point is placed in the edit word between the entries for the third and fourth digits. As can be seen from the example, the decimal point will be included in the output in the same relative position as it is placed within the edit word.

A comma may be inserted in the same manner as a period, that is, by placing it in the proper relative location within the edit word. This is illustrated below.

EXAMPLE

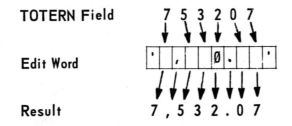

Figure 3-20 Example of Inserting Comma in Edited Field

In the example above it can be seen that a comma is placed in the Edit Word in the location where it is to appear in the edited field on the report, that is, between the first and second digit. When the field is edited, the comma is placed between the first and second digit because this is where it is placed in the edit word.

7. If punctuation is to appear in an edit word which also includes zero-suppression, the punctuation will be printed if it appears to the right of the first significant digit. If it appears to the left of the first significant digit, it will be replaced by a blank. This is illustrated in Figure 3-20.

EXAMPLE

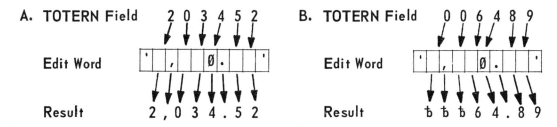

Figure 3-21 Example of Zero-Suppression with Punctuation

Note in the example in Figure 3-21 that the edit words for both editing operations are the same. In Example A, the value in TOTERN contains a significant digit to the left of the comma, that is, in the first position of the number. Therefore, the comma is included in the edited field which will appear on the report. In Example B, however, the first significant digit, which is the third digit in the number 006489, is to the right of the point where the comma is to be inserted. Therefore, the comma is replaced with a blank.

8. If a dollar sign is to be included in the output field to indicate a dollar value, it may be either a "fixed dollar sign" or a "floating dollar sign". A "fixed" dollar sign will always appear in the same location in the edited output field, regardless of the value which is to be edited. A "floating" dollar sign is one which is printed to the left of and adjacent to the first significant character of an edited output field. The use of a fixed dollar sign and a floating dollar sign are illustrated in Figure 3-22.

EXAMPLE

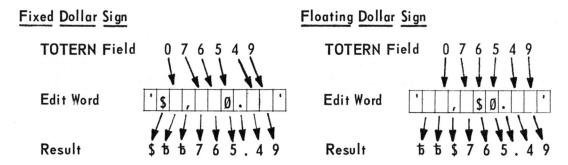

Figure 3-22 Example of Fixed and Floating Dollar Signs

Note from the example in Figure 3-22 that the fixed dollar sign will always appear as the left-most character in the edited field regardless of the value in the field and regardless of whether zero-suppression is to occur. In order to cause a fixed dollar sign to be included in the edited output, a dollar sign must be the first value which is placed in the edit word within the apostrophes. The remainder of the edit word is formed as if a dollar sign were not to be included.

A floating dollar sign, as illustrated in Figure 3-22, is obtained by placing a dollar sign to the immediate left of the zero which specifies the last digit to be zero-suppressed in a number. Thus, as can be seen, the dollar sign is placed to the left of the zero in the Edit Word. When the field is edited, the dollar sign is placed to the left of and adjacent to the first significant digit in the field to be edited. Note that zero-suppression takes place in the same manner as if a floating dollar sign were not being used, that is, the comma is replaced by a blank because there are no significant digits to the left of the position of the comma in the edit word. Note also that an additional blank is included in the edit word to the left of the comma. When a floating dollar sign is being used, there must be space for it in case the entire field to be edited contains significant digits. This is illustrated below.

EXAMPLE

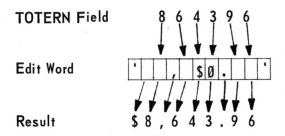

Figure 3-23 Example of Floating Dollar Sign

Note in the example above that there are no insignificant digits in the value to be edited. Thus, the dollar sign must appear to the left of the high-order digit in the edited output. In order for this to occur, two blanks must be specified to the left of the comma in the edit word so that there is space for the floating dollar sign.

9. There must be enough blanks and zeros in the edit word to accomodate all of the digits which are in the field to be edited. Thus, as illustrated previously, if there are six digits in the field to be edited, there must be six blanks in the edit word if zero-suppression is not to occur or five blanks and one zero if zero-suppression is to occur. If a floating dollar sign is to be used, there must still be the same amount of blanks and zeros in the edit word as there are digits to be edited.

10. All fields which are to be edited must be defined as numeric fields on either the Input Specifications form or the Calculation Specifications form, that is, there must be a value specified in the "Decimal Positions" entry on these forms for the field to be edited.

The example below illustrates some of the typical uses of the Editing feature of the RPG language.

EXAMPLE – OUTPUT SPECIFICATIONS

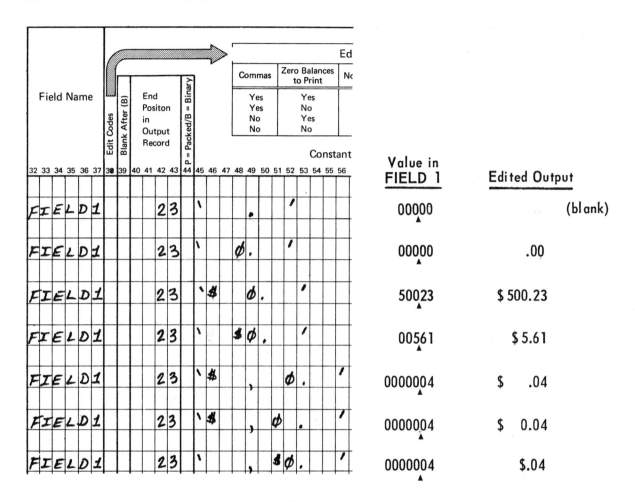

Figure 3-24 Examples of Editing

PRINTING TOTAL LINES

As was noted previously, two totals are accumulated during the processing of the input data – a total of the number of employees processed and the total pay for all of the employees. These totals are to be printed after all of the input records have been processed. In order to print them, a specification must be made on the Output-Format Specifications form to indicate that a total line is to be printed. The Output-Format Specifications form used in the sample program is illustrated in Figure 3-25.

EXAMPLE

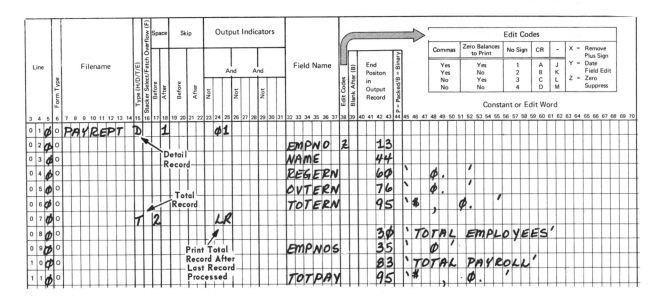

Figure 3-25 Example of Total Lines

As noted previously, when a line is to be printed on the report after each input record is read, the line is considered a Detail Line and the letter of the alphabet "D" is entered in Column 15 of the Output-Format Specifications form to indicate this. When a Total Line is to be printed, that is, a line which will be printed only at a specified time and not for each input record which is read, the letter "T" must be entered in the "Type" field (column 15). As can be seen from the example above, the letter "T" is entered in column 15 after the specifications of the Detail lines. Note also that the filename PAYREPT is not entered in columns 7-13 on coding line 070. This is because the filename is specified on line 010 and if the total line is to be written or printed on the same file as the detail line, the filename need not be repeated.

It can be seen from the example in Figure 3-25 that the total line is to be printed on the report after two lines are spaced because the value "2" is entered in column 17 ("Space Before"). Thus, as illustrated in Figure 3-2, the total line is separated from the detail lines by two spaces. The total lines are to be printed only after all of the detail records have been processed. The fact that they are to be printed after the Last Record has been processed is indicated by the entry "LR" in the Output Indicators portion of the form in columns 24-25. The "LR" entry specifies that the total line is to be printed only after the Last Record has been processed. Thus, by making the LR entry, a total line will be processed only after all of the input cards have been read and processed.

Note that the field specifications for the total line, as with the detail line, are placed on the next subsequent coding line from the entries to define the type of record to be printed, that is, the specifications for the fields to be printed are on line 080 of the coding form and the specifications for the type of record to be printed are on line 070.

The Total Line in Figure 3-25 introduces the use of "constant" values which are to be printed on a printed line. The use of these constant values is illustrated in Figure 3-26.

3.24

EXAMPLE

Output – Format Specifications

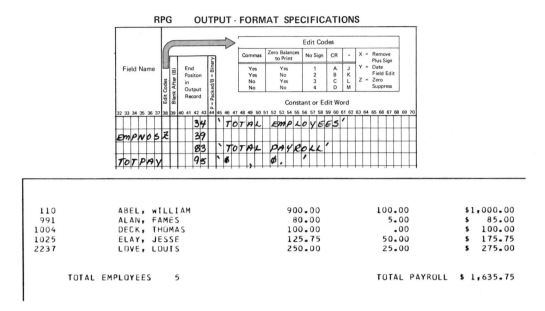

RPG   OUTPUT - FORMAT SPECIFICATIONS

				110	ABEL, WILLIAM	900.00	100.00	$1,000.00
				991	ALAN, FAMES	80.00	5.00	$ 85.00
				1004	DECK, THOMAS	100.00	.00	$ 100.00
				1025	ELAY, JESSE	125.75	50.00	$ 175.75
				2237	LOVE, LOUIS	250.00	25.00	$ 275.00

```
     110        ABEL, WILLIAM          900.00      100.00      $1,000.00
     991        ALAN, FAMES             80.00        5.00      $    85.00
    1004        DECK, THOMAS           100.00         .00      $   100.00
    1025        ELAY, JESSE            125.75       50.00      $   175.75
    2237        LOVE, LOUIS            250.00       25.00      $   275.00

        TOTAL EMPLOYEES     5                         TOTAL PAYROLL  $ 1,635.75
```

Figure 3-26 Example of the Use of Constant Values

As can be seen from the report above, the constant values "TOTAL EMPLOYEES" and
"TOTAL PAYROLL" are printed on the Total line of the report in order to identify the
total values. In order to specify a constant value which is to be printed, the ending
position of the constant in the output record is specified in columns 40-43 in the same
manner as used with values which are to be printed from fields. Note in the example above
that the constant "TOTAL EMPLOYEES" will end in column 34 and the constant "TOTAL
PAYROLL" will end in column 83. The constant to be printed is placed in the "Constant
or Edit Word" portion of the form (columns 45-70). The constants to be printed must be
enclosed within apostrophes as illustrated in Figure 3-26. Within the apostrophes, any
alphabetic, numeric, or special character desired by the programmer may be specified. As
illustrated, blanks may also be included within the apostrophes. When the constant is
printed, the value within the apostrophes is printed but the apostrophes are not printed.

Subtraction

Although not illustrated in the sample problem, the entries for a subtraction operation are very similar to addition. As noted, the ADD operation code is used to add the values in two fields together. In order to subtract the values in two fields from one another, the SUB operation is used. This is illustrated in Figure 3-27.

EXAMPLE – CALCULATION SPECIFICATIONS

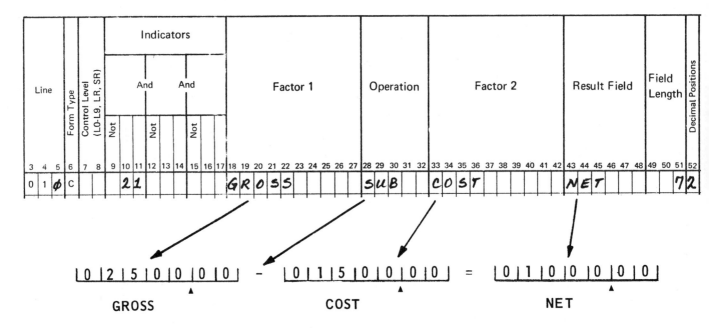

Figure 3-27 Example of SUB Operation

In the example above, it can be seen that the Subtraction operation is to take place if indicator 21 is "on". It will not take place if indicator 21 is "off" because the value 21 is placed in the indicator columns 10-11. The field which is specified in the Factor 1 columns (columns 18-27) is the subtrahend of the subtraction operation and the field which is specified in the Factor 2 columns (column 33-42) is the minuend, that is, the value in the field in the Factor 2 specification will be subtracted from the value in the field in the Factor 1 specification. Thus, in the example above, the value in the field COST will be subtracted from the value in the field GROSS. The difference, or the answer to the subtraction operation, is stored in the Result field specified in columns 43-48. Thus, the difference between GROSS and COST will be stored in the field NET. As can be seen, the length of the NET field is 7 digits with two digits to the right of the decimal place. In the example above, the value 1500 in the COST field is subtracted from the value 2500 in the GROSS field and the answer, 1000.00, is stored in the NET field.

SAMPLE PROBLEM

The following pages illustrate the complete documentation for the sample problem developed in this chapter. Input consists of the Employee Earnings Cards, containing the Employee Number, Employee Name, Regular Earnings, and Overtime Earnings. Total Earnings are to be calculated by adding Regular Earnings to Overtime Earnings. If there are no Overtime Earnings, the field will contain zeros.

Output is to consist of a printed report.

Input

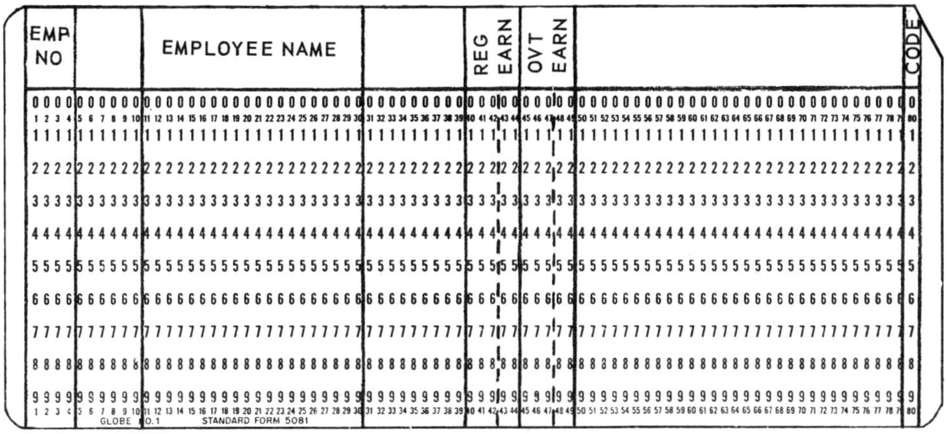

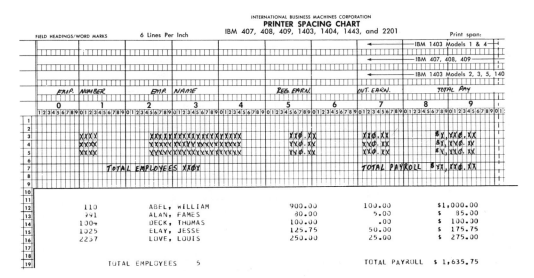

Figure 3 - 28 Input

Output

Figure 3 - 29 Output

RPG Coding

The RPG coding from the sample problem is illustrated below.

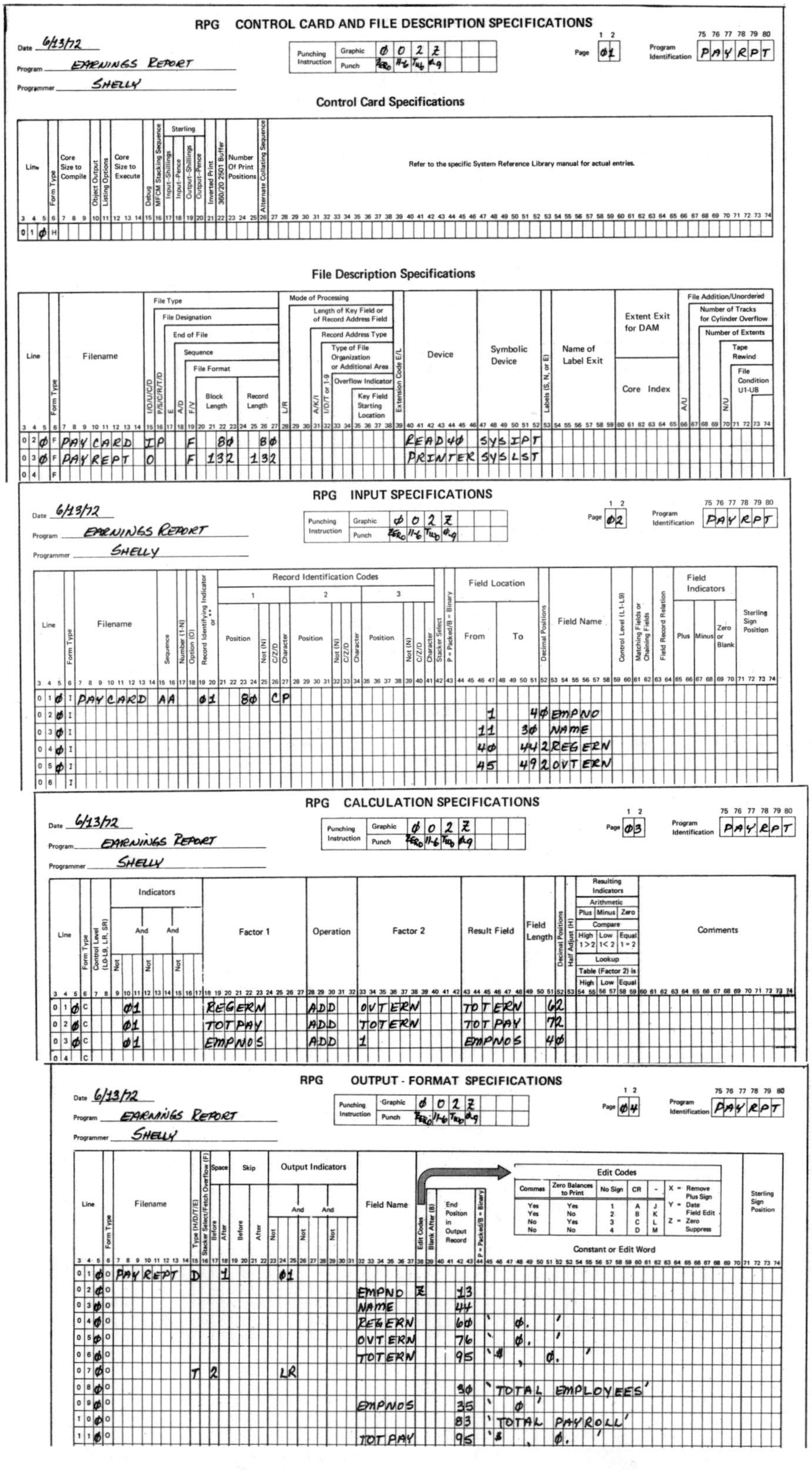

Figure 3-30 RPG Coding

Program

The following is the source program listing printed by the RPG compiler.

```
DUS/360*RPG*CL 3-9                  NO NAME                    09/11/72        PAGE 0001

         01 010 H                                                              PAYRPT
001      01 020 FPAYCARD IP   F   80   80              READ40 SYSIPT           PAYRPT
002      01 030 FPAYREPT O    F  132  132              PRINTERSYSLST           PAYRPT
003      02 010 IPAYCARD AA    01   80 CP                                      PAYRPT
004      02 020 I                                         1     40EMPNO        PAYRPT
005      02 030 I                                        11   30 NAME          PAYRPT
006      02 040 I                                        40  442REGERN         PAYRPT
007      02 050 I                                        45  492OVTERN         PAYRPT
008      03 010 C     01      REGERN     ADD  OVTERN    TOTERN  62             PAYRPT
009      03 020 C     01      TOTPAY     ADD  TOTERN    TOTPAY  72             PAYRPT
010      03 030 C     01      EMPNOS     ADD  1         EMPNOS  40             PAYRPT
011      04 010 OPAYREPT D   1      01                                        PAYRPT
012      04 020 O                          EMPNO Z  13                         PAYRPT
013      04 030 O                          NAME     44                         PAYRPT
014      04 040 O                          REGERN   60 '  0. '                 PAYRPT
015      04 050 O                          OVTERN   76 '  0. '                 PAYRPT
016      04 060 O                          TOTERN   95 '$ ,  0. '              PAYRPT
017      04 070 O      T 2      LR                                             PAYRPT
018      04 080 O                                   30 'TOTAL EMPLOYEES'       PAYRPT
019      04 090 O                          EMPNOS   35 ' 0 '                    PAYRPT
020      04 100 O                                   83 'TOTAL PAYROLL'         PAYRPT
021      04 110 O                          TOTPAY   95 '$ ,  0. '              PAYRPT
```

Figure 3-31 RPG Program Listing

CHAPTER 3

REVIEW QUESTIONS

1. How is a field defined as a numeric field? When is it required that a field be defined as a numeric field?

2. How is a field which is to be used as a final total counter initially set to zero?

3. Why can't a literal be specified in the Result Field of the Add operation?

4. What is the difference between a fixed dollar sign and a floating dollar sign? How does the compiler know whether a dollar sign is to be fixed or floating?

5. What values may be placed in a constant which is defined on the Output-Format Specifications? What values may be placed in a literal which is used in Factor 2 of an Add operation on the Calculation Specifications?

CHAPTER 3

STUDENT EXERCISES

1. Write the entries on the Input Specifications to set on indicator 35 if there is the character "T" in column 5 and the character "S" in column 80 of a card read from the PAYCD file.

RPG INPUT SPECIFICATIONS

Line	Form Type	Filename	Sequence	Number (1-N)	Option (O)	Record Identifying Indicator or **	Record Identification Codes												Stacker Select	P = Packed/B = Binary	Field Location		Decimal Positions	Field Name
							1				2				3									
							Position	Not (N)	C/Z/D	Character	Position	Not (N)	C/Z/D	Character	Position	Not (N)	C/Z/D	Character			From	To		
01	I																							
02	I																							
03	I																							
04	I																							

2. Write the entries on the Calculation Specifications to add the value 6.00 to the value stored in the field ACCUM and have the sum stored in the field TOTFLD. The maximum size answer which can be stored in TOTFLD is 9999.99.

RPG CALCULATION SPECIFICATIONS

Line	Form Type	Control Level (L0-L9, LR, SR)	Indicators						Factor 1	Operation	Factor 2	Result Field	Field Length	Decimal Positions	Half Adjust (H)
				And		And									
			Not		Not		Not								
01	C														
02	C														
03	C														
04	C														

3.31

3. The following are the names of the fields which are to be printed on the file PRTOUT.

Beginning Print Position	Field Name	Format to be printed
Col 3	DIV	X0X (zero suppress first 2 digits)
Col 23	NAME	XXXXXXXXXXXXXXXXXXXX
Col 55	TOTFLD	$X,XX0.XX (print a dollar sign, comma, decimal point and zero suppress up to the decimal point)

The report is to be single spaced whenever the card defined in Question #1 is read. Write the entries required to print this line on the Output-Format Specifications.

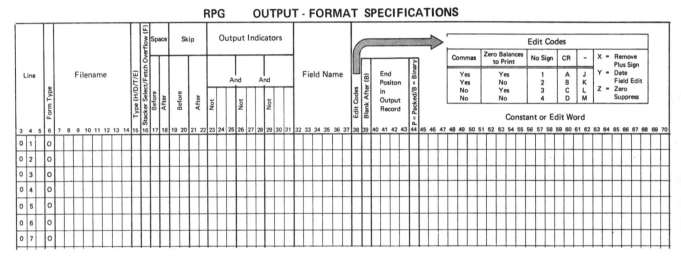

RPG   OUTPUT - FORMAT SPECIFICATIONS

4. After the last card is to be processed, the message "END OF REPORT" is to be printed on the report which is produced in Question #3. Write the entries on the Output-Format Specifications to cause this line to be printed.

RPG   OUTPUT - FORMAT SPECIFICATIONS

Debugging RPG Programs

Problem 1

Instructions: The following RPG program contains an error or errors which have occurred during compilation. Circle each error and record the corrected entries directly on the listing. Explain the error and method of correction in the space provided below.

```
DOS/360*RPG*CL 3-9                    CASHMAN                      10/05/72           PAGE 0001

           01 120 H                                                                    PAYRPT
001        01 130 FPAYCARD IP   F  80   80          READ40 SYSIPT                      PAYRPT
002        01 140 FPAYREPT O    F 132  132          PRINTERSYSLST                      PAYRPT
003        02 150 IPAYCARD AA   01   80 CP                                             PAYRPT
004        02 160 I                                 1    4 EMPNO                        PAYRPT
005        02 170 I                                11   30 NAME                         PAYRPT
006        02 180 I                                     40  442REGERN                   PAYRPT
007        02 190 I                                     45  492OVTERN                   PAYRPT
008        03 200 C     01      REGERN     ADD  OVTERN   TOTERN  62                     PAYRPT
009        03 210 C     01      TOTPAY     ADD  TOTERN   TOTPAY  72                     PAYRPT
           03 220 C     01      EMPNOS     ADD  1        EMPNOS  40                     PAYRPT
                                                                                     NOTE 086
010        04 230 OPAYREPT D  1      01                                                PAYRPT
011        04 240 O                            EMPNO Z  13                             PAYRPT
012        04 250 O                            NAME     44                             PAYRPT
013        04 260 O                            REGERN   60 ' 0. '                      PAYRPT
014        04 270 O                            OVTERN   76 ' 0. '                      PAYRPT
015        04 280 O                            TOTERN   95 '$ , 0. '                   PAYRPT
           04 290 O           2      LR                                                PAYRPT
                                                                                     NOTE 167
016        04 300 O                                     30 'TOTAL EMPLOYEES'           PAYRPT
           04 310 O                            EMPNOS   35 ' 0 '                        PAYRPT
                                                                                     NOTE 179
017        04 320 O                                     83 'TOTAL PAYROLL'             PAYRPT
018        04 330 O                            TOTPAY   95 '$ , 0. '                   PAYRPT
```

```
DOS/360*RPG*CL 3-9                    CASHMAN                      10/05/72           PAGE 0002

                                     SYMBOL   TABLES

RESULTING  INDICATORS

ADDRESS RI       ADDRESS RI       ADDRESS RI       ADDRESS RI       ADDRESS RI       ADDRESS RI       ADDRESS RI

000014 1P        000015 LR        000016 00        000017 01        00007A L0        000085 H0        000086 H1
000087 H2        000088 H3        000089 H4        00008A H5        00008B H6        00008C H7        00008D H8
00008E H9
FIELD  NAMES

ADDRESS FIELD        ADDRESS FIELD        ADDRESS FIELD        ADDRESS FIELD        ADDRESS FIELD

000123  EMPNO        000127  NAME         00013B  REGERN        00013E  OVTERN       000141  TOTERN
000145  TOTPAY

LITERALS

ADDRESS LITERAL              ADDRESS LITERAL              ADDRESS LITERAL

000149   --/.--              000150   - -,--/.--          00015B  TOTAL EMPLOYEES
00016A  TOTAL PAYROLL        000177  --,--/.--
    011                                                                      NOTE 227

NOTE  086   OPERATION CODE (COLUMNS 28-32) IS INVALID OR MISSING.  SPECIFICATION IS NOT
            PROCESSED.

NOTE  167   RECORD TYPE (COLUMN 15) IS NOT H, D, OR T.  SPECIFICATION IS NOT PROCESSED.

NOTE  179   FIELD NAME (COLUMNS 32-37) IS UNDEFINED.  SPECIFICATION IS NOT PROCESSED.

NOTE  227   IMPROPER USE OF PACKING OR ZERO SUPPRESSION ON ALPHAMERIC OR PACKED FIELD.
            ENTRY OF BLANK IS ASSUMED FOR INVALID CODE.
```

EXPLANATION _____

_____

Instructions: The following RPG program contains an error or errors which occur during execution. Circle each error and record the corrected entries directly on the listing. Explain the error and method of correction in the space provided below.

```
DOS/360*RPG*CL 3-9              CASHMAN                    10/05/72        PAGE 0001
                                                                          PAYRPT
          01 120 H                                                        PAYRPT
001       01 130 FPAYCARD IP  F   80  80          READ40 SYSIPT           PAYRPT
002       01 140 FPAYREPT O   F  132 132          PRINTERSYSLST           PAYRPT
003       02 150 IPAYCARD AA  01  80 CP                                   PAYRPT
004       02 160 I                                  1    40EMPNO          PAYRPT
005       02 170 I                                 11    30 NAME          PAYRPT
006       02 180 I                                 40    442REGERN        PAYRPT
007       02 190 I                                 45    492OVTERN        PAYRPT
008       03 200 C    01       REGERN  ADD  OVTERN  TOTERN  62            PAYRPT
009       03 210 C    01       TOTPAY  ADD  TOTERN  TOTPAY  72            PAYRPT
010       03 220 C    01       EMPNOS  ADD  1       EMPNOS  40            PAYRPT
011       04 230 OPAYREPT D  1      01                                    PAYRPT
012       04 240 O                              EMPNO Z  13               PAYRPT
013       04 250 O                              NAME     44               PAYRPT
014       04 260 O                              REGERN   60 '  0. '       PAYRPT
015       04 270 O                              OVTERN   76 '  0. '       PAYRPT
016       04 280 O                              TOTERN   95 '$ , 0. '     PAYRPT
017       04 290 O       T 2      LR                                      PAYRPT
018       04 300 O                                       30 'TOTAL EMPLOYEES'  PAYRPT
019       04 310 O                              EMPNOS   35 ' 0 '         PAYRPT
020       04 320 O                                       83 'TOTAL PAYROLL'    PAYRPT
021       04 330 O                              TOTPAY   95 '$ , 0. '     PAYRPT
```

```
DOS/360*RPG*CL 3-9              CASHMAN                    10/05/72        PAGE 0002

                                     SYMBOL  TABLES

RESULTING  INDICATORS

ADDRESS RI      ADDRESS RI      ADDRESS RI      ADDRESS RI      ADDRESS RI      ADDRESS RI      ADDRESS RI

000014 1P       000015 LR       000016 00       000017 01       00007A L0       000085 H0       000086 H1
0000R7 H2       000088 H3       000089 H4       00008A H5       00008B H6       00008C H7       00008D H8
00008E H9
FIELD NAMES

ADDRESS FIELD       ADDRESS FIELD       ADDRESS FIELD       ADDRESS FIELD       ADDRESS FIELD

000123 EMPNO        000126 NAME         00013A REGERN       00013D OVTERN       000140 TOTERN
000144 TOTPAY       000148 EMPNOS

LITERALS

ADDRESS LITERAL           ADDRESS LITERAL           ADDRESS LITERAL

00014B  1                 00014C  --/.--            000153    -,-/.--
00015C  TOTAL EMPLOYEES   00016B  ---/-             000171  TOTAL PAYROLL
00017E  - --,--/.-                                                          NOTE 230
   016                                                                      NOTE 230
   021

NOTE  230  FIELD TO BE EDITED IS GREATER THAN THE EDIT WORD.  SIGNIFICANT DIGITS MAY BE
           LOST.
```

```
       110        ABEL, WILLIAM        900.00        100.00        $   10.00      NOTE: Answers are
       991        ALAN, FAMES           80.00          5.00        $     .85            Incorrect
      1004        DECK, THOMAS         100.00           .00        $    1.00
      1025        ELAY, JESSE          125.75         50.00        $    1.75
      2237        LOVF, LOUIS          250.00         25.00        $    2.75

           TOTAL EMPLOYEES    5                       TOTAL PAYROLL     $16,357.5
```

EXPLANATION _____

CHAPTER 3

PROGRAMMING ASSIGNMENT 1

INSTRUCTIONS

Write the RPG program which will produce a Gross Profit Report.

INPUT

The input is to consist of Sales Cards containing the Item Number, Description, Sales Amount, and Cost Amount. The format of the cards is illustrated below.

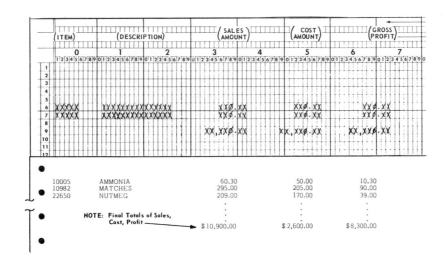

OUTPUT

Output is to consist of a listing of the Item Number, Description, Sales Amount, Cost Amount and Gross Profit. Gross Profit is to be calculated by subtracting the Cost Amount field from the Sales Amount field. Final Totals are to be taken for the Sales Amount field, the Cost Amount field, and the Gross Profit. A printer spacing chart and a segment of the report is illustrated below.

TEST DATA — ASSIGNMENT NO. 1

Item (col 1-5)	Description (col 6-20)	Sales Amount (col 21-25)	Cost Amount (col 26-30)
10005	Ammonia	06030	05000
10982	Matches	29500	20500
22650	Nutmeg	20900	17000
33569	Bleach	57809	22156
44521	Detergent	05607	02178
55903	Cleanser	42175	36598
69340	Sponges	04487	03905

DOS JOB CONTROL

```
// JOB jobname
// OPTION LINK
// EXEC RPG

  — Student Source Deck —

/*
// EXEC LNKEDT
// EXEC

  — Test Data —

/*
/&
```

Note: This assumes that the assignment for the card read and printer are standard assignments known to the student.

PROGRAMMING ASSIGNMENT

INSTRUCTIONS

Write the RPG program to produce a Sales Listing Report.

INPUT

The input consists of Sales Cards which contain the Salesman Number, the Salesman Name, the Current Sales, the Previous Year-To-Date Sales, and the Sales Returns.

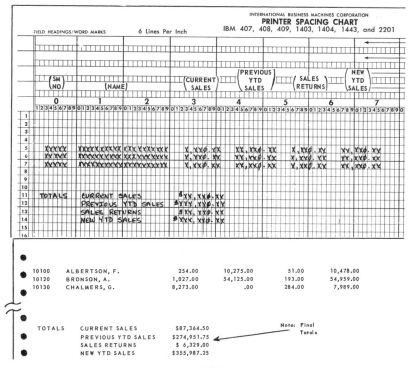

OUTPUT

The output is to consist of a Sales Listing which contains the Salesman Number, the Salesman Name, the Current Sales, the Previous Year-To-Date Sales, the Sales Returns, and the New Year-To-Date Sales. The New Year-To-Date Sales are calculated by adding the Current Sales and the Previous Year-To-Date Sales and then subtracting the Sales Returns. Final Totals are to be taken for the Current Sales, the Previous Year-To-Date Sales, the Sales Returns, and the New Year-To-Date Sales.

		Current Sales	Previous YTD Sales	Sales Returns	New YTD Sales
10100	ALBERTSON, F.	254.00	10,275.00	51.00	10,478.00
10120	BRONSON, A.	1,027.00	54,125.00	193.00	54,959.00
10130	CHALMERS, G.	8,273.00	.00	284.00	7,989.00

TOTALS	CURRENT SALES	$87,364.50	
	PREVIOUS YTD SALES	$274,951.75	Note: Final Totals
	SALES RETURNS	$ 6,329.00	
	NEW YTD SALES	$355,987.25	

TEST DATA – ASSIGNMENT NO. 2

Salesman Number (col 1-5)	Name (col 6-25)	Current Sales (col 26-31)	Previous YTD Sales (col 32-38)	Sales Returns (col 39-44)
10100	Albertson, F.	025400	1027500	00 5100
10120	Bronson, A.	102700	5412500	019300
10130	Chalmers, G.	827300	0000000	028400
10140	Delvertz, H.	398700	3890600	003250
10150	Fritz, C.	653098	3452876	013290
10160	Lilum, R.	126750	0387690	003189

DOS JOB CONTROL

// JOB jobname

// OPTION LINK

// EXEC RPG

  – Student Source Deck –

/*

// EXEC LNKEDT

// EXEC

  – Test Data –

/*

/&

Note: This assumes that the assignment for the card read and printer are standard assignments known to the student.

3.38

CHAPTER 4

MULTIPLICATION – DIVISION

INTRODUCTION

In many programming applications, the use of division and multiplication are essential to produce the required output. When programming in RPG, multiplication and division are easily accomplished through the use of the MULT and DIV operations on the Calculation Specifications form.

In performing any multiplication operation, manually or with a computer, the maximum size of the answer that may develop may be determined by adding the number of digits in the multiplier to the number of digits in the multiplicand. For example, if multiplying a 3-digit Rate field by a 2-digit Hours field in order to obtain the pay of an employee, the maximum size of the answer that may develop is an answer 5-digits in length.

EXAMPLE

$3.20 **RATE** (Multiplicand)
 40 **HOURS** (Multiplier)
_____
$128.00   (Maximum size answer — 5 digits in length

It is important that the programmer understand this basic concept of arithmetic to properly perform multiplication operations using the computer.

Rounding

In programming for business applications involving decimal positions in the answer it is frequently desirable to round off the answer. For example, in a problem if the answer is developed as $1.254, it may be desirable to round the answer to $1.25 so that the amount can be expressed in terms of dollars and cents. If the answer is developed as $1.255, the amount would normally be rounded upward to $1.26. Note in the preceeding examples that if the low-order position is less than 5, the amount is not rounded upward. If the low-order position is 5 or greater, the amount is rounded upward.

Both the multiplication operation and the process of rounding an answer are easily accomplished through the entries on the Calculation Specifications form. The following example illustrates the entries which would be required to multiply a 3-digit rate field by a 3-digit hours field (XX.X) in order to obtain the pay.

EXAMPLE

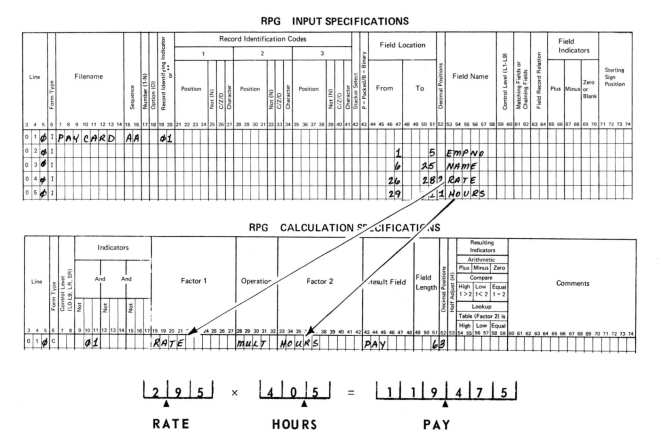

Figure 4-1 Example of Multiplication Operation

In the example above it can be seen that the value in the field RATE is to be multiplied by the value in the field HOURS and the answer is to be stored in the field PAY. The RATE field contains 3 digits with two digits to the right of the decimal point, as defined on the Input Specifications illustrated. The HOURS field also contains three digits with one digit to the right of the decimal point. The answer, therefore, will be 6 digits in length with three digits to the right of the decimal point.

With the Multiply operation (MULT) the contents of the field or literal specified in FACTOR 1 is multiplied by the contents of the field or literal specified in FACTOR 2. The result of this operation is placed in the RESULT FIELD.

In the example in Figure 4-1 it can be seen that the multiplicand (RATE) and the multiplier (HOURS) are specified in the Factor 1 (columns 18-27) and Factor 2 (columns 33-42) portions of the calculation specifications form. The names specified in the Factor 1 and Factor 2 areas must have been previously defined either on the Input Specifications, such as in the example, or on the Calculation Specifications form. As noted previously, all fields used in an arithmetic operation must be defined as numeric fields, that is, a value must be entered in the "Decimal Positions" column of the form. The operation code to cause multiplication to take place is MULT and this value is placed in columns 28-31 of the Calculation Specifications.

The result field in the example is named PAY. As noted previously, it must be six digits in length in order to store the answer from the Multiplication operation. Thus, the field length is specified as "6" in columns 49-51. Since the RATE field contains two digits to the right of the decimal point and the HOURS field contains one digit to the right of the decimal point, the answer in the PAY field will contain three digits to the right of the decimal point. This is indicated by the value "3" being entered in the Decimal Positions field in column 52 of the Calculation Specifications form. When the value in RATE is multiplied by the value in HOURS, the six digit answer will be stored in the field PAY with three digits to the right of the implied decimal point.

As mentioned previously, it is many times desirable to round off the result of a multiplication or division operation. In the previous example, the value in the field PAY contains three digits to the right of the decimal point. Normally, when dealing with dollar amounts, the result of the multiplication would be rounded off so that there were only two digits to the right of the decimal point. The entries to accomplish this are illustrated in Figure 4-2.

EXAMPLE – CALCULATION SPECIFICATIONS

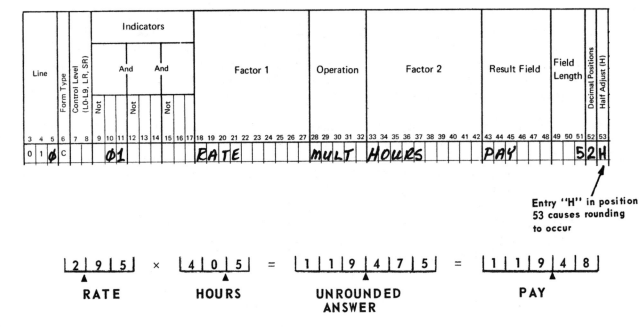

Figure 4-2 *Example of Rounding Answer in Multiplication Operation*

Note from the example above that the values in the RATE and HOURS field are multiplied in the same manner as illustrated in Figure 4-1. The answer to the multiplication operation is stored in a "work area" which is used by the object program. The answer stored in the work area is then rounded off to two decimal positions and is stored in the PAY field.

In order to request that an answer is to be rounded, the value "H" is placed in the "Half Adjust" column (column 53) on the Calculation Specifications. This value indicates that Half-Adjusting or Rounding is to occur on the answer of the arithmetic operation specified in the Operation columns (columns 28-32). Note also in the example above that the length of the PAY field is specified as 5 and the number of decimal positions is specified as 2, rather than the 6 for the length and the 3 for the decimal positions as specified in the example in Figure 4-1. Whenever rounding is to take place, the length specified and the number of decimal positions specified must refer to the length of the field after the half-adjusting has taken place. Thus, as can be seen from the example in Figure 4-2, the PAY field is 5 digits in length with two positions to the right of the decimal place.

DIVISION

When division is to be performed in the RPG program, the DIV operation is specified on the Calculation Specifications form. In the example below, a Year-To-Date Sales field is to be divided by the Months Employed field to determine an average monthly sales for the employee. The Year-To-Date Sales field forms the DIVIDEND, the Months Employed field forms the DIVISOR, and the answer or QUOTIENT reflects the Average Monthly Sales. The REMAINDER after dividing is zero.

EXAMPLE

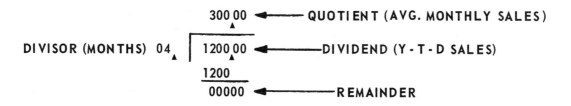

Figure 4-3 Example of Division

Note from the example above that the value 1200.00 is divided by the value 04 and the answer is 300.00 with a remainder of zero. In any division problem the maximum number of digits which may be found in the answer to a division problem is equal to the number of digits in the Dividend. This is illustrated in the following example.

EXAMPLE

Figure 4-4 Example of Maximum Size of Quotient

Note from the example above that the maximum number of digits which may be contained in the quotient is equal to the number of digits in the Dividend.

The maximum number of digits which may be contained in the remainder after a division operation is the number of digits contained in the Divisor. This is illustrated below.

EXAMPLE

Figure 4-5 Example of Remainder

Note in the example above that the Remainder, 1111, contains the same number of digits as the divisor, 2222. It is important that the programmer understand these functions of the division operation in order to properly use the Divide Instruction in RPG.

DIV Operation

In order to divide two numbers using the RPG language, the DIV operation is specified on the Calculation Specifications form. This is illustrated below.

EXAMPLE – CALCULATION SPECIFICATIONS

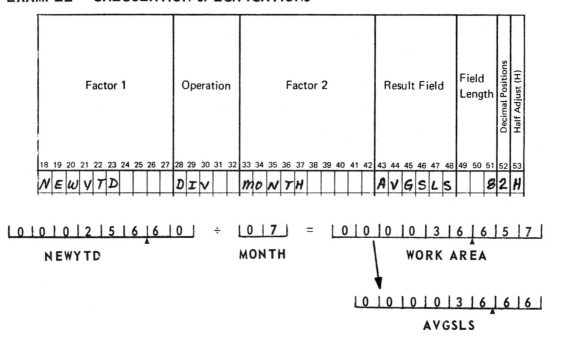

Figure 4-6 Example of DIV Operation

With the Divide operation (DIV) the contents of the field or literal specified in FACTOR 1 is divided by the contents of the field or literal specified in FACTOR 2. The result of this operation (the quotient) is placed in the area specified in the RESULT FIELD. The contents of the field or literal in FACTOR 2 cannot be zero.

Note in the example in Figure 4-6 that the value in the field NEWYTD is divided by the value in the field MONTH and the answer is stored in the field AVGSLS. As can be seen from the example, the dividend is placed in the Factor 1 portion of the form (columns 18-27), the divisor is placed in the Factor 2 portion of the form (columns 33-42) and the field to be used for the quotient is placed in the Result Field area (columns 43-48). The length of the field to be used for the quotient is specified in columns 49-51. As noted previously, it must be equal to the size of the dividend, which, in the example, is eight digits with two digits to the right of the decimal point. Note also that Half-Adjusting is specified by placing the character "H" in column 53. Thus, the division will be carried out to three places to the right of the decimal place and then the quotient will be rounded to two decimal places as specified by the "2" in column 52. As when rounding is used with Multiplication, the field length and Decimal positions specified for the receiving field in a Division operation must be the values which are to be used after the half-adjusting has taken place.

MVR Operation

In the previous example, it was illustrated how the quotient may be half-adjusted to a given number of places to the right of the decimal point. When half-adjusting is to take place, the remainder value from the division is not available. If half-adjusting is not to take place, however, it is possible to retrieve the remainder after the division operation has taken place. This is accomplished with the MVR operation on the Calculation Specifications form and is illustrated in Figure 4-7.

EXAMPLE – CALCULATION SPECIFICATIONS

Factor 1	Operation	Factor 2	Result Field	Field Length	Decimal Positions
18 19 20 21 22 23 24 25 26 27	28 29 30 31 32	33 34 35 36 37 38 39 40 41 42	43 44 45 46 47 48	49 50 51	52
N E W Y T D	D I V	M O N T H	A V G S L S	8	2
	M V R		R E M A I N	2	2

Results

$$\lfloor 0 \mid 0 \mid 0 \mid 2 \mid 5 \mid 6 \mid 6 \mid 0 \rfloor \div \lfloor 0 \mid 7 \rfloor = \lfloor 0 \mid 0 \mid 0 \mid 0 \mid 3 \mid 6 \mid 6 \mid 5 \rfloor \quad \lfloor 0 \mid 5 \rfloor$$

NEWYTD   MONTH   AVGSLS   REMAIN

Division

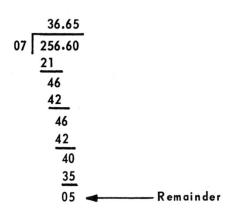

```
              36.65
        07 | 256.60
             21
             ___
             46
             42
             ___
              46
              42
              ___
               40
               35
               ___
               05  ◄────── Remainder
```

Figure 4-7 Example of MVR Operation

In the example above it can be seen that the value in the NEWYTD field is to be divided by the value in the MONTH field and the quotient is to be stored in the AVGSLS field. Note that since half-adjusting is not specified, the answer in the AVGSLS field is not rounded upward. Instead, the low-order positions are truncated. Immediately following the DIV operation is the MVR (MoVe Remainder) operation code. This instruction causes the remainder which resulted from the Division operation to be moved to the field which is specified in the Result Field of the Calculation Specifications (columns 43-48). In the example above, this is the field REMAIN. The MVR instruction must always immediately follow the DIV instruction from which the remainder is to be retrieved.

The size of the field to be used for the remainder value is quite important in order for the MVR operation to take place properly. The value specified in the Field Length portion of the form (columns 49-51) must be equal to the length of the field specified in Factor 2 of the Division operation. In the example, this is the MONTH field and it is 2 digits in length. Thus, the length specified for the Result Field (REMAIN) of the MVR operation is 2.

4.8

The reason that the lengths of these two fields must be the same is illustrated in Figure 4-5, where it is shown that the maximum size of the remainder is equal to the number of digits contained in the Divisor. On the calculation specifications form, of course, the Divisor field is specified in the Factor 2 portion of the form.

The number of decimal positions to the right of the decimal place for the remainder is determined in one of two ways: if the sum of the decimal places in Factor 2 of the division operation and the number of decimal places in the Result field is greater than the number of decimal places in Factor 1, then this sum is used. Otherwise, the number of decimal places in the remainder should be equal to the number of decimal places in Factor 1 of the division operation. In the example in Figure 4-7, it can be seen that two digits will be to the right of the decimal place (column 52). The reason for the number of digits to the right of the decimal place is because the remainder is always the value which must be added to the product of the divisor times the quotient in order to obtain the dividend. The following example illustrates this.

EXAMPLE 1

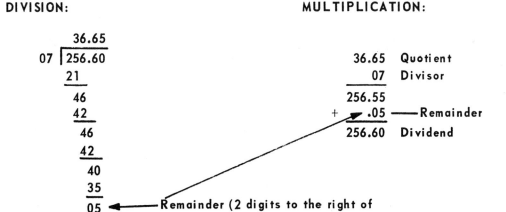

Figure 4-8 Example of Remainder

Note in the example above that the product of the quotient and the divisor plus the remainder is equal to the dividend. In the example, the remainder is 2 digits in length because there are two digits in the Divisor, which is the field specified in the Factor 2 field on the Calculation Specifications form. The remainder has two digits to the right of the decimal place because the sum of the decimal places in the divisor plus the sum of the decimal places in the quotient is 2.

SAMPLE PROGRAM

The sample program in this chapter illustrates the use of the Divide Operation in a problem. The RPG program reads a file of Sales Cards and produces a Sales Report. The input cards are illustrated below.

Input

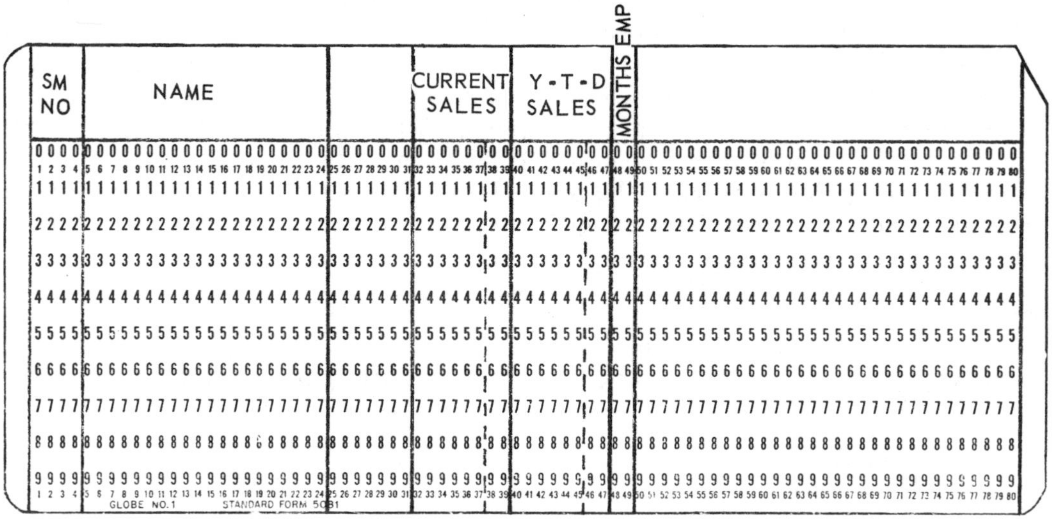

Figure 4-9 Input

Note from the card illustrated above that it contains a Salesman Number, a Salesman Name, the Current Sales, the Year-To-Date Sales, and the Months Employed. The report which is to be prepared contains the Salesman Number, the Salesman Name, the Current Sales, the Old Year-To-Date Sales, the New Year-To-Date Sales (Current Sales + Old Year-To-Date Sales), the Months Employed, and the Average Monthly Sales (New Year-To-Date Sales ÷ Months Employed). In addition, final totals are taken for the Current Sales, the Old Year-To-Date Sales, and the New Year-To-Date Sales. The report is illustrated below.

Report

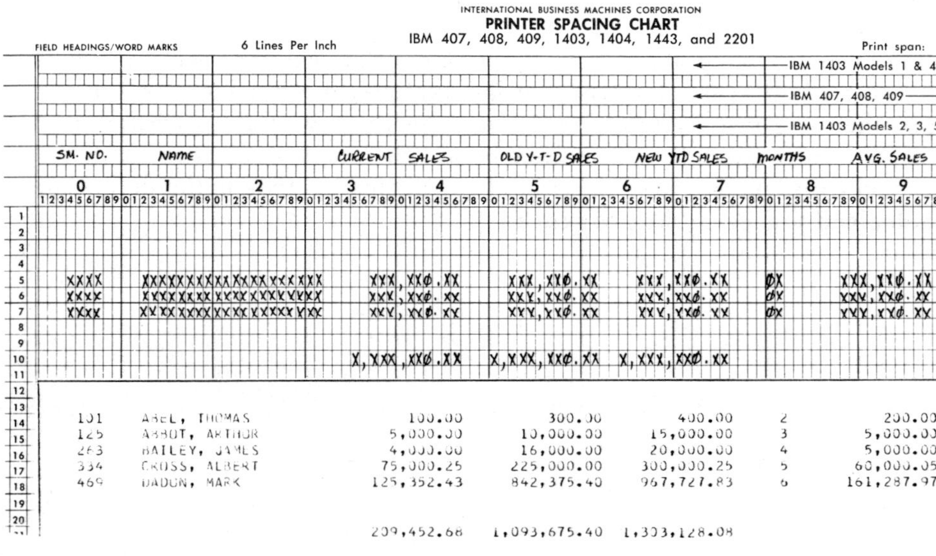

Figure 4-10 Output

4.10

RPG CODING

The entries for the sample program are similar to those used in previous programs. The File Description Specifications for the sample program are illustrated below.

EXAMPLE

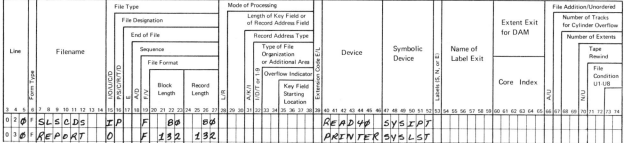

File Description Specifications

Figure 4-11 File Description Specifications

Note from the File Description Specifications illustrated above that the card input file is named SLSCDS and the printer output file is named REPORT. As noted previously, these filenames may be any desired by the programmer as long as the rules for forming a filename are followed. The remainder of the entries are the same as in previous programs.

The Input Specifications must be used to define the input card illustrated in Figure 4-9. The Input Specifications utilized in the sample program are shown below.

EXAMPLE

RPG   INPUT SPECIFICATIONS

Date 6/20/72
Program AVERAGE SALES REPORT
Programmer SHELLY

Punching Instruction — Graphic: Ø 0 2 2 — Punch: ZERO 11-6 Two 8-9

Page Ø2   Program Identification AVGSLS

Line	Form Type	Filename	Sequence	Number (1-N)	Option (O)	Record Identifying Indicator or **	Position	Not (N)	C/Z/D	Character	Position	Not (N)	C/Z/D	Character	Position	Not (N)	C/Z/D	Character	P = Packed/B = Binary	From	To	Decimal Positions	Field Name	Control Level (L1-L9)	Matching Fields or Chaining Fields	Field Record Relation	Plus	Minus	Zero or Blank	Sterling Sign Position
0 1	Ø	I	SLSCDS	AA		Ø1																									
0 2	Ø	I																		1	4	Ø	SLSMAN							
0 3	Ø	I																		5	24		NAME							
0 4	Ø	I																		32	39	2	CURSLS							
0 5	Ø	I																		40	47	2	YTDSLS							
0 6	Ø	I																		48	49	Ø	MONTH							

Figure 4-12 Input Specifications

In the Input Specifications illustrated above, it can be seen that there is no given sequence in which the input cards will appear and whenever a card is read, indicator 01 will be turned "on". The fields within the input card are defined as has been illustrated in previous programs. Note that the SLSMAN field is defined as a numeric field (zero in column 52) because it is to be edited on the report. The CURSLS field, the YTDSLS field, and the MONTH field are all numeric because they are to be used in arithmetic calculations and they are also to be edited on the report. Whenever a field is to be edited or used in an arithmetic operation, it must be defined as a numeric field.

The entries on the Calculation Specifications are used to determine the New Year-To-Date Sales by adding the Old Year-To-Date Sales and the Current Sales. The Average Sales are then determined by dividing the New Year-To-Date Sales by the Months Employed. Totals are then taken for the three fields as illustrated in Figure 4-10. The Calculation Specifications are illustrated below.

EXAMPLE

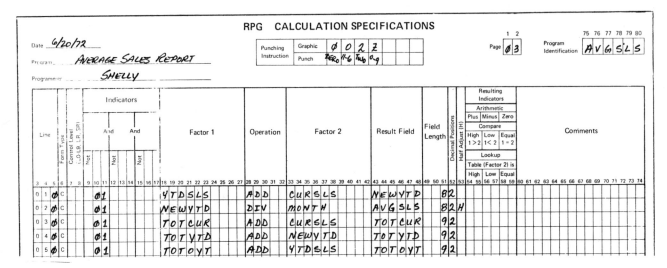

Figure 4-13 Calculation Specifications

Note in the Calculation Specifications in Figure 4-13 that all of the calculations necessary to derive the information on the printed report are performed. The Average Sales, which is calculated by dividing the New Year-To-Date Sales by the Months Employed, is to be rounded after the division takes place.

The Output Specifications for the Sample Program are illustrated in Figure 4-14.

EXAMPLE

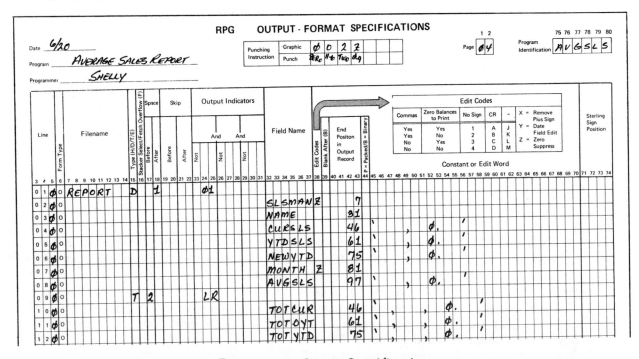

Figure 4-14 Output Specifications

4.12

Program

The program listing for the sample program is illustrated below.

```
DOS/360*RPG*CL 3-9                    NO NAME                    09/11/72            PAGE 0001

             01 010 H                                                                AVGSLS
001          01 020 FSLSCDS   IP  F  80  80              READ40 SYSIPT               AVGSLS
002          01 030 FREPORT   O   F 132 132              PRINTERSYSLST               AVGSLS
003          02 010 ISLSCDS   AA   01                                                AVGSLS
004          02 020 I                                      1     40SLSMAN            AVGSLS
005          02 030 I                                      5     24 NAME             AVGSLS
006          02 040 I                                     32     392CURSLS           AVGSLS
007          02 050 I                                     40     472YTDSLS           AVGSLS
008          02 060 I                                     48     490MONTH            AVGSLS
009          03 010 C    01       YTDSLS    ADD  CURSLS   NEWYTD  82                 AVGSLS
010          03 020 C    01       NEWYTD    DIV  MONTH    AVGSLS  82H                AVGSLS
011          03 030 C    01       TOTCUR    ADD  CURSLS   TOTCUR  92                 AVGSLS
012          03 040 C    01       TOTYTD    ADD  NEWYTD   TOTYTD  92                 AVGSLS
013          03 050 C    01       TOTOYT    ADD  YTDSLS   TOTOYT  92                 AVGSLS
014          04 010 OREPORT   O   1     01                                          AVGSLS
015          04 020 O                         SLSMANZ   7                            AVGSLS
016          04 030 O                         NAME     31                            AVGSLS
017          04 040 O                         CURSLS   46 '  ,  0.  '                AVGSLS
018          04 050 O                         YTDSLS   61 '  ,  0.  '                AVGSLS
019          04 060 O                         NEWYTD   75 '  ,  0.  '                AVGSLS
020          04 070 O                         MONTH Z  81                            AVGSLS
021          04 080 O                         AVGSLS   97 '  ,  0.  '                AVGSLS
022          04 090 O      T 2      LR                                               AVGSLS
023          04 100 O                         TOTCUR   46 ' ,  ,  0.  '              AVGSLS
024          04 110 O                         TOTOYT   61 ' ,  ,  0.  '              AVGSLS
025          04 120 O                         TOTYTD   75 ' ,  ,  0.  '              AVGSLS
```

Figure 4-15 Computer Listing

4.13

CHAPTER 4

REVIEW QUESTIONS

1. State the rule concerning the size of the area which must be reserved for the answer of a multiplication operation.

2. State the rule concerning the size of the area which must be reserved for the answer (quotient) of a divide operation. State the rule concerning the size of the area which must be reserved for the remainder in a divide operation.

3. Explain the method of deciding the number of decimal places to the right of the decimal point which must be reserved for a remainder in a divide operation.

4. How does "half-adjusting" or rounding take place in an RPG program?

5. If rounding is to take place in a divide operation, can the MVR instruction be used? Why?

CHAPTER 4

STUDENT EXERCISES

1. A RATE field (XX.XX) is to be multiplied by an HOURS field (XX.X) and the answer is to be stored in the PAY field (XXXX.XX). Write the Multiply statement which will cause this to occur. The RATE field and the HOURS field are defined in the Input Specifications but the PAY field has not been defined. The answer should be rounded off. Multiplication is to take place when indicator 01 is "ON".

RPG   CALCULATION SPECIFICATIONS

Line	Form Type	Control Level (L0-L9, LR, SR)	Indicators And Not	And Not	And Not	Factor 1	Operation	Factor 2	Result Field	Field Length	Decimal Positions	Half Adjust (H)	Resulting Indicators Arithmetic Plus / Compare High 1>2	Minus / Low 1<2	Zero / Equal 1=2
0 1	C														
0 2	C														
0 3	C														
0 4	C														
0 5	C														
0 6	C														

2. Divide the field TOTAL (XXXX.XX) by 2.25 and store the answer in HALFTOT. Do not half adjust. Store the remainder in REMAIN. HALFTOT and REMAIN have not been previously defined. This division should take place when indicator 22 is "on".

RPG   CALCULATION SPECIFICATIONS

Line	Form Type	Control Level (L0-L9, LR, SR)	Indicators And Not	And Not	And Not	Factor 1	Operation	Factor 2	Result Field	Field Length	Decimal Positions	Half Adjust (H)	Resulting Indicators Arithmetic Plus / Compare High 1>2	Minus / Low 1<2	Zero / Equal 1=2
0 1	C														
0 2	C														
0 3	C														
0 4	C														
0 5	C														
0 6	C														
0 7	C														
0 8	C														
0 9	C														

3. Multiply the RATE field (X.XX) by the HOURS field (XX.X) and divide the answer by PARTS (XXXX) giving the COSTPT answer. The Rate field, Hours field and Parts field are defined on the input specifications. The COSTPT answer should be rounded, as it is a dollar amount. The multiply and divide operation are to occur when Indicator 10 is "on".

RPG   CALCULATION SPECIFICATIONS

Line	Form Type	Control Level (L0-L9, LR, SR)	Indicators And Not	And Not	And Not	Factor 1	Operation	Factor 2	Result Field	Field Length	Decimal Positions	Half Adjust (H)	Resulting Indicators Arithmetic Plus / High 1>2	Minus / Low 1<2	Zero / Equal 1=2
0 1	C														
0 2	C														
0 3	C														
0 4	C														
0 5	C														
0 6	C														
0 7	C														
0 8	C														
0 9	C														

4. Divide the PAY field (XXX.XX) by the PIECES field (XXXX) and <u>add</u> the remainder to the REMAIN field. The PAY field and the PIECES field are defined on the Input Specifications. Perform the operations when Indicator 25 is "ON".

RPG   CALCULATION SPECIFICATIONS

Line	Form Type	Control Level (L0-L9, LR, SR)	Indicators And Not	And Not	And Not	Factor 1	Operation	Factor 2	Result Field	Field Length	Decimal Positions	Half Adjust (H)	Resulting Indicators Arithmetic Plus / High 1>2	Minus / Low 1<2	Zero / Equal 1=2
0 1	C														
0 2	C														
0 3	C														
0 4	C														
0 5	C														
0 6	C														
0 7	C														
0 8	C														
0 9	C														

Debugging RPG Programs

Problem 1

Instructions: The following RPG program contains an error or errors which have occurred during compilation. Circle each error and record the corrected entries directly on the listing. Explain the error and method of correction in the space provided below.

```
DOS/360*RPG*CL 3-9              CASHMAN                    10/05/72           PAGE 0001

                                                                             AVGSLS
        01 950 H                                                             AVGSLS
001     01 960 FSLSCDS  IP  F  80  80          READ40 SYSIPT                 AVGSLS
002     01 970 FREPORT   O  F 132 132          PRINTERSYSLST                 AVGSLS
        02 980  SLSCDS  AA  01                                              NOTE 200
                                                                             AVGSLS
        02 990 I                                  1    40SLSMAN            NOTE 130
                                                                             AVGSLS
     S  02 000 I                                  5    24 NAME             NOTE 130
                                                                             AVGSLS
        02 010 I                                 32   392CURSLS           NOTE 130
                                                                             AVGSLS
        02 020 I                                 40   472YTDSLS           NOTE 130
                                                                             AVGSLS
        02 030 I                                 48   490MONTH            NOTE 130
                                                                            NOTE 077
                                           SLSCDS                          NOTE 210
003     03 040 C   01      YTDSLS   ADD  CURSLS   NEWYTD  82                 AVGSLS
004     03 050 C   01      NEWYTD   DIV  MONTH    AVGSLS  82H                AVGSLS
005     03 060 C   01      TOTCUR   ADD  CURSLS   TOTCUR  92                 AVGSLS
006     03 070 C   01      TOTYTD   ADD  NEWYTD   TOTYTD  92                 AVGSLS
007     03 080 C   01      TOTOYT   ADD  YTDSLS   TOTOYT  92                 AVGSLS
008     04 090 OREPORT  D  1     01                                         AVGSLS
                                                                            NOTE 192
        04 100 O                       SLSMANZ   7                           AVGSLS
                                                                            NOTE 179
        04 110 O                       NAME     31                           AVGSLS
                                                                            NOTE 179
009     04 120 O                       CURSLS   46 '  ,  0. '                AVGSLS
010     04 130 O                       YTDSLS   61 '  ,  0. '                AVGSLS
011     04 140 O                       NEWYTD   75 '  ,  0. '                AVGSLS
012     04 150 O                       MONTH Z  81                           AVGSLS
013     04 160 O                       AVGSLSZ  97 '  ,  0. '                AVGSLS
                                                                            NOTE 178
014     04 170 O   T 2      LR                                              AVGSLS
015     04 180 O                       TOTCUR   46 ' ,  ,  0. '             AVGSLS
016     04 190 O                       TOTOYT   61 ' ,  ,  0. '             AVGSLS
017     04 200 O                       TOTYTD   75 ' ,  ,  0. '             AVGSLS
```

SYMBOL   TABLES

RESULTING INDICATORS

ADDRESS	RI	ADDRESS	RI	ADDRESS	RI	ADDRESS	RI	ADDRESS	RI	ADDRESS	RI	ADDRESS	RI
000014	1P	000015	LR	000016	00	000017	01	00007A	L0	000085	H0	000086	H1
000087	H2	000088	H3	000089	H4	00008A	H5	00008B	H6	00008C	H7	00008D	H8
00008E	H9												

FIELD NAMES

ADDRESS	FIELD	ADDRESS	FIELD	ADDRESS	FIELD	ADDRESS	FIELD	ADDRESS	FIELD
000123	YTDSLS	000127	CURSLS	00012B	NEWYTD	000130	MONTH	000134	AVGSLS
000139	TOTCUR	00013E	TOTYTD	000143	TOTOYT				

LITERALS

ADDRESS	LITERAL	ADDRESS	LITERAL	ADDRESS	LITERAL		
000148	----,--/.--	000154	-,---,--/.--				
	003				01		NOTE 212
	003				YTDSLS		NOTE 214
	003				CURSLS		NOTE 214
	004				01		NOTE 212
	004				MONTH		NOTE 214
	005				01		NOTE 212
	005				CURSLS		NOTE 214
	006				01		NOTE 212
	007				01		NOTE 212
	007				YTDSLS		NOTE 214
	008				01		NOTE 212
	009				CURSLS		NOTE 214
	010				YTDSLS		NOTE 214
	012				MONTH		NOTE 214

NOTE   077   THERE ARE NO VALID INPUT SPECIFICATIONS IN THIS PROGRAM. EXECUTION IS DELETED.

NOTE   130   RECORD IDENTIFICATION IS OUT OF SEQUENCE - I.E., FIRST INPUT SPECIFICATION OR
             FOLLOWING AN INVALID 'OR', 'AND', OR FILE NAME. SPECIFICATION IS NOT
             PROCESSED.

NOTE   178   ZERO SUPPRESSION (COLUMN 38) MAY NOT BE SPECIFIED FOR CONSTANTS OR EDIT WORDS.
             ENTRY OF BLANK IN COLUMN 38 IS ASSUMED.

NOTE   179   FIELD NAME (COLUMNS 32-37) IS UNDEFINED. SPECIFICATION IS NOT PROCESSED.

NOTE   192   OUTPUT INDICATOR (COLUMNS 24-25, 27-28, OR 30-31) IS INVALID OR UNDEFINED.
             ENTRY OF L0 IS ASSUMED.

NOTE   200   FORM TYPE (COLUMN 6) IS INVALID OR OUT OF SEQUENCE. SPECIFICATION IS NOT
             PROCESSED.

NOTE   210   WARNING - FILENAME (COLUMNS 7-14) IS DEFINED BUT NEVER USED.

NOTE   212   RESULTING INDICATOR IS INVALID OR UNDEFINED. ENTRY OF L0 IS ASSUMED.

NOTE   214   FIELD NAME IS UNDEFINED. FIELD IS PROCESSED WITH ASSUMED LENGTH OF 004.

'END OF COMPILATION'

EXPLANATION_____

_____

_____

_____

Debugging RPG Programs

Problem 2

Instructions: The following RPG program contains an error or errors which occur during execution. Circle each error and record the corrected entries directly on the listing. Explain the error and method of correction in the space provided below.

```
DOS/360*RPG*CL 3-9                 CASHMAN                    10/05/72            PAGE 0001
           01 950 H                                                              AVGSLS
001        01 960 FSLSCDS  IP  F  80  80              READ40 SYSIPT             AVGSLS
002        01 970 FREPORT  O   F 132 132              PRINTERSYSLST             AVGSLS
003        02 980 ISLSCDS  AA   01                                             AVGSLS
004        02 990 I                               1    40SLSMAN                AVGSLS
005      S 02 000 I                               5    24 NAME                 AVGSLS
006        02 010 I                              32   392CURSLS                AVGSLS
007        02 020 I                              40   472YTDSLS               AVGSLS
008        02 030 I                              48   490MONTH                AVGSLS
009        03 040 C    01     YTDSLS    ADD  CURSLS   NEWYTD  82              AVGSLS
010        03 050 C    01     MONTH     DIV  NEWYTD   AVGSLS  82H             AVGSLS
011        03 060 C    01     TOTCUR    ADD  CURSLS   TOTCUR  92              AVGSLS
012        03 070 C    01     TOTYTD    ADD  NEWYTD   TOTYTD  92              AVGSLS
013        03 080 C    01     TOTOYT    ADD  YTDSLS   TOTOYT  92              AVGSLS
014        04 090 OREPORT  D  1    01                                        AVGSLS
015        04 100 O                       SLSMANZ  7                          AVGSLS
016        04 110 O                       NAME    31                          AVGSLS
017        04 120 O                       CURSLS  46 '   ,   0. '             AVGSLS
018        04 130 O                       YTDSLS  61 '   ,   0. '             AVGSLS
019        04 140 O                       NEWYTD  75 '   ,   0. '             AVGSLS
020        04 150 O                       MONTH Z 81                          AVGSLS
021        04 160 O                       AVGSLS  97 '   ,   0. '             AVGSLS
022        04 170 O    T 2     LR                                            AVGSLS
023        04 180 O                       TOTCUR  46 ' ,   ,   0. '           AVGSLS
024        04 190 O                       TOTOYT  61 ' ,   ,   0. '           AVGSLS
025        04 200 O                       TOTYTD  75 ' ,   ,   0. '           AVGSLS
```

```
101    ABEL, THOMAS            100.00        300.00        400.00     2        .01
125    ABBOT, ARTHUR         5,000.00     10,000.00     15,000.00     3        .00
263    BAILEY, JAMES         4,000.00     16,000.00     20,000.00     4        .00
334    CROSS, ALBERT        75,000.25    225,000.00    300,000.25     5        .00
469    DADON, MARK         125,352.43    842,375.40    967,727.83     6        .00

                           209,452.68  1,093,675.40  1,303,128.08   NOTE: Average is
                                                                          Incorrect
```

EXPLANATION _____

_____

_____

_____

PROGRAMMING ASSIGNMENT 1

INSTRUCTIONS

Write the RPG program to produce a Budget Report. The Input and Output are illustrated below.

INPUT

The input to the program consists of a file of Budget Expense Cards. They contain the Employee Number, the Employee Name, the Budget Amount, and the Current Expenses.

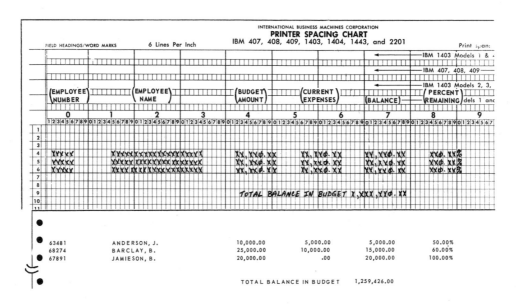

OUTPUT

The output from the program is a Budget Report containing the Employee Number, the Employee Name, the Budget Amount, the Current Expenses, the Balance in the Budget, and the Percentage of the Budget Remaining. The Balance is calculated by subtracting the Current Expenses from the Budget Amount. The Percentage is calculated by dividing the Balance by the Budget Amount, that is, Balance ÷ Amount = Percentage.

TEST DATA – ASSIGNMENT NO. 1

Emp. No. (col 1-5)	Name (col 6-25)	Budget Amount (col 29-35)	Expenses (col 36-42)
63481	Anderson, J.	1000000	0500000
68274	Barclay, B.	2500000	1000000
67891	Jamieson, B.	2000000	0000000
74310	Kiler, G.	4500000	1123400
89763	Milner, F.	1000000	0135896
99784	Ziepak, K.	3500000	2976509

DOS JOB CONTROL

```
// JOB jobname
// OPTION LINK
// EXEC RPG

  – Student Source Deck –

/*
// EXEC LNKEDT
// EXEC

  – Test Data –

/*
/&
```

Note: This assumes that the assignments for the card read and printer
are standard assignments known to the student.

PROGRAMMING ASSIGNMENT 2

INSTRUCTIONS

A computer billing report is to be produced from card input which specifies the number of minutes which the computer is used for a given application. The billing rate for the computer is $50.00 per hour of usage.

INPUT

The input consists of a card containing the Job Name, the Customer Name to which the job is to be billed, and the number of minutes which the job used on the computer.

OUTPUT

The output is to consist of the Computer Billing Report. The fields on the report are the Job Name, the Customer Name, the Hours and Minutes which the computer job used, the cost per hour, and the Total Billing Cost. Note that the minutes which are contained in the input card must be converted to hours and minutes in order to use the per hour billing rate and also to be printed on the report.

4.22

TEST DATA – ASSIGNMENT NO. 2

Job Name (col 1-8)	Customer Name (col 9-28)	Minutes (col 29-32)
P782301A	Absco, Inc.	0210
P821024C	Jackson's Co.	1236
Q903478D	Nelson Electronics	0462
S5326710	Quarry Gloves	0973
S853421B	Simmons Inc.	2896
T098876R	Timonson, Inc.	0032

DOS JOB CONTROL

// JOB jobname

// OPTION LINK

// EXEC RPG

  – Student Source Deck –

/*

// EXEC LNKEDT

// EXEC

  – Test Data –

/*

/&

Note: This assumes that the assignments for the card read and printer
are standard assignments known to the student.

CHAPTER 5

COMPARING

INTRODUCTION

The ability of the computer to compare numeric or alphanumeric values and perform alternative operations based upon the results of this comparison provides electronic data processing systems with great flexibility in the solution of business and mathematical problems.

Comparisons are normally made on data which is stored in main storage and alternative operations are performed based upon conditions which result from the comparisons. These comparisons may be made to determine if data in one portion of main storage is less than or greater than data stored in another portion of main storage. The examples below illustrate how these comparisons may be made. In the examples, an area called SALAMT (Sales Amount) is compared to an area called QUOTA (Sales Quota).

Example 1: Numeric data is equal.

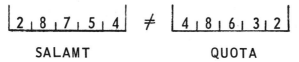

Figure 5-1 *Example of Equal Numeric Data*

Note in the example above that the values contained in the main storage areas called SALAMT and QUOTA are equal, that is, both areas contain the value 17354. When the two values above are compared, the computer would indicate that they are equal and the program could then process data based upon the fact that the values are equal.

Example 2: Numeric data is unequal.

$$\lfloor 2 \mid 8 \mid 7 \mid 5 \mid 4 \rfloor \neq \lfloor 4 \mid 8 \mid 6 \mid 3 \mid 2 \rfloor$$

SALAMT   QUOTA

Figure 5-2 *Example of Unequal Numeric Data*

Note in Figure 5-2 that the numeric data stored in SALAMT and QUOTA are not equal. When this condition occurs, certain indicators could be set to control the processing of the program.

It can also be seen that the data in the area SALAMT is less than the data contained in the area QUOTA. This is illustrated in Figure 4-3.

Example 3: Numeric data in one area is less than numeric data in the second area.

$$\lfloor 2\,|\,8\,|\,7\,|\,5\,|\,4 \rfloor \quad < \quad \lfloor 4\,|\,8\,|\,6\,|\,3\,|\,2 \rfloor$$

SALAMT   QUOTA

Figure 5-3 Example of Less Than Condition

As noted, the value in SALAMT is less than the value in QUOTA. It should be noted also that all of the comparisons illustrated begin with the high-order value in the field, that is, the left-most number in the field. Thus, in the example above, since the "2", which is the high-order value in the SALAMT field, is less than the "4", which is the high-order value in the QUOTA field, the entire SALAMT field is considered smaller than the QUOTA field. Comparisons are always performed on a high-order to low-order basis.

Example 4: Numeric data in one area is greater than numeric data in a second area.

$$\lfloor 6\,|\,4\,|\,0\,|\,9\,|\,1 \rfloor \quad > \quad \lfloor 4\,|\,1\,|\,2\,|\,7\,|\,3 \rfloor$$

SALAMT   QUOTA

Figure 5-4 Example of Greater Than Condition

In the example above it can be seen that the numeric data in the field SALAMT is greater than the numeric data in QUOTA since the high-order value in SALAMT is "6" and the high-order value in QUOTA is "4".

Alphabetic data may also be compared. The example below illustrates the comparison of alphabetic data.

Example 5: Comparison of Alphabetic Data.

$$\lfloor J\,|\,O\,|\,N\,|\,E\,|\,S \rfloor \quad < \quad \lfloor S\,|\,M\,|\,I\,|\,T\,|\,H \rfloor$$

DATA1   DATA2

Figure 5-5 Example of Alphabetic Comparison

In the example above it can be seen that the value JONES in the area DATA1 is compared to the value SMITH in the area DATA2. When alphabetic comparisons are made, the "value" of each letter of the alphabet is greater as the alphabet progresses from A-Z. Thus, in the example above, the "J" which begins the name JONES is considered less than the letter "S" which begins the name SMITH. Therefore, the entire field in DATA1 is considered less than the field in DATA2.

COMP Operation

In order to compare two values when programming in RPG, the COMP operation is used and is specified on the Calculation Specifications form. The example below illustrates the use of the COMP Operation.

EXAMPLE

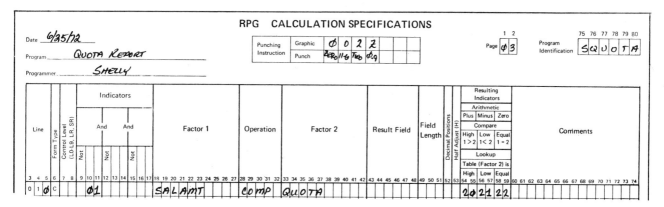

Figure 5-6 Example of COMP Operation

With the compare operation (COMP) the contents of the field or the literal specified in FACTOR 1 is compared to the contents of the field or literal specified in FACTOR 2. The outcome of this operation can be used to set on an indication that has been specified in positions 54-59, (Resulting Indicators High, Low, or Equal).

In the example above, the value in the field SALAMT is to be compared to the value in the field QUOTA. Note that the fieldname SALAMT is placed in the Factor 1 field on the Calculation Specifications form (columns 18-27) and the fieldname QUOTA is placed in the Factor 2 field (columns 33-42). Note that no entry is made in the Result field in Columns 43-48. The operation code to compare two values is COMP and this word must be placed in columns 28-31 of the Calculation Specifications form.

When comparisons between the value in two fields are performed, there must be some indication of the results of the comparisons so that alternative processing may take place based upon the results. When programming in RPG, these results are indicated through the use of the Resulting Indicators which are specified in columns 54-59 on the Calculation Specifications form. The Resulting Indicators utilized in the example in Figure 5-6 are again illustrated below.

EXAMPLE 1: Setting Resulting Indicators.

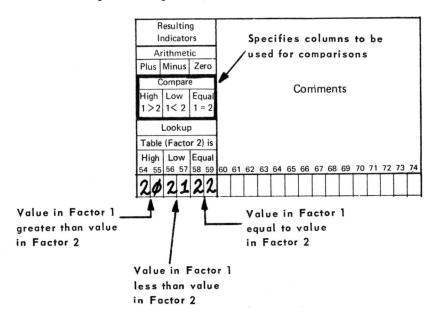

EXAMPLE 2: Possible conditions when comparing.

SALES AMOUNT HIGH — (Factor 1 > Factor 2)

| 6 4 0 9 1 | > | 4 1 2 7 3 |
| SALAMT | | QUOTA |

INDICATOR 20 — "ON"
INDICATOR 21 — "OFF"
INDICATOR 22 — "OFF"

SALES AMOUNT LOW — (Factor 1 < Factor 2)

| 2 8 7 5 4 | < | 4 8 6 3 2 |
| SALAMT | | QUOTA |

INDICATOR 20 — "OFF"
INDICATOR 21 — "ON"
INDICATOR 22 — "OFF"

EQUAL — (Factor 1 = Factor 2)

| 1 7 3 5 4 | = | 1 7 3 5 4 |
| SALAMT | | QUOTA |

INDICATOR 20 — "OFF"
INDICATOR 21 — "OFF"
INDICATOR 22 — "ON"

Figure 5-7 Example of Resulting Indicators from COMP Operation

In the example in Figure 5-7 it can be seen that there is the possibility of three different conditions after the comparison has taken place — the value in the Factor 1 field may be greater than the value in the Factor 2 field, it may be less than the value in the Factor 2 field, or the values in the two fields may be equal. In order that the program may test for these conditions, Resulting Indicators are used. As will be recalled, an Indicator was specified on the Input Specifications of previous sample programs to indicate the type of record which has been read. This indicator may then be tested on both the Calculation Specifications form and the Output-Format Specifications form to determine if Calculations are to be performed or if data output lines are to be written. The Resulting Indicators from a Comparison Operation are used in the same manner, that is, by testing the status of a given Resulting Indicator, different processing may take place within the program.

In the example in Figure 5-7, note that if the value in the Factor 1 field is greater than the value in the Factor 2 field, Indicator 20 will be turned on. If the value in the Factor 1 field is less than the value in the Factor 2 field, then Indicator 21 is to be turned on and if the fields contain equal values, Indicator 22 will be turned on. These indicators may then be tested as illustrated below.

EXAMPLE

RPG   CALCULATION SPECIFICATIONS

Line	Form Type	Control Level (L0-L9, LR, SR)	Indicators And Not	And Not	And Not	Factor 1	Operation	Factor 2	Result Field	Field Length	Decimal Positions	Half Adjust (H)	Resulting Indicators Arithmetic Plus High 1>2	Minus Low 1<2	Zero Equal 1=2
0 1	0	C		Ø1		SALAMT	COMP	QUOTA					2Ø	21	22
0 2	0	C		2Ø		SALAMT	SUB	QUOTA	DIFF	62					
0 3	0	C		21		QUOTA	SUB	SALAMT	DIFF						

Figure 5-8 Example of Testing Resulting Indicators

As was noted previously, the entries made in the "Indicators" field (columns 9-17) can be used to specify when an operation on the Calculation Specifications is to be performed. Thus, in the example above, the Comparison will take place only when the 01 Indicator is "on". After the comparison is performed, either Indicator 20, 21, or 22 will be "on", depending upon the results of the comparison. These indicators may then be specified in columns 9-17 in order to control other operations. In the example in Figure 5-8 it can be seen that if the Sales Amount is greater than the Quota, that is, if Indicator 20 is "on", the value in Quota will be subtracted from the value in SALAMT. If the value in QUOTA is greater than the value in SALAMT, the sales amount is subtracted from the quota value. Note that no operations are to be performed if the values are equal (indicator 22 is "on"). Thus, through the use of the Indicators, different operations may be performed based upon the results of a comparison.

5.5

COMPARISON RULES

When using the COMP operation on the Calculation Specifications form, there are several conditions of which the programmer should be aware so that all comparisons will take place properly. These deal primarily with fields of different lengths and numeric values with a different number of digits to the right of the decimal place. The following are several examples which illustrate these points.

Example 1: Different size numeric fields.

Input Specifications

Field Location			
From	To	Decimal Positions	Field Name
44 45 46 47	48 49 50 51	52	53 54 55 56 57 58
1	40		MOEMP
5	60		MOLEFT

Calculation Specifications

Factor 1	Operation	Factor 2	Result Field	Field Length	Decimal Positions	Half Adjust (H)	Resulting Indicators		
							Arithmetic		
							Plus	Minus	Zero
							Compare		
							High 1>2	Low 1<2	Equal 1=2
							Lookup		
							Table (Factor 2) is		
							High	Low	Equal
18 19 20 21 22 23 24 25 26 27	28 29 30 31 32	33 34 35 36 37 38 39 40 41 42	43 44 45 46 47 48	49 50 51	52	53	54 55	56 57	58 59
MOEMP	COMP	MOLEFT					20	21	22

	MOEMP	NOLEFT	INDICATOR ON
A.	0010	10	22
B.	0100	10	20
C.	2321	99	20
D.	0061	83	21
E.	0051 (−)	0051 (+)	21

Figure 5-9 Example of Numeric Comparisons

5.6

From the examples in Figure 5-9 it can be seen that numeric fields are always compared beginning with the low-order position of the number and moving to the left. Thus, in Example A, even though the field MOEMP contains four digits and the field MOLEFT contains two digits, the numbers are considered equal because the two high-order zeros in the MOEMP field are meaningless in the comparison.

In the second example, the value in MOEMP is one hundred and the value in MOLEFT is ten. Again, the comparison begins with the low-order value and procedes to the left. The two digit number is "filled" with high-order zeros so that the comparison will take place. Thus, when the computer compares the numbers, they are considered to have the following configuration:

MOEMP   0100   MOLEFT   0010

**High-order
"Filled" Zeros**

Note from the example above that the two digit field is "filled" with two high-order zeros so that when the comparison is performed, the fields are of equal length. It should be noted that this "filling" process takes place internally and the programmer need not be concerned with this process. The other examples in Figure 5-9 further illustrate this concept. Note in Example E that a negative value is considered less than a positive value when numeric fields are compared.

Example 2: Non-aligned decimal places.

Calculation Specifications

Factor 1	Operation	Factor 2	Result Field	Field Length	Decimal Positions	Half Adjust (H)	Resulting Indicators		
							Arithmetic		
							Plus	Minus	Zero
							Compare		
							High 1>2	Low 1<2	Equal 1=2
							Lookup		
							Table (Factor 2) is		
							High 54 55	Low 56 57	Equal 58 59
18 19 20 21 22 23 24 25 26 27	28 29 30 31 32	33 34 35 36 37 38 39 40 41 42	43 44 45 46 47 48	49 50 51	52	53			
CURSLS	ADD	YTDSLS	NEWYTD	72					
COMM	MULT	.04	COMPCT	43					
NEWYTD	COMP	COMPCT					20 21 22		

	NEWYTD	COMPCT	INDICATOR ON
A.	00725.25	2.931	20
B.	00006.24	6.243	21
C.	00000.28	0.028	20
D.	00008.91	8.910	22

Figure 5-10 Non-aligned Decimal Comparisons

In the examples in Figure 5-10, the comparisons are made on fields which are defined on the Calculation Specifications form. Note that the NEWYTD field has seven digits, two of which are to the right of the decimal place. The COMPCT field has four digits, three of which are to the right of the decimal place. When numeric fields are compared which do not have the same number of digits and which are not decimally aligned, the RPG compiler will align the fields to the implied decimal point prior to the comparison. After the decimal alignment has taken place, the high-order and low-order positions of each number will be zero-filled in order to make the fields the same length. The comparisons will then take place. Thus, in the fields illustrated in Figure 5-10, a low-order zero will then be added to each value in the NEWYTD field and four high-order zeros will be added to the values in the COMPCT field. The comparisons are then made based upon the aligned values in the fields. For example, note that the value 6.24 is considered less than the value 6.243 (Example B) because the value in the NEWYTD field will acctually be 6.240 when the comparison takes place and is less than 6.243.

It is also possible to compare alphabetic data. This is illustrated in the following example.

Example 3: Alphabetic data comparisons.

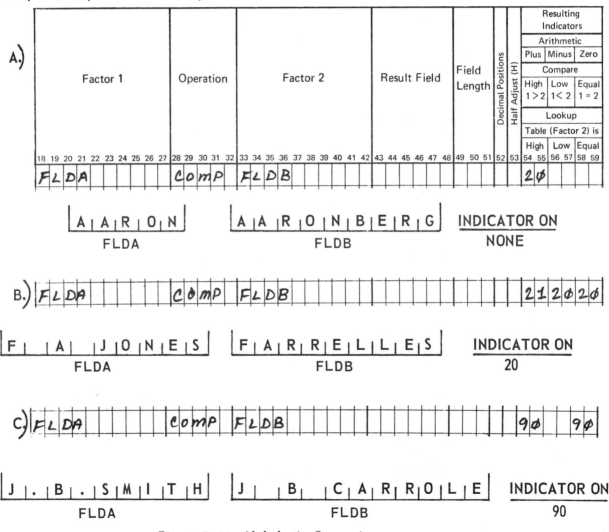

Figure 5-11 Alphabetic Comparisons

When an alphabetic comparison is performed, the first character in each field is compared. If they are equal, the comparison proceeds one character at a time to the right until all of the characters are found to be equal to until an unequal condition is found. If one of the fields contains fewer characters than the other, the field with the lesser number of characters is padded with blanks in the low-order positions of the field. Thus, in Example A in Figure 5-10, the field FLDA would be padded with four blanks in the low-order positions in order to make the field the same length as FLDB. The comparison would then take place and the value in FLDB is greater than the value in FLDA because a blank is the lowest character in the collating scheme of most computers. Thus, the "B" in the name AARONBERG is greater than the blank which is inserted following the name AARON. Because of the result of the comparison, indicator 20 is turned off and no indicators are turned on. Note that indicator 20 would have been turned on had the value in the first field been greater than the value in the second field. Since it is not, however, indicator 20 is turned off and no indicators are turned on. As can be seen, it is not required to have an indicator in each of the Resulting Indicator fields.

In the second example, the value in FLDB is again greater than the value in FLDA because the "A" in FARRELLES is greater than the blank in the second position of the value in FLDA. Again, the blank is always considered less than any special characters, letters of the alphabet, or numbers.

In the Example C, indicator 90 will be turned on because the value in FLDA is greater than the value in FLDB. This is because the period in the second position of the value in FLDA is greater than the blank in the second position of FLDB. The following list contains many of the common special characters used and their collating sequence on the System/360, System/370 and System/3.

Character

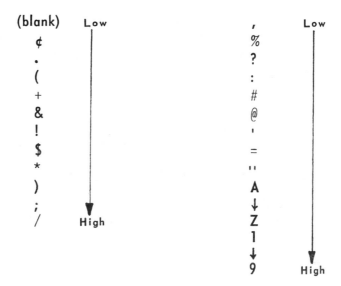

Figure 5-12 Collating Sequence

SAMPLE PROBLEM

The sample program presented at the end of this chapter illustrates the use of the Comparison and Multiply operations. In this problem, a sales commission report is to be prepared. The input to the program is a file of sales cards containing the salesman number, the salesman name, and the amount of sales by the salesman. The format of the card is illustrated below.

Input Cards

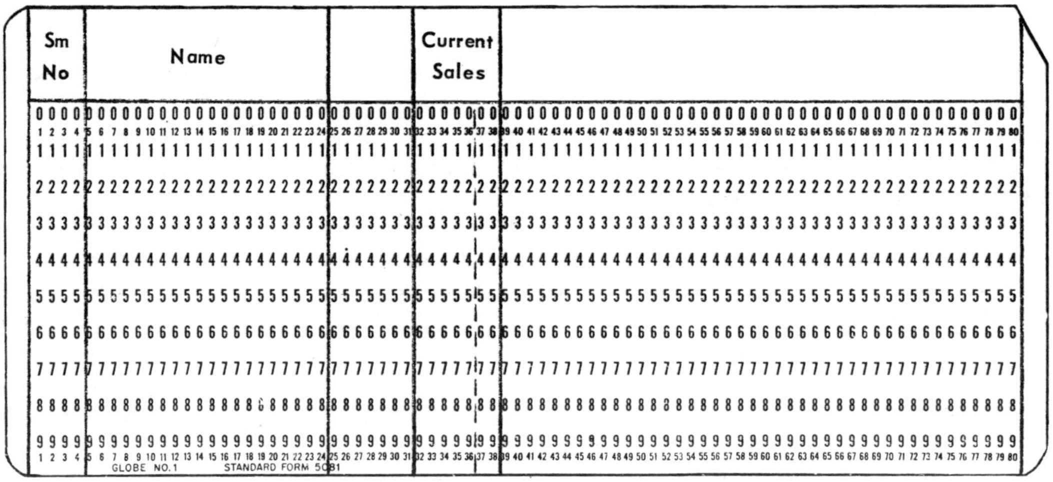

Figure 5-13 Input Card

Note in the example above that the input card contains a Salesman Number field, a Salesman Name field, and a Current Sales field. The printed report is to contain the Salesman Number, the Salesman Name, the Sales, the Percentage of Commission and the Actual Commission. The percentage of commission is determined as follows: If the Sales in the input card is greater than $1000.00, then the percentage of commission is 5%. If the sales are equal to or less than 1000.00, then the percentage of commission is 3%. The Salesman's commission is then computed by multiplying the commission percentage by the Sales. In addition, final totals are taken for the current sales and the total commissions paid. The report is illustrated below.

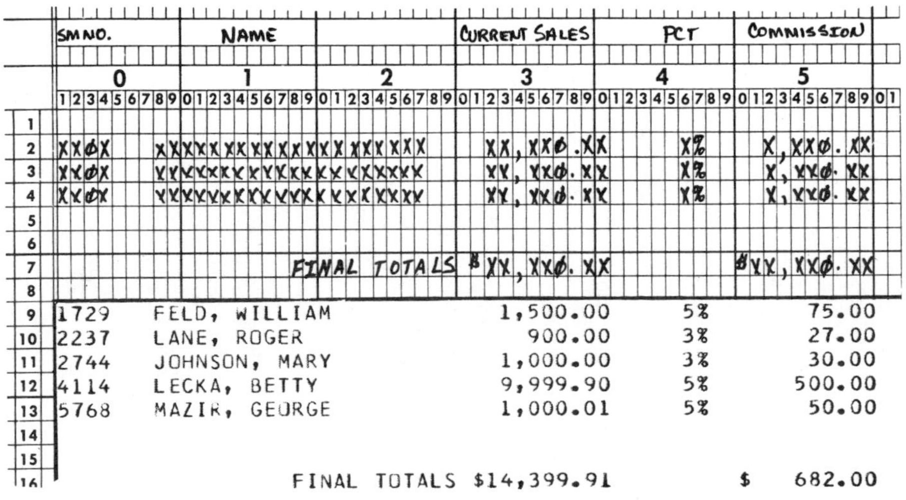

Figure 5-14 Commission Report

5.10

RPG CODING

As with all RPG programs, the input and output files must be defined on the File Description Specifications and the format of the input records must be defined on the Input Specifications. These two forms which are utilized in the sample program are illustrated in Figure 5-15.

EXAMPLE

RPG CONTROL CARD AND FILE DESCRIPTION SPECIFICATIONS

Date 6/25/72

Program SALESMAN REPORT

Programmer SHELLY

Punching Instruction	Graphic	Ø	O	2	Z
	Punch	ZERO	11-6	TWO	0-9

Page Ø1 — Program Identification (75–80): SMREPT

Control Card Specifications

Line (3–5)	Form Type (6)	Core Size to Compile (7–9)	Object Output (10)	Listing Options (11)	Core Size to Execute (12–14)	Debug (15)	MFCM Stacking Sequence (16)	Sterling: Input-Shillings (17)	Input-Pence (18)	Output-Shillings (19)	Output-Pence (20)	Inverted Print (21)	360/20 2501 Buffer (22)	Number Of Print Positions (23–25)	Alternate Collating Sequence (26)	27–74
01Ø	H															

Refer to the specific System Reference Library manual for actual entries.

File Description Specifications

Line (3–5)	Form Type (6)	Filename (7–14)	File Type I/O/U/C/D (15)	File Designation P/S/C/R/T/D (16)	End of File E (17)	Sequence A/D (18)	File Format F/V (19)	Block Length (20–23)	Record Length (24–27)	Mode of Processing L/R (28)	Length of Key Field or of Record Address Field (29–30)	Record Address Type A/K/I (31)	Type of File Organization or Additional Area I/D/T or 1-9 (32)	Overflow Indicator (33–34)	Key Field Starting Location (35–38)	Extension Code E/L (39)	Device (40–46)	Symbolic Device (47–52)	Labels (S, N, or E) (53)	Name of Label Exit (54–59)	Extent Exit for DAM / Core Index (60–65)	File Addition/Unordered A/U (66)	Number of Tracks for Cylinder Overflow (67–68)	Number of Extents (69–70)	Tape Rewind N/U (71–72)	File Condition U1-U8 (73–74)
02Ø	F	SMCARDS	I	P			F	8Ø	8Ø								READ4Ø	SYSIPT								
03Ø	F	SALERPT	O				F	132	132								PRINTER	SYSLST								

RPG INPUT SPECIFICATIONS

Date 6/25/72

Program SALESMAN REPORT

Programmer SHELLY

Punching Instruction	Graphic	Ø	O	2	Z
	Punch	ZERO	11-6	TWO	0-9

Page Ø2 — Program Identification (75–80): SMREPT

Line (3–5)	Form Type (6)	Filename (7–14)	Sequence (15–16)	Number (1-N) (17)	Option (O) (18)	Record Identifying Indicator or ** (19–20)	Record Identification Codes 1: Position / Not (N) / C/Z/D / Character (21–27)	2: Position / Not (N) / C/Z/D / Character (28–34)	3: Position / Not (N) / C/Z/D / Character (35–41)	Stacker Select (42)	P = Packed/B = Binary (43)	Field Location From (44–47)	To (48–51)	Decimal Positions (52)	Field Name (53–58)	Control Level (L1-L9) (59–60)	Matching Fields or Chaining Fields (61–62)	Field Record Relation (63–64)	Field Indicators Plus (65–66)	Minus (67–68)	Zero or Blank (69–70)	Sterling Sign Position (71–74)
01Ø	I	SMCARDS	AA			Ø1																
02Ø	I											1	4	Ø	SMNO							
03Ø	I											5	24		NAME							
04Ø	I											32	38	2	CURSLS							

Figure 5-15 File Description and Input Specifications

CALCULATION SPECIFICATIONS

As noted, the sales in the input card is to be compared to $1000.00. If the sales are greater, a commission rate of 5% is to be used. Otherwise, a commission rate of 3% is to be used. In addition, final totals are to be taken for the total sales and the total commission. The Calculation Specifications used for the sample program are illustrated below.

EXAMPLE

RPG CALCULATION SPECIFICATIONS

Line	Form Type	Control Level	And	And	Factor 1	Operation	Factor 2	Result Field	Field Length	Decimal Positions	Half Adjust (H)	Resulting Indicators	Comments
010	C	01			CURSLS	COMP	1000.00					20 21 21	IS CURR > 1000
020	C	01	20		CURSLS	MULT	.05	Commis	62H				YES, PCT = .05
030	C	01	21		CURSLS	MULT	.03	Commis	62H				NO, PCT = .03
040	C	01			TOTCUR	ADD	CURSLS	TOTCUR	72				TAKE SALES TOT
050	C	01			TOTCOM	ADD	Commis	TOTCOM	72				TAKE COMM TOTAL

Figure 5-16 Calculation Specifications Form

Note from the example above that there are five different operations to be performed. These are explained below by line number on the coding form.

Line 010: If the 01 Indicator is "on", as it will be when each input record is read, the value in the CURSLS field, which contains the current sales from the input card, is compared with the value 1000.00. Note the use of a literal in the COMP statement. A literal may be used in a comparison in the same manner as it is used with arithmetic operations as illustrated previously. Note also that a decimal point is included within the literal to indicate where the decimal place is to be. This decimal point is used merely to indicate to the RPG compiler where the decimal point should be assumed to be. Thus, it performs the same function for a literal as the "Decimal Positions" field on the Input Specifications and the Calculation Specifications performs for fields.

Note from the example above that if the value in the CURSLS field is greater than 1000.00, Indicator 20 will be turned "on". If it is equal to or less than 1000.00, indicator 21 will be turned "on".

Line 020: If both indicator 01 and indicator 20 are "on", it indicates that the value in CURSLS is greater than 1000.00 because indicator 20 would be turned on in the comparison operation. If this is the case, the commission rate is to be 5%. Thus, if both of these indicators are "on", the value in CURSLS is multiplied by .05 in order to get the commission for the salesman (ie. Sales × Rate = Commission). Note that the literal .05 is used in the multiplication. As noted, literals may be used in any arithmetic or comparison operations. The result of the multiplication will be rounded to two decimal places and be placed in the COMMIS field.

Line 030: If the sales are less than or equal to 1000.00, then the commission rate to be used is 3%. Note from Figure 5-11 that if the value in CURSLS is less than or equal to 1000.00, then indicator 21 will be turned "on". When indicator 21 is "on", it indicates that the sales are less than or equal to 1000.00 and the commission rate is to be 3%. Thus, on line 030, the value in the CURSLS field is multiplied by .03 and the commission is stored in the field COMMIS.

Line 040 and 050: After the commission has been calculated, the current sales from the input card (CURSLS) is added to the final total counter for the total sales (TOTCUR). The commission (COMMIS) is then added to the final total counter for the commission (TOTCOM).

Note also from the example in Figure 5-11 that comments are entered in columns 60-74. This portion of the Calculation Specifications form may be used by the programmer to insert meaningful comments to describe the processing which is to occur with each statement. Thus, as can be seen, a description of the comparison is included as well as the processing which is to occur as a result of the comparison. Comments help document the source program and should normally be included whenever possible to clarify the processing to be performed.

Output - Format Specifications

The data to be printed on the output report may vary based upon the results of the comparison between the current sales field and the value 1000.00. The output-format specifications form used in the program illustrates the entries which must be made in order to print the proper data.

EXAMPLE

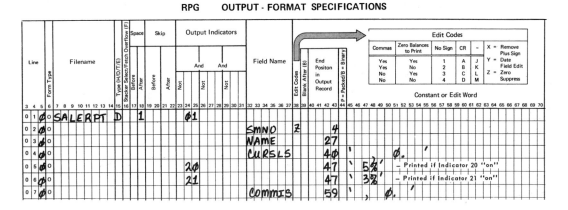

Figure 5-17 Output-Format Specifications Form

Note from the example in Figure 5-17 that the filename of the report is SALERPT and that the print line described is a Detail line. Note also that the print line will be printed each time the 01 Indicator is "on" (column 24-25). As was mentioned previously, the report is to consist of the salesman number (SMNO), the salesman name, the current sales (CURSLS), the commission rate, and the commission (COMMIS). The commission rate is not known until the comparison on the Calculation Specifications takes place and the corresponding indicator is set "on". Thus, the commission rate printed will depend upon whether indicator 20 or indicator 21 is "on". In the example in Figure 5-17 it can be seen that there are two entries for the value which is to print in the field ending in column 47 of the report. One is the constant value "5%" and the other is the constant value "3%". The determination as to which of these values will be printed on any given line of the report is made by the status of indicators 20 and 21. As will be noted, the value "20" is specified in columns 24-25 (Output Indicators) on the same line as the 5% constant. This indicator number appearing on the same line as a constant or field to be printed indicates that the field or constant will be printed only if the corresponding indicator is "on". If the indicator is not "on", the value will not be printed. Thus, as can be seen, the value 5% will be printed if indicator 20 is "on" and the value 3% will be printed if indicator 21 is "on". It must be noted that the indicators which are specified for a single field or constant on the report have nothing to do with whether the output record will be written or not. This is controlled by the Indicator which is specified on the same line as the filename. In the example in Figure 5-17, this is indicator 01 and each time indicator 01 is "on", the output record will be printed regardless of the indicators specified for each field.

Program

The source listing generated by the RPG compiler for the sample program is illustrated below.

```
DOS/360*RPG*CL 3-9                    CASHMAN                        09/12/72          PAGE 0001

        01 010 H                                                                      SMREPT
001     01 020 FSMCARDS IP  F  80  80            READ40 SYSIPT                        SMREPT
002     01 030 FSALERPT O   F 132 132            PRINTERSYSLST                        SMREPT
003     02 010 ISMCARDS AA  01                                                        SMREPT
004     02 020 I                                      1    40SMNO                      SMREPT
005     02 030 I                                      5    24 NAME                     SMREPT
006     02 040 I                                     32   382CURSLS                    SMREPT
007     03 010 C     01     CURSLS   COMP 1000.00                202121IS CURR > 1000  SMREPT
008     03 020 C     01 20  CURSLS   MULT .05    COMMIS   62H     YES,PCT = .05        SMREPT
009     03 030 C     01 21  CURSLS   MULT .03    COMMIS   62H     NO,PCT = .03         SMREPT
010     03 040 C     01     TOTCUR   ADD  CURSLS TOTCUR   72      TAKE TOTALS          SMREPT
011     03 050 C            TOTCOM   ADD  COMMIS TOTCOM   72                           SMREPT
012     04 010 OSALERPT D   1       01                                                SMREPT
013     04 020 O                         SMNO  Z   4                                   SMREPT
014     04 030 O                         NAME     27                                   SMREPT
015     04 040 O                         CURSLS   40 ' , 0. '                          SMREPT
016     04 050 O                   20              47 ' 5%'                            SMREPT
017     04 060 O                   21              47 ' 3%'                            SMREPT
018     04 070 O                         COMMIS   59 ' , 0. '                          SMREPT
019     04 080 O     T 2    LR                                                         SMREPT
020     04 090 O                              29 'FINAL TOTALS'                        SMREPT
021     04 100 O                         TOTCUR   40 '$ , 0. '                         SMREPT
022     04 110 O                         TOTCOM   59 '$ , 0. '                         SMREPT
```

Figure 5-18 Source Listing

CHAPTER 5

REVIEW QUESTIONS

1. In the collating sequence illustrated in Figure 5-12, why are numeric values which are stored in the zoned-decimal format considered higher than alphabetic values stored in the zoned-decimal format (see Appendix A)?

2. Will a comparison of numeric data stored in a field defined as an alphameric field take place properly with numeric data stored in a field defined as a numeric field? Why?

3. Why isn't there a Resulting Indicator which can be set if the two fields in a comparison contain unequal values? What entries should be used if an indicator is to be set "on" if two fields contain unequal values?

4. What is the difference between an Output Indicator which is specified on the same line as the filename and an Output Indicator which is specified on the same line as a fieldname?

CHAPTER 5

STUDENT EXERCISES

1. Specify the results of the following comparisons.

	FieldA	FieldB	Result (A>B, B>A, A=B)
a.	James, Frank	James, Frank	_____
b.	12.879	127.89	_____
c.	.000005	000.050	_____
d.	5.1	005.09875	_____
e.	Art	Arthur	_____
f.	X'09873D'	X'00006C'	_____
g.	3.9987	03.998700	_____
h.	0095.8700	95.87	_____

2. Write the compare statement on the calculation specifications to compare the field AMOUNT to the field MAX. If AMOUNT is less than MAX, turn on indicator 30. If AMOUNT is equal to MAX, turn on indicator 31 and if AMOUNT is greater then MAX turn on indicator 32.

RPG   CALCULATION SPECIFICATIONS

Line	Form Type	Control Level (L0-L9, LR, SR)	Indicators						Factor 1	Operation	Factor 2	Result Field	Field Length	Decimal Positions	Half Adjust (H)	Resulting Indicators		
			And		And											Arithmetic		
																Plus	Minus	Zero
			Not		Not		Not									Compare		
																High 1 > 2	Low 1 < 2	Equal 1 = 2
																Lookup		
																Table (Factor 2) is		
																High	Low	Equal
3 4 5	6	7 8	9 10 11	12 13 14	15 16 17	18 19 20 21 22 23 24 25 26 27	28 29 30 31 32	33 34 35 36 37 38 39 40 41 42	43 44 45 46 47 48	49 50 51	52	53	54 55	56 57	58 59
0 1	C														
0 2	C														
0 3	C														
0 4	C														
0 5	C														
0 6	C														
0 7	C														

3. One of three fields (FIELDA, FIELDB, or FIELDC) will be printed depending upon the values stored in the three fields. Write the COMP statements to set the indicators which specify which field is to be printed and the entries on the Output Specifications to print the proper field. The conditions to be tested are:

a. If the value in FIELDA is less than the value in FIELDB and the value in FIELDC is greater than the value in FIELDA, then FIELDA is to be printed.

b. If the value in FIELDA is greater than the value in FIELDB and is less than the value in FIELDC, then FIELDB is to be printed.

c. If the value in FIELDA is greater than the value in FIELDB and is greater than the value in FIELDC, then FIELDC is to be printed.

FIELDA will be printed on the report ending in column 15, FIELDB should end in column 56, and FIELDC will end in column 90.

RPG   CALCULATION SPECIFICATIONS

Line		Form Type	Control Level (L0-L9, LR, SR)	Indicators						Factor 1	Operation	Factor 2	Result Field	Field Length	Decimal Positions	Half Adjust (H)	Resulting Indicators		
				And		And											Arithmetic		
																	Plus	Minus	Zero
																	Compare		
				Not		Not		Not									High 1>2	Low 1<2	Equal 1=2
																	Lookup		
																	Table (Factor 2) is		
																	High	Low	Equal
3	4 5	6	7 8	9 10 11	12 13 14	15 16 17	18 19 20 21 22 23 24 25 26 27	28 29 30 31 32	33 34 35 36 37 38 39 40 41 42	43 44 45 46 47 48	49 50 51 52	53	54 55	56 57	58 59
0	1	C											
0	2	C											
0	3	C											
0	4	C											
0	5	C											
0	6	C											
0	7	C											
0	8	C											

Debugging RPG Programs

Problem 1

Instructions: The following RPG program contains an error or errors which have occurred during compilation. Circle each error and record the corrected entries directly on the listing. Explain the error and method of correction in the space provided below.

```
DOS/360*RPG*CL 3-9              CASHMAN                    10/13/72        PAGE 0001

       01 210 H                                                            SMREPT
001    01 220 FSMCARDS IP  F  80  80          READ40 SYSIPT               SMREPT
002    01 230 FSALERPT O   F 132 132          PRINTERSYSLST               SMREPT
003    02 240 ISMCARDS AA  01                                             SMREPT
004    02 250 I                            1    40SMNU                     SMREPT
005    02 260 I                            5    24 NAME                    SMREPT
006    02 270 I                           32    382CURSLS                  SMREPT
       03 280 C   01    CURSLS   COMP $1000.00      2021211S CURR > 1000  SMREPT
                                                                          NOTE 088
       03 290 C   01 20 CURSLS   MUL  .05    COMMIS 62H    YES,PCT = .05   SMREPT
                                                                          NOTE 086
       03 310 C   01 21 CURSLS   MUL  .03    COMMIS 62H    NO,PCT = .03    SMREPT
                                                                          NOTE 086
007    03 320 C   01    TOTCUR   ADD  CURSLS TOTCUR 72     TAKE TOTALS     SMREPT
008    03 330 C         TOTCOM   ADD  COMMIS TOTCOM 72                     SMREPT
009    04 340 OSALERPT O  1    01                                         SMREPT
010    04 350 O                    SMNO  Z  4                              SMREPT
011    04 360 O                    NAME     27                             SMREPT
012    04 370 O                    CURSLS   40 ' , 0. '                    SMREPT
013    04 380 O            20                47 ' 5%'                       SMREPT
014    04 390 O            21                47 ' 3%'                       SMREPT
015    04 400 O                    COMMIS   59 ' , 0. '                    SMREPT
016    04 410 O       1 2  LR                                              SMREPT
017    04 420 O                    29 'FINAL TOTALS'                       SMREPT
018    04 430 O                    TOTCUR   40 '$ , 0. '                   SMREPT
019    04 440 O                    TOTCOM   59 '$ , 0. '                   SMREPT
```

```
DOS/360*RPG*CL 3-9              CASHMAN                    10/13/72        PAGE 0002

                              SYMBOL  TABLES

RESULTING  INDICATORS

ADDRESS RI      ADDRESS RI      ADDRESS RI      ADDRESS RI      ADDRESS RI      ADDRESS RI      ADDRESS RI

000014 1P       000015 LR       000016 00       000017 01       00002A 20       00002B 21       00007A L0
000085 H0       000086 H1       000087 H2       000088 H3       000089 H4       0000BA H5       00008B H6
00008C H7       00008D H8       00008E H9
FIELD  NAMES

ADDRESS FIELD      ADDRESS FIELD      ADDRESS FIELD      ADDRESS FIELD      ADDRESS FIELD

000123  SMNO       000126  NAME       00013A  CURSLS      00013E  TOTCUR      000142  TOTCOM
000146  COMMIS

LITERALS

ADDRESS LITERAL            ADDRESS LITERAL            ADDRESS LITERAL

00014A  --,--/.--           000154  5%                  000157  3%
00015A  FINAL TOTALS        000166  --,--/.--
     008                                    COMMIS                  NOTE 214
     015                                    COMMIS                  NOTE 214
     015                                                            NOTE 230

NOTE  0P6  OPERATION CODE (COLUMNS 28-32) IS INVALID OR MISSING.  SPECIFICATION IS NOT
           PROCESSED.

NOTE  088  REQUIRED ENTRY IN FACTOR 2 (COLUMNS 33-42) IS MISSING OR INVALID.  SPECIFICATION
           IS NOT PROCESSED.

NOTE  214  FIELD NAME IS UNDEFINED.  FIELD IS PROCESSED WITH ASSUMED LENGTH OF 004.

NOTE  230  FIELD TO BE EDITED IS GREATER THAN THE EDIT WORD.  SIGNIFICANT DIGITS MAY BE
           LOST.
```

EXPLANATION _____

_____

_____

Debugging RPG Programs

Problem 2

Instructions: The following RPG program contains an error or errors which occur during execution. Circle each error and record the corrected entries directly on the listing. Explain the error and method of correction in the space provided below.

```
DOS/360*RPG*CL 3-9              CASHMAN                    10/13/72        PAGE 0001

        01 210 H                                                          SMREPT
001     01 220 FSMCARDS IP  F  80  80              READ40 SYSIPT          SMREPT
002     01 230 FSALERPT O   F 132 132              PRINTERSYSLST          SMREPT
003     02 240 ISMCARDS AA  01                                           SMREPT
004     02 250 I                             1  40SMNO                    SMREPT
005     02 260 I                             5  24 NAME                   SMREPT
006     02 270 I                            32  382CURSLS                 SMREPT
007     03 280 C  01    CURSLS   COMP 1000.00          202021IS CURR > 1000 SMREPT
008     03 300 C  01 20 CURSLS   MULT .05   COMMIS 62H    YES,PCT = .05   SMREPT
009     03 310 C  01 21 CURSLS   MULT .03   COMMIS 62H    NO,PCT = .03    SMREPT
010     03 320 C  01    TOTCUR   ADD  CURSLS TOTCUR 72    TAKE TOTALS     SMREPT
011     03 330 C        TOTCOM   ADD  COMMIS TOTCOM 72                    SMREPT
012     04 340 OSALERPT D  1     01                                      SMREPT
013     04 350 O                         SMNO Z   4                       SMREPT
014     04 360 O                         NAME     27                      SMREPT
015     04 370 O                         CURSLS   40 ' , 0. '             SMREPT
016     04 380 O                    20              47 ' 5%'              SMREPT
017     04 390 O                    21              47 ' 3%'              SMREPT
018     04 400 O                         COMMIS   59 ' , 0. '             SMREPT
019     04 410 O     T 2    LR                                           SMREPT
020     04 420 O                              29 'FINAL TOTALS'          SMREPT
021     04 430 O                         TOTCUR   40 '$  , 0. '           SMREPT
022     04 440 O                         TOTCOM   59 '$  , 0. '           SMREPT
```

Note: 5% commission calculated for amounts less than $1000.00 and greater than $1000.00.

```
// EXEC
1729   FELD, WILLIAM      1,500.00    5%      75.00
2237   LANE, ROGER          900.00    5%      45.00
2744   JOHNSON, MARY      1,000.00    3%      30.00
4114   LECKA, BETTY       9,999.90    5%     500.00
5768   MAZIK, GEORGE      1,000.01    5%      50.00

        FINAL TOTALS $14,399.91        $     700.00
```

EXPLANATION _____

_____

_____

_____

PROGRAMMING ASSIGNMENT 1

INSTRUCTIONS

From the Sales Cards illustrated below, a Sales Quota Report is to be prepared. This report is to list all employees employed six months or more that have a Y-T-D Sales below $6,000.00, Employees employed less than six months or with Sales $6,000.00 or more are NOT to be included on the report.

The Salesman Number, Salesman Name, Y-T-D Sales, and the Months Employed are to be printed on the report. The Amount below quota is to be calculated and printed on the right side of each report.

A "final total line" is to be printed indicating the total number of employees, and the total number of employees below quota.

INPUT — Sales Card

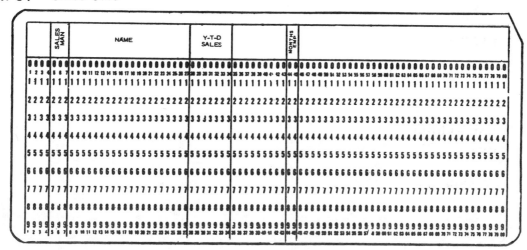

OUTPUT — Sales Quota Report

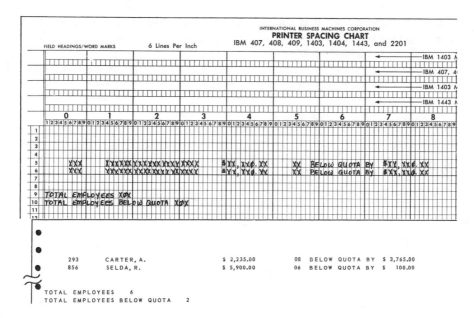

TEST DATA — ASSIGNMENT NO. 1

Salesman (col 5-7)	Name (col 8-27)	YTD Sales (col 28-34)	Months (col 44-45)
164	Adams, B.	0286700	3
293	Carter, A.	0223500	8
539	Gallagher, F.	0600000	8
792	Router, Y.	0965400	4
856	Selda, R.	0590000	6
908	Williams, K.	0798000	6

DOS JOB CONTROL

```
// JOB jobname
// OPTION LINK
// EXEC RPG

  — Student Source Deck —

/*
// EXEC LNKEDT
// EXEC

  — Test Data —

/*
/&
```

Note: This assumes that the assignments for the card reader and printer are standard assignments known to the student.

CHAPTER 5

PROGRAMMING ASSIGNMENT 2

INSTRUCTIONS

Write the RPG program to prepare a Weekly Payroll Report. Employees are to receive time and one-half for all work in excess of 40 hours. For example, an employee working 42 hours at $2.00 per hour would be paid for 40 hours work at $2.00 per hour and 2 hours work at $3.00 per hour.

INPUT – Payroll Cards

Input is to consist of Payroll cards containing the Employee Number, Employee Name, Hours Worked, Rate of Pay and Deductions. The format of the card is illustrated below.

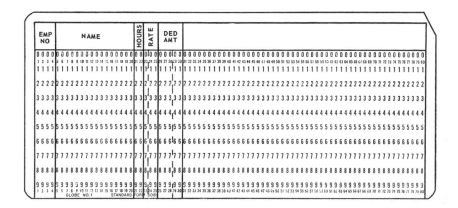

OUTPUT – Payroll Report

Output is to consist of a Payroll Report. The report is to contain the Employee Number, Employee Name, Total Hours Worked, Regular Rate of Pay, Regular Earnings, Overtime Earnings, Deductions, and Net Pay. Regular Earnings added to Overtime Earnings minus the Deductions will give the Net Pay. Final Totals are to be taken of Regular Earnings, Overtime Earnings, Deductions, and Net Pay.

EMPLOYEE NUMBER	NAME	HOURS	RATE OF PAY	REGULAR EARNINGS	OVERTIME EARNINGS	DEDUCTIONS	NET PAY
1539	ALL, WILLIAM C.	42	2.00	80.00	6.00	10.00	76.00
1901	AKER, JAMES C.	30	2.50	75.00	.00	7.00	68.00
3343	BRYANT, ANDREW W.	45	3.00	120.00	22.50	20.00	122.50
FINAL TOTALS				$27,650.00	$350.00	$4,000.00	$24,000.00

5.23

TEST DATA — ASSIGNMENT NO. 2

Emp No (col 1-4)	Name (col 5-20)	Hours (col 21-22)	Rate (col 23-25)	Deductions (col 26-30)
1539	All, William C.	42	200	01000
1901	Aker, James C.	30	250	00700
3343	Bryant, Andrew C.	45	300	02000
4439	Clayborne, Walter	59	375	04200
5593	Ellisin, William A.	20	270	00000
7894	Gelden, Robert A.	48	580	00500

DOS JOB CONTROL

```
// JOB jobname
// OPTION LINK
// EXEC RPG

  — Student Source Deck —

/*
// EXEC LNKEDT
// EXEC

  — Test Data —

/*
/&
```

Note: This assumes that the assignments for the card reader and printer are standard assignments known to the student.

CHAPTER 6

CONTROL CODES

REPORT HEADINGS

INTRODUCTION

It was noted in Chapter 3 that different codes in an input record can be checked by recording selected entries in the Input Specifications form and then alternate processing accomplished based upon the Record Identifying Indicators which have been set "on". The use of multiple Record Identifying Indicators will be illustrated by the sample program in this chapter. The input to the program is a file of Payroll Cards. The format of these cards is illustrated below.

Input

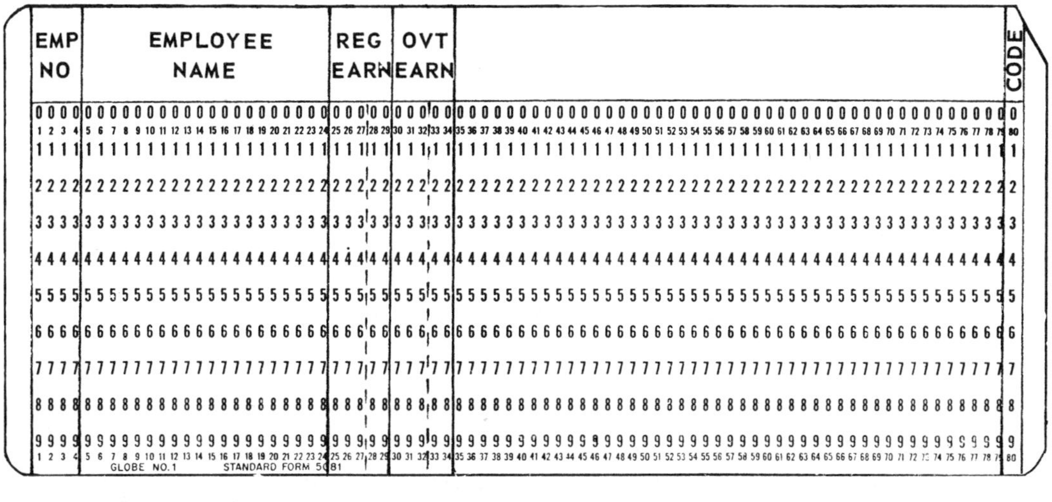

Figure 6-1 Input Card

Note that the input card contains the Employee Number field, the Employee Name field, the Regular Earnings field, the Overtime Earnings field, and a Code field. The code, in column 80, is used to indicate the shift on which an employee works. The value "1" indicates that an employee works the first shift, thc code "2" indicates the second shift, and the code "3" indicates the third shift.

A report is to be generated which includes the Employee Number, the Employee Name, the Shift, the Regular Earnings, the Overtime Earnings, the Bonus Earnings which an employee is entitled to if he works on the second or third shift, and the total pay of an employee. The format of the report is illustrated in Figure 6-2.

INTERNATIONAL BUSINESS MACHINES CORPORATION
PRINTER SPACING CHART
IBM 407, 408, 409, 1403, 1404, 1443, and 2201

FIELD HEADINGS/WORD MARKS   6 Lines Per Inch

```
  XX/XX/XX                    P A Y R O L L   R E P O R T          PAGE XX0X

      EMP                              REGULAR     OVERTIME                  TOTAL
      NO           NAME        SHIFT   EARNINGS    EARNINGS    BONUS     EARNINGS

      XX0X    XXXXXXXXXXXXXXXXXXXXX   XXXXXX    XXX0.XX    XX0.XX   0XX.XX    XXX0.XX
      XX0X    XXXXXXXXXXXXXXXXXXXXX   XXXXXX    XXX0.XX    XX0.XX   0XX.XX    XXX0.XX
      XX0X    XXXXXXXXXXXXXXXXXXXXX   XXXXXX    XXX0.XX    XX0.XX   0XX.XX    XXX0.XX

  END OF PAYROLL REPORT
```

```
  9/19/72                     P A Y R O L L   R E P O R T          PAGE     1

      EMP                              REGULAR     OVERTIME                  TOTAL
      NO           NAME        SHIFT   EARNINGS    EARNINGS    BONUS     EARNINGS

      25      BAKER, ROGER         FIRST    $125.00    $50.00    $.00     $175.00
      98      DAVIS, FRED          SECOND   $150.00    $.00      $5.00    $155.00
     101      GRANGER, THOMAS      THIRD    $135.35    $5.00     $10.00   $150.35
     522      LAFET, RAYMOND   INVALID SHIFT
    1257      ZABO, ALEX           FIRST    $250.30    $253.30   $.00     $503.60

  END OF PAYROLL REPORT
```

Figure 6-2 Output Report

Note from the example above that, in addition to the printing of the fields on the card and the calculated amounts, report and column headings are also printed in order to identify the various fields on the report. The RPG programming technique used to cause heading lines on a report will be covered in this chapter. Note also from the example that the bonus values that an employee is to receive varies according to the shift the employee has worked. An employee working on the first shift receives no shift bonus; an employee working on the second shift receives a $5.00 bonus and an employee working on the third shift receives a $10.00 bonus.

In order to produce the report illustrated in Figure 6-2, the Record Identifying Indicators and Record Identification Codes portions of the Input Specifications must be utilized to identify the shift the employee worked by recognizing the punches "1", "2", or "3" in the Code field of the input data cards. The use of these RPG programming features is explained on subsequent pages.

RECORD IDENTIFYING INDICATORS

As noted, the "code" field in the input cards will contain the value "1" if the employee works the first shift, the value "2" if he works the second shift, and the value "3" if he works the third shift. These codes may be tested through the use of the Record Identification Codes and the Record Identifying Indicators. A segment of the Input Specifications form used in the sample program is illustrated below.

EXAMPLE   **RPG   INPUT SPECIFICATIONS**

Line	Form Type	Filename	Sequence	Number (1-N)	Option (O)	Record Identifying Indicator or **	Record Identification Codes 1 Position	Not (N)	C/Z/D	Character	2 Position	Not (N)	C/Z/D	Character	3 Position	Not (N)	C/Z/D	Character
3 4 5	6	7 8 9 10 11 12 13 14	15 16	17	18	19 20	21 22 23 24	25	26	27	28 29 30 31	32	33	34	35 36 37 38	39	40	41
0 1 0	I	PAYCARD	AA			01	80		C	1								
0 2 0	I	OR				02	80		C	2								
0 3 0	I	OR				03	80		C	3								
0 4 0	I	OR				04	80	N	C	1	80	N	C	2	80	N	C	3

Figure 6-3 Example of Input Specifications

In the example above it can be seen that the filename is **PAYCARD** and that there is no prescribed sequence for the input cards ("AA" in columns 15-16). The record identification codes portion of the form is used to specify the values which will be found in the Code field of the input record. In the example, note that column 80 is specified as the column which will contain the identification code. As noted previously, whenever the given code is found in a record, the corresponding Record Identifying Indicator is set "on". Thus, if the character "1" is found in column 80, Indicator 01 will be set "on".

In column 14 and column 15 of every line except the first line, the word "OR" is entered on the form. This entry specifies that the card to be processed may contain more than one code in column 80 and that a different record identifying indicator is to be set when a particular card type is read. Thus, the entries above may be read as follows:

    If there is the character "1" in column 80, turn on indicator 01;
OR If there is the character "2" in column 80, turn on indicator 02;
OR If there is the character "3" in column 80, turn on indicator 03;
OR If there is not a "1" in column 80 and if there is not a "2" in
    column 80 and if there is not a "3" in column 80, turn on
    indicator 04.

Note in the example on line 040 the use of the "N" in columns 25, 32, and 39. This entry specifies "NOT" when used in the Record Identification Codes portion of the form. Thus, as mentioned above, the entries on line 040 state that record identifying indicator 04 is to be "on" if none of the values specified in the three positions are found in the input card. Resulting Indicator 04 is used to identify invalid card types, that is, cards that do not contain a "1", "2", or "3" in card column 80.

CALCULATION SPECIFICATIONS FORM

When the record identifying indicators have been set after a card has been read, they can be referenced on the Calculation Specifications and the Output - Format Specifications form. It is important to understand the logic of the processing that is to take place prior to coding the calculation specifications. In the sample problem the Regular Earnings Field and the Overtime Earnings Field are to be added together for all valid cards, that is, for all cards that contain a "1", "2", or "3" punch in card column 80. In RPG this may be stated by indicating that this add operation is to be performed when Indicator "04" is NOT "on". If there is a "2" punch in card column 80, $5.00 is to be added to the total of the Regular Earnings and Overtime Earnings, and if there is a "3" punch in card column 80, $10.00 is to be added to the total of Regular Earnings and Overtime Earnings. The Calculation Specifications form used in the program to calculate the total pay of an employee is illustrated below.

EXAMPLE.

RPG   CALCULATION SPECIFICATIONS

Line			Form Type	Control Level (L0-L9, LR, SR)	Indicators							Factor 1	Operation	Factor 2	Result Field	Field Length	Decimal Positions
					And			And								
					Not			Not		Not						
3	4	5	6	7 8	9	10 11	12 13 14	15 16 17	18 19 20 21 22 23 24 25 26 27	28 29 30 31 32	33 34 35 36 37 38 39 40 41 42	43 44 45 46 47 48	49 50 51	52
0 1 0			C		N 0 4				REGERN	ADD	OVTERN	TOTERN	5 2	
0 2 0			C		0 2				TOTERN	ADD	5 . 0 0	TOTERN		
0 3 0			C		0 3				TOTERN	ADD	1 0 . 0 0	TOTERN		

Figure 6-4 Calculation Specifications Form

Note in the example above that Indicators are used in the Indicators portion of the form (Columns 9-17) in order to specify which calculations are to be performed. On line 010, the value "N04" is specified. This means that the corresponding ADD operation is to take place if the 04 Indicator is NOT "on". If the 04 Indicator is "on", the addition will not occur. This is the desired situation because when the 04 Indicator is on, it means that a card with an invalid code in column 80 has been read, that is, the code is not equal to "1", "2", or "3". When this occurs, no arithmetic should take place because the data in the card is probably not valid. If any indicator except 04 is "on", then the value in the REGERN field (Regular Earnings) will be added to the value in the OVTERN (Overtime Earnings) field and the result is stored in the TOTERN field (Total Earnings).

As mentioned previously, if the employee has worked the second shift, he receives a bonus of $5.00 and if he works the third shift, he receives a bonus of $10.00. If Indicator 02 is "on", it indicates that employee has worked the second shift because the value in card column 80 is "2". Thus, as can be seen from the example above, when indicator 02 is "on", the value 5.00 is added to the total earnings field in order to include the $5.00 bonus in the employee's earnings. If indicator 03 is "on", the value 10.00 is added to the total earnings to incorporate the $10.00 bonus. Note that no value is added to the Total Earnings field if the 01 Indicator is "on" because there is no bonus when the first shift is worked.

OUTPUT-FORMAT SPECIFICATIONS

As was noted previously, in addition to the data which is to be printed on the report, headings are also to be printed indicating the current date and a page number. In order to print headings, Heading lines must be specified on the Output-Format Specifications form. This is illustrated below.

EXAMPLE

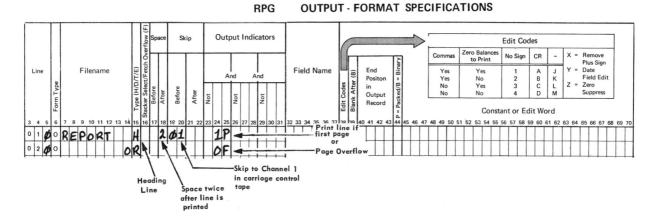

Figure 6-5 Output-Format Specifications

Note from the Output-Format Specifications form illustrated above that the filename for the output report is REPORT. The fact that the line to be printed on the REPORT file is a "heading" is indicated by the value "H" in the Type field (column 15). Whenever the "H" appears, it indicates that the line described is a Heading line, not a Detail line or a Total line. It should be noted that all heading lines for an output file must precede the first detail line described for the same file.

The spacing and skipping of a Heading line is handled in the same manner as a Detail line or a Total line, that is, entries are made in the Space (columns 17-18) and Skip (columns 19-22) fields of the Output-Format Specifications form. Note in Figure 6-5 the entry "01" in columns 19-20. This entry specifies that before the heading line is printed, the printer is to be skipped to Channel 1 in the Carriage control tape.

A carriage control tape is a tape which is positioned on the printer, and when used in conjunction with entries in Columns 19-22, can cause the page to be positioned at various lines. Typically, the first line which is to be printed on a page of a report is identified by a punch in channel 1 of the carriage control tape. This is illustrated in Figure 6-6.

EXAMPLE

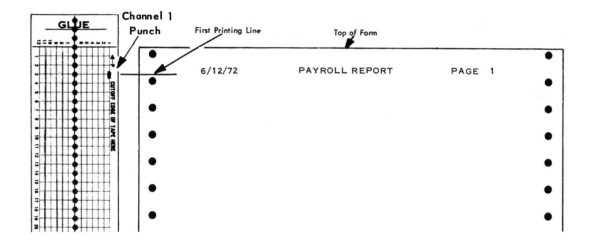

Figure 6-6 Example of Carriage Control Tape

Note in the example above that the first line on the page is printed on the same line which corresponds to the punch in channel 1 of the carriage control tape. Thus, before the heading line is printed on the report, a skip to channel 1 in the carriage control tape must occur so that the page is positioned properly for the first heading line. Again, this skip is specified by entering the value "01" in columns 19-20 of the Output-Format Specifications form.

As can be seen from the example in Figure 6-5, the printer is to be spaced twice after the line is printed because the value "2" is entered in column 18 of the form. Thus, after the first heading line is printed, the printer will be spaced twice so that the next heading line may be printed.

In addition to specifying what spacing and skipping is to occur for a heading line, the Output-Format Specifications form must be used to indicate when a heading line is to be printed. It will be recalled that the Output Indicators portion of the form (columns 23-31) are used to indicate when a line is to be written on an output file. When processing heading lines, two special indicators are used: the "1P" indicator (first page), and the "OF" indicator (Overflow). Note from Figure 6-5 that the value "1P" is entered in columns 24-25 to indicate that when the "1P" indicator is "on", the heading line should be printed. The "1P", or first page, indicator is "on" when the execution of the program begins and remains on until just before the first data card is read. Thus, before the first data card is read, the heading line will be printed on the report. After the "1P" indicator is turned off automatically by the object program, it is not normally turned on again.

After the headings have been printed on the first page, the data is printed. When the first page has been filled with data, it is normally desirable to skip to the head of forms for the second page and again write the headings. In order to specify where the end of a page is and to signal when headings should be written on the next page, the "12" punch in the carriage control tape is utilized. This is illustrated in Figure 6-7.

EXAMPLE

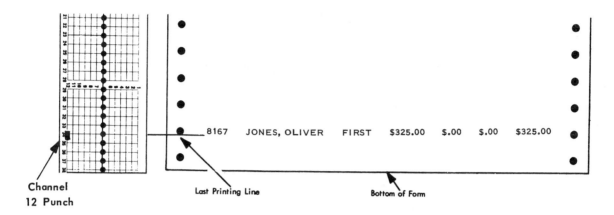

Channel
12 Punch

Last Printing Line

Bottom of Form

8167   JONES, OLIVER   FIRST $325.00 $.00 $.00 $325.00

Figure 6-7 Example of End-of-Forms

Note in the example above that the last line of printing on a page of the report is indicated through the use of a punch in the Channel 12 column of the carriage control tape. This punch has been placed in the tape where the last possible line on the report is to be printed.

When the punch in channel 12 of the carriage control tape is sensed, a special "OF" (overflow) Indicator is set "on". This indicator is a special indicator used to indicate that the end of the page has been reached. When this occurs, of course, it is desired to print headings on the next page after skipping to head of forms. Thus, the "OF" entry is also made on the Output-Format Specifications form to indicate that headings are to be printed. This entry is illustrated in Figure 6-8 together with the entry which must be placed in the File Description Specifications form.

EXAMPLE

FILE DESCRIPTION SPECIFICATIONS

Line	Form Type	Filename	I/O/U/C/D — P/S/C/R/T/D	E	A/D	F/V	Block Length	Record Length	L/R	A/K/I	I/D/T or 1-9	Overflow Indicator / Key Field Starting Location	Extension Code E/L	Device	Symbolic Device
0 1	Ø F	PAYCARD	IP			F	8Ø	8Ø						READ4Ø	SYSIPT
0 2	Ø F	REPORT	O			F	132	132				OF		PRINTER	SYSLST

File Type · File Designation · End of File · Sequence · File Format · Mode of Processing · Length of Key Field or of Record Address Field · Record Address Type · Type of File Organization or Additional Area

→ Printing heading when page overflow occurs

RPG OUTPUT - FORMAT SPECIFICATIONS

Line	Form Type	Filename	Type (H/D/T/E)	Stacker Select/Fetch Overflow (F)	Space Before	Space After	Skip Before	Skip After	Not	(And)	Not	(And)	Not			
0 1	Ø O	REPORT	H		2	Ø	1		1P							
0 2	Ø O		OR						OF							

Output Indicators

Figure 6-8 File Description Specification and Output Specifications

Note in the example above that the indicator "OF" is specified in columns 24-25 of the Output-Format Specifications form. It is contained on the second line of the form and is joined with the first line through the use of the word "OR" in columns 14-15. When the "OR" is used in columns 14-15 it indicates that the output line is to be written if either the indicator "1P" is "on" or the indicator "OF" is "on". This is the situation desired because headings should be written on the first page and on each subsequent page when the last line of the previous page has been written.

When the "OF" indicator is to be used in conjunction with a printer file, an entry must also be made on the File Description Specifications in order to associate the "OF" indicator with the correct file. Note from the example above that the value "OF" is placed in the Overflow Indicator portion of the File Description Specification (columns 33-34). It should be noted also that the value "OF" is not the only indicator which may be used to indicate form overflow. Any value OA-OG and OV may be used as the forms overflow indicator. Regardless of the value used, however, it must be specified both on the File Description Specifications and on the Output-Format Specifications.

After the spacing of the heading lines has been defined and the indicators to determine when the printing is to occur have been specified, the data which is to be printed in the heading is defined. The entries to perform this function are illustrated below.

EXAMPLE

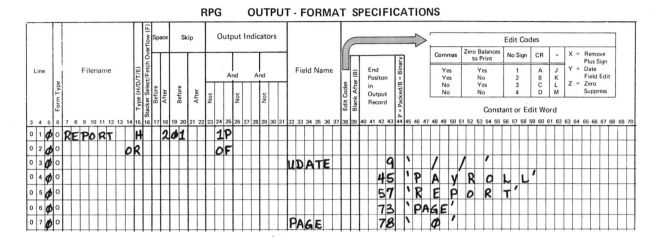

Figure 6-9 Entries for Heading Line

Note from the example in Figure 6-9 that the values to be printed on the first line of the heading are specified following the entries describing the form spacing and the indicators, that is, the first entry is on line 030 of the coding form. As can be seen from the example in Figure 6-2, the first entry in the heading is the date in the format MM/DD/YY. In order to retrieve the current date, the Field Name UDATE is specified in the Field Name portion of the form (columns 32-37). This Field Name need not be used on any other forms within the program. It is a special field name which references the current date which is normally stored in the memory unit of the computer. This date is a six-digit value with two digits for the month, two digits for the day, and two digits for the year. As may be noted from the example in Figure 6-9, this six-digit field is to be edited because of the Edit Word specified in columns 46-53. The editing of the date is illustrated below.

EXAMPLE

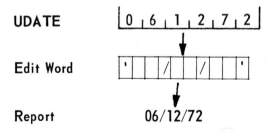

Figure 6-10 Editing of Current Date in UDATE Field

Note from the example that the slashes in the edit word will be inserted in the printed output between the Month and the Day and between the Day and the Year. It should be noted also that the date may be edited with characters other than slashes if desired.

The next three lines on the Output-Format Specifications form are used to specify the constant values which are to be included in the heading. The entry on line 070 specifies a Field Name of PAGE, and, like the Field Name UDATE, is a special field name which is not used elsewhere in the program. The field PAGE is used to keep a page count of each page which is printed and this page count is kept automatically by the object program. When the first page is printed, the value in PAGE is one and it is incremented by one each time a new page is printed. Thus, the value in PAGE for the second page is 2, for the third page is 3, etc. The PAGE field is always a four-digit numeric field. Thus, four positions must be reserved for it on the printed output line. The numeric PAGE field may be edited or zero-suppressed if desired. Note in the Output-Format Specifications form illustrated in Figure 6-9 that the field is edited with an edit word specified in columns 46-49, which is four characters in length.

The second and subsequent heading lines are specified in the same manner as the first heading line with the same Output Indicators (1P or OF). The only difference is in the spacing of the lines. The entries for the heading lines are illustrated in Figure 6-11.

In the example in Figure 6-11 it can be seen that the second and third heading lines are identified by the value "H" in column 15 and that each of them will be written when either the first page indicator (1P) or the overflow indicator (OF) are "on". The printer will be spaced one space after the second line is written and will be spaced twice after the third line is printed.

EXAMPLE: RPG Coding for Headings

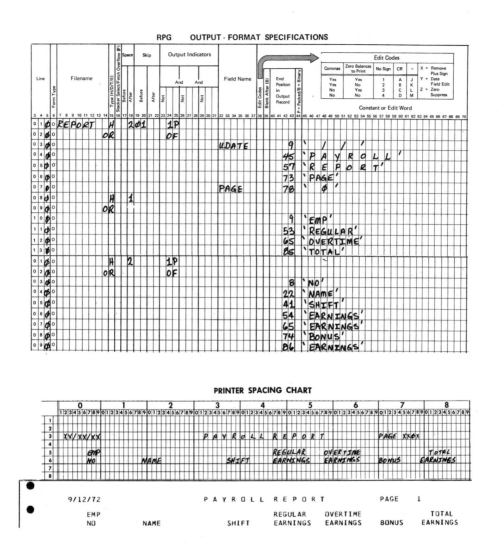

Figure 6-11 Specifications for Heading Lines and a Segment of the Report

Detail Lines

The Detail lines of the report contain the actual processed data which has been read from the input cards and the values which have been calculated on the Calculation Specifications form. In addition, depending upon the indicators which are on, certain constants are also included on the detail line. The Output-Format Specifications entries for the detail line and a segment of the report is illustrated below.

EXAMPLE

RPG OUTPUT-FORMAT SPECIFICATIONS

Edit Codes: Commas	Zero Balances to Print	No Sign	CR	-
Yes	Yes	1	A	J
Yes	No	2	B	K
No	Yes	3	C	L
No	No	4	D	M

X = Remove Plus Sign
Y = Date Field Edit
Z = Zero Suppress

Line (3-5)	Form Type (6)	Filename (7-14)	Type (H/D/T/E) (15)	Stacker Select/Fetch Overflow (F) (16)	Space Before (17)	Space After (18)	Skip Before (19-20)	Skip After (21-22)	Output Indicators (23-31)	Field Name (32-37)	Edit Codes (38)	Blank After (B) (39)	End Position in Output Record (40-43)	P = Packed/B = Binary (44)	Constant or Edit Word (45-70)
01Ø	O		D			1			Ø1						
02Ø	O		OR						Ø2						
03Ø	O		OR						Ø3						
04Ø	O		OR						Ø4						
05Ø	O									EMPNO	Z		9		
06Ø	O									NAME			33		
07Ø	O								Ø1				41		'FIRST'
08Ø	O								Ø2				42		'SECOND'
09Ø	O								Ø3				41		'THIRD'
10Ø	O								Ø4				45		'INVALID SHIFT'
11Ø	O								NØ4	REGERN			53		' $Ø. '
12Ø	O								NØ4	OVTERN			64		' $Ø. '
13Ø	O								Ø1				74		' $.ØØ'
14Ø	O								Ø2				74		' $5.ØØ'
15Ø	O								Ø3				74		'$1Ø.ØØ'
16Ø	O								NØ4	TOTERN			85		' $Ø. '

9/19/72 PAYROLL REPORT PAGE 1

EMP NO	NAME	SHIFT	REGULAR EARNINGS	OVERTIME EARNINGS	BONUS	TOTAL EARNINGS
25	BAKER, ROGER	FIRST	$125.00	$50.00	$.00	$175.00
98	DAVIS, FRED	SECOND	$150.00	$.00	$5.00	$155.00
101	GRANGER, THOMAS	THIRD	$135.35	$5.00	$10.00	$150.35
522	LAFET, RAYMOND	INVALID SHIFT				
1257	ZABU, ALEX	FIRST	$250.30	$253.30	$.00	$503.60

END OF PAYROLL REPORT

Figure 6-12 Detail Line Specifications and Output Report

Note from the Output-Format Specifications form in Figure 6-12 that the line to be printed is specified as a Detail line (column 15). Note also that the filename entry is not included. This is because it was specified previously for the Heading lines and need not be repeated. As can be seen from the entries in the Output Indicators portion of the form and the use of the "OR" entry, a detail line is to be printed if any of the indicators 01, 02, 03 or 04 are "on". Thus, a detail line is to be printed for each input record which is read.

Note that the Employee Number (EMPNO) and the Employee Name (NAME) will be printed for each detail line, that is, when Indicator "01", "02", "03", or "04" are "ON". No entries are required in Output Indicators, positions 24-25 of the coding form, for lines 050 and 060.

Beginning with line 070 entries are recorded in Output Indicators, positions 24-25, to cause specific information to be printed depending upon the indicators which have been set.

As was noted earlier, when the 01 indicator is "on", the input card is for an employee which worked the first shift. Thus, if indicator 01 is "on", the value FIRST will be printed on the report to indicate the first shift. Similarly, if indicator 02 is "on", the value SECOND will be printed for the Shift and if indicator 03 is "on", the value THIRD will be printed. It will be recalled that if the value in the Code field (column 80) of the input card is not one of the valid numbers (1, 2, or 3) indicator 04 will be turned "on". Thus, indicator 04 indicates an invalid code in column 80 of the input card and the value INVALID SHIFT will be printed on the report instead of the shift identification.

When a card with an invalid shift code is read, that is, when indicator 04 is "on", the calculations which are required to determine the pay for the employee are not performed (see Figure 6-4). Thus, the pay information for a card with an invalid code is not to be printed. The suppression of the printing of this information is accomplished by specifying that the information will be printed only if the 04 Indicator is Not on. Note in Figure 6-12 that the value "N04" is placed in the Output Indicator portion of the form (columns 23-25). This value indicates that the corresponding fields are to be printed only if the 04 indicator is not "on". If it is "on", the Regular Earnings, the Overtime Earnings, the Bonus, and the Total Employee Pay will not be printed on the report.

The entry on line 130 causes the constant $.00 to print when Indicator 01 is "on". The entry on line 140 causes the constant $5.00 to print when Indicator 02 is "on", and the entry on line 150 causes the constant $10.00 to print when Indicator 03 is "on".

SAMPLE PROBLEM

The complete documentation for the sample problem discussed in this chapter is illustrated on the following pages.

INPUT: Payroll Cards

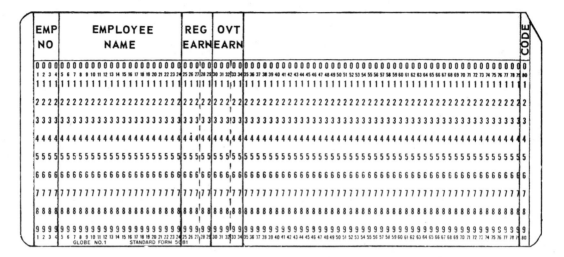

Figure 6 - 13 Input

OUTPUT: Payroll Report

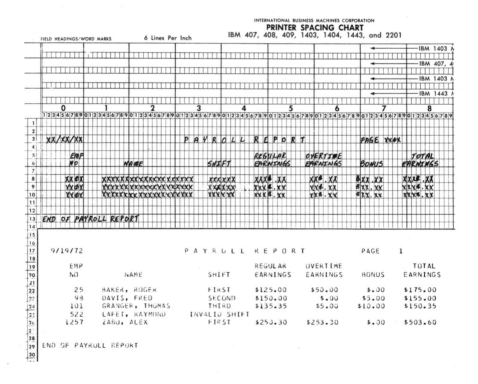

Figure 6 - 14 Output

RPG Program

RPG CONTROL CARD AND FILE DESCRIPTION SPECIFICATIONS

Date 4/25/72
Program PAYROLL REPORT
Programmer SHELLY

Punching Instruction — Graphic 0 0 2 2 — Punch Zero 11-6 Two 2-9
Page 01 — Program Identification PAYRPT

Control Card Specifications

Refer to the specific System Reference Library manual for actual entries.

Line	Form Type
0 1 0	H

File Description Specifications

Line	Form Type	Filename	I/O/U/C/D	P/S/C/R/T/D	E	A/D F/V	Block Length	Record Length	L/R	Device	Symbolic Device
0 2 0	F	PAYCARD	IP			F	80	80		READ40	SYSIPT
0 3 0	F	REPORT	O			F	132	132	OF	PRINTER	SYSLST

RPG INPUT SPECIFICATIONS

Date 4/25/72
Program PAYROLL REPORT
Programmer SHELLY

Punching Instruction — Graphic 0 0 2 2 — Punch Zero 11-6 Two 2-9
Page 02 — Program Identification PAYRPT

Line	Form Type	Filename	Sequence	Number (1/N)	Option (O)	Record Identifying Indicator	Position	Not (N)	C/Z/D	Character	Position	Not (N)	C/Z/D	Character	Position	Not (N)	C/Z/D	Character	From	To	Decimal Positions	Field Name
0 1 0	I	PAYCARD	AA			01	80		C	1												
0 2 0	I	OR				02	80		C	2												
0 3 0	I	OR				03	80		C	3												
0 4 0	I	OR				04	80	N	C	1	80	N	C	2	80	N	C	3				
0 5 0	I																		1	40		EMPNO
0 6 0	I																		5	24		NAME
0 7 0	I																		25	292		REGERN
0 8 0	I																		30	342		OVTERN

RPG CALCULATION SPECIFICATIONS

Date 4/25/72
Program PAYROLL REPORT
Programmer SHELLY

Punching Instruction — Graphic 0 0 2 2 — Punch Zero 11-6 Two 2-9
Page 03 — Program Identification PAYRPT

Line	Form Type	Control Level (L0-L9, LR, SR)	Not	And	Not	And	Factor 1	Operation	Factor 2	Result Field	Field Length	Decimal Positions	Half Adjust (H)	Comments
0 1 0	C	N04					REGERN	ADD	OVTERN	TOTERN	52			
0 2 0	C	02					TOTERN	ADD	5.00	TOTERN				
0 3 0	C	03					TOTERN	ADD	10.00	TOTERN				

Figure 6-15a File Description, Input, Calculation Specifications

RPG OUTPUT - FORMAT SPECIFICATIONS

Date 6/25/72 Program PAYROLL REPORT Programmer SHELLY
Punching Instruction — Graphic: 0 0 2 Z Punch: ZERO 14-6 TWO R9
Page 04 Program Identification PAYRPT

Line	Form Type	Filename	Type (H/D/T/E)	Stacker Select/Fetch Overflow (F)	Space Before	Space After	Skip Before	Skip After	And (Not)	And (Not)	(Not)	Field Name	Edit Codes	End Position in Output Record	P = Packed/B = Binary	Constant or Edit Word
010	O	REPORT	H		2		0	1	1P							
020	O		OR						OF							
030	O											UDATE		9		' / / '
040	O													45		'PAYROLL'
050	O													57		'REPORT'
060	O													73		'PAGE'
070	O											PAGE		78		' 0'
080	O		H		1				1P							
090	O		OR						OF							
100	O													9		'EMP'
110	O													53		'REGULAR'
120	O													65		'OVERTIME'
130	O													85		'TOTAL'
140	O		H		2				1P							
150	O		OR						OF							

RPG OUTPUT - FORMAT SPECIFICATIONS

Date 6/25/72 Program PAYROLL REPORT Programmer SHELLY
Punching Instruction — Graphic: 0 0 2 Z Punch: ZERO 14-6 TWO R9
Page 05 Program Identification PAYRPT

Line	Form Type	Filename	Type	Space B/A	Skip	And (Not)	And (Not)	(Not)	Field Name	Edit Codes	End Position	P/B	Constant or Edit Word
010	O										8		'NO'
020	O										22		'NAME'
030	O										41		'SHIFT'
040	O										54		'EARNINGS'
050	O										65		'EARNINGS'
060	O										74		'BONUS'
070	O										86		'EARNINGS'
080	O		D	1		01							
090	O		OR			02							
100	O		OR			03							
110	O		OR			04							
120	O								EMPNO	Z	9		
130	O								NAME		33		
140	O					01					41		'FIRST'
150	O					02					42		'SECOND'

RPG OUTPUT - FORMAT SPECIFICATIONS

Date 6/25/72 Program PAYROLL REPORT Programmer SHELLY
Punching Instruction — Graphic: 0 0 2 Z Punch: ZERO 14-6 TWO R9
Page 06 Program Identification PAYRPT

Line	Form Type	Filename	Type	Space B/A	Skip	And (Not)	And (Not)	(Not)	Field Name	Edit Codes	End Position	P/B	Constant or Edit Word
010	O					03					41		'THIRD'
020	O					04					45		'INVALID SHIFT'
030	O					N04			REGERN		53		' $0. '
040	O					N04			OVTERN		64		' $0. '
050	O					01					74		' $.00'
060	O					02					74		'$5.00'
070	O					03					74		'$10.00'
080	O					N04			TOTERN		85		' $0.'
090	O		T	2		LR							
100	O										21		'END OF PAYROLL REPORT'

Figure 6-15b Output Specifications

6.16

PROGRAM

The source listing of the sample program is illustrated below.

```
DDS/360*RPG*CL 3-9                    CASHMAN                      09/19/72          PAGE 0001
        01 010 H                                                                    PAYRPT
001     01 020 FPAYCARD IP  F  80  80              READ40 SYSIPT                    PAYRPT
002     01 030 FREPORT   O  F 132 132       OF     PRINTERSYSLST                    PAYRPT
003     02 010 IPAYCARD AA  01  80 C1                                              PAYRPT
004     02 020 I           OR  02  80 C2                                           PAYRPT
005     02 030 I           OR  03  80 C3                                           PAYRPT
006     02 040 I           OR  04  80NC1  80NC2  80NC3                             PAYRPT
007     02 050 I                                         1   40EMPNO               PAYRPT
008     02 060 I                                         5   24 NAME               PAYRPT
009     02 070 I                                        25   292REGERN             PAYRPT
010     02 080 I                                        30   342OVTERN             PAYRPT
011     03 010 C  NO4       REGERN    ADD  OVTERN   TOTERN   52                    PAYRPT
012     03 020 C   02       TOTERN    ADD  5.00     TOTERN                         PAYRPT
013     03 030 C   03       TOTERN    ADD  10.00    TOTERN                         PAYRPT
014     04 010 OREPORT   H  201        1P                                          PAYRPT
015     04 020 O          OR           OF                                          PAYRPT
016     04 030 O                             UDATE      9 ' / / '                   PAYRPT
017     04 040 O                                       45 'P A Y R O L L '          PAYRPT
018     04 050 O                                       57 'R E P O R T'             PAYRPT
019     04 060 O                                       73 'PAGE'                    PAYRPT
020     04 070 O                             PAGE      78 ' O '                     PAYRPT
021     04 080 O          H  1         1P                                          PAYRPT
022     04 090 O          OR           OF                                          PAYRPT
023     04 100 O                                        9 'EMP'                     PAYRPT
024     04 110 O                                       53 'REGULAR'                 PAYRPT
025     04 120 O                                       65 'OVERTIME'                PAYRPT
026     04 130 O                                       85 'TOTAL'                   PAYRPT
027     04 140 O          H  2         1P                                          PAYRPT
028     04 150 O          OR           OF                                          PAYRPT
029     05 010 O                                        8 'NO'                      PAYRPT
030     05 020 O                                       22 'NAME'                    PAYRPT
031     05 030 O                                       41 'SHIFT'                   PAYRPT
032     05 040 O                                       54 'EARNINGS'               PAYRPT
033     05 050 O                                       65 'EARNINGS'               PAYRPT
034     05 060 O                                       74 'BONUS'                   PAYRPT
035     05 070 O                                       86 'EARNINGS'               PAYRPT
036     05 080 O          D  1         01                                          PAYRPT
037     05 090 O          OR           02                                          PAYRPT
038     05 100 O          OR           03                                          PAYRPT
039     05 110 O          OR           04                                          PAYRPT
040     05 120 O                             EMPNO Z    9                           PAYRPT
041     05 130 O                             NAME      33                           PAYRPT
042     05 140 O                        01               41 'FIRST'                 PAYRPT
043     05 150 O                        02               42 'SECOND'                PAYRPT
044     06 010 O                        03               41 'THIRD'                 PAYRPT
045     06 020 O                        04               45 'INVALID SHIFT'         PAYRPT
046     06 030 O                        NO4  REGERN      53 '  $0.  '               PAYRPT
047     06 040 O                        NO4  OVTERN      64 '  $0.  '               PAYRPT
048     06 050 O                        01               74 '  $.00'               PAYRPT
049     06 060 O                        02               74 ' $5.00'               PAYRPT
050     06 070 O                        03               74 '$10.00'               PAYRPT
051     06 080 O                        NO4  TOTERN      85 '  $0.  '               PAYRPT
052     06 090 O          T  2          LR                                          PAYRPT
053     06 100 O                                         21 'END OF PAYROLL REPORT' PAYRPT
```

Figure 6-16 RPG Computer Listing

6.17

CHAPTER 6

REVIEW QUESTIONS

1. What is the difference between the 1P and the OF indicator? Must both of them be specified in order for a heading line to be printed?

2. When an OF indicator is to be used, where must the entries be specified in order to cause page overflow to occur properly?

3. Why isn't it necessary to define the UDATE or PAGE fields on the Input Specifications or the Calculation Specifications like it is for other fields?

4. Explain the difference between the processing caused by an entry in the Space portion of the Output-Format Specifications and an entry in the Skip portion of the Output-Format Specifications.

STUDENT EXERCISES

1. Write the entries on the Input Specifications to turn on indicator 45 if there is the character "I" in column 43 and the character "Y" in column 45 or to turn on indicator 48 if there is the character "P" in column 43 and a blank in column 45.

RPG INPUT SPECIFICATIONS

Line	Form Type	Filename	Sequence	Number (1-N)	Option (O)	Record Identifying Indicator or *‍	Record Identification Codes 1 Position	Not (N)	C/Z/D	Character	Record Identification Codes 2 Position	Not (N)	C/Z/D	Character	Record Identification Codes 3 Position	Not (N)	C/Z/D	Character	Stacker Select	P = Packed/B = Binary	Field Location From	Field Location To	Decimal Positions	Field Name
3 4 5	6	7 8 9 10 11 12 13 14	15 16	17	18	19 20	21 22 23 24	25	26	27	28 29 30 31	32	33	34	35 36 37 38	39	40	41	42	43	44 45 46 47	48 49 50 51	52	53 54 55 56 57 58
0 1	I																							
0 2	I																							
0 3	I																							
0 4	I																							
0 5	I																							
0 6	I																							
0 7	I																							
0 8	I																							
0 9	I																							

2. If, from question #1, there is an "I" in column 43 and a "Y" in column 45, the value in FIELDA is to be added to the value in FIELDB and the result is to be stored in FIELDA. If there is the character "P" in column 43 and a blank in column 45, then the value in FIELDB is to be subtracted from the value in FIELDA and the result stored in FIELDA. Assuming that these fields are defined on the Input Specifications, write the entries on the Calculation Specifications to cause this processing.

RPG CALCULATION SPECIFICATIONS

Line	Form Type	Control Level (L0-L9, LR, SR)	Indicators Not	And	And Not	And Not	Factor 1	Operation	Factor 2	Result Field	Field Length	Decimal Positions	Half Adjust (H)	Resulting Indicators Arithmetic Plus	Minus	Zero Compare High 1>2	Low 1<2	Equal 1=2 Lookup Table (Factor 2) is High	Low	Equal
3 4 5	6	7 8	9 10 11	12 13 14	15 16 17		18 19 20 21 22 23 24 25 26 27	28 29 30 31 32	33 34 35 36 37 38 39 40 41 42	43 44 45 46 47 48	49 50 51	52	53	54 55	56 57	58 59				
0 1	C																			
0 2	C																			
0 3	C																			
0 4	C																			
0 5	C																			
0 6	C																			
0 7	C																			
0 8	C																			
0 9	C																			

3. Given the following headings on the printer spacing chart, record the entries on the Output-Format Specifications to cause the headings to print for the OUTFLE file. Assume that the overflow indicator, OA, has been properly specified on the File Description

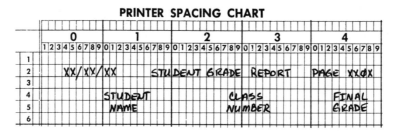

PRINTER SPACING CHART

	0 (1-9,0)	1	2	3	4
1					
2	XX/XX/XX	STUDENT GRADE	REPORT		PAGE XXØX
3					
4	STUDENT		CLASS		FINAL
5	NAME		NUMBER		GRADE
6					

RPG   OUTPUT - FORMAT SPECIFICATIONS

Line	Form Type	Filename	Type (H/D/T/E)	Stacker Select/Fetch Overflow (F)	Space Before	Space After	Skip Before	Skip After	Output Indicators Not	And Not	And Not	Field Name	Edit Codes	Blank After (B)	End Position in Output Record	P = Packed/B = Binary	Constant or Edit Word
0 1	O																
0 2	O																
0 3	O																
0 4	O																
0 5	O																
0 6	O																
0 7	O																
0 8	O																
0 9	O																
1 0	O																
1 1	O																
1 2	O																
1 3	O																
1 4	O																
1 5	O																

Edit Codes

Commas	Zero Balances to Print	No Sign	CR	-	
Yes	Yes	1	A	J	X = Remove Plus Sign
Yes	No	2	B	K	Y = Date Field Edit
No	Yes	3	C	L	Z = Zero Suppress
No	No	4	D	M	

Instructions: The following RPG program contains an error or errors which have occurred during compilation. Circle each error and record the corrected entries directly on the listing. Explain the error and method of correction in the space provided below.

```
LOS/360*RPG*CL 3-9                    CASHMAN                   10/13/72            PAGE 0001

        01 010 H                                                              PAYRPT
001     01 020 FPAYCARD IP  F  80  80              READ40 SYSIPT               PAYRPT
002     01 030 FREPORT  O   F 132 132              PRINTERSYSLST               PAYRPT
003     02 010 IPAYCARD AA   01  80 C1                                         PAYRPT
004     02 020 I        OR   02  80 C2                                         PAYRPT
005     02 030 I        OR   03  80 C3                                         PAYRPT
006     02 040 I        OR   C4  80NC1 80NC2 80NC3                             PAYRPT
007     02 050 I                              1   40EMPNO                      PAYRPT
008     02 060 I                              5   24 NAME                      PAYRPT
009     02 070 I                             25   292REGERN                    PAYRPT
010     02 080 I                             30   342OVTERN                    PAYRPT
011     03 010 C    NO4    REGERN   ADD  OVTERN   TOTERN  52                    PAYRPT
012     03 020 C    02     TOTERN   ADD  5.00     TOTERN                        PAYRPT
013     03 030 C    03     TOTERN   ADD  10.00    TOTERN                        PAYRPT
014     04 010 OREPORT H  2O1  1P                                              PAYRPT
015     04 020 O        OR   OF                                                PAYRPT
                                                                              NOTE 192
016     04 030 O                    UDATE     9 ' / / '                         PAYRPT
017     04 040 O                             45 'P A Y R O L L '                PAYRPT
018     04 050 O                             57 'R E P O R T'                   PAYRPT
019     04 060 O                             73 'PAGE'                          PAYRPT
020     04 070 O                    PAGE     78 ' O '                           PAYRPT
021     04 080 O        H   1    1P                                            PAYRPT
022     04 090 O        OR   OF                                                PAYRPT
                                                                              NOTE 192
023     04 100 O                              9 'EMP'                           PAYRPT
024     04 110 O                             53 'REGULAR'                       PAYRPT
025     04 120 O                             65 'OVERTIME'                      PAYRPT
026     04 130 O                             85 'TOTAL'                         PAYRPT
027     04 140 O        H   2    1P                                            PAYRPT
028     04 150 O        OR   OF                                                PAYRPT
                                                                              NOTE 192
029     05 010 O                              8 'NO'                            PAYRPT
030     05 020 O                             22 'NAME'                          PAYRPT
031     05 030 O                             41 'SHIFT'                         PAYRPT
032     05 040 O                             54 'EARNINGS'                      PAYRPT
033     05 050 O                             65 'EARNINGS'                      PAYRPT
034     05 060 O                             74 'BONUS'                         PAYRPT
035     05 070 O                             86 'EARNINGS'                      PAYRPT
036     05 080 O        D   1    01                                           PAYRPT
        05 090 O                  02                                           PAYRPT
                                                                              NOTE 197
        05 100 O                  03                                           PAYRPT
                                                                              NOTE 197
        05 110 O                  04                                           PAYRPT
                                                                              NOTE 197
037     05 120 O                    EMPNO Z   9                                 PAYRPT
038     05 130 O                    NAME     33                                 PAYRPT
039     05 140 O                  01         41 'FIRST'                         PAYRPT
040     05 150 O                  02         42 'SECOND'                        PAYRPT
041     06 010 O                  03         41 'THIRD'                         PAYRPT
042     06 020 O                  04         45 'INVALID SHIFT'                 PAYRPT
043     06 030 O                  NO4  REGERN 53 '  $0.  '                      PAYRPT
044     06 040 O                  NO4  OVTERN 64 '  $0.  '                      PAYRPT
045     06 050 O                  01         74 '  $.00'                        PAYRPT
046     06 060 O                  02         74 '  $5.00'                       PAYRPT
047     06 070 O                  03         74 '$10.00'                        PAYRPT
048     06 080 O                  NO4  TOTERN 85 '  $0.  '                      PAYRPT
049     06 090 O    T   2    LR                                               PAYRPT
050     06 100 O                             21 'END OF PAYROLL REPORT'         PAYRPT
```

SYMBOL   TABLES

RESULTING INDICATORS

ADDRESS RI	ADDRESS RI	ADDRESS RI	ADDRESS RI	ADDRESS RI	ADDRESS RI	ADDRESS RI
000011 OF	000014 1P	000015 LR	000016 00	000017 01	000018 02	000019 03
00001A 04	00007A L0	000085 H0	000086 H1	000087 H2	000088 H3	000089 H4
00008A H5	00008B H6	00008C H7	00008D H8	00008E H9		

FIELD NAMES

ADDRESS FIELD	ADDRESS FIELD	ADDRESS FIELD	ADDRESS FIELD	ADDRESS FIELD
000123 EMPNO	000126 NAME	00013A REGERN	00013D OVTERN	000140 TOTERN
000143 UDATE	000147 PAGE			

LITERALS

ADDRESS LITERAL	ADDRESS LITERAL	ADDRESS LITERAL
00014A 5.00	00014C 10.00	00014F ---/--/--
000159 P A Y R O L L	000167 R E P O R T	000172 PAGE
000176 ---/-	00017C EMP	00017F REGULAR
000186 OVERTIME	00018E TOTAL	000193 NO
000195 NAME	000199 SHIFT	00019E EARNINGS
0001A6 BONUS	0001AB FIRST	0001B0 SECOND
0001B6 THIRD	0001BB INVALID SHIFT	0001C8 ----/.--
0001D1 $.00	0001D7 $5.00	0001DD $10.00
0001E3 END OF PAYROLL REPORT		

015	OF	NOTE 212
022	OF	NOTE 212
028	OF	NOTE 212

NOTE 192   OUTPUT INDICATOR (COLUMNS 24-25, 27-28, OR 30-31) IS INVALID OR UNDEFINED.
            ENTRY OF LO IS ASSUMED.

NOTE 197   SPECIFICATION TYPE CANNOT BE DETERMINED. RECORD AND FIELD DEFINITIONS ARE
            SPECIFIED IN SAME LINE OR BOTH ARE BLANK. SPECIFICATION IS NOT PROCESSED.

NOTE 212   RESULTING INDICATOR IS INVALID OR UNDEFINED. ENTRY OF LO IS ASSUMED.

EXPLANATION _____

_____

_____

_____

Debugging RPG Programs

Problem 2

Instructions: The following RPG program contains an error or errors which occur during execution. Circle each error and record the corrected entries directly on the listing. Explain the error and method of correction in the space provided below.

```
DOS/360*RPG*CL 3-9                    CASHMAN              10/13/72        PAGE 0001

           01 010 H                                                       PAYRPT
001        01 020 FPAYCARD IP  F  80  80            READ40 SYSIPT         PAYRPT
002        01 030 FREPORT  O   F 132 132     OF     PRINTERSYSLST         PAYRPT
003        02 010 IPAYCARD AA   01   80 C1                                PAYRPT
004        02 020 I        OR   02   80 C2                                PAYRPT
005        02 030 I        OR   03   80 C3                                PAYRPT
006        02 040 I        OR   04   80NC1  80NC2  80NC3                  PAYRPT
007        02 050 I                             1   40EMPNO               PAYRPT
008        02 060 I                             5   24 NAME               PAYRPT
009        02 070 I                            25  292REGERN              PAYRPT
010        02 080 I                            30  342OVTERN              PAYRPT
011        03 010 C   04     REGERN   ADD  OVTERN   TOTERN  52            PAYRPT
012        03 020 C   02     TOTERN   ADD  5.00     TOTERN                PAYRPT
013        03 030 C   03     TOTERN   ADD  10.00    TOTERN                PAYRPT
014        04 010 OREPORT   H  201     1P                                 PAYRPT
015        04 020 O         OR          OF                                PAYRPT
016        04 030 O                            UDATE    9 ' / / '         PAYRPT
017        04 040 O                                    45 'P A Y R O L L 'PAYRPT
018        04 050 O                                    57 'R E P O R T'   PAYRPT
019        04 060 O                                    73 'PAGE'          PAYRPT
020        04 070 O                            PAGE    78 ' 0 '           PAYRPT
021        04 080 O         H  1     1P                                   PAYRPT
022        04 090 O         OR          OF                                PAYRPT
023        04 100 O                                     9 'EMP'           PAYRPT
024        04 110 O                                    53 'REGULAR'       PAYRPT
025        04 120 O                                    65 'OVERTIME'      PAYRPT
026        04 130 O                                    85 'TOTAL'         PAYRPT
027        04 140 O         H  2     1P                                   PAYRPT
028        04 150 O         OR          OF                                PAYRPT
029        05 010 O                                     8 'NO'            PAYRPT
030        05 020 O                                    22 'NAME'          PAYRPT
031        05 030 O                                    41 'SHIFT'         PAYRPT
032        05 040 O                                    54 'EARNINGS'      PAYRPT
033        05 050 O                                    65 'EARNINGS'      PAYRPT
034        05 060 O                                    74 'BONUS'         PAYRPT
035        05 070 O                                    86 'EARNINGS'      PAYRPT
036        05 080 O         D  1     01                                   PAYRPT
037        05 090 O         OR       02                                   PAYRPT
038        05 100 O         OR       03                                   PAYRPT
039        05 110 O         OR       04                                   PAYRPT
040        05 120 O                           EMPNO Z   9                 PAYRPT
041        05 130 O                           NAME     33                 PAYRPT
042        05 140 O                    01               41 'FIRST'        PAYRPT
043        05 150 O                    02               42 'SECOND'       PAYRPT
044        06 010 O                    03               41 'THIRD'        PAYRPT
045        06 020 O                    04               45 'INVALID SHIFT'PAYRPT
046        06 030 O                    N04  REGERN      53 '  $0. '       PAYRPT
047        06 040 O                    N04  OVTERN      64 '  $0. '       PAYRPT
048        06 050 O                    01               74 '  $.00'       PAYRPT
049        06 060 O                    02               74 '  $5.00'      PAYRPT
050        06 070 O                    03               74 '$10.00'       PAYRPT
051        06 080 O                    N04  TOTERN      85 '  $0. '       PAYRPT
052        06 090 O         T  2     LR                                   PAYRPT
053        06 100 O                                     21 'END OF PAYROLL REPORT' PAYRPT
```

P A Y R O L L   R E P O R T   PAGE   1

EMP NO	NAME	SHIFT	REGULAR EARNINGS	OVERTIME EARNINGS	BONUS	TOTAL EARNINGS	
25	HAKER, ROGER	FIRST	$125.00	$50.00	$.00	$.00	Note: Totals incorrect
98	DAVIS, FRED	SECOND	$150.00	$.00	$5.00	$5.00	
101	GRANGER, THOMAS	THIRD	$135.35	$5.00	$10.00	$15.00	
522	LAFET, RAYMOND	INVALID SHIFT					
1257	ZAGU, ALEX	FIRST	$250.30	$253.30	$.00	$100.75	

END OF PAYROLL REPORT

EXPLANATION

_____

_____

_____

_____

CHAPTER 6

PROGRAMMING ASSIGNMENT 1

INSTRUCTIONS

Write the RPG program to produce a Customer Sales Report. Input cards will contain a control code indicating whether the customer balance punched on the card is current, whether the balance is over 30 days old, or whether the balance is over 60 days old. A "1" punch indicates a current account, a "2" punch indicates an account 30-60 days past due, and a "3" punch indicates an account over 60 days past due. If the account is current, a 3% cash discount is given. If the account is 30-60 days past due, no cash discount is given. For accounts over 60 days past due, a 1.5% service charge is added to the account.

INPUT — Customer Sales Cards

Input is to consist of Customer Sales Cards containing the Customer Number, the Customer Name, the Balance, and a Code field containing a "1", "2", or "3" punch. The format of the Sales Cards is illustrated below.

OUTPUT — Customer Sales Report

Output is to consist of a Customer Sales Report. The report is to contain the Customer Number, the Customer Name, the Balance, the Discount Percentage or Service Charge, and the Balance Due. The Balance Due is obtained by multiplying the Balance by the Discount Percentage and subtracting the answer obtained from the original balance or by multiplying the balance by the Service Charge and adding the answer to the original balance. Each customer is to be identified as being "Current", "30-60 Days", or "Over 60 Days". Notice also that headings are to be included on the report.

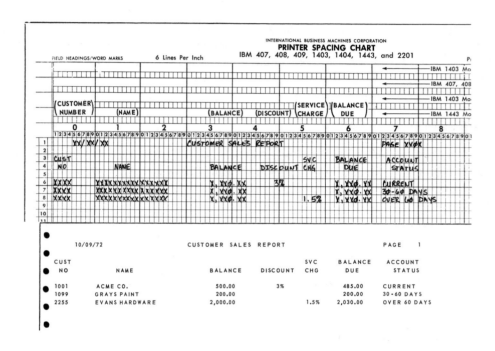

TEST DATA — ASSIGNMENT NO. 1

Cust No (col 1-4)	Name (col 5-20)	Balance (col 21-26)	Code (col 27)
1001	Acme Co.	050000	1
1099	Grays Paint	020000	2
2255	Evans Hardware	200000	3
3463	Finigan's, Inc.	002490	1
7439	Holman Furn.	345200	3
8675	Masonary Brick	008750	2

DOS JOB CONTROL

```
// JOB jobname
// OPTION LINK
// EXEC RPG

  — Student Source Deck —

/*
// EXEC LNKEDT
// EXEC

  — Test Data —

/*
/&
```

Note: This assumes that the assignments for the card read and printer are standard assignments known to the student.

CHAPTER 6

PROGRAMMING ASSIGNMENT 2

INSTRUCTIONS

Write the RPG program to produce a Sales Commission Report. Input cards will contain a control code indicating the type of Employee. A "1" code indicates a part-time employee. No commission is paid to   part-time employees. A "2" punch indicates a fulltime salaried employee. Fulltime salaried employees receive a 5% commission on all sales. A "3" punch indicates employees working on a commission only. Employees working on a commission only basis receive a 5% commission on all sales up to $1000.00 and a 7% commission on all sales in excess of $1000.00. For example, a "commission only" employee with sales of $1200.00 would receive a commision of 5% on $1000.00 and a 7% commission on $200.00.

INPUT — Sales Cards

Input is to consist of Sales Cards containing the Salesman Number, Salesman Name, Sales Amount, and a Code. The format of the Sales Cards is illustrated below.

OUTPUT — Sales Commission Report

Output is to consist of a Sales Commission Report. The report is to contain the Salesman Number, Salesman Name, Sales Amount, and Commission. Employee cards which contain a "1" punch are to be identified as PART-TIME on the report. Employee cards containing a "2" punch are to be identified as FULL-TIME on the report and cards containing a "3" punch are to be identified as COMMISSION on the report. Final Totals are to be taken of the Sales Amount and Commission Amount.

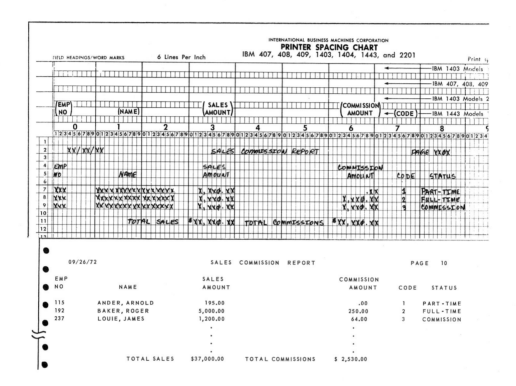

TEST DATA – ASSIGNMENT NO. 2

Salesman Number (col 1-3)	Name (col 4-20)	Sales Amount (col 21-26)	Code (col 80)
115	Ander, Arnold	019500	1
192	Baker, Roger	500000	2
237	Louie, James	120000	3
376	Menton, Robert	326500	3
657	Operit, Fred	099500	3
961	Talbott, Mike	539000	2

DOS JOB CONTROL

```
// JOB jobname
// OPTION LINK
// EXEC RPG

  – Student Source Deck

/*
// EXEC LNKEDT
// EXEC

  – Test Data –

/*
/&
```

Note: This assumes that the assignments for the card reader and printer are standard assignments known to the student.

6.30

CHAPTER 7

CONTROL BREAKS

INTRODUCTION

In the previous examples of RPG programs, the data which was read as input to the program was then printed as output on a report, that is, all of the data was treated as detail data, except for the heading and final total lines. In many business applications, it is necessary to print intermediate data, such as totals, on the report which has been calculated from the input data. The printing of this information normally takes place when a control break occurs.

A CONTROL BREAK occurs when the value in a given input field changes from the value read on a previous input record. This is illustrated in the following example.

EXAMPLE

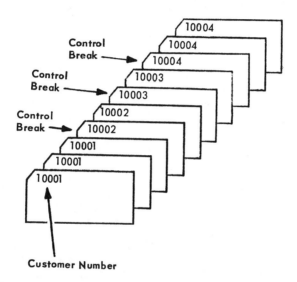

Figure 7-1 Example of CONTROL BREAK

Note in the example above that a customer number field is contained on each card which is to be read. The first three cards have the customer number 10001. The fourth input card, however, contains the customer number 10002. When the fourth card is read, therefore, a control break is said to occur because the value in the control field, in this case the customer number, has changed.

When a control break occurs, it is normally desirable to perform some type of unique processing, for example, taking a total of sales for the customer just processed. When programming in RPG, the indication that a control break has occured is performed by Control Level Indicators. The use of Control Level Indicators will be explained in this chapter.

The sample program in this chapter is designed to prepare an Accounts Receivable Register report from a file of Accounts Receivable Cards. Within the Accounts Receivable file, there may be more than one card for each customer which is to be processed. Each card for each customer is to be printed and, in addition, a total is to be taken for each customer. A "summary" card, which contains the customer number and the customer total, will also be punched on the card punch.

EXAMPLE

Input

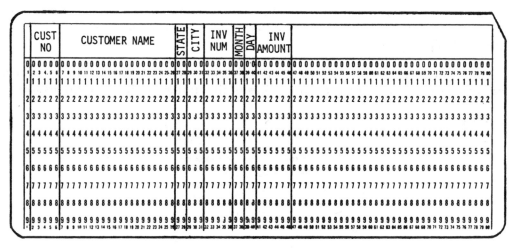

Output

INTERNATIONAL BUSINESS MACHINES CORPORATION
PRINTER SPACING CHART
IBM 407, 408, 409, 1403, 1404, 1443, and 2201

9/15/72	ACCOUNTS RECEIVABLE REGISTER							PAGE	1

CUSTOMER NUMBER	CUSTOMER NAME	LOCATION STATE	CITY	INVOICE NUMBER	INVOICE MONTH	DATE DAY		INVOICE AMOUNT
7163	ALCO INC.	36	471	12267	12	18		100.00
7163	ALCO INC.	36	471	12285	12	19		506.79
						CUSTOMER TOTAL	$	606.79*
11897	LOGAN MFG.	47	771	00521	11	50		14.59
11897	LOGAN MFG.	47	771	10936	12	06		63.82
11897	LOGAN MFG.	47	771	10901	10	18		27.63
						CUSTOMER TOTAL	$	106.04*
20395	MODAR CO.	13	353	12299	12	19		75.00
20395	MODAR CO.	13	353	12275	12	18		125.50
20395	MODAR CO.	13	353	12252	12	17		500.25
						CUSTOMER TOTAL	$	700.75*
						FINAL TOTAL	$	1,413.58**

Figure 7-2 Input and Output for Accounts Receivable Register

Note from the example report in Figure 7-2 that each time the customer number changes, a total of the invoice amount is taken for the previous customer. This total, sometimes referred to as a Minor Total, will be printed each time a control break occurs within the input data.

INPUT SPECIFICATIONS

In order to process control breaks, the control field or fields in each input record must be specified on the Input Specifications. The Input Specifications for the sample program is illustrated below.

EXAMPLE

RPG INPUT SPECIFICATIONS

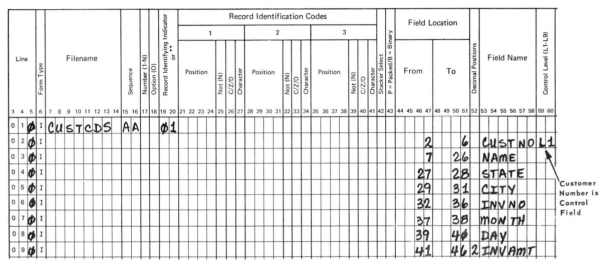

Figure 7-3 Input Specifications for Control Break

Note in the example above that the entries for the definition of the file and the Record Identifying Indicator are similar to previous problems. The only additional entry which is required to indicate that a control break is to be processed is the "L1" entry in the Control Level field of the form (columns 59-60). This entry identifies the field which is to be the control field for each input record and also specifies the indicator which will be "on" when a control break occurs in the input data. Note that the remainder of the record is defined in the same manner as used previously.

CALCULATION SPECIFICATIONS

When a total is to be printed at a control break, the total must be accumulated from each detail card which is read for a given customer. This is illustrated in the following example.

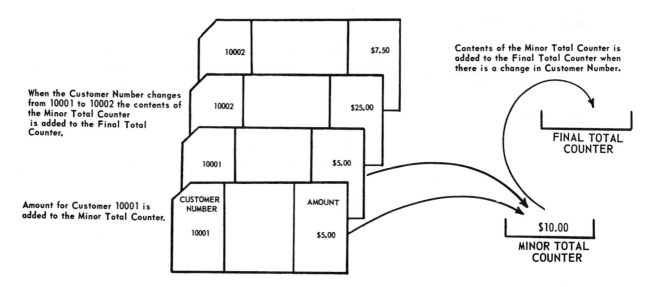

Figure 7-4 Example of Adding to Minor Total Counter and Final Total Counter

Note in the example above that, when the cards with the customer number 10001 are read, the invoice amount in each detail card is added to the "minor total counter", which is used to accumulate the invoice amounts for customer 10001. When a control break is found, that is, when the first card with the customer number 10002 is read, the value which has been accumulated for customer 10001, and which is stored in the minor total counter area, will be added to the final total counter. Thus, the value in the final total counter area will be the sum of the values in the minor total counter area. The entries on the Calculation Specifications in order to cause this arithmetic to take place are illustrated in Figure 7-5.

EXAMPLE

CALCULATION SPECIFICATIONS

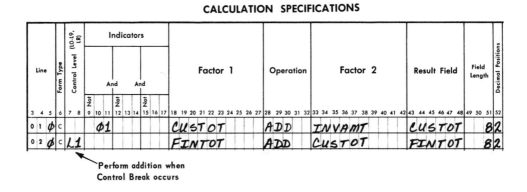

Figure 7-5 Calculation Specifications

Note from the example in Figure 7-5 that two addition operations are to be performed in the program. The first is performed when indicator 01 is "on", that is, each time an input card is read. This operation adds the invoice amount which is found in the input card into the minor total counter (CUSTOT). The second addition operation is performed when the L1 indicator is "on" (columns 7-8), that is, when a control break occurs. Note that the entry "L1" is made in the Control Level field on the form, not in the Indicators portion of the form. It performs the same function as an indicator, however, in that when the L1 indicator is "on", the addition will take place. Thus, as can be seen from the entries in Figure 7-5, the addition operations which are required to take a minor total as illustrated in Figure 7-4 can be specified by entering the proper indicators on the Calculation Specifications form.

OUTPUT SPECIFICATIONS

The headings on the report are printed when indicators "1P" and "OF" are on as illustrated in the previous chapters. In order to print the report with detail lines, minor totals, and a final total, three different print lines must be defined: a detail line for each card which is processed, a total line for the L1 control break, and a total line for the last record, which is used to print the final total. The entries for the detail line and the L1 total line are illustrated below.

EXAMPLE

RPG   OUTPUT - FORMAT SPECIFICATIONS

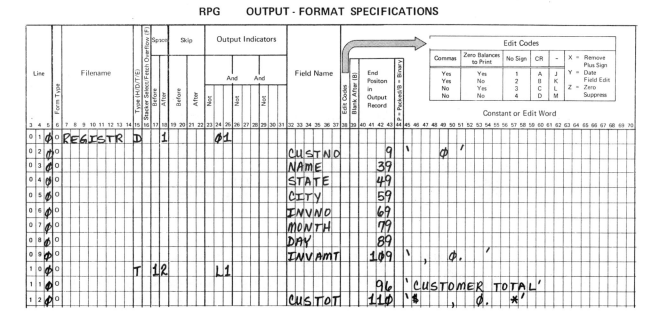

Figure 7-6 Output Specification for Detail and L1 Total Lines

Note in the example above that the detail line, as identified by the "D" in column 15, will be printed each time the 01 Indicator is "on", that is, each time a detail card is read. The total line, on the other hand, will be printed only when the L1 indicator is "on", that is, only when a control break occurs. This is because the value "L1" is entered in columns 24-25, indicating that the line should be printed only when L1 is "on". This, of course, is the desired result because the total line will contain the total for the customer just processed (see Figure 7-2).

Summary Cards

As was noted previously, in addition to the printed report, a Summary Card is to be punched for each customer. A Summary Card is an output card which is punched from the program and contains certain information which has been calculated in the program. In this example, the summary card will contain the customer number and the amount totals of the invoices for the customer, that is, the same customer total which is printed as a minor total on the report. The entries in the File Description Specifications and the Output-Format Specifications for the card output file are illustrated below.

EXAMPLE

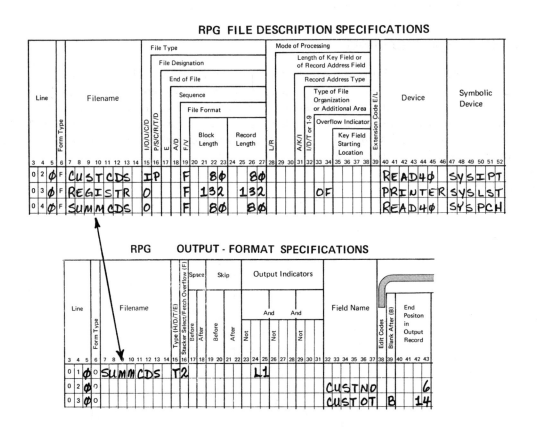

Figure 7-7 Specifications for Summary Cards

Note from the example above that the file **SUMMCDS** must be defined on the File Description Specifications as an output file (column 15). The block and record lengths are both 80 characters, as this is the number of columns in a punched card. The device on which the cards are to be punched is a 2540 (READ40) and the symbolic unit name is SYSPCH. This symbolic unit name may normally always be used for punched output from an RPG program.

The entries on the Output-Format Specifications form specify that the card to be punched from the SUMMCDS file is to be punched at "total" time by the entry "T" in column 15. The entry in column 16 is used to specify the "stacker" where the output card will be placed after it is punched. The entry "2" specifies that the card will be placed in stacker 2 of the three stackers available on a 2540 Card Read-Punch. If this entry is omitted, that is, the column is left blank, the card will be placed in stacker 1.

The output indicator which is specified in columns 24-25, L1, indicates that the card is to be punched when an L1 control break takes place. Thus, it will take place at the same time the customer total is printed on the report (see Figure 7-6). Note that the two fields which will be punched in the Summary Card are the Customer Number (CUSTNO), and the Total amount for the invoices of the customer (CUSTOT).

As noted, when a minor total is being accumulated, the invoice amount from each detail record is added to a "counter". In the example, this is the field CUSTOT (see Figure 7-4). After the customer total has been printed on the report and punched on the summary card, the value in the CUSTOT field must be reset to the value zero so that when the invoice amounts for the next customer are added to the field, it will not contain the totals for both of the customers — rather, it will contain only the total for the new customer. In order to "zero" the field after the minor total has been printed and punched, the entry "B" is placed in the "Blank After" field (column 39) on the Output-Format Specifications form. This entry causes a numeric field to be set to zeros after the field has been printed or punched. It will also cause an alphanumeric field to be set to blanks after processing if it is specified for an alphanumeric field. It should be noted that the "B" entry is placed with the CUSTOT field when the field is specified for the Summary Card, not when it is specified for the Customer Total on the printed report. This is because the field is "zeroed" immediately after the specified field is printed or punched. If the "B" had been placed with the CUSTOT field when it is specified for the printed total line, the value in CUSTOT would be zero when it is punched. This is illustrated in Figure 7-8.

EXAMPLE

Incorrect

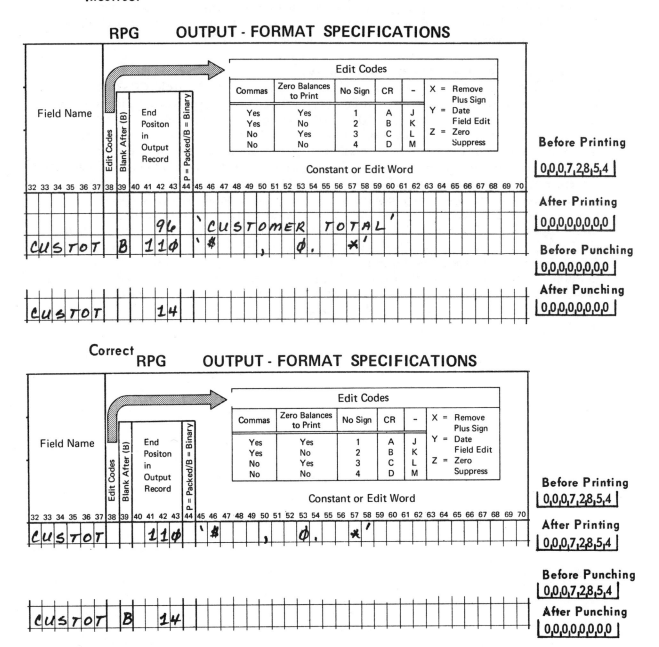

Figure 7-8 Example of "BLANK AFTER" Entries

Note in the example above that if the Blank After entry is made prior to the punching of the CUSTOT field in the Summary Card, it will be equal to zero when punched on the card. Again, when a field is to be used more than one time at any given level, such as the CUSTOT field which is used at L1 total time for both the printed report and the summary summary card, the last use of the field must contain the Blank After entry.

Final Total

After the last input card has been processed, a final total is to be printed. The portion of the printed report below illustrates the final total.

EXAMPLE

```
INVOICE          DATE                  INVOICE
MONTH            DAY                   AMOUNT

  12              18                   100.00
  12              19                   506.79

         CUSTOMER  TOTAL    $    606.79*

  11              50                    14.59
  12              06                    63.82
  10              18                    27.63

         CUSTOMER  TOTAL    $    106.04*

  12              19                    75.00
  12              18                   125.50
  12              17                   500.25

         CUSTOMER  TOTAL    $    700.75* ◄────── L1 Total


         FINAL  TOTAL       $  1,413.58** ────── LR Total
```

Figure 7-9 Example of Final Total

Note in the example above that after the Customer Total for the last customer processed is printed, the Final Total is printed. This final total will be printed because this is the print line which is to be printed when the LR Last Record indicator is "on". It should be noted, however, that the minor total for the last customer must be printed when the last card is read but before the final total is printed. In order to accomplish this, the RPG object program will turn on all total indicators when the last card is read, that is, when the LR indicator is turned on. Thus, when the LR indicator is turned "on" when the last card is read, the L1 indicator for the customer will be turned on at the same time. The totals will then be printed beginning with the lowest numbered indicator and continuing through the LR indicator. Thus, the L1 total will be printed on the report before the LR total is printed. This is the desired result in order to have the Customer Total for the last customer print before the Final Total.

RPG FIXED LOGIC

In the previous example, it can be seen that the processing takes place in a prescribed sequence, that is, the detail cards are processed until a control break occurs, at which time the total lines are printed and the summary card is punched. The detail cards are then again processed and so on. This prescribed sequence follows the RPG FIXED LOGIC, which is the logic used by the RPG compiler to translate the symbolic coding on the RPG Specification forms into a step-by-step object program. The RPG programmer should have a basic knowledge of the RPG Fixed Logic because an understanding of which indicators will be "on" and when they will be "on" many times influences the manner in which the source program is written.

The flowchart in Figure 7-10 illustrates the portion of the RPG Fixed Logic which is applicable to the sample program in this chapter.

Note from the flowchart that each process which is to occur within the RPG program takes place in a given sequence within the program and that the source coding written by the programmer in no way changes this sequence. Thus, the sequence in which indicators are turned on or off and are checked is fixed and may not be altered. The programmer should, therefore, be aware of this sequence so that checks for appropriate indicators will be made at the proper time within the program. The example on the following pages illustrates the steps which occur in the processing of the sample program. It may be useful to refer to the flowchart in Figure 7-10 as well as the portions of the flowchart illustrated in the next example in order to get the overall view of the processing.

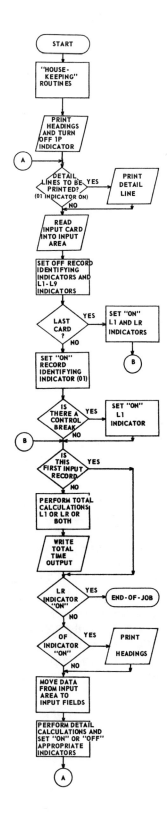

Figure 7 - 10   RPG Fixed Logic - Control Break

Step 1: Housekeeping routines are processed and headings, if required, are written.

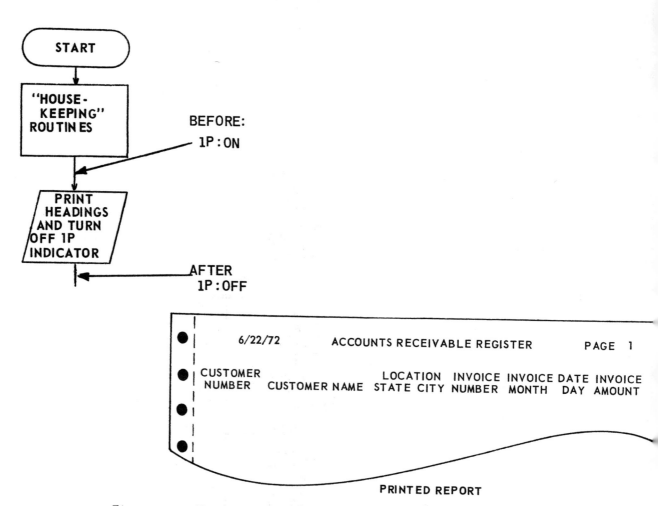

Figure 7-11 Headings are printed because 1P Indicator is "on"

When the RPG program is begun, certain routines must always be processed before the main processing of the program may take place. These routines are termed "House-keeping" routines and are always the first processing which take place within the program. After the housekeeping routines, the headings are printed because the 1P indicator is "on". It will be recalled that when the program begins, the 1P (First Page) indicator is always "on". After the headings are printed, the 1P indicator is turned "off" and will remain "off" for the duration of the program.

Step 2: A check is made to determine if detail lines are to be printed and then a card is read into the input area.

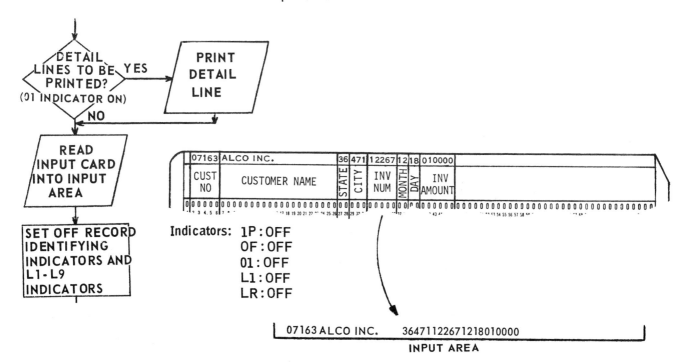

Figure 7-12 Input Card Is Read

Note from the example in Figure 7-12 that the indicators within the program are tested to determine if a detail line is to be printed. As can be seen from the Output-Format Specifications in Figure 7-6, the detail line is to be printed when Indicator 01 is "on". Since an input card has not been read, the 01 indicator will be "off". Therefore, no detail lines will be printed on the report.

The first input card is then read into the input area. It should be noted that the input area in an RPG program is merely 80 bytes which are established by the RPG compiler in which to store the card. The data in the input area is not available to be processed. It is merely stored in the input area as a temporary hold area. Only after the data in the input area is moved to the individual input fields is the data in the input card available for processing.

Note also that all Record Identifying Indicators and the Control Break Indicators (L1-L9) are set "off". These will not be "on" when the first card is read but this step is always performed to ensure that only the proper indicators will be "on" for the current input record being processed.

Step 3: A test for the last card is performed and the record is identified. A
check is then performed for a control break.

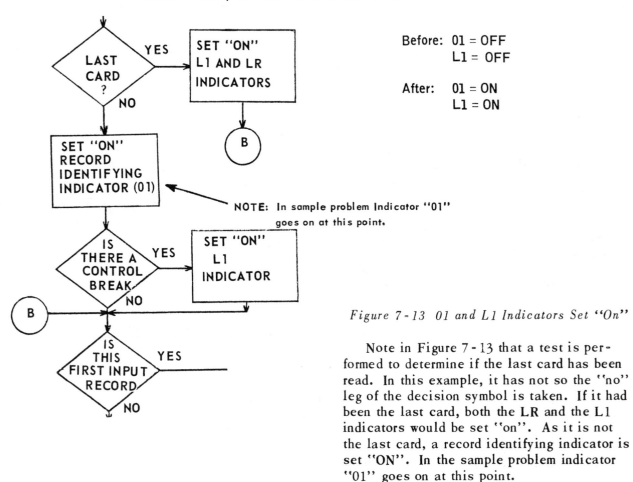

Before: 01 = OFF
          L1 = OFF

After: 01 = ON
         L1 = ON

NOTE: In sample problem Indicator "01" goes on at this point.

Figure 7-13 01 and L1 Indicators Set "On"

Note in Figure 7-13 that a test is performed to determine if the last card has been read. In this example, it has not so the "no" leg of the decision symbol is taken. If it had been the last card, both the LR and the L1 indicators would be set "on". As it is not the last card, a record identifying indicator is set "ON". In the sample problem indicator "01" goes on at this point.

A test is then made to determine if a control break has occurred. Whenever the first data card is read, a control break will always occur because the value read on the card, that is, the customer number on the card, has not been read previously. Therefore, the L1 indicator will be set "on" specifying that an L1 control break has occurred. A test is then made to determine if the card being processed is the first card read by the program. If, as in this example, it is the first card, none of the total processing routines are entered. This is because no values have been accumulated since no previous customer numbers have been processed by the program. Thus, when the first data card is read, none of the total routines are processed. It should be noted, however, that the L1 indicator is still "on" even though none of the total calculations or total lines will be processed. Note also from the example above that the 01 Indicator is set "on" because a data card corresponding to the Record Identifying Indicator 01 has been read.

Step 4: The data in the input area is moved to each of the individual input fields and the detail calculations are processed.

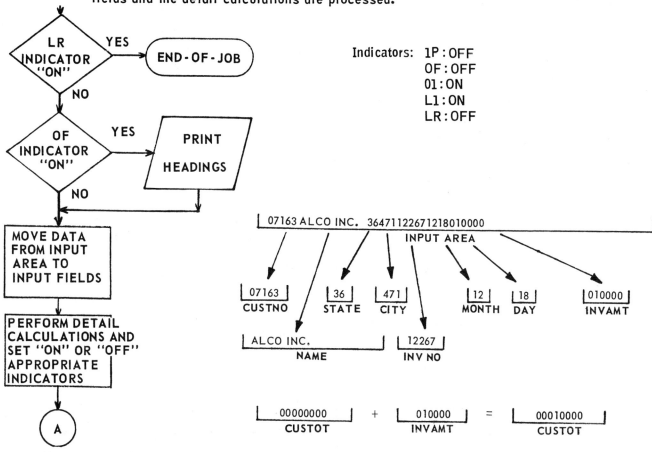

Figure 7-14 Data is Moved to Input Areas and Detail Calculations are Performed

The first step in the example above is to determine if the last data record has been read. This would be indicated by the LR indicator being "on". In the example, the last card has not been read so the LR indicator is "off" and the "no" path is taken. The OF indicator is then checked to determine if the total lines, heading lines, and detail lines which may be conditioned by the OF indicator are to be printed. In the example, the OF indicator is "off" so the heading lines which are to be printed in the program when it is "on" are not printed. After the LR and OF indicators have been checked and processed, the data which is stored in the Input Area, where it was placed when it was read from the card in Figure 7-12, is moved into the individual data fields. When data is moved to the input fields, it is available for processing within the program. Thus, after the data is moved, the detail calculations are performed. Note in the example above that this means that the value in the INVAMT field is added to the value in the CUSTOT field. The value in the CUSTOT field prior to the addition will be zero because all numeric fields defined on the Calculation Specifications are set to zero prior to the execution of the program. After the arithmetic has been completed, CUSTOT will contain the value in the invoice amount field of the first card read.

It should be noted also that any indicators which may be specified on the Calculation Specifications as a result of detail calculations are also set at this time. Thus, in the sample programs in previous chapters, the indicators for the Compare operations which took place at detail time would be set.

When the detail calculations have been completed, control is returned to the connector A which specifies that a check is to be performed to determine if a detail line should be printed. This is illustrated in Figure 7-15.

Step 5: Detail lines are printed on the report.

Indicators: 1P = OFF
OF = OFF
01 = ON
L1 = ON
LR = OFF

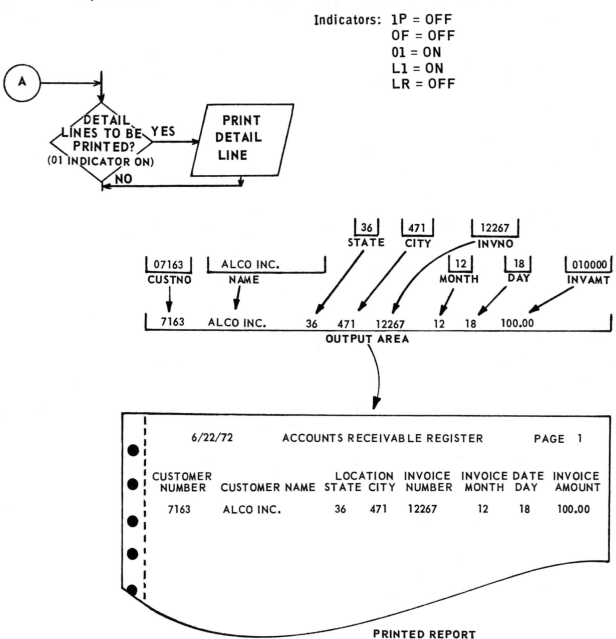

Figure 7 - 15 Detail Line is Printed

Note from the indicators illustrated above that the 01 Indicator is "on". Therefore, the detail line will be printed on the report. In order to print the detail line, the data in the input fields is moved to an output area which is reserved by the RPG compiler. The data in this output area is then printed on the report.

It should be noted also from the example above that the L1 indicator is still "on", that is, it has not been turned "off" when the detail line is printed. This factor becomes important when group indication is to be performed on a printed report, as will be illustrated in Chapter 8.

After the detail line has been printed, a card will be read into the input area. This is illustrated in Figure 7-16.

Step 6: Input card is read.

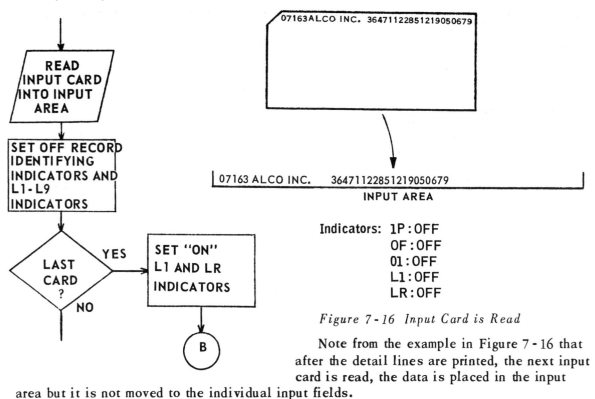

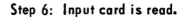

READ
INPUT CARD
INTO INPUT
AREA

SET OFF RECORD
IDENTIFYING
INDICATORS AND
L1-L9
INDICATORS

LAST
CARD
?

YES → SET "ON"
L1 AND LR
INDICATORS

NO

B

Indicators: 1P : OFF
OF : OFF
01 : OFF
L1 : OFF
LR : OFF

Figure 7-16 Input Card is Read

Note from the example in Figure 7-16 that after the detail lines are printed, the next input card is read, the data is placed in the input area but it is not moved to the individual input fields.

The record identifying indicator and the total indicators are reset to an "off" status when the new card is read. This is so that these indicators may be properly set by the instructions which follow.

Step 7: The record identifying indicator is set "on".

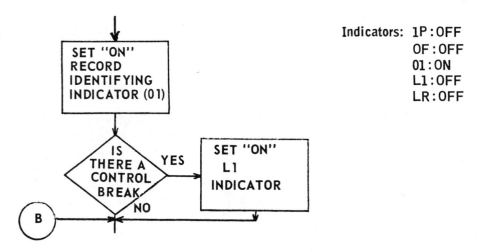

SET "ON"
RECORD
IDENTIFYING
INDICATOR (01)

IS
THERE A
CONTROL
BREAK

YES → SET "ON"
L1
INDICATOR

NO

B

Indicators: 1P : OFF
OF : OFF
01 : ON
L1 : OFF
LR : OFF

Figure 7-17 Indicators are Set on and Control Break is Tested

Note from Figure 7-17 that since an input record which is identified by the 01 Indicator is read from the card reader, the 01 Indicator is set "on". If, as in Chapter 6, different input cards were identified by different codes and different indicators, the appropriate indicator would be turned "on" at this point.

A test is then made to determine if a control break has occurred. Since the customer number in the card just read is the same as the customer number in the previous card, no control break has occurred. It should be recalled that the field which is used to determine if a control break has occurred is identified by the appropriate level indicator in columns 59-60 of the Input Specifications (see Figure 7-3). When the second card is read, the control level indicator L1 is not turned on because a control break has not occurred.

> Step 8: If applicable, the total calculations and total output are processed and then the detail calculations are performed.

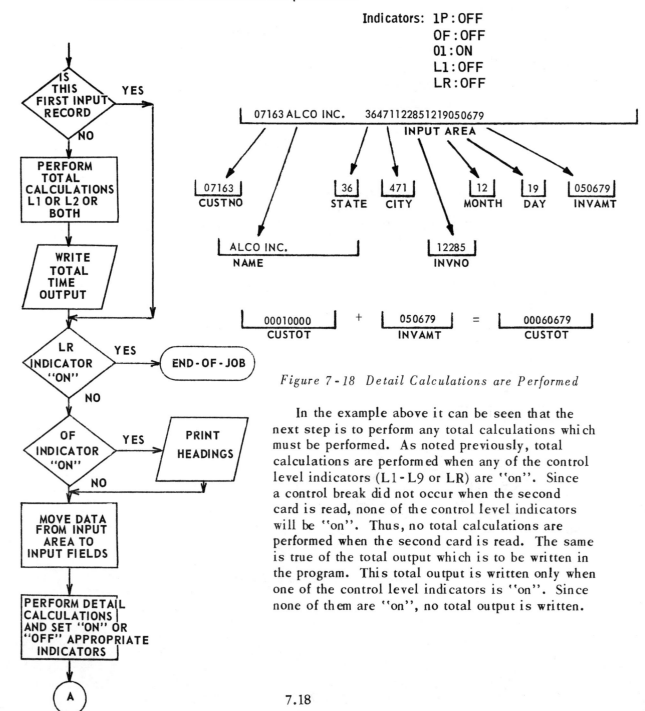

Figure 7-18 Detail Calculations are Performed

In the example above it can be seen that the next step is to perform any total calculations which must be performed. As noted previously, total calculations are performed when any of the control level indicators (L1-L9 or LR) are "on". Since a control break did not occur when the second card is read, none of the control level indicators will be "on". Thus, no total calculations are performed when the second card is read. The same is true of the total output which is to be written in the program. This total output is written only when one of the control level indicators is "on". Since none of them are "on", no total output is written.

Since the LR indicator is not "on", the data in the input area is moved to the input fields and the detail calculations are performed. In the sample program, these calculations consist of adding the invoice amount in the input card to the minor total counter. As can be seen from the example, prior to the addition, the field CUSTOT contains the invoice amount from the first card processed (00010000). After the addition, it contains the total of the first and second cards (00060679). Thus, this field is being used to accumulate the invoice amounts for each customer.

Step 9: The detail lines are printed.

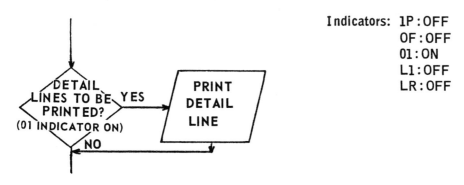

Indicators: 1P: OFF
             OF: OFF
             01: ON
             L1: OFF
             LR: OFF

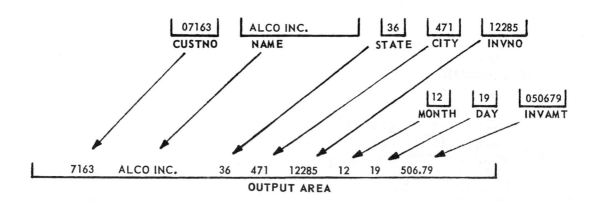

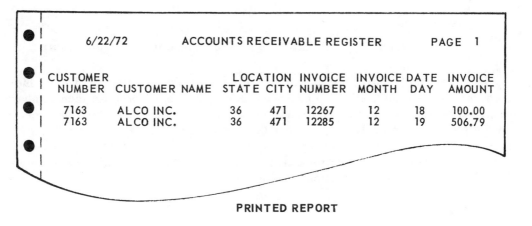

PRINTED REPORT

Figure 7-19 Detail Line is Printed

Note from Figure 7-19 that a detail line will be printed because the 01 indicator is "on" and the detail line is to be printed when the 01 Indicator is "on". Thus, the second detail line is printed on the report. After the detail line is printed, the next data card is read.

Step 10: The next data card is read and it contains a new customer number.

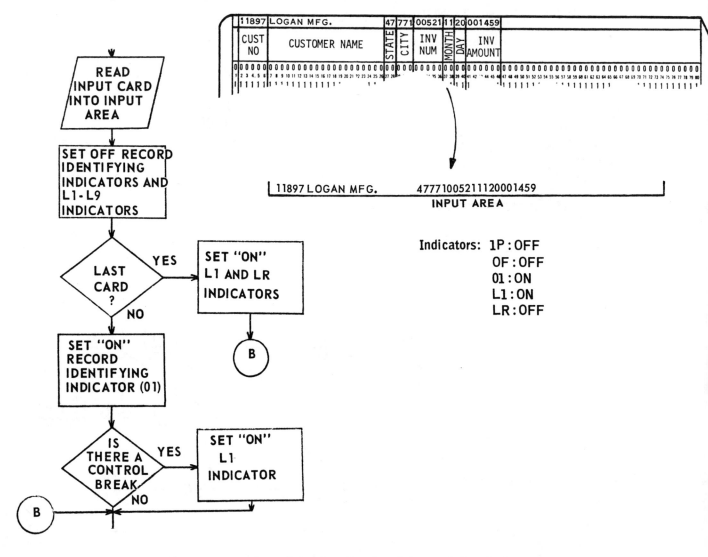

Figure 7-20 Detail Card is Read and Control Break Occurs

In the example above, the input card is read into the input area. The 01 Indicator is then set "on" because the card has been read. The object program then compares the customer number of the card just read with the customer number which has been contained on the previous cards. It is found that the customer in the card just read, 11897, is different than the customer number in the previous card, 07163. Thus, a control break has occurred because the control fields are different. The L1 indicator, therefore, is set "on" to indicate that the control break has occurred.

Step 11: The L1 total calculations are performed, the L1 total lines are printed, and then the detail time calculations are performed.

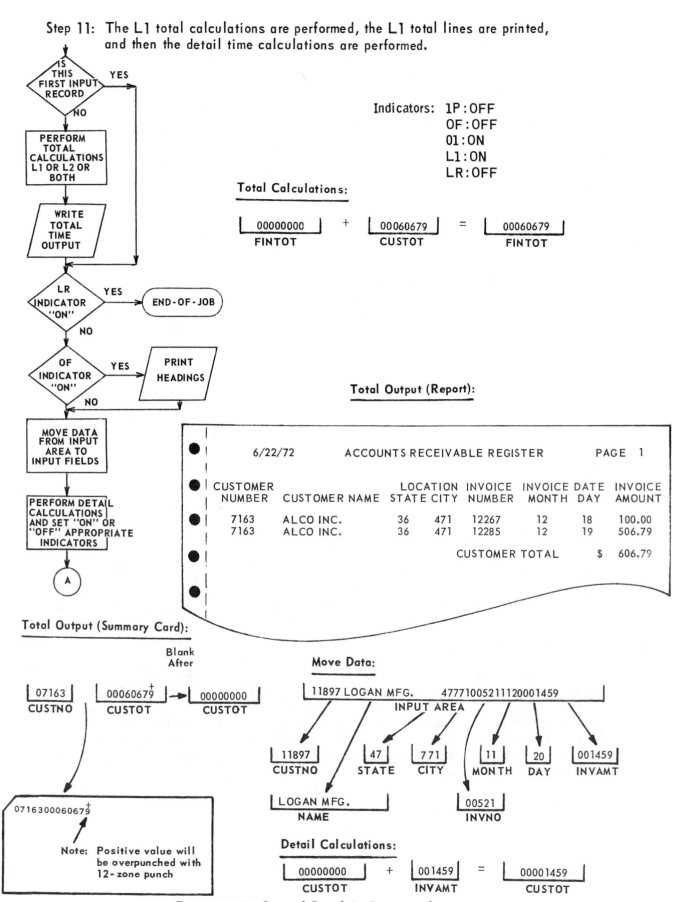

Figure 7-21 Control Break is Processed

Note in the example in Figure 7‑21 that the L1 indicator is "on" when it is checked to determine if total calculations and total output should be processed. Therefore, the total calculations specified on the Calculation Specifications form for the L1 indicator will be processed. In the sample program, the only calculation required involves adding the value in the field CUSTOT, which is the total for the customer just processed, to the value in the field FINTOT, which is the total of all of the customers. When this is completed, the output which is to be written at total time is processed

The total output in the sample program consists of two different items — the Customer Total which is to be printed on the report and the Summary Card which is to be punched on the card punch. These output functions will take place in the sequence in which they are specified on the Output‑Format Specifications form. Thus, as can be seen from Figure 7‑6 and 7‑7, the customer total on the report will be written first. Note in Figure 7‑21 that the total printed is the sum of the invoice amounts for customer number 7163. The Summary Card is then punched on the card punch. It contains the customer number and the customer total. In Figure 7‑21 it can be seen that the value in the CUSTOT field is a positive number and, when the value is punched in the output card, it will contain a 12‑zone over the low‑order digit. Unless a special technique is used to remove the zone punch, it will always appear in punched output. It does not appear on the printed report because the field is edited.

Another important thing to note about the Summary Card is that it will contain the customer number 07163 even though a new customer has been read into the card input area. The new customer number is what caused the L1 control break. The reason that the old customer number is still in the CUSTNO field is that the new data is not moved to the input fields until after the total calculations and the total output has been processed. This can be seen by the flowchart in Figure 7‑21. Thus, in all cases when a control break occurs, the input fields contain the data from the previous card, not from the card which caused the control break.

After the total processing has been completed, a check is made to determine if the LR indicator is "on". As can be seen from the example, it is not, so the input data is moved from the input area to the input fields. As can be seen again, this takes place after the total processing routines have been completed. The detail calculations are then performed which means that the value in the field INVAMT is added to the value in the CUSTOT field. Note from Figure 7‑21 that the CUSTOT field has been cleared to zeros prior to the addition operation. It was cleared to zeros after the Summary Card was punched because of the Blank After specification on the Output‑Format Specifications form (see Figure 7‑7).

The remainder of the input cards will be processed as illustrated in this example. When the end‑of‑file card is read, the LR indicator will be turned on as well as the L1 indicator. As noted previously, whenever the LR indicator is turned on, all of the other total indicators are turned on as well. The totals are then processed in ascending order, that is, the L1 totals are processed first, followed by an L2 totals, etc. When all of the control break totals have been processed, the LR total processing is completed and the program terminates.

Although it is important to see the logic used by the RPG program in order to process data, the most important feature to note in the previous example is when indicators are set on and when they are turned off. Since, when writing the source code of an RPG program, all processing is "keyed" by the status of an indicator, it is absolutely vital that the programmer realize when certain indicators are on and when they are off. The following is a summary of the various types of indicators illustrated in this chapter.

Heading Indicators:

a) 1P — This indicator is automatically turned "on" before the program begins processing. It remains "on" until just before the first data card is read, at which time it is automatically turned "off". It remains "off" for the duration of the program.

b) OF — This indicator is turned "on" when a punch in channel 12 of the carriage control tape is sensed. It is turned off after the headings for a given file have been printed. In the previous example, it was never turned "on" because no page overflow was sensed.

Record Identifying Indicators:

c) 01 — This record identifying indicator is turned "on" whenever a card is read which satisfies the conditions specified on the Input Specifications form. It is turned "on" immediately after it is found that the input card read was not the end-of-file card. It remains "on" during any total time processing and during the detail processing. Thus, if the 01 indicator, or any record identifying indicator, is tested in a total calculation routine or a total output routine, it will be "on" if the record which caused the control break was an 01 record. The record identifying indicator will also, of course, be "on" during the detail time calculations and detail time output routines.

Control Level Indicators:

d) L1 — Any control level indicator is set "on" when it is determined that a corresponding control break has occurred, that is, if the L1 indicator is specified on the Input Specifications form for a given field, whenever the value of that field changes, a control break is said to have occurred. The determination as to whether a control break has occurred is made prior to the input data being moved from the input area to the input fields. Thus, when the L1 indicator is turned "on", the data from the last input record of the old group is still in the input fields. The L1 indicator remains on during the processing of the total time routines and also for the processing of the detail time routines for the record which caused the control break. This fact, as will be seen in Chapter 8, allows the printing of group indicated reports. The L1 or any Control Level indicator is turned "off" at the same time the Record Identifying Indicators are turned "off" and it is not turned "on" again until another control break occurs.

e) LR — The last record indicator is turned "on" only when the last input record has been read. When the LR indicator is turned "on" as a result of reading the last record, all of the other control level indicators are turned on as well. Thus, when the last record is read, the L1 totals as well as any other control break totals will be processed prior to the LR routines.

SAMPLE PROGRAM

The input and output to the sample problem which takes control breaks and punches a summary card are illustrated below.

Input

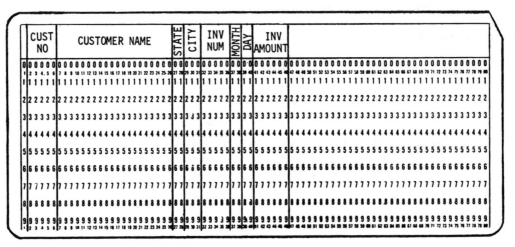

Figure 7-22 Input

Output

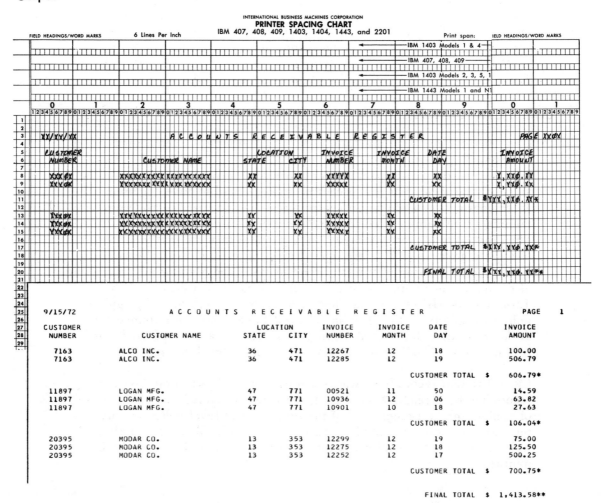

Figure 7-23 Output

RPG Coding:

The complete RPG coding is illustrated on the following pages.

RPG CONTROL CARD AND FILE DESCRIPTION SPECIFICATIONS

Date 7/8/72

Program ACCOUNTS RECEIVABLE REGISTER

Programmer SHELLY

Punching Instruction — Graphic: Ø 0 2 Z — Punch: ZERO 11-6 Two 0-9

Page Ø1   Program Identification ACCREC

Control Card Specifications

Refer to the specific System Reference Library manual for actual entries.

Line	Form Type										
0 1 Ø	H										

File Description Specifications

Line	Form Type	Filename	File Type	File Designation	Block Length	Record Length	Mode of Processing	Device	Symbolic Device
0 2 Ø	F	CUSTCDS	IP	F	80	80		READ40	SYSIPT
0 3 Ø	F	REGISTR	O	F	132	132	OF	PRINTER	SYSLST
0 4 Ø	F	SUMMCDS	O	F	80	80		READ40	SYSPCH

RPG INPUT SPECIFICATIONS

Date 7/8/72

Program ACCOUNTS RECEIVABLE REGISTER

Programmer SHELLY

Punching Instruction — Graphic: Ø 0 2 Z — Punch: ZERO 11-6 Two 0-9

Page Ø2   Program Identification ACCREC

Line	Form Type	Filename	Sequence	Number (1-N)	Option (O)	Record Identifying Indicator	Position	Field Location From	To	Decimal Positions	Field Name	Control Level (L1-L9)
0 1 Ø	I	CUSTCDS	AA			Ø1						
0 2 Ø	I							2	6	Ø	CUSTNO	L1
0 3 Ø	I							7	26		NAME	
0 4 Ø	I							27	28		STATE	
0 5 Ø	I							29	31		CITY	
0 6 Ø	I							32	36		INVNO	
0 7 Ø	I							37	38		MONTH	
0 8 Ø	I							39	40		DAY	
0 9 Ø	I							41	46	2	INVAMT	

RPG CALCULATION SPECIFICATIONS

Date 7/8/72

Program ACCOUNTS RECEIVABLE REGISTER

Programmer SHELLY

Punching Instruction — Graphic: Ø 0 2 Z — Punch: ZERO 11-6 Two 0-9

Page Ø3   Program Identification ACCREC

Line	Form Type	Control Level (L0-L9, LR, SR)	Indicators	Factor 1	Operation	Factor 2	Result Field	Field Length	Decimal Positions
0 1 Ø	C		Ø1	CUSTOT	ADD	INVAMT	CUSTOT	8	2
0 2 Ø	C	L1		FINTOT	ADD	CUSTOT	FINTOT	8	2

7.25

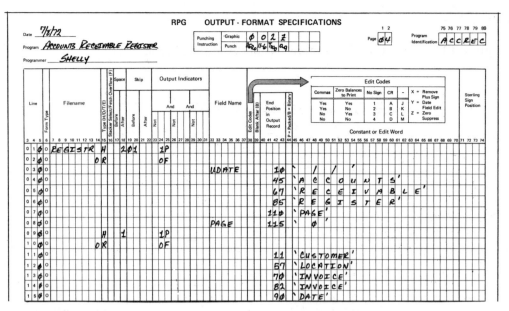

RPG OUTPUT - FORMAT SPECIFICATIONS

Date 7/8/72
Program ACCOUNTS RECEIVABLE REGISTER
Programmer SHELLY
Punching Instruction — Graphic Ø 0 2 Z — Punch ZERO 11-6 TWO 0-9
Page Ø4 — Program Identification A C C R E C

Line	Form Type	Filename	Type (H/D/T/E)	Space Before	Space After	Skip Before	Skip After	Output Indicators	Field Name	Edit Codes	End Position in Output Record	Constant or Edit Word
0 1	Ø 0	REGISTR H		2 0 1			1P					
0 2	Ø 0	OR					OF					
0 3	Ø 0							UDATE		1Ø	' / / '
0 4	Ø 0									45	'ACCOUNTS'
0 5	Ø 0									67	'RECEIVABLE'
0 6	Ø 0									85	'REGISTER'
0 7	Ø 0									11Ø	'PAGE'
0 8	Ø 0							PAGE		115	' Ø '
0 9	Ø 0		H	1			1P				
1 0	Ø 0	OR					OF				
1 1	Ø 0									11	'CUSTOMER'
1 2	Ø 0									57	'LOCATION'
1 3	Ø 0									70	'INVOICE'
1 4	Ø 0									82	'INVOICE'
1 5	Ø 0									90	'DATE'

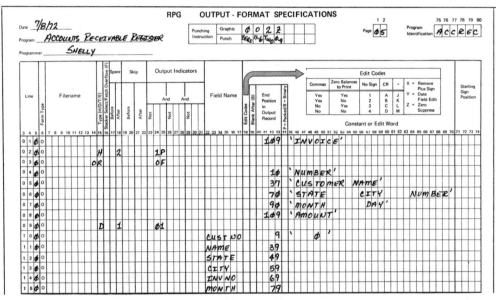

RPG OUTPUT - FORMAT SPECIFICATIONS

Date 7/8/72
Program ACCOUNTS RECEIVABLE REGISTER
Programmer SHELLY
Punching Instruction — Graphic Ø 0 2 Z — Punch ZERO 11-6 TWO 0-9
Page Ø5 — Program Identification A C C R E C

Line	Form Type	Filename	Type (H/D/T/E)	Space Before	Output Indicators	Field Name	Edit Codes	End Position in Output Record	Constant or Edit Word
0 1	Ø 0							1Ø9	'INVOICE'
0 2	Ø 0		H	2	1P				
0 3	Ø 0	OR			OF				
0 4	Ø 0							1Ø	'NUMBER'
0 5	Ø 0							37	'CUSTOMER NAME'
0 6	Ø 0							70	'STATE CITY NUMBER'
0 7	Ø 0							9Ø	'MONTH DAY'
0 8	Ø 0							1Ø9	'AMOUNT'
0 9	Ø 0		D	1	Ø1				
1 0	Ø 0					CUSTNO		9	Ø
1 1	Ø 0					NAME		39	
1 2	Ø 0					STATE		49	
1 3	Ø 0					CITY		59	
1 4	Ø 0					INVNO		69	
1 5	Ø 0					MONTH		79	

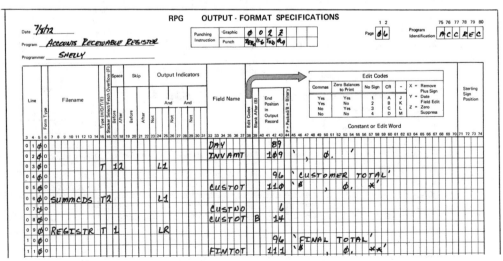

RPG OUTPUT - FORMAT SPECIFICATIONS

Date 7/8/72
Program ACCOUNTS RECEIVABLE REGISTER
Programmer SHELLY
Punching Instruction — Graphic Ø 0 2 Z — Punch ZERO 11-6 TWO 0-9
Page Ø6 — Program Identification A C C R E C

Line	Form Type	Filename	Type (H/D/T/E)	Output Indicators	Field Name	Edit Codes	Blank After (B)	End Position in Output Record	Constant or Edit Word
0 1	Ø 0				DAY			89	
0 2	Ø 0				INVAMT			1Ø9	' , Ø. '
0 3	Ø 0		T 12	L1					
0 4	Ø 0							96	'CUSTOMER TOTAL'
0 5	Ø 0				CUSTOT			11Ø	'# , Ø. *'
0 6	Ø 0	SUMMCDS T2		L1					
0 7	Ø 0				CUSTNO			6	
0 8	Ø 0				CUSTOT		B	14	
0 9	Ø 0	REGISTR T 1		LR					
1 0	Ø 0							96	'FINAL TOTAL'
1 1	Ø 0				FINTOT			111	'# , Ø. **'

7.26

Program

The source listing of the sample program is illustrated below.

```
DOS/360*RPG*CL 3-9            CASHMAN                    09/15/72         PAGE 0001

          01 010 H                                                       ACCREC
001       01 020 FCUSTCDS IP  F  80  80             READ40 SYSIPT        ACCREC
002       01 030 FREGISTR  O  F 132 132      OF     PRINTERSYSLST        ACCREC
003       01 040 FSUMMCDS  O  F  80  80             READ40 SYSPCH        ACCREC
004       02 010 ICUSTCDS AA  01                                        ACCREC
005       02 020 I                              2   60CUSTNOL1           ACCREC
006       02 030 I                              7   26 NAME              ACCREC
007       02 040 I                             27   28 STATE             ACCREC
008       02 050 I                             29   31 CITY              ACCREC
009       02 060 I                             32   36 INVNO             ACCREC
010       02 070 I                             37   38 MONTH             ACCREC
011       02 080 I                             39   40 DAY               ACCREC
012       02 090 I                             41  462INVAMT             ACCREC
013       03 010 C    01      CUSTOT   ADD INVAMT   CUSTOT   82          ACCREC
014       03 020 CL1          FINTOT   ADD CUSTOT   FINTOT   82          ACCREC
015       04 010 OREGISTR H  201     1P                                 ACCREC
016       04 020 O        OR         OF                                 ACCREC
017       04 030 O                        UDATE  10 ' / / '             ACCREC
018       04 040 O                               45 'A C C O U N T S'    ACCREC
019       04 050 O                               67 'R E C E I V A B L E' ACCREC
020       04 060 O                               85 'R E G I S T E R'    ACCREC
021       04 070 O                              110 'PAGE'               ACCREC
022       04 080 O                        PAGE  115 ' 0 '                ACCREC
          04 090 O*                                                     ACCREC
023       04 100 O        H  1      1P                                  ACCREC
024       04 110 O        OR         OF                                 ACCREC
025       04 120 O                               11 'CUSTOMER'           ACCREC
026       04 130 O                               57 'LOCATION'           ACCREC
027       04 140 O                               70 'INVOICE'            ACCREC
028       04 150 O                               82 'INVOICE'            ACCREC
029       05 010 O                               90 'DATE'               ACCREC
030       05 020 O                              109 'INVOICE'            ACCREC
          05 030 O*                                                     ACCREC
031       05 040 O        H  2      1P                                  ACCREC
032       05 050 O        OR         OF                                 ACCREC
033       05 060 O                               10 'NUMBER'             ACCREC
034       05 070 O                               37 'CUSTOMER NAME'      ACCREC
035       05 080 O                               70 'STATE    CITY    NUMBER' ACCREC
036       05 090 O                               90 'MONTH    DAY'       ACCREC
037       05 100 O                              109 'AMOUNT'             ACCREC
          05 110 O*                                                     ACCREC
038       05 120 O        D  1      01                                  ACCREC
039       05 130 O                        CUSTNO  9 ' 0 '                ACCREC
040       05 140 O                        NAME   39                     ACCREC
041       05 150 O                        STATE  49                     ACCREC
042       06 010 O                        CITY   59                     ACCREC
043       06 020 O                        INVNO  69                     ACCREC
044       06 030 O                        MONTH  79                     ACCREC
045       06 040 O                        DAY    89                     ACCREC
046       06 050 O                        INVAMT 109 ' , 0. '           ACCREC
          06 060 O*                                                     ACCREC
047       06 070 O        T 12      L1                                  ACCREC
048       06 080 O                               96 'CUSTOMER TOTAL'     ACCREC
049       06 090 O                        CUSTOT 110 '$   , 0. *'        ACCREC
          06 100 O*                                                     ACCREC
050       06 110 OSUMMCDS T2      L1                                    ACCREC
051       06 120 O                        CUSTNO  6                     ACCREC
052       06 130 O                        CUSTOT B 14                   ACCREC
053       06 140 OREGISTR T 1      LR                                  ACCREC
054       06 150 O                               96 'FINAL TOTAL'        ACCREC
055       07 010 O                        FINTOT 111 '$   , 0.  **'      ACCREC
```

CHAPTER 7

REVIEW QUESTIONS

1. Define a Control Break and given an example.

2. When a control break occurs within an RPG program, when will the total routines be processed?

3. What values are in the input fields of the RPG program when totals are being processed?

4. In the sample program illustrated in this chapter, state all of the indicators which are "on" when the total calculations and total output are processed, assuming that page overflow has not occurred.

5. Can a Control Level indicator be tested in detail calculations accurately? Why? What columns should be used to specify the control level indicator, if any?

6. In the output of an RPG program will there ever be a total line as the first line on a new page? Why?

CHAPTER 7

STUDENT EXERCISES

1. Record the entries to define the fields within a card file named SALES. The following fields are found in the card:

    a. Card columns 1-4 — Division Field, Control Level 1.
    b. Card columns 6-8 — Department Number. Zeros are to be suppressed on the printed output.
    c. Card columns 9-14 — Salesman Number. Zeros are to be suppressed on the printed output.
    d. Card columns 29-32 — Quantity. One decimal position.
    e. Card columns 35-41 — Amount. Two decimal positions.

The input card must contain a 12-zone punch in column 79, otherwise it is not to be processed. The fieldnames to be used should be determined by the programmer.

RPG INPUT SPECIFICATIONS

Line	Form Type	Filename	Sequence	Number (1-N)	Option (O)	Record Identifying Indicator or **	Record Identification Codes 1 — Position	Not (N)	C/Z/D	Character	2 — Position	Not (N)	C/Z/D	Character	3 — Position	Not (N)	C/Z/D	Character	Stacker Select	P = Packed/B = Binary	Field Location From	To	Decimal Positions	Field Name	Control Level (L1-L9)	Matching Fields or Chaining Fields
0 1	I																									
0 2	I																									
0 3	I																									
0 4	I																									
0 5	I																									
0 6	I																									
0 7	I																									
0 8	I																									
0 9	I																									
1 0	I																									
1 1	I																									
1 2	I																									
1 3	I																									

2. As was noted in the text, the "Blank After" entry on the Output Specifications may be used to zero a field after it has been printed on a total line. On the Calculation Specifications below, specify the entries which could be made during detail or total time calculations in order to cause the same thing, that is, zero the field after it has been printed on a total line and before it is used to begin accumulating another total. Use the field definitions in the sample program.

RPG   CALCULATION SPECIFICATIONS

Line	Form Type	Control Level (L0-L9, LR, SR)	Indicators And Not	And Not	And Not	Factor 1	Operation	Factor 2	Result Field	Field Length	Decimal Positions	Half Adjust (H)	Resulting Indicators Arithmetic Plus / Minus / Zero	Compare High 1>2 / Low 1<2 / Equal 1=2	Lookup Table (Factor 2) is High / Low / Equal
0 1	C														
0 2	C														
0 3	C														

3. After you write the RPG program in Programming Assignment 1 list, in order, the steps which are executed after a control break occurs. These steps should begin when a control break is found and continue until the detail record which caused the control break has been printed.

Instructions: The following RPG program contains an error or errors which have occurred during compilation. Circle each error and record the corrected entries directly on the listing. Explain the error and method of correction in the space provided below.

```
DOS/360*RPG*CL 3-9              CASHMAN                    10/10/72           PAGE 0001

         01 340 H                                                            ACCREC
001      01 350 FCUSTCDS IP  F  80  80            READ40 SYSIPT              ACCREC
002      01 360 FREGISTR O   F 132 132     OF     PRINTERSYSLST              ACCREC
003      01 370 FSUMMCDS O   F  80  80            READ40 SYSPCH              ACCREC
004      02 380 ICUSTCDS AA  01                                             ACCREC
005      02 390 I                                2    60CUSTNO               ACCREC
006      02 400 I                                7  26 NAME                  ACCREC
007      02 410 I                               27  28 STATE                 ACCREC
008      02 420 I                               29  31 CITY                  ACCREC
009      02 430 I                               32  36 INVNO                 ACCREC
010      02 440 I                               37  38 MONTH                 ACCREC
011      02 450 I                               39  40 DAY                   ACCREC
012      02 460 I                               41  462INVAMT                ACCREC
013      03 470 C   01       CUSTOT   ADD INVAMT CUSTOT   82                 ACCREC
014      03 480 CL1          FINTOT   ADD CUSTOT FINTOT   82                 ACCREC
015      04 490 OREGISTR H   201    1P                                      ACCREC
016      04 500 O        OR        OF                                       ACCREC
         04 510 O                        DATE   10 ' / / '                  ACCREC
                                                                            NOTE 179
017      04 520 O                                45 'A C C O U N T S'       ACCREC
018      04 530 O                                67 'R E C E I V A B L E'   ACCREC
019      04 540 O                                85 'R E G I S T E R'       ACCREC
020      04 550 O                               110 'PAGE'                   ACCREC
021      04 560 O                        PAGE   115 ' 0 '                    ACCREC
         04 570 O*                                                          ACCREC
022      04 580 O        H  1     1P                                        ACCREC
023      04 590 O        OR        OF                                       ACCREC
024      04 600 O                                11 'CUSTOMER'              ACCREC
025      04 610 O                                57 'LOCATION'              ACCREC
026      04 620 O                                70 'INVOICE'               ACCREC
027      04 630 O                                82 'INVOICE'               ACCREC
028      05 640 O                                90 'DATE'                  ACCREC
029      05 650 O                               109 'INVOICE'               ACCREC
         05 660 O*                                                          ACCREC
030      05 670 O        H  2     1P                                        ACCREC
031      05 680 O        OR        OF                                       ACCREC
032      05 690 O                                10 'NUMBER'                ACCREC
033      05 700 O                                37 'CUSTOMER NAME'         ACCREC
034      05 710 O                                70 'STATE     CITY     NUMBER'  ACCREC
035      05 720 O                                90 'MONTH     DAY'         ACCREC
036      05 730 O                               109 'AMOUNT'                ACCREC
         05 740 O*                                                          ACCREC
037      05 750 O        D  1     01                                        ACCREC
038      05 760 O                        CUSTNO   9 ' 0 '                    ACCREC
039      05 770 O                        NAME    39                          ACCREC
040      05 780 O                        STATE   49                          ACCREC
041      06 790 O                        CITY    59                          ACCREC
042      06 800 O                        INVNO   69                          ACCREC
043      06 810 O                        MONTH   79                          ACCREC
044      06 820 O                        DAY     89                          ACCREC
045      06 830 O                        INVAMT 109 ' , 0. '                 ACCREC
         06 840 O*                                                          ACCREC
046      06 850 O        T 12     L1                                        ACCREC
                                                                            NOTE 192
047      06 860 O                                96 'CUSTOMER TOTAL'        ACCREC
048      06 870 O                        CUSTOT 110 '$ , 0. *'              ACCREC
         06 880 O*                                                          ACCREC
049      06 890 OSUMMCDS T2    L1                                           ACCREC
                                                                            NOTE 192
050      06 900 O                        CUSTNO   6                          ACCREC
051      06 910 O                        CUSTOT B 14                         ACCREC
052      06 920 OREGISTR T 1   LR                                           ACCREC
053      06 930 O                                96 'FINAL TOTAL'           ACCREC
054      07 940 O                        FINTOT 111 '$ , 0. **'             ACCREC
```

SYMBOL TABLES

RESULTING INDICATORS

ADDRESS RI	ADDRESS RI	ADDRESS RI	ADDRESS RI	ADDRESS RI	ADDRESS RI	ADDRESS RI
000011 0F	000014 1P	000015 LR	000016 00	000017 01	00007A L0	00007B L1
000085 H0	000086 H1	000087 H2	000088 H3	000089 H4	00008A H5	00008B H6
00008C H7	00008D H8	00008E H9				

FIELD NAMES

ADDRESS FIELD	ADDRESS FIELD	ADDRESS FIELD	ADDRESS FIELD	ADDRESS FIELD
000123 CUSTNO	000126 NAME	00013A STATE	00013C CITY	00013F INVNO
000144 MONTH	000146 DAY	000148 INVAMT	00014C CUSTOT	000151 FINTOT
000156 PAGE				

LITERALS

ADDRESS LITERAL	ADDRESS LITERAL	ADDRESS LITERAL
000159 A C C O U N T S	000168 R E C E I V A B L E	00017B R E G I S T E R
00018A PAGE	00018E ---/-	000194 CUSTOMER
00019C LOCATION	0001A4 INVOICE	0001AB DATE
0001AF NUMBER	0001B5 CUSTOMER NAME	0001C2 STATE CITY NUMBER
0001DA MONTH DAY	0001E8 AMOUNT	0001EE --,--/.--
0001F8 CUSTOMER TOTAL	000206 - ---,--/.--*	000214 FINAL TOTAL
00021F - ---,--/.--**		

014	L1	NOTE 212
046	L1	NOTE 212
049	L1	NOTE 212

NOTE 179 FIELD NAME (COLUMNS 32-37) IS UNDEFINED. SPECIFICATION IS NOT PROCESSED.

NOTE 192 OUTPUT INDICATOR (COLUMNS 24-25, 27-28, OR 30-31) IS INVALID OR UNDEFINED.
          ENTRY OF L0 IS ASSUMED.

NOTE 212 RESULTING INDICATOR IS INVALID OR UNDEFINED. ENTRY OF L0 IS ASSUMED.

EXPLANATION _____

_____

_____

_____

CHAPTER 7

Debugging RPG Programs

Problem 2

Instructions: The following RPG program contains an error or errors which occur during execution. Circle each error and record the corrected entries directly on the listing. Explain the error and method of correction in the space provided below.

```
DOS/360*RPG*CL 3-9                    CASHMAN                    10/10/72         PAGE 0001
                                                                                 ACCREC
        01 340 H                                                                  ACCREC
001     01 350 FCUSTCDS IP  F  80  80            READ40 SYSIPT                    ACCREC
002     01 360 FREGISTR O   F 132 132     OF     PRINTERSYSLST                    ACCREC
003     01 370 FSUMMCDS O   F  80  80            READ40 SYSPCH                    ACCREC
004     02 380 ICUSTCDS AA  01                                                    ACCREC
005     02 390 I                                  2   60CUSTNOL1                  ACCREC
006     02 400 I                                  7   26 NAME                     ACCREC
007     02 410 I                                 27   28 STATE                    ACCREC
008     02 420 I                                 29   31 CITY                     ACCREC
009     02 430 I                                 32   36 INVNO                    ACCREC
010     02 440 I                                 37   38 MONTH                    ACCREC
011     02 450 I                                 39   40 DAY                      ACCREC
012     02 460 I                                 41   462INVAMT                   ACCREC
013     03 470 C    01      CUSTOT     ADD  INVAMT    CUSTOT   82                 ACCREC
014     03 480 CL1          FINTOT     ADD  CUSTOT    FINTOT   82                 ACCREC
015     04 490 OREGISTR H   201     1P                                           ACCREC
016     04 500 O        OR           OF                                          ACCREC
017     04 510 O                           UDATE      10 ' / / '                  ACCREC
018     04 520 O                                      45 'A C C O U N T S'        ACCREC
019     04 530 O                                      67 'R E C E I V A B L E'    ACCREC
020     04 540 O                                      85 'R E G I S T E R'        ACCREC
021     04 550 O                                     110 'PAGE'                   ACCREC
022     04 560 O                           PAGE      115 ' 0 '                    ACCREC
        04 570 O*                                                                 ACCREC
023     04 580 O        H  1     1P                                              ACCREC
024     04 590 O        OR          OF                                           ACCREC
025     04 600 O                                      11 'CUSTOMER'               ACCREC
026     04 610 O                                      57 'LOCATION'               ACCREC
027     04 620 O                                      70 'INVOICE'                ACCREC
028     04 630 O                                      82 'INVOICE'                ACCREC
029     05 640 O                                      90 'DATE'                   ACCREC
030     05 650 O                                     109 'INVOICE'               ACCREC
        05 660 O*                                                                 ACCREC
031     05 670 O        H  2     1P                                              ACCREC
032     05 680 O        OR          OF                                           ACCREC
033     05 690 O                                      10 'NUMBER'                 ACCREC
034     05 700 O                                      37 'CUSTOMER NAME'          ACCREC
035     05 710 O                                      70 'STATE      CITY     NUMBER'  ACCREC
036     05 720 O                                      90 'MONTH        DAY'       ACCREC
037     05 730 O                                     109 'AMOUNT'                 ACCREC
        05 740 O*                                                                 ACCREC
038     05 750 O        D  1     01                                              ACCREC
039     05 760 O                           CUSTNO     9 ' 0 '                     ACCREC
040     05 770 O                           NAME      39                           ACCREC
041     05 780 O                           STATE     49                           ACCREC
042     06 790 O                           CITY      59                           ACCREC
043     06 800 O                           INVNO     69                           ACCREC
044     06 810 O                           MONTH     79                           ACCREC
045     06 820 O                           DAY       89                           ACCREC
046     06 830 O                           INVAMT   109 ' , 0. '                  ACCREC
        06 840 O*                                                                 ACCREC
047     06 850 O        T 12     L1                                              ACCREC
048     06 860 O                                      96 'CUSTOMER TOTAL'         ACCREC
049     06 870 O                           CUSTOT   110 '$  , 0. *'               ACCREC
        06 880 O*                                                                 ACCREC
050     06 890 OSUMMCDS T2            L1                                          ACCREC
051     06 900 O                           CUSTNO     6                           ACCREC
052     06 910 O                           CUSTOT    14                           ACCREC
053     06 920 OREGISTR T 1            LR                                         ACCREC
054     06 930 O                                      96 'FINAL TOTAL'            ACCREC
055     07 940 O                           FINTOT   111 '$  , 0. **'              ACCREC
```

7.33

A C C O U N T S   R E C E I V A B L E   R E G I S T E R   PAGE   1

CUSTOMER NUMBER	CUSTOMER NAME	LOCATION STATE	CITY	INVOICE NUMBER	INVOICE MONTH	DATE DAY	INVOICE AMOUNT	
7163	ALCO INC.	36	471	12267	12	18	100.00	
7163	ALCO INC.	36	471	12285	12	19	506.79	NOTE: TOTALS ARE NOT CORRECT
					CUSTOMER TOTAL	$	606.79*	
11897	LOGAN MFG.	47	771	00521	11	50	14.59	
11897	LOGAN MFG.	47	771	10936	12	06	63.82	
11897	LOGAN MFG.	47	771	10901	10	18	27.63	
					CUSTOMER TOTAL	$	712.83*	
20395	MODAR CO.	13	353	12299	12	19	75.00	
20395	MODAR CO.	13	353	12275	12	18	125.50	
20395	MODAR CO.	13	353	12252	12	17	500.25	
					CUSTOMER TOTAL	$	1,413.58*	
					FINAL TOTAL	$	2,733.20**	

EXPLANATION
_____

_____

_____

_____

7.34

CHAPTER 7

PROGRAMMING ASSIGNMENT 1

INSTRUCTIONS

From the Sales Cards illustrated below, a Sales Analysis Report is to be prepared. The report is to list the Department Number, Salesman Number, Name, and Current Sales. When there is a change in Department Number, a total for the department is to be taken. After all of the cards have been processed, a Final Total is to be printed.

INPUT — Sales Cards

The fields to be used in the Sales Cards are the Department Number, the Salesman Number, the Name, and the Current Sales.

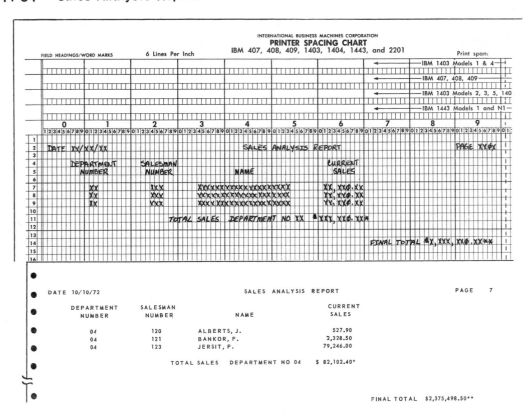

OUTPUT — Sales Analysis Report

TEST DATA — ASSIGNMENT NO. 1

Department (Col 3-4)	Salesman (Col 5-7)	Name (Col 8-27)	Current Sales (Col 35-41)
04	120	Alberts, J.	0052790
04	121	Bankor, F.	0232850
04	123	Jersit, P.	7924600
05	096	Peters, P.	0045692
05	236	Metyrs, T.	0987400
19	774	Snider, T.	0093101

DOS JOB CONTROL

```
// JOB jobname
// OPTION LINK
// EXEC RPG

  — Student Source Deck —

/*
// EXEC LNKEDT
// EXEC

  — Test Data —

/*
/&
```

Note: This job stream assumes that there are standard assignments for the card reader and printer of which the student is aware.

PROGRAMMING ASSIGNMENT 2

INSTRUCTIONS

Write the RPG program to produce a weekly Payroll Register. The input to the program and the desired output are illustrated below.

INPUT — Payroll Cards

The input is to consist of a file of Payroll Cards. The format of the card is illustrated below.

OUTPUT — Weekly Payroll Register

The output is to consist of the Weekly Payroll Register with the Division field, the Employee Number field, the Gross Earnings field (Hours × Rate = Gross Earnings), the Insurance Deduction field, the FICA deduction field, the Federal Tax Deduction field, the State Tax Deduction field, a Union Dues Deduction field, and the Net Earnings field (Net Earnings = Gross Earnings – Insurance – FICA – Federal Tax – State Tax – Union Dues). The Union Dues are 2% of the Gross Earnings if the Union Code field contains the value "1". If it contains a blank, then there are no union dues to be deducted from the Gross Earnings.

The format of the Weekly Payroll Report is illustrated below.

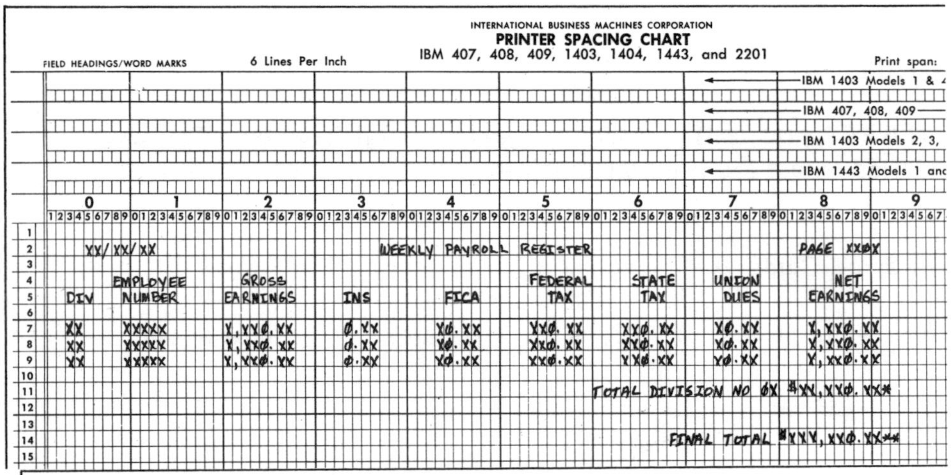

INTERNATIONAL BUSINESS MACHINES CORPORATION
PRINTER SPACING CHART
IBM 407, 408, 409, 1403, 1404, 1443, and 2201

	10/20/72			WEEKLY PAYROLL REGISTER				PAGE 1
		EMPLOYEE	GROSS			FEDERAL	STATE	UNION	NET
DIV	NUMBER	EARNINGS	INS	FICA	TAX	TAX	DUES	EARNINGS
12	231	200.00	1.25	10.00	30.00	5.50	4.00	149.25
12	442	135.00	1.40	7.50	20.00	4.50		101.60
12	553	100.00	.75	5.00	18.00	4.00	2.00	70.25

TOTAL DIVISION NO 12 $ 321.10 *

FINAL TOTAL $ 23,743.51 * *

Note from the sample report illustrated above that a Minor Total is to be taken whenever the Division Number changes and a Final Total for the Net Earnings is to be taken after all of the input cards have been processed.

TEST DATA – ASSIGNMENT NO. 2

Div (col 1-2)	Emp No (col 3-5)	Hours (col 6-8)	Rate (col 9-12)	Ins (col 13-15)	FICA (col16-19)	Fed Tax (col 20-24)	State Tax (col 25-29)	Union Code (col 30)
12	231	400	0500	125	1000	03000	00550	1
12	442	450	0300	140	0750	02000	00450	
12	553	400	0250	075	0500	01800	00400	1
13	369	416	0275	125	0520	02300	00475	
13	430	302	0345	100	0490	01950	00385	1
14	549	519	0890	275	2020	08900	01210	1

DOS JOB CONTROL

// JOB jobname

// OPTION LINK

// EXEC RPG

– Source Deck –

/*

// EXEC LNKEDT

// EXEC

– Test Data –

/*

/&

CHAPTER 8

GROUP INDICATION

GROUP PRINTING

INTRODUCTION

In the sample program in Chapter 7, a group of cards were read for each customer and the information on these cards was listed as detail records on the printed report. From an examination of the report created in that program, it will be noted that certain information on the report is duplicated each time a detail line is printed. In particular, the Customer Number, the Customer Name, the State, and the City are always the same for each customer which is processed. In many business reports, it is not desired to repeat this information for each customer, that is, it is more desirable to identify the customer on the first line of the detail lines for the customer and to leave these columns blank on each subsequent line for a given customer. This concept of printing one identification line for each group of detail lines is called GROUP INDICATION and is illustrated in Figure 8-1.

EXAMPLE

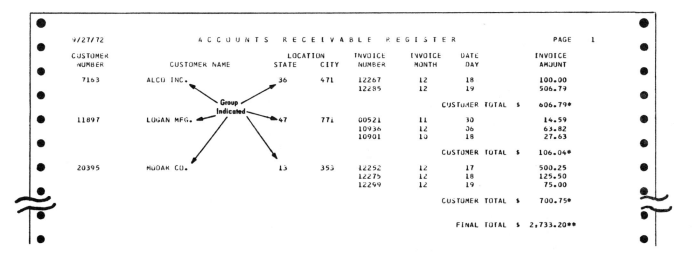

Figure 8-1 Group Indication

Note in the example above that the first detail line for each customer contains the Customer Number, the Customer Name, the State, and the City. Each subsequent line for the same customer is blank in these columns. Thus, the report is said to be group-indicated because the entire group of detail lines for a given customer is identified by one line printed with the first detail line of a customer. As can be seen from the example above in comparison with the report in Chapter 7, the group-indicated report is often considered easier to read.

8.1

Output - Format Specifications Form

A group indicated report will only be produced when one or more control breaks are to occur within the program. Obviously, if there are no control breaks, there are no "groups" which may be identified by a single line on the report. Therefore, the control level indicators must be specified on the Input Specifications in the same manner as is used when a report is not to be group-indicated, such as in Chapter 7. They are placed in columns 59-60 on the same coding line as the field(s) which determine when a control break has occurred.

The entries on the Output - Format Specifications, however, differ from those where a report is not to be group-indicated. The entries which are used to create the report illustrated in Figure 8-1 are illustrated below.

EXAMPLE

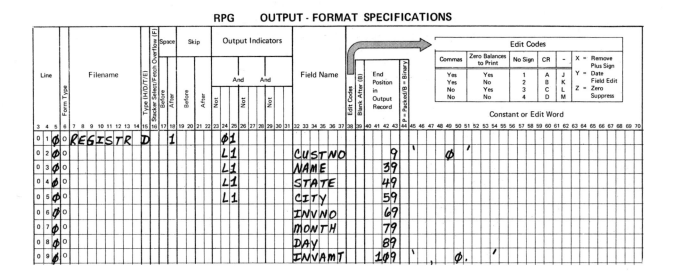

Figure 8 - 2 Entries for Group Indicated Report

Note from the example above that the detail line for the report is defined in the same manner as used previously, that is, the entry "D" is specified in column 15 to indicate that the line is a detail line and the indicator 01 is specified in columns 24-25 to specify that the line is to be printed whenever the 01 Indicator is "on".

The entries which differ from those of a report which is not group-indicated are the Output Indicators which are specified for the fields which are to appear only once in each group of customers. Note from the example in Figure 8-2 that the L1 indicator is specified for the fields CUSTNO, NAME, STATE, and CITY. Thus, these fields will be printed on the detail line only when the L1 indicator is "on". If it is "off", these fields will not be printed when the 01 Indicator is "on" and the remainder of the detail line is printed. Note the similarity between the use of the L1 indicator with the group-indicated fields and the use of the Indicators in Chapter 6 to determine which fields will be printed on the report. The concept is identical — the entire detail line will be printed whenever the 01 Indicator is "on" but the individual fields will be printed only when the L1 indicator is "on", as well as the 01 Indicator.

The key to the ability to group-indicate a report is the fact that the L1 indicator which indicates a control break remains "on" during the processing of the detail record which caused the control break. This is illustrated in the following example.

EXAMPLE

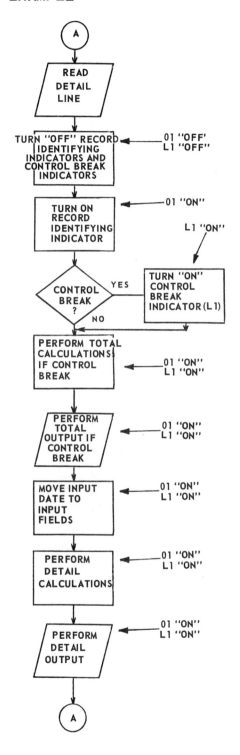

In the example in Figure 8-3 it can be seen that the L1 and 01 Indicators are turned "off" immediately after an input card is read. The Record Identifying Indicator is then turned "on" to identify the input record (01 Indicator). A test is then performed to determine if a control break has occurred. Assume in the example that a control break did occur. Thus, the L1 control level indicator would be turned "on". Since a control break did occur, the total calculations routine and the total output routines would be executed. The data in the input area which caused the control break would then be moved to the input fields. Note that both the 01 Indicator and the L1 Indicator are still "on". The Detail calculations are performed and the detail output is then written. Note that when the detail output lines are written on the report, both the 01 Indicator and the L1 Indicator are "on". This is the combination which must occur in order for the Customer Number, the Customer Name, the State, and the City to be printed on the detail line. Thus, the first detail line for a new customer will contain this information. In subsequent printings of detail lines for the same customer, the L1 indicator will not be on, so the fields will not be printed. Thus, group indication will be achieved.

Figure 8-3 Flowchart of Logic for Group-Indicated Report

EDITING TO ELIMINATE SIGNS

In the sample program in Chapter 7, it was noted that the customer amount which was punched on the Summary Card would contain a 12-zone punch in the low-order position of the field because the field was not edited on the output card. One method of removing the over-punch is to edit the field. The field must be edited, however, with an edit word which is one character larger than the field to be edited. This is illustrated in Figure 8-4.

EXAMPLE

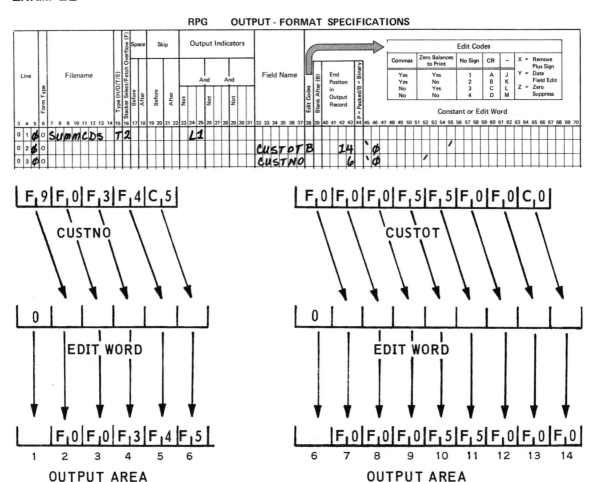

Figure 8-4 Editing to Eliminate the Sign

Note from the example in Figure 8-4 that the edit word which is defined on the Output Specifications is one character longer than the input field, that is, there is a leading zero which indicates where zero-suppression should end and then there are the five bytes which correspond to the size of the input field and the size of the field in the output area. The reason that the edit word is one byte larger than the input field is that when a field is punched in an output card, zero-suppression is not desired, that is, all five numeric digits are required in the punched output field. The only way to eliminate the sign, however, is to edit the field. Thus, since the zero in the edit word is required to indicate where zero suppression is to stop, the zero must be in the left-most position of a digit edit word. By specifying the edit word one more byte than the size of the field to be edited and placing the zero in the high-order byte of the edit word, the entire field to be edited will be edited without zero-suppression and the sign in the input field will be removed.

There is one aspect of this editing technique which must be considered. Since, as illustrated in Figure 8-4, the high-order position of the output area will always contain a blank, care must be taken when editing two adjacent fields such as the CUSTNO field and the CUSTOT field. The field which is the right-most of the two adjacent fields must be moved to the output area first, that is, it must be specified first on the output specifications. This is because the blank in the output field for the CUSTOT field will appear in column 6 of the output area. If the CUSTNO field has already been moved to the output area, then the blank in column 6 which results from the editing operation would destroy the low-order digit in the CUSTNO field. By specifying the CUSTOT field first on the Output Specifications, and then the CUSTNO field, the value in the low-order position of the CUSTNO field will not be replaced by the blank in the edit word for the CUSTOT field and the numbers will appear as adjacent numbers in the output area.

SAMPLE PROBLEM – GROUP INDICATION

The following is an illustration of the input, program, and output of the sample problem to produce a group indicated report.

Input:

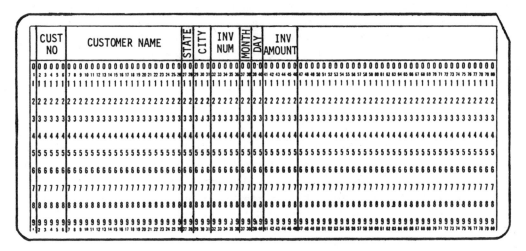

Figure 8-5 Input

Output:

INTERNATIONAL BUSINESS MACHINES CORPORATION
PRINTER SPACING CHART
IBM 407, 408, 409, 1403, 1404, 1443, and 2201

	9/19/72	ACCOUNTS RECEIVABLE REGISTER						PAGE 1

```
 9/19/72            ACCOUNTS  RECEIVABLE  REGISTER                    PAGE   1

 CUSTOMER                            LOCATION      INVOICE   INVOICE   DATE       INVOICE
 NUMBER          CUSTOMER NAME     STATE   CITY    NUMBER     MONTH    DAY        AMOUNT

  7163           ALCU INC.          36      471    12267      12       18          100.00
                                                   12285      12       19          506.79

                                                            CUSTOMER TOTAL  $      606.79*

 11897           LUGAN MFG.         47      771    00521      11       30           14.59
                                                   10936      12       06           63.82
                                                   10901      10       18           27.63

                                                            CUSTOMER TOTAL  $      106.04*

 20395           MODAR CO.          13      353    12252      12       17          500.25
                                                   12275      12       18          125.50
                                                   12299      12       19           75.00

                                                            CUSTOMER TOTAL  $      700.75*

                                                              FINAL TOTAL  $    2,733.20**
```

Figure 8-6 Group Indicated Report

Program:

```
DOS/360*RPG*CL 3-9                    CASHMAN                      09/19/72            PAGE 0001
            01 010 H                                                                  ACCREC
001         01 020 FCUSTCDS IP  F  80   80                    READ40 SYSIPT           ACCREC
002         01 030 FREGISTR O   F 132  132         OF         PRINTERSYSLST           ACCREC
003         01 040 FSUMMCDS O   F  80   80                    READ40 SYSPCH           ACCREC
004         02 010 ICUSTCDS AA   01                                                   ACCREC
005         02 020 I                                     2   60CUSTNOL1               ACCREC
006         02 030 I                                     7   26 NAME                  ACCREC
007         02 040 I                                    27   28 STATE                 ACCREC
008         02 050 I                                    29   31 CITY                  ACCREC
009         02 060 I                                    32   36 INVNO                 ACCREC
010         02 070 I                                    37   38 MONTH                 ACCREC
011         02 080 I                                    39   40 DAY                   ACCREC
012         02 090 I                                    41  462INVAMT                 ACCREC
013         03 010 C    01       CUSTOT    ADD  INVAMT  CUSTOT   82                    ACCREC
014         03 020 CL1           FINTOT    ADD  CUSTOT  FINTOT   82                    ACCREC
015         04 010 OREGISTR H    201      1P                                          ACCREC
016         04 020 O        OR         OF                                             ACCREC
017         04 030 O                                   UDATE  10 ' / / '              ACCREC
018         04 040 O                                          45 'A C C O U N T S'    ACCREC
019         04 050 O                                          67 'R E C E I V A B L E'ACCREC
020         04 060 O                                          85 'R E G I S T E R'    ACCREC
021         04 070 O                                         110 'PAGE'               ACCREC
022         04 080 O                                   PAGE  115 ' 0 '                ACCREC
            04 090 O*                                                                 ACCREC
023         04 100 O        H  1       1P                                             ACCREC
024         04 110 O        OR         OF                                             ACCREC
025         04 120 O                                          11 'CUSTOMER'           ACCREC
026         04 130 O                                          57 'LOCATION'           ACCREC
027         04 140 O                                          70 'INVOICE'            ACCREC
028         04 150 O                                          82 'INVOICE'            ACCREC
029         05 010 O                                          90 'DATE'               ACCREC
030         05 020 O                                         109 'INVOICE'            ACCREC
            05 030 O*                                                                 ACCREC
031         05 040 O        H  2       1P                                             ACCREC
032         05 050 O        OR         OF                                             ACCREC
033         05 060 O                                          10 'NUMBER'             ACCREC
034         05 070 O                                          37 'CUSTOMER NAME'      ACCREC
035         05 080 O                                          70 'STATE    CITY    NUMBER'ACCREC
036         05 090 O                                          90 'MONTH     DAY'      ACCREC
037         05 100 O                                         109 'AMOUNT'             ACCREC
            05 110 O*                                                                 ACCREC
038         05 120 O        D  1        01                                            ACCREC
039         05 130 O                    L1     CUSTNO   9 '  0 '                       ACCREC
040         05 140 O                    L1     NAME    39                             ACCREC
041         05 150 O                    L1     STATE   49                             ACCREC
042         06 010 O                    L1     CITY    59                             ACCREC
043         06 020 O                           INVNO   69                             ACCREC
044         06 030 O                           MONTH   79                             ACCREC
045         06 040 O                           DAY     89                             ACCREC
046         06 050 O                           INVAMT 109 ' , 0. '                    ACCREC
            06 060 O*                                                                 ACCREC
047         06 070 O        T 12        L1                                            ACCREC
048         06 080 O                                          96 'CUSTOMER TOTAL'     ACCREC
049         06 090 O                           CUSTOT 110 '$  , 0. *'                  ACCREC
            06 100 O*                                                                 ACCREC
050         06 110 OSUMMCDS T2           L1                                           ACCREC
051         06 120 O                           CUSTNO   6 '0  '                        ACCREC
052         06 130 O                           CUSTOT B 14 '0   '                      ACCREC
053         06 140 OREGISTR T  1         LR                                           ACCREC
054         06 150 O                                          96 'FINAL TOTAL'        ACCREC
055         07 010 O                           FINTOT 111 '$  , 0. **'                 ACCREC
```

Figure 8-7 Source Listing — Group Indication

GROUP PRINTING

Previously in this chapter it was illustrated how a report may be group indicated. Another commonly used technique which is used on business reports is GROUP PRINTING. Group Printing means that no detail lines are printed on the report. Instead, a line is printed on the report only when a control break occurs. The line which is printed contains the totals for a given customer number. The example in Figure 8-8 illustrates the difference between a group indicated report and a group printed report.

Group Indicated

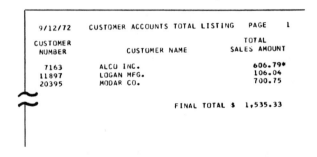

```
9/27/72                  A C C O U N T S   R E C E I V A B L E   R E G I S T E R           PAGE    1

CUSTOMER                                      LOCATION      INVOICE    INVOICE   DATE            INVOICE
NUMBER          CUSTOMER NAME             STATE    CITY     NUMBER     MONTH     DAY             AMOUNT

  7163          ALCO INC.                   36      471     12267        12       18             100.00
                                                           12285        12       19             506.79

                                                                       CUSTOMER TOTAL  $        606.79*

 11897          LOGAN MFG.                  47      771     00521        11       30              14.59
                                                           10936        12       06              63.82
                                                           10901        10       18              27.63

                                                                       CUSTOMER TOTAL  $        106.04*

 20395          MODAR CO.                   13      353     12252        12       17             500.25
                                                           12275        12       18             125.50
                                                           12299        12       19              75.00

                                                                       CUSTOMER TOTAL  $        700.75*

                                                                          FINAL TOTAL  $      2,733.20**
```

Group Printed

```
9/12/72    CUSTOMER ACCOUNTS TOTAL LISTING    PAGE    1

CUSTOMER                                    TOTAL
NUMBER            CUSTOMER NAME          SALES AMOUNT

  7163          ALCO INC.                   606.79*
 11897          LOGAN MFG.                  106.04
 20395          MODAR CO.                   700.75

                          FINAL TOTAL  $  1,535.33
```

Figure 8-8 Group Indicated and Group Printed Reports

Note in the example above that the group indicated report contains one printed line for each card which is read. When the customer number changes, a customer total is printed on the report. The group printed report, on the other hand, does not contain a printed line for each card which is read. Instead, it contains a line on the report only when the customer number changes. Note that the Sales Amount on the group printed report corresponds to the Customer Total Amount on the Group Indicated report. Thus, as can be seen, the sales amount on the Group Printed report corresponds to the total amount for the group indicated report.

In order to cause a Group Printed report to be produced, the proper entries must be made on the Output-Format Specification form. Entries on the other forms are not changed from those used for the Group Indicated report. The entries to cause a Group Printed report are illustrated below.

EXAMPLE

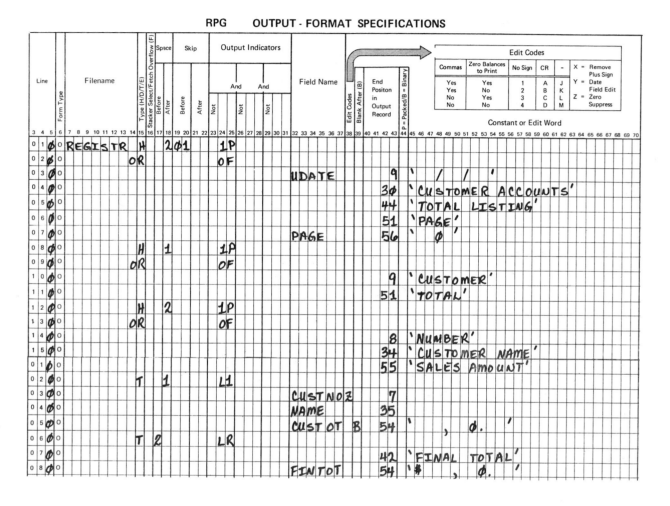

Figure 8-9 Specifications for Group Printed Report

Note in the example above that the heading lines are specified in the same manner as for other reports produced previously. Note also, however, that there are no detail lines to be printed on the report. The only lines which are to be written on the report are total lines, as indicated by the value "T" in the type field (column 15). Thus, the Customer Number, the Customer Name, and the Customer Total will be printed only when the customer number changes. The total of each of the customer cards will be accumulated because the detail calculation of adding the invoice amount to the customer total still takes place as before. Note also that the "blank after" entry is made following the CUSTOT field so that the field will be reset to zeros prior to the next customer being processed.

SAMPLE PROGRAM – GROUP PRINTING

The following pages illustrate the complete documentation for a program to produce a group printed report.

Input

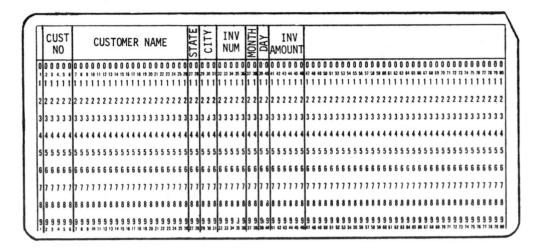

Figure 8-10 Input Cards

Output

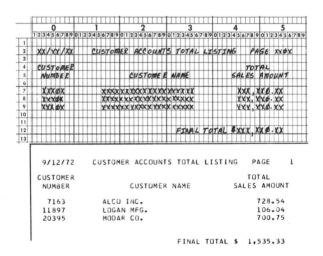

Figure 8-11 Group Printed Report

Source Listing

The following is the source listing of the program to create a group printed report.

```
DOS/360*RPG*CL 3-9                      CASHMAN                          09/12/72                PAGE 0001

            01 010 H                                                                             ACCTOT
001         01 020 FCUSTCDS IP  F  80  80              READ40 SYSIPT                             ACCTOT
002         01 030 FREGISTR  O  F 132 132      OF      PRINTERSYSLST                             ACCTOT
003         02 010 ICUSTCDS AA  01                                                              ACCTOT
004         02 020 I                                    2   60CUSTNOL1                           ACCTOT
005         02 030 I                                    7   26 NAME                              ACCTOT
006         02 040 I                                   41   462INVAMT                            ACCTOT
007         03 010 C    01      CUSTOT    ADD  INVAMT  CUSTOT  82                                ACCTOT
008         03 020 CL1          FINTOT    ADD  CUSTOT  FINTOT  82                                ACCTOT
009         04 010 OREGISTR H  201    1P                                                        ACCTOT
010         04 020 O       OR          OF                                                       ACCTOT
011         04 030 O                          UDATE     9 ' / / '                                ACCTOT
012         04 040 O                                   30 'CUSTOMER ACCOUNTS'                    ACCTOT
013         04 050 O                                   44 'TOTAL LISTING'                        ACCTOT
014         04 060 O                                   51 'PAGE'                                 ACCTOT
015         04 070 O                          PAGE     56 ' 0 '                                  ACCTOT
016         04 080 O       H  1    1P                                                           ACCTOT
017         04 090 O       OR          OF                                                       ACCTOT
018         04 100 O                                    9 'CUSTOMER'                             ACCTOT
019         04 110 O                                   51 'TOTAL'                                ACCTOT
020         04 120 O       H  2    1P                                                           ACCTOT
021         04 130 O       OR          OF                                                       ACCTOT
022         04 140 O                                    8 'NUMBER'                               ACCTOT
023         04 150 O                                   34 'CUSTOMER NAME'                        ACCTOT
024         05 010 O                                   55 'SALES AMOUNT'                         ACCTOT
025         05 020 O       T  1    L1                                                           ACCTOT
026         05 030 O                          CUSTNOZ   7                                        ACCTOT
027         05 040 O                          NAME     35                                        ACCTOT
028         05 050 O                          CUSTOT B 54 '   ,  0. '                            ACCTOT
029         05 060 O       T  2    LR                                                           ACCTOT
030         05 070 O                                   42 'FINAL TOTAL'                          ACCTOT
031         05 080 O                          FINTOT   54 '$   ,  0. '                           ACCTOT
```

Figure 8-12 Source Listing

CHAPTER 8

REVIEW QUESTIONS

1. Why can't a report be group indicated if there are no control breaks?

2. Since the L1 indicator is "on" during both total time and detail time, why must the group indicated information be printed at detail time instead of total time?

3. Explain the difference between a group indicated report and a group printed report.

4. Why, when editing numeric fields in card output, must the edit word be one character longer than the field to be edited if zero-suppression is not to take place?

CHAPTER 8

STUDENT EXERCISES

1. Write the entries on the Input Specifications to define an input card with the following fields:

        Col 1-5: Employee Number
        Col 6-25: Name
        Col 50-52: Division
        Col 55-70: Date Worked (Example: October 1, 1972)

The control break is to occur when the Employee Number changes. The filename is EMPCDS and indicator 37 should be turned on when the card is read. The field names should be determined by the programmer.

RPG INPUT SPECIFICATIONS

Line	Form Type	Filename	Sequence	Number (1-N) Option (O)	Record Identifying Indicator or **	Record Identification Codes 1 Position	Not (N)	C/Z/D	Character	2 Position	Not (N)	C/Z/D	Character	3 Position	Not (N)	C/Z/D	Character	Stacker Select	P = Packed/B = Binary	Field Location From	To	Decimal Positions	Field Name	Control Level (L1-L9)	Matching Fields or Chaining Fields	Field Record Relation
0 1	I																									
0 2	I																									
0 3	I																									
0 4	I																									
0 5	I																									
0 6	I																									
0 7	I																									

2. Write the entries on the Calculation Specifications to add the value "1" to the EMPNO counter when a card is read and the entries to add this total to the TOTDAYS counter when the Employee Number changes.

RPG CALCULATION SPECIFICATIONS

Line	Form Type	Control Level (L0-L9, LR, SR)	Indicators And Not	And Not	And Not	Factor 1	Operation	Factor 2	Result Field	Field Length	Decimal Positions	Half Adjust (H)	Resulting Indicators Arithmetic Plus	Minus	Zero	Compare High 1>2	Low 1<2	Equal 1=2	Lookup Table (Factor 2) is High 54 55	Low 56 57	Equal 58 59
0 1	C																				
0 2	C																				
0 3	C																				
0 4	C																				
0 5	C																				
0 6	C																				
0 7	C																				
0 8	C																				

3. Write the Output Specification for the REPORT file which is to contain a report listing the Employee Number, the Employee Name, the Division, the Date Worked, and the total number of days worked for each employee. At the end of the report, the total number of days worked for all of the employees is to be printed. The format of the report and the field names used on the Input Specifications are to be designed by the programmer. The Employee Number, Name and Division are to be group indicated.

RPG OUTPUT - FORMAT SPECIFICATIONS

Line	Form Type	Filename	Type (H/D/T/E) Stacker Select/Fetch Overflow (F)	Space Before	Space After	Skip Before	Skip After	Output Indicators And Not	And Not	Not	Field Name	Edit Codes	Blank After (B)	End Positon in Output Record	P = Packed/B = Binary	Edit Codes / Constant or Edit Word
0 1	O															
0 2	O															
0 3	O															
0 4	O															
0 5	O															
0 6	O															
0 7	O															
0 8	O															
0 9	O															
1 0	O															
1 1	O															
1 2	O															
1 3	O															
1 4	O															
1 5	O															

Edit Codes

Commas	Zero Balances to Print	No Sign	CR	–	
Yes	Yes	1	A	J	X = Remove Plus Sign
Yes	No	2	B	K	Y = Date Field Edit
No	Yes	3	C	L	Z = Zero Suppress
No	No	4	D	M	

CHAPTER 8

Debugging RPG Programs

Problem 1

Instructions: The following RPG program contains an error or errors which have occurred during compilation. Circle each error and record the corrected entries directly on the listing. Explain the error and method of correction in the space provided below.

```
DOS/360*RPG*CL 3-9              CASHMAN              10/11/72         PAGE 0001

          01 010 H                                                   ACCREC
001       01 020 FCUSTCDS IP  F  80  80              READ40 SYSIPT   ACCREC
002       01 030 FREGISTR O   F 132 132      OF      PRINTERSYSLST   ACCREC
          01 040 FSUMMCDS O   F  80  80              READ40 SYSPNH   ACCREC
                                                                     NOTE 026
003       02 010 ICUSTCDS AA  01                                    ACCREC
004       02 020 I                               2   60CUSTNOL1      ACCREC
005       02 030 I                               7   26 NAME         ACCREC
006       02 040 I                              27   28 STATE        ACCREC
007       02 050 I                              29   31 CITY         ACCREC
008       02 060 I                              32   36 INVNO        ACCREC
009       02 070 I                              37   38 MONTH        ACCREC
010       02 080 I                              39   40 DAY          ACCREC
011       02 090 I                              41   462INVAMT       ACCREC
012       03 010 C    01       CUSTOT   ADD  INVAMT  CUSTOT  82      ACCREC
013       03 020 CL1           FINTOT   ADD  CUSTOT  FINTOT  82      ACCREC
014       04 010 OREGISTR H    201      1P                          ACCREC
015       04 020 O        OR           OF                           ACCREC
016       04 030 O                           UDATE   10             ACCREC
017       04 040 O                              45 'A C C O U N T S' ACCREC
018       04 050 O                              67 'R E C E I V A B L E' ACCREC
019       04 060 O                              85 'R E G I S T E R' ACCREC
020       04 070 O                             110 'PAGE'           ACCREC
          04 080 O                   PAGENO     115 '  0 '          ACCREC
                                                                     NOTE 179
          04 090 O*                                                 ACCREC
021       04 100 O        H   1       1P                            ACCREC
022       04 110 O        OR          OF                            ACCREC
023       04 120 O                              11 'CUSTOMER'       ACCREC
024       04 130 O                              57 'LOCATION'       ACCREC
025       04 140 O                              70 'INVOICE'        ACCREC
026       04 150 O                              82 'INVOICE'        ACCREC
027       05 010 O                              90 'DATE'           ACCREC
028       05 020 O                             109 'INVOICE'        ACCREC
          05 030 O*                                                 ACCREC
029       05 040 O        H   2       1P                            ACCREC
030       05 050 O        OR          OF                            ACCREC
031       05 060 O                              10 'NUMBER'         ACCREC
032       05 070 O                              37 'CUSTOMER NAME'  ACCREC
033       05 080 O                              70 'STATE    CITY      NUMBER' ACCREC
034       05 090 O                              90 'MONTH      DAY'  ACCREC
035       05 100 O                             109 'AMOUNT'         ACCREC
          05 110 O*                                                 ACCREC
036       05 120 O        D   1       01                            ACCREC
037       05 130 O                   L1  CUSTNO   9 '  0 '          ACCREC
038       05 140 O                   L1  NAME    39                 ACCREC
039       05 150 O                   L1  STATE   49                 ACCREC
040       06 010 O                   L1  CITY    59                 ACCREC
041       06 020 O                       INVNO   69                 ACCREC
042       06 030 O                       MONTH   79                 ACCREC
043       06 040 O                       DAY     89                 ACCREC
044       06 050 O                       INVAMT 109 ' , 0.  '       ACCREC
          06 060 O*                                                 ACCREC
045       06 070 O        T  12       L1                            ACCREC
046       06 080 O                              96 'CUSTOMER TOTAL' ACCREC
047       06 090 O                   CUSTOT    110 '$  , 0. *'      ACCREC
          06 100 O*                                                 ACCREC
048       06 110 OSUMMCDS T2       L1                               ACCREC
049       06 120 O                   CUSTNO     6 '0      '         ACCREC
050       06 130 O                   CUSTOT    14 '0        '       ACCREC
051       06 140 OREGISTR T  1       LR                             ACCREC
052       06 150 O                              96 'FINAL TOTAL'    ACCREC
053       07 010 O                   FINTOT    111 '$  , 0. **'     ACCREC
```

SYMBOL   TABLES

RESULTING   INDICATORS

ADDRESS RI	ADDRESS RI	ADDRESS RI	ADDRESS RI	ADDRESS RI	ADDRESS RI	ADDRESS RI
000011 OF	000014 1P	000015 LR	000016 00	000017 01	00007A L0	00007B L1
000085 H0	000086 H1	000087 H2	000088 H3	000089 H4	00008A H5	00008B H6
00008C H7	00008D H8	00008E H9				

FIELD   NAMES .

ADDRESS FIELD	ADDRESS FIELD	ADDRESS FIELD	ADDRESS FIELD	ADDRESS FIELD
000123 CUSTNO	000126 NAME	00013A STATE	00013C CITY	00013F INVNO
000144 MONTH	000146 DAY	000148 INVAMT	00014C CUSTOT	000151 FINTOT
000156 ODATE				

LITERALS

ADDRESS LITERAL	ADDRESS LITERAL	ADDRESS LITERAL
00015A A C C O U N T S	000169 R E C E I V A B L E	00017C R E G I S T E R
000188 PAGE	00018F CUSTOMER	000197 LOCATION
00019F INVOICE	0001A6 DATE	0001AA NUMBER
0001B0 CUSTOMER NAME	0001BD STATE CITY NUMBER	0001D5 MONTH DAY
0001E3 AMOUNT	0001E9 ---/-	0001EF --,--/.--
0001F9 CUSTOMER TOTAL	000207 - ---,--/.--*	000215 -/-----
00021D /--------	000227 FINAL TOTAL	000232 - ---,--/.--**

    048   NOTE 220

NOTE   026   SYMBOLIC DEVICE (COLUMNS 47-52) IS INVALID.   SPECIFICATION IS NOT PROCESSED.

NOTE   179   FIELD NAME (COLUMNS 32-37) IS UNDEFINED.   SPECIFICATION IS NOT PROCESSED.

NOTE   220   FILE SPECIFIED ON OUTPUT FORMAT SPECIFICATIONS IS UNDEFINED OR NOT AN OUTPUT
             FILE (U, C, OR O).   ENTIRE FILE IS DELETED FROM PROCESSING.

EXPLANATION _____

_____

_____

_____

Debugging RPG Programs

Problem 2

Instructions: The following RPG program contains an error or errors which occur during execution. Circle each error and record the corrected entries directly on the listing. Explain the error and method of correction in the space provided below.

```
DOS/360*RPC*CL 3-9              CASHMAN                    10/13/72          PAGE 0001

      01 010 H                                                              ACCREC
001   01 020 FCUSTCDS IP  F  80  80              READ40 SYSIPT              ACCREC
002   01 030 FREGISTR O   F 132 132      OF      PRINTERSYSLST              ACCREC
003   01 040 FSUMMCDS O   F  80  80              READ40 SYSPCH              ACCREC
004   02 010 ICUSTCDS AA  01                                               ACCREC
005   02 020 I                              2   60CUSTNOL1                  ACCREC
006   02 030 I                              7   26 NAME                     ACCREC
007   02 040 I                             27   28 STATE                    ACCREC
008   02 050 I                             29   31 CITY                     ACCREC
009   02 060 I                             32   36 INVNO                    ACCREC
010   02 070 I                             37   38 MONTH                    ACCREC
011   02 080 I                             39   40 DAY                      ACCREC
012   02 090 I                             41   462INVAMT                   ACCREC
013   03 010 C     01      CUSTOT   ADD  INVAMT  CUSTOT    82               ACCREC
014   03 020 CL1           FINTOT   ADD  CUSTOT  FINTOT    82               ACCREC
015   04 010 OREGISTR H  201    1P                                         ACCREC
016   04 020 O        OR        OF                                         ACCREC
017   04 030 O                           UDATE   10 ' / / '                 ACCREC
018   04 040 O                                   45 'A C C O U N T S'       ACCREC
019   04 050 O                                   67 'R E C E I V A B L E'   ACCREC
020   04 060 O                                   85 'R E G I S T E R'       ACCREC
021   04 070 O                                  110 'PAGE'                  ACCREC
022   04 080 O                           PAGE   115 ' 0 '                   ACCREC
      04 090 O*                                                            ACCREC
023   04 100 O        H  1    1P                                           ACCREC
024   04 110 O        OR        OF                                         ACCREC
025   04 120 O                                   11 'CUSTOMER'              ACCREC
026   04 130 O                                   57 'LOCATION'              ACCREC
027   04 140 O                                   70 'INVOICE'               ACCREC
028   04 150 O                                   82 'INVOICE'               ACCREC
029   05 010 O                                   90 'DATE'                  ACCREC
030   05 020 O                                  109 'INVOICE'               ACCREC
      05 030 O*                                                            ACCREC
031   05 040 O        H  2    1P                                           ACCREC
032   05 050 O        OR        OF                                         ACCREC
033   05 060 O                                   10 'NUMBER'                ACCREC
034   05 070 O                                   37 'CUSTOMER NAME'         ACCREC
035   05 080 O                                   70 'STATE    CITY    NUMBER'  ACCREC
036   05 090 O                                   90 'MONTH     DAY'         ACCREC
037   05 100 O                                  109 'AMOUNT'                ACCREC
      05 110 O*                                                            ACCREC
038   05 120 O        D  1    L1                                           ACCREC
039   05 130 O                 L1      CUSTNO     9 '   0   '               ACCREC
040   05 140 O                 L1      NAME      39                         ACCREC
041   05 150 O                 L1      STATE     49                         ACCREC
042   06 010 O                 L1      CITY      59                         ACCREC
043   06 020 O                         INVNO     69                         ACCREC
044   06 030 O                         MONTH     79                         ACCREC
045   06 040 O                         DAY       89                         ACCREC
046   06 050 O                         INVAMT   109 ' , 0. '                ACCREC
      06 060 O*                                                            ACCREC
047   06 070 O        T 12    L1                                           ACCREC
048   06 080 O                                   96 'CUSTOMER TOTAL'        ACCREC
049   06 090 O                         CUSTOT   110 '$  , 0. *'             ACCREC
      06 100 O*                                                            ACCREC
050   06 110 OSUMMCDS T2      L1                                           ACCREC
051   06 120 O                         CUSTNO     6 '0   '                  ACCREC
052   06 130 O                         CUSTOT    14 '0       '              ACCREC
053   06 140 OREGISTR T 1     LR                                           ACCREC
054   06 150 O                                   96 'FINAL TOTAL'           ACCREC
055   07 010 O                         FINTOT   111 '$  , 0. **'            ACCREC
```

10/13/72 ACCOUNTS RECEIVABLE REGISTER PAGE 1

CUSTOMER NUMBER	CUSTOMER NAME	LOCATION STATE	LOCATION CITY	INVOICE NUMBER	INVOICE MONTH	DATE DAY			INVOICE AMOUNT
7163	ALCO INC.	36	471	12267	12	18			100.00
						CUSTOMER TOTAL		$	606.79*
11897	LOGAN MFG.	47	771	00521	11	30			14.59
						CUSTOMER TOTAL		$	712.83*
20395	MODAR CO.	13	353	12252	12	17			500.25
						CUSTOMER TOTAL		$	1,413.58*
						FINAL TOTAL		$	2,733.20**

Note: Totals and Detail do not match

EXPLANATION ____________________

____

____

____

CHAPTER 8

PROGRAMMING ASSIGNMENT 1

INSTRUCTIONS

A group indicated Account Balance Report is to be created. From the input, a balance for each account is to be accumulated and printed.

INPUT

The input consists of a file of Transaction cards which indicate the deposits and withdrawls which have taken place for a given account. The format of the input card is illustrated below.

```
1 = OLD BALANCE
2 = WITHDRAWL
3 = DEPOSIT
```

In the example above it can be seen that the input card contains an Account Number, the date of the transaction, and an amount field which contains either the old balance, the amount withdrawn from the account, or the amount deposited to the account. The Code field in column 79 identifies the type of transaction — if the card contains the old balance, then the code is equal to "1", a withdrawl is identified by the code "2", and a deposit is identified by the code "3".

The cards are sorted in an ascending sequence by account number.

OUTPUT

The Output is to consist of the Account Balance Report and a Summary card for the new balance. The format of the report is illustrated below.

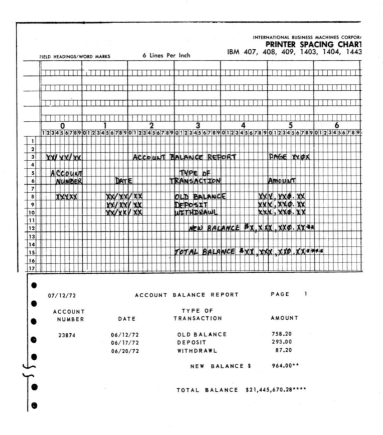

The New Balance is calculation by the following formula: New Balance = Old Balance + Deposits – Withdrawls. The Total Balance is the sum of all of the New Balances. Note that the report is group indicated by Account Number.

In addition to the report illustrated above, a summary card containing the Account Number (columns 1-5), the Current Date (columns 6-11), the New Balance (columns 12-19) and the Code "1" in column 79 should be punched. The New Balance should not be zero-suppressed in the card and should not be overpunched.

TEST DATA — ASSIGNMENT NO. 1 AND ASSIGNMENT NO. 2

Account Number (col 1-5)	Date (col 6-11)	Amount (col 12-19)	Code (col 79)
23874	061272	00075820	1
23874	061772	00029300	3
23874	062072	00008720	2
45397	061272	09976356	1
45397	070172	00876567	2
67549	061272	34378398	1

DOS JOB CONTROL

// JOB jobname

// OPTION LINK

// EXEC RPG

— Student Source Deck —

/*

// EXEC LNKEDT

// EXEC

— Test Data —

/*

/&

Note: This job stream assumes that there are standard assignments for the card reader and the printer of which the student is aware.

CHAPTER 8

PROGRAMMING ASSIGNMENT 2

INSTRUCTIONS

Modify the program in Assignment No. 1 to make the report be a group-printed report. In addition, the interest for each account is to be calculated as follows: If the balance is less than $2500.00, the interest is 5%. If the balance is between 2500.00 and 10,000.00, the interest is 5 ¾%. If the balance is greater than $10,000.00, the interest is 6 ¼%. The input data is the same as in the first assignment. The format of the output report is illustrated below.

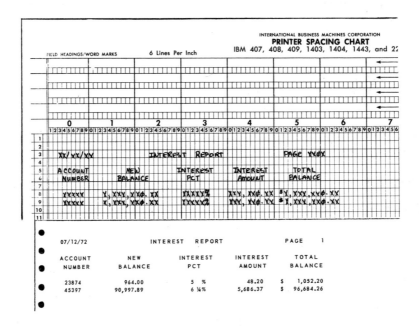

Note from the output illustrated above that there is one line per account. There are no Summary Cards to be punched from this program.

CHAPTER 9

MULTIPLE CONTROL BREAKS

INTRODUCTION

In previous chapters it was illustrated how totals may be taken at a control break and how group indication and group printed reports may also be produced based upon the change in value of a field. There is no limitation that only one field may be used to cause a control break. RPG allows up to nine different control breaks to be processed.

The sample program in this chapter is to be used to create a Sales Report in which there are three fields to be used for control breaks. The input to the program is a file of Sales cards. The format of these cards is illustrated below.

Card Input

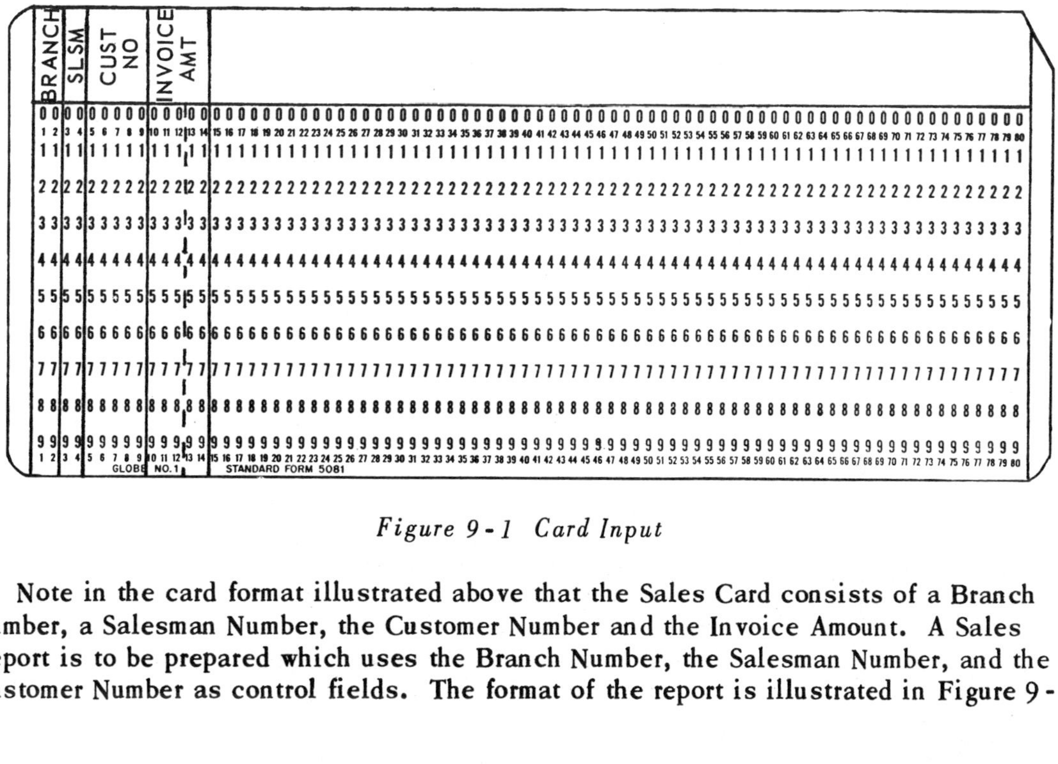

Figure 9-1 Card Input

Note in the card format illustrated above that the Sales Card consists of a Branch Number, a Salesman Number, the Customer Number and the Invoice Amount. A Sales Report is to be prepared which uses the Branch Number, the Salesman Number, and the Customer Number as control fields. The format of the report is illustrated in Figure 9-2.

```
 10/16/72     SALES REPORT           PAGE    1

 BRANCH       SALESMAN       CUSTOMER        SALES
   NO            NO             NO          AMOUNT
   15           21            6432           5.00
   15           21            6432          10.00
   15           21            6432          15.00
                                            30.00*

   15           21            7263          20.00
   15           21            7263          10.00
                                            30.00*

   15           21           11897         500.00
                                           500.00*

                         TOTAL SALESMAN NO 21    560.00**

   15           79           11897         100.00
   15           79           11897          60.00
                                           160.00*

   15           79            7163           5.00
                                             5.00*

                         TOTAL SALESMAN NO 79    165.00**

                             TOTAL BRANCH NO 15      725.00 ***

   39           12            7163           7.50
   39           12            7163          90.00
                                            97.50*

   39           12           11899         200.00
                                           200.00*

                         TOTAL SALESMAN NO 12    297.50**

   39           54           11147         150.00
                                           150.00*

   39           54            6432         175.00
                                           175.00*

                         TOTAL SALESMAN NO 54    325.00**

                             TOTAL BRANCH NO 39      622.50 ***


                             FINAL TOTAL  $  1,347.50 ****
```

Figure 9-2 Sales Report

From the report illustrated in Figure 9-2 it can be seen that there are three fields which are to cause control breaks — the Customer Number, the Salesman Number, and the Branch Number. As a result of the control breaks, totals are taken for each customer number, for each salesman number, and for each branch number.

MULTIPLE CONTROL BREAKS

Control breaks are to be taken on three fields — the Branch Number, the Salesman Number, and the Customer Number. A Customer total is to be taken where there is a change in Customer Number, a Salesman total is to be taken when there is a change in Salesman Number, and a Branch total is to be taken when there is a change in Branch Number.

Note that the Salesman Total may be obtained by adding the individual customer totals for that Salesman. The Branch Total may be obtained by adding the totals for each of the Salesmen working in that Branch. For example in Figure 9-2 it can be seen that the total for Branch 15 may be obtained by adding the total sales for salesman 21 and salesman 79. The final total may be obtained by adding the totals of each of the branches. This method of accumulating totals should be thoroughly understood for this technique is utilized in the RPG Calculation Specifications for the sample problem.

9.2

The concept is illustrated below and on the following pages.

Input File

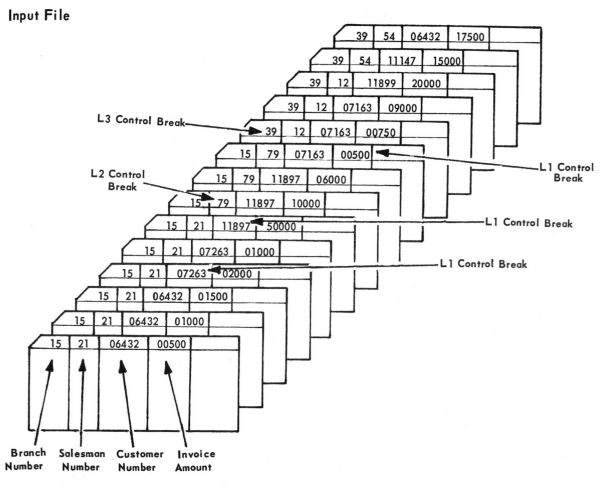

Figure 9-3 Input File

Note from the input file illustrated in Figure 9-3 that an L1 control break will occur when a change in Customer Number takes place, an L2 control break will take place when there is a change in the Salesman Total, and an L3 control break occurs when the Branch Number changes. When each detail card is read, the invoice amount for each customer number is added into a counter to accumulate a total for each customer. The following steps illustrate the process of accumulating various lines of totals.

Step 1: A card is read and the invoice amount from the card is added to a customer total counter (CUSTOT).

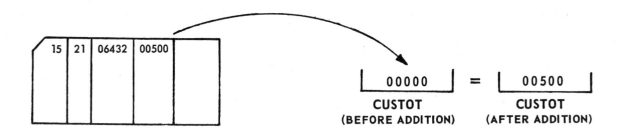

Figure 9-4 Customer Total Is Accumulated

Step 2: A second card is read and the invoice amount is added to the customer total counter.

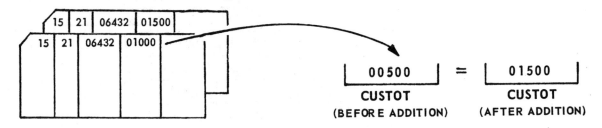

Figure 9-5 Second Card is Read

Note from Figure 9-4 and Figure 9-5 that when each customer card is read, the invoice amount is added to the counter called CUSTOT. Each time a card with the same customer number is read, the counter will be incremented by the value in the invoice amount field of the input card. When a change in customer number is found, that is, when an L1 control break occurs, the total will be printed and the total value which is in the CUSTOT field will be added to a salesman total counter to reflect the sales for the salesman. This is illustrated below.

Step 3: A card containing Customer Number 07263 is read causing an L1 Control Break.

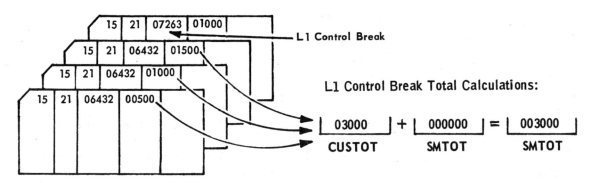

Figure 9-6 An L1 Control Break Occurs

Note in the example above that when a card with a new customer number is read, the total which was accumulated for the customer number 06432 is added to the salesman total counter (SMTOT). Thus, in the example, the salesman total counter contains the total sales to customer 06432 by salesman number 21. The CUSTOT field will then be reset to zero so that the totals for the new customer number (07263) may be accumulated.

From the example in Figure 9-3, it can be seen that there are three customers for salesman number 21. These are customer number 06432, customer number 07263, and customer number 11897. Each time the customer number changes, the customer total which is accumulated each time a detail card is read will be added to the SMTOT counter. When a new salesman is read, an L2 control break occurs, that is, a change in Salesman Number is defined as an L2 control break. When an L2 control break occurs, both the total processing for an L1 control break and an L2 control break occurs. This is illustrated below.

Step 4: The Salesman Number changes (L2 and L1 control break).

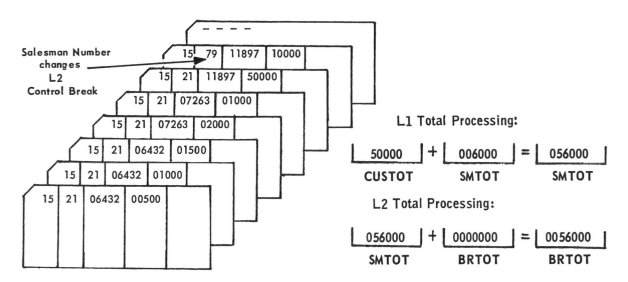

Figure 9-7 L2 and L1 Control Break Processing

Note in Figure 9-7 that when a change in Salesman Number occurs, both the L1 total processing and the L2 total processing is performed. The L1 processing is accomplished before the L2 total processing. Thus, the value in the CUSTOT field is added to the value in the SMTOT field. This, as illustrated in Figure 9-6, is the L1 total processing. The L2 total processing consists of adding the value in the Salesman Total counter (SMTOT) to the value in the Branch Total counter (BRTOT). This occurs at L2 total time so that the total for all of the salesmen within the branch will be accumulated.

When an L3 control break occurs, the Branch Total which is accumulated in the BRTOT counter is added to the Final Total counter (FINTOT) which will be printed at the conclusion of the processing of all of the input file. It should be noted that in addition to the calculations which are illustrated in the previous examples, any output which is defined as Total output on the Output Specifications will be printed if the appropriate control break indicator is "on". Thus, at L1 control break time, the Total lines with an L1 output indicator will be printed. At an L2 control break, both the L1 and L2 Total lines will be printed. At L3 time, the L1, L2, and L3 Total lines will be printed.

INPUT SPECIFICATIONS

In order to define the fields to be used for control breaks, the proper entries must be made on the Input Specifications. The entries used for the sample program are illustrated below.

EXAMPLE

Line	Form Type	Filename	Sequence	Number (1-N)	Option (O)	Record Identifying Indicator or **	Record Identification Codes 1 Position	Not (N)	C/Z/D	Character	2 Position	Not (N)	C/Z/D	Character	3 Position	Not (N)	C/Z/D	Character	Stacker Select	P = Packed/B = Binary	Field Location From	To	Decimal Positions	Field Name	Control Level (L1-L9)
0 1	Ø I	SLSCARD	A A			Ø1																			
0 2	Ø I																				1	2Ø		BRANCH	L3
0 3	Ø I																				3	4Ø		SLSMAN	L2
0 4	Ø I																				5	9Ø		CUSTNO	L1
0 5	Ø I																				1Ø	142		INVAMT	

Figure 9-8 Input Specifications

Note from the example above that the fields in the input record are defined in the same manner as used previously, that is, the field names are specified and the field locations in the input record are defined. The Control Level field on the Input Specifications form (columns 59-60) is used to indicate the fields which are to be used when determining if a control break has occurred. Note in the example that the control level indicator L1 is used with the Customer Number field, the control level indicator L2 with the Salesman Number field, and the control level indicator L3 is used with the Branch Number.

The highest numbered control level indicator indicates the major field of the fields which are to be used as control fields, that is, the field which will be checked first to determine if a control break has occurred. Thus, in the sample program, the value in the BRANCH field will be compared with the previous value in the BRANCH field to determine if a control break has occurred. If the branches are the same, the value in the SLSMAN field will be compared with the previous value because it has the control level indicator L2. If the salesman numbers are the same, the customer numbers are compared because of the L1 control level indicator. If the customer numbers are the same, no control breaks have occurred and the detail processing will occur.

When a control break is found, the appropriate total processing is executed. If an L1 control break occurs, only the L1 total processing is accomplished and a minor total is printed. If an L2 control break occurs, both the L1 and the L2 processing takes place and a minor and intermediate totals are printed because the L2 control break turns on both the L1 and L2 indicators. If an L3 control break is found, the L1, the L2 and the L3 processing takes place because an L3 control break will turn on the L1, L2, and L3 indicators. It should be noted also that the total processing always takes place in an ascending sequence that is, if an L3 control break is found, the L1 total processing will be executed, followed by the L2 total processing and then the L3 total processing. This is illustrated in the following flowchart.

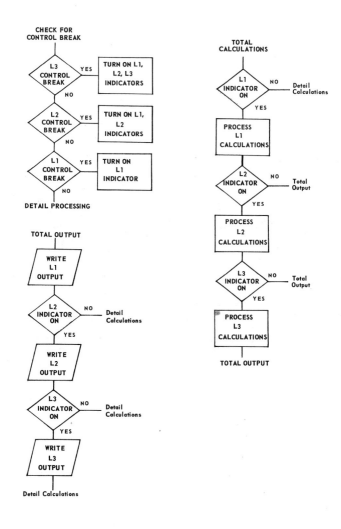

Figure 9-9 Flowcharts for Total Processing

9.7

In the Check for Control Break portion of the flowchart illustrated in Figure 9-9, it can be seen that the L3 control break is checked first. If an L3 control break is found, it and all indicators with a lesser value are turned on. Thus, when an L3 control break is found, the L1, L2, and L3 indicators are all turned "on". Note that this implies that if an L3 control break occurs, an L1 and an L2 control break automatically occur. Thus, in the sample program, even if the salesman number is the same, if a change occurs in the branch number, a change is assumed to occur in all of the control fields.

When the total calculations are performed, the lowest numbered level is processed first. Thus, the sequence of processing the total calculations is exactly opposite to the sequence used when the control fields are checked for a control break. The L1 total calculations are performed first. If there was only an L1 control break, the remainder of the total calculations are not executed and control is passed to the total output routines. The same type of check is done for an L2 control break and an L3 control break. The Calculation Specifications used to indicate the processing to be performed are illustrated below.

EXAMPLE

Line	Form Type	Control Level (L0-L9, LR, SR)	Indicators						Factor 1	Operation	Factor 2	Result Field	Field Length	Decimal Positions	Half Adjust (H)	Resulting Indicators
0 1	C		01						CUSTOT	ADD	INVAMT	CUSTOT	62			
0 2	C	L1							SMTOT	ADD	CUSTOT	SMTOT	72			
0 3	C	L2							BRTOT	ADD	SMTOT	BRTOT	72			
0 4	C	L3							FINTOT	ADD	BRTOT	FINTOT	82			

Figure 9-10 Calculation Specifications

In the Calculation Specifications illustrated above, it can be seen that when a detail record is read and no control break occurs, that is, when the 01 indicator only is "on", then the invoice amount in the record is added to the CUSTOT field. If an L1 control break occurs, the value in the CUSTOT field is added to the value in the SMTOT field. If an L2 control break occurs, the L1 and L2 processing will be performed, that is, the value in the CUSTOT field will be added to the SMTOT field and the value in the SMTOT field will be added to the value in the BRTOT field. When an L3 control break is found, all three total calculations will be performed, beginning with the L1 total processing. Thus, as can be seen, the processing which is to be performed is dependent upon the control break which is found and the specification on the Calculation Specifications.

When control is passed to the total output routines, the same type of checking is performed as was done in the total calculation routines, that is, the L1 total output is written and then a check is performed to determine if an L2 control break has occurred. If it has, the L2 output is written. If it has not, control is passed to the routine which moves the data in the detail input area to the input fields and the detail calculations are performed. The same processing is performed for the L3 totals. The entries on the Output Specifications for these total routines are illustrated below.

EXAMPLE

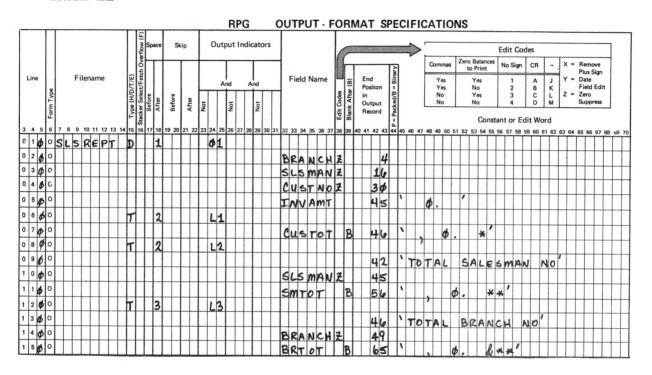

Figure 9-11 Output Specifications

As can be seen from Figure 9-11, the processing for the second and third control breaks is specified in the same manner as was used for the single level control break in Chapter 7, that is, the line is defined as a Total line ("T" in column 15) and the Output Indicator specified is the appropriate control break indicator.

As noted, up to nine control levels may be specified for input records. These will be processed in the same manner as illustrated for the L1, L2, and L3 control level indicators. It should also be noted that when the LR indicator, that is, the Last Record indicator, is turned on when the end of data card is read, all of the control level indicators will be turned "on". Thus, when the LR indicator is turned "on", all levels of totals will be processed beginning with the L1 control level and continuing up to whatever level is specified in the program. After all of the control level processing has been completed, the Last Record processing takes place.

SAMPLE PROGRAM

The source listing for the program to process multi-level control breaks is illustrated below.

```
DOS/360*RPG*CL 3-9              CASHMAN                  10/16/72          PAGE 0001

          01 010 H                                                        SLSRPT
001       01 020 FSLSCARD IP  F  80   80                  READ40 SYSIPT   SLSRPT
002       01 030 FSLSREPT O   F 132  132          OF      PRINTERSYSLST   SLSRPT
003       02 010 ISLSCARD AA  01                                          SLSRPT
004       02 020 I                                1  20BRANCHL3           SLSRPT
005       02 030 I                                3  40SLSMANL2           SLSRPT
006       02 040 I                                5  90CUSTNOL1           SLSRPT
007       02 050 I                               10 142INVAMT            SLSRPT
008       03 010 C      01       CUSTOT    ADD INVAMT   CUSTOT  62         SLSRPT
009       03 020 CL1             SMTOT     ADD CUSTOT   SMTOT   72         SLSRPT
010       03 030 CL2             BRTOT     ADD SMTOT    BRTOT   72         SLSRPT
011       03 040 CL3             FINTOT    ADD BRTOT    FINTOT  82         SLSRPT
012       04 010 OSLSREPT H   201    1P                                   SLSRPT
013       04 020 O       OR         OF                                    SLSRPT
014       04 030 O                               UDATE     9 ' / / '       SLSRPT
015       04 040 O                                        25 'SALES REPORT' SLSRPT
016       04 050 O                                        38 'PAGE'         SLSRPT
017       04 060 O                               PAGE     43 ' 0 '         SLSRPT
          04 070 O*                                                       SLSRPT
018       04 080 O       H   1   1P                                       SLSRPT
019       04 090 O       OR         OF                                    SLSRPT
020       04 100 O                                         6 'BRANCH'      SLSRPT
021       04 110 O                                        19 'SALESMAN'    SLSRPT
022       04 120 O                                        32 'CUSTOMER'    SLSRPT
023       04 130 O                                        43 'SALES'       SLSRPT
          04 140 O*                                                       SLSRPT
024       04 150 O       H   2   1P                                       SLSRPT
025       05 010 O       OR         OF                                    SLSRPT
026       05 020 O                                         4 'NO'          SLSRPT
027       05 030 O                                        16 'NO'          SLSRPT
028       05 040 O                                        29 'NO'          SLSRPT
029       05 050 O                                        44 'AMOUNT'      SLSRPT
030    S  05 040 O       D   1    01             BRANCHZ   4               SLSRPT
031       05 050 O                               SLSMANZ  16               SLSRPT
032       05 060 O                               CUSTNOZ  30               SLSRPT
033       05 070 O                               INVAMT   45 ' 0. '        SLSRPT
034       05 080 O                                                        SLSRPT
035       05 090 O       T   2   L1             CUSTOT  B  46 ' , 0. *'    SLSRPT
036       05 120 O                                                        SLSRPT
037       05 130 O       T   2   L2                       42 'TOTAL SALESMAN NO' SLSRPT
038       05 140 O                               SLSMANZ  45               SLSRPT
039       05 150 O                               SMTOT  B  56 ' , 0. **'   SLSRPT
040       06 100 O                                                        SLSRPT
041       06 120 O       T   3   L3                       46 'TOTAL BRANCH NO' SLSRPT
042       06 130 O                               BRANCHZ  49               SLSRPT
043       06 140 O                               BRTOT  B  65 ' , 0. &***' SLSRPT
044       06 150 O                                                        SLSRPT
045       07 020 O       T  11   LR                       46 'FINAL TOTAL' SLSRPT
046       07 030 O                                                        SLSRPT
047       07 040 O                               FINTOT   64 '$ , 0. &****' SLSRPT
```

Figure 9-12 Source Listing

GROUP INDICATED AND GROUP PRINTED REPORTS

In the sample programs in Chapter 8 it was seen how a report may be group indicated or group printed. In some business applications, it is desirable to create a report which is both group indicated and group printed. Such is the case in the second sample program in this chapter. Using the same input as in the first program, the Branch Number and the Salesman Number are to be group indicated on the report and the Customer Number is to be group printed. Thus, more than one input record for each customer may be processed but only one line will be printed on the report for each customer. The report to be generated from the program is illustrated below.

EXAMPLE

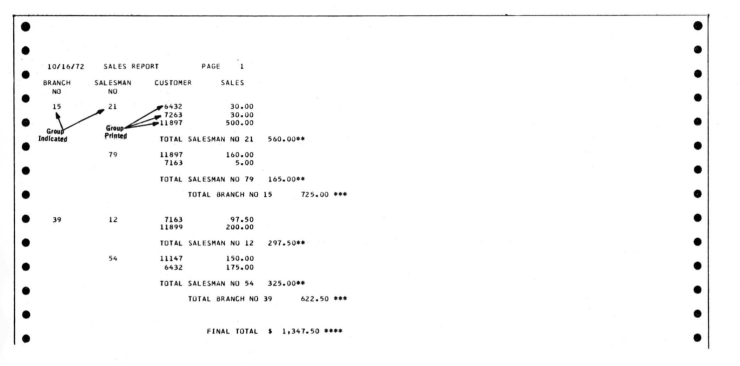

Figure 9-13 Group Indicated and Group Printed Report

Note from the report illustrated in Figure 9-13 that there is only one output line for each customer which is processed. Since there may be more than one input record for each customer, the customer line on the output is group iprinted. As can also be seen, the salesman number and the branch number are group indicated on the report.

In order to have both group printing and group indication on the same report, certain entries must be included on the Output Specifications. The entries used in the sample program are illustrated in Figure 9-14.

Line	Form Type	Filename	Type (H/D/T/E)	Stacker Select/Fetch Overflow (F)	Space Before	Space After	Skip Before	Skip After	Output Indicators And Not	And Not	Not	Field Name	Edit Codes	Blank After (B)	End Position in Output Record	Packed/P = Binary	Constant or Edit Word
010	0		D			0			01								
020	0								L3			BRANCH	Z		4		
030	0								L2			SLSMAN	Z		16		
040	0		T		1				L1								
050	0											CUSTNO	Z		30		
060	0											CUSTOT		B	45		' , 0. '
070	0		T		12				L2								
080	0														32		'TOTAL SALESMAN NO'
090	0											SLSMAN	Z		35		
100	0											SMTOT		B	45		' , 0. '
110	0		T		2				L3								
120	0														41		'TOTAL BRANCH NO'
130	0											BRANCH	Z		44		
140	0											BRTOT		B	56		' , 0. &*'

Edit Codes:

	Commas	Zero Balances to Print	No Sign	CR	-	
	Yes	Yes	1	A	J	X = Remove Plus Sign
	Yes	No	2	B	K	Y = Date Field Edit
	No	Yes	3	C	L	Z = Zero Suppress
	No	No	4	D	M	

Figure 9-14 Entries for Group Indicated and Group Printed Report

Note from the example above that both detail lines and total lines are to be printed on the report. As has been noted previously, a detail line is printed each time an input record is read. The detail line in this example, however, has additional conditions placed upon it before any data will be printed. The branch number (BRANCH) will only be printed if the L3 indicator is "on", and the Salesman Number (SLSMAN) will only be printed if the L2 indicator is "on". Note that these specifications are similar to those entries made for detail lines in Chapter 8 when a group indicated report is to be produced, that is, the fields which are to be group indicated are qualified with a control level indicator.

One other factor which should be noted for the detail line specified in the example in Figure 9-14 is that the printer will not be spaced after the line is printed. This is indicated by the value "0" in column 18. Thus, after the detail line is printed, the printer will be positioned to print the first total line on the same print line. This is necessary because the customer number is to be group printed. As has been noted previously, the total indicators (L2 and L3) will be "on" for the first detail record which is to be printed. When the report is to be group indicated without group printing, the group indicated information will be printed along with the first line of the detail data as has been illustrated. When the report is group printed, however, there may be more than one detail record read before the L1 total line is to be printed. In this case, the L2 and/or L3 indicators would not be on when the group printed customer number is to be printed. Thus, if a line were spaced after the detail line is printed, the branch and salesman numbers would not be on the same print line as the first line containing the Customer Number, which is group printed. Thus, whenever group indication and group printing is to take place on the same report, the data to be group indicated must be specified as a detail line with the proper control level indicators specified for each field to be group indicated. The detail line must not be spaced after the line is printed. The group printed information, as can be seen from the example above, is to be printed when the proper control break occurs and the total line to group print the report is specified in the same manner as if group indication were not to take place.

It should be noted also that an ampersand (&) is included in the edit word on coding line 140. Whenever an ampersand appears in an edit word, a blank will be placed in the edited output (see Figure 9-13).

The source listing of the sample program is illustrated below.

```
DOS/360*RPG*CL 3-9              CASHMAN                    10/16/72           PAGE 0001

         01 010 H                                                              SLSRPT
001      01 020 FSLSCARD IP  F  80  30                READ40 SYSIPT            SLSRPT
002      01 030 FSLSREPT O   F 132 132       OF       PRINTERSYSLST            SLSRPT
003      02 010 ISLSCARD AA  01                                               SLSRPT
004      02 020 I                                     1    20BRANCHL3          SLSRPT
005      02 030 I                                     3    40SLSMANL2          SLSRPT
006      02 040 I                                     5    90CUSTNOL1          SLSRPT
007      02 050 I                                    10   142INVAMT           SLSRPT
008      03 010 C      01          CUSTOT   ADD  INVAMT    CUSTOT  62          SLSRPT
009      03 020 CL1                SMTOT    ADD  CUSTOT    SMTOT   72          SLSRPT
010      03 030 CL2                BRTOT    ADD  SMTOT     BRTOT   72          SLSRPT
011      03 040 CL3                FINTOT   ADD  BRTOT     FINTOT  82          SLSRPT
012      04 010 OSLSREPT H     201       1P                                   SLSRPT
013      04 020 O          OR           OF                                    SLSRPT
014      04 030 O                                  UDATE    9  ' / / '         SLSRPT
015      04 040 O                                          25 'SALES REPORT'   SLSRPT
016      04 050 O                                          38 'PAGE'           SLSRPT
017      04 060 O                                  PAGE    43 '  0 '           SLSRPT
         04 070 O*                                                            SLSRPT
018      04 080 O       H   1       1P                                        SLSRPT
019      04 090 O          OR           OF                                    SLSRPT
020      04 100 O                                           6 'BRANCH'         SLSRPT
021      04 110 O                                          19 'SALESMAN'       SLSRPT
022      04 120 O                                          32 'CUSTOMER'       SLSRPT
023      04 130 O                                          43 'SALES'          SLSRPT
         04 140 O*                                                            SLSRPT
024      04 150 O       H   2       1P                                        SLSRPT
025      05 010 O          OR           OF                                    SLSRPT
026      05 020 O                                           4 'NO'             SLSRPT
027      05 030 O                                          16 'NO'             SLSRPT
028      05 040 O       D   0       01                                        SLSRPT
029      05 050 O                          L3     BRANCHZ   4                  SLSRPT
030      05 060 O                          L2     SLSMANZ  16                  SLSRPT
031      05 070 O       T   1       L1                                        SLSRPT
032      05 080 O                                 CUSTNOZ  30                  SLSRPT
033      05 090 O                                 CUSTOT B 45 ' , 0. '         SLSRPT
034      05 100 O       T  12       L2                                        SLSRPT
035      05 140 O                                          42 'TOTAL SALESMAN NO' SLSRPT
036      05 150 O                                 SLSMANZ  45                  SLSRPT
037      06 010 O                                 SMTOT  B 56 ' , 0. **'       SLSRPT
038      06 020 O       T   3       L3                                        SLSRPT
039      06 030 O                                          46 'TOTAL BRANCH NO' SLSRPT
040      06 040 O                                 BRANCHZ  49                  SLSRPT
041      06 050 O                                 BRTOT  B 65 ' , 0. &***'     SLSRPT
042      06 060 O       T  11       LR                                        SLSRPT
043      06 070 O                                          46 'FINAL TOTAL'    SLSRPT
044      06 080 O                                 FINTOT   64 '$ , 0. &****'   SLSRPT
```

Figure 9-15 Source Listing

CHAPTER 9

REVIEW QUESTIONS

1. What control break indicators will be "on" when an L3 control break occurs? Why is this done?

2. In what sequence are totals processed when an L3 control break occurs? Why is this done?

3. What indicators are "on" at detail output time when an L2 control break occurs? Why is this done?

4. How are counters which are used to accumulate totals reset to zero after the data has been printed? Why can't the following subtract statement be used at total time to zero the field?

3	4	5	6	7	8	9	10	11	12	13	14	15	16	17	18	19	20	21	22	23	24	25	26	27	28	29	30	31	32	33	34	35	36	37	38	39	40	41	42	43	44	45	46	47	48	49	50	51	52	53	54	55	56	57	58	59
0	1	Ø	C		L	1									C	O	U	N	T					S	U	B		C	O	U	N	T					C	O	U	N	T															

CHAPTER 9

STUDENT EXERCISES

1. The following fields should be defined for the INPUT file on the input specifications:

> col 1-5:   Customer Number (XXXXX)
> col 6-8:   Sales District (XXX)
> col 9-11: State (XXX)
> col 12-16: Sales Amount (XXX.XX)

The cards are sorted in a sequence with State the major field, Sales District the intermediate field, and Customer Number the minor field. Totals are to be taken for the Customer Number, the Sales District, and the State whenever these values change. Write the entries on the input specifications to define the fields and cause the proper control breaks.

RPG   INPUT SPECIFICATIONS

Line	Form Type	Filename	Sequence	Number (1-N)	Option (O)	Record Identifying Indicator or **	Position (1)	Not (N)	C/Z/D	Character	Position (2)	Not (N)	C/Z/D	Character	Position (3)	Not (N)	C/Z/D	Character	Stacker Select	P = Packed/B = Binary	From	To	Decimal Positions	Field Name	Control Level (L1-L9)	Matching Fields or Chaining Fields	Field Record Relation	Plus	Minus	Zero or Blank
0 1	I																													
0 2	I																													
0 3	I																													
0 4	I																													
0 5	I																													
0 6	I																													

2. Write the entries on the Calculation Specifications to total the Sales Amount for each customer, total the sales amount for each Sales District when the customer number changes, and total the sales amount for the state when the Sales District changes. In addition, a final total is to be taken for all of the states.

RPG   CALCULATION SPECIFICATIONS

Line	Form Type	Control Level (L0-L9, LR, SR)	Not	And	Not	And	Not	Factor 1	Operation	Factor 2	Result Field	Field Length	Decimal Positions	Half Adjust (H)	Plus	Minus	Zero	High 1>2	Low 1<2	Equal 1=2
0 1	C																			
0 2	C																			
0 3	C																			
0 4	C																			
0 5	C																			
0 6	C																			
0 7	C																			

3. Write the Output Specification entries for the output report. The state, which is to be group indicated, is to end in column 5. The sales district, which is also to be group indicated, ends in column 15. The customer number, which is to be group printed, ends in column 25 and the sales amount for each customer, which is also group printed, ends in column 39. Totals are to be taken for the sales district and the state.

RPG   OUTPUT - FORMAT SPECIFICATIONS

Edit Codes					
Commas	Zero Balances to Print	No Sign	CR	–	X = Remove Plus Sign
Yes	Yes	1	A	J	Y = Date Field Edit
Yes	No	2	B	K	
No	Yes	3	C	L	Z = Zero Suppress
No	No	4	D	M	

Constant or Edit Word

Line | Form Type | Filename | Type (H/D/T/E) | Stacker Select/Fetch Overflow (F) | Space Before/After | Skip Before/After | Output Indicators And/And Not | Field Name | Edit Codes | Blank After (B) | End Position in Output Record | P = Packed/B = Binary | Constant or Edit Word

Columns: 3 4 5 | 6 | 7 8 9 10 11 12 13 14 | 15 | 16 | 17 18 | 19 20 21 22 | 23 24 25 26 27 28 29 30 31 | 32 33 34 35 36 37 | 38 | 39 | 40 41 42 43 | 44 | 45 46 47 48 49 50 51 52 53 54 55 56 57 58 59 60 61 62 63 64 65 66 67 68 69 70

Line	Form Type
0 1	O
0 2	O
0 3	O
0 4	O
0 5	O
0 6	O
0 7	O
0 8	O
0 9	O
1 0	O
1 1	O
1 2	O
1 3	O
1 4	O
1 5	O
0 1	O
0 2	O
0 3	O
0 4	O
0 5	O
0 6	O
0 7	O
0 8	O
0 9	O
1 0	O
1 1	O
1 2	O
1 3	O
1 4	O
1 5	O

Debugging RPG Programs

Problem 1

INSTRUCTIONS: The following RPG program contains an error or errors which occur during execution. Circle each error and record the corrected entries directly on the listing. Explain the error and method of correction in the space provided below.

```
DOS/360*RPG*CL 3-9              CASHMAN                    10/16/72              PAGE 0001

          01 010 H                                                              SLSRPT
001       01 020 FSLSCARD IP  F  80   80              READ40 SYSIPT             SLSRPT
002       01 030 FSLSREPT O   F 132  132      OF      PRINTERSYSLST             SLSRPT
003       02 010 ISLSCARD AA   01                                              SLSRPT
004       02 020 I                             1    20BRANCHL3                 SLSRPT
005       02 030 I                             3    40SLSMANL2                 SLSRPT
006       02 040 I                             5    90CUSTNOL1                 SLSRPT
007       02 050 I                            10   142INVAMT                   SLSRPT
008       03 010 C     01    CUSTOT    ADD  INVAMT    CUSTOT  62                SLSRPT
009       03 020 CL1         SMTOT     ADD  CUSTOT    SMTOT   72                SLSRPT
010       03 030 CL2         BRTOT     ADD  SMTOT     BRTOT   72                SLSRPT
011       03 040 CL3         FINTOT    ADD  BRTOT     FINTOT  82                SLSRPT
012       04 010 OSLSREPT H  201    1P                                         SLSRPT
013       04 020 O       OR         OF                                         SLSRPT
014       04 030 O                            UDATE    9 ' / / '               SLSRPT
015       04 040 O                                    25 'SALES REPORT'        SLSRPT
016       04 050 O                                    38 'PAGE'                SLSRPT
017       04 060 O                            PAGE     43 ' 0 '                SLSRPT
          04 070 O*                                                            SLSRPT
018       04 080 O       H   1     1P                                          SLSRPT
019       04 090 O       OR        OF                                         SLSRPT
020       04 100 O                                     6 'BRANCH'              SLSRPT
021       04 110 O                                    19 'SALESMAN'            SLSRPT
022       04 120 O                                    32 'CUSTOMER'            SLSRPT
023       04 130 O                                    43 'SALES'               SLSRPT
          04 140 O*                                                            SLSRPT
024       04 150 O       H   2     1P                                          SLSRPT
025       05 010 O       OR        OF                                         SLSRPT
026       05 020 O                                     4 'NO'                  SLSRPT
027       05 030 O                                    16 'NO'                  SLSRPT
028       05 040 O                                    29 'NO'                  SLSRPT
029       05 050 O                                    44 'AMOUNT'              SLSRPT
030     S 05 040 O       D   1     01                                         SLSRPT
031       05 050 O                          BRANCHZ    4                       
032       05 060 O                          SLSMANZ   16                       
033       05 070 O                          CUSTNOZ   30                       
034       05 080 O                          INVAMT    45 ' 0. '                
035       05 090 O       T   2     01                                         
036       05 120 O                          CUSTOT  B 46 ' , 0. *'             
037       05 130 O       T   2     L2                                         
038       05 140 O                                    42 'TOTAL SALESMAN NO'   
039       05 150 O                          SLSMANZ   45                       
040       06 100 O                          SMTOT   B 56 ' , 0. **'            
041       06 120 O       T   3     L3                                         
042       06 130 O                                    46 'TOTAL BRANCH NO'     SLSRPT
043       06 140 O                          BRANCHZ   49                       SLSRPT
044       06 150 O                          BRTOT   B 65 ' , 0. &***'          
045       07 020 O       T  11     LR                                         SLSRPT
046       07 030 O                                    46 'FINAL TOTAL'         SLSRPT
047       07 040 O                          FINTOT    64 '$ , 0. &****'        
```

```
10/16/72    SALES REPORT        PAGE   1

BRANCH      SALESMAN     CUSTOMER       SALES
  NO          NO           NO          AMOUNT

  15          21          6432          5.00
                                        5.00*

  15          21          6432         10.00
                                       10.00*

  15          21          6432         15.00
                                       15.00*

  15          21          7263         20.00
                                       20.00*

  15          21          7263         10.00
                                       10.00*

  15          21         11897        500.00
                                      500.00*

                    TOTAL SALESMAN NO 21    525.00**

  15          79         11897        100.00
                                      100.00*

  15          79         11897         60.00
                                       60.00*

  15          79          7163          5.00
                                        5.00*

                    TOTAL SALESMAN NO 79     65.00**

                        TOTAL BRANCH NO 15      590.00 ***
```

EXPLANATION: _____

_____

_____

_____

INSTRUCTIONS: The following RPG program contains an error or errors which occur
during execution. Circle each error and record the corrected entries
directly on the listing. Explain the error and method of correction
in the space provided below.

```
DOS/360*RPG*CL 3-9                    CASHMAN                    10/16/72          PAGE 0001

        01 010 H                                                                  SLSRPT
001     01 020 FSLSCARD IP  F  80  80                      READ40 SYSIPT          SLSRPT
002     01 030 FSLSREPT O   F 132 132        OF            PRINTERSYSLST          SLSRPT
003     02 010 ISLSCARD AA  01                                                    SLSRPT
004     02 020 I                                  1   20BRANCHL3                  SLSRPT
005     02 030 I                                  3   40SLSMANL2                  SLSRPT
006     02 040 I                                  5   90CUSTNOL1                  SLSRPT
007     02 050 I                                 10  142INVAMT                    SLSRPT
008     03 010 C    01      CUSTOT     ADD  INVAMT   CUSTOT  62                    SLSRPT
009     03 020 CL1          SMTOT      ADD  CUSTOT   SMTOT   72                    SLSRPT
010     03 030 CL2          BRTOT      ADD  SMTOT    BRTOT   72                    SLSRPT
011     03 040 CL3          FINTOT     ADD  BRTOT    FINTOT  82                    SLSRPT
012     04 010 OSLSREPT H   201    1P                                             SLSRPT
013     04 020 O       OR          OF                                             SLSRPT
014     04 030 O                                 UDATE     9 ' / / '              SLSRPT
015     04 040 O                                          25 'SALES REPORT'       SLSRPT
016     04 050 O                                          38 'PAGE'               SLSRPT
017     04 060 O                                 PAGE     43 ' 0 '                SLSRPT
        04 070 O*                                                                 SLSRPT
018     04 080 O        H   1    1P                                               SLSRPT
019     04 090 O       OR          OF                                             SLSRPT
020     04 100 O                                           6 'BRANCH'             SLSRPT
021     04 110 O                                          19 'SALESMAN'           SLSRPT
022     04 120 O                                          32 'CUSTOMER'           SLSRPT
023     04 130 O                                          43 'SALES'              SLSRPT
        04 140 O*                                                                 SLSRPT
024     04 150 O        H   2    1P                                               SLSRPT
025     05 010 O       OR          OF                                             SLSRPT
026     05 020 O                                           4 'NO'                 SLSRPT
027     05 030 O                                          16 'NO'                 SLSRPT
028     05 040 O        T   0    01                                               SLSRPT
029     05 050 O                   L3            BRANCHZ   4                       SLSRPT
030     05 060 O                   L2            SLSMANZ  16                       SLSRPT
031     05 070 O        T   1    L1                                               SLSRPT
032     05 080 O                                 CUSTNOZ  30                       SLSRPT
033     05 090 O                                 CUSTOT B 45 ' , 0. '             SLSRPT
034     05 100 O        T  12    L2                                               SLSRPT
035     05 140 O                                          42 'TOTAL SALESMAN NO   SLSRPT
036     05 150 O                                 SLSMANZ  45                       SLSRPT
037     06 010 O                                 SMTOT  B 56 ' , 0. **'           SLSRPT
038     06 020 O        T   3    L3                                               SLSRPT
039     06 030 O                                          46 'TOTAL BRANCH NO'    SLSRPT
040     06 040 O                                 BRANCHZ  49                       SLSRPT
041     06 050 O                                 BRTOT  B 65 ' , 0. &***'         SLSRPT
042     06 060 O        T  11    LR                                               SLSRPT
043     06 070 O                                          46 'FINAL TOTAL'        SLSRPT
044     06 080 O                                 FINTOT   64 '$ , 0. &****'       SLSRPT
```

```
10/16/72    SALES REPORT        PAGE    1

BRANCH     SALESMAN     CUSTOMER     SALES
  NO          NO
                          6432        30.00
                          7263        30.00
              21         11897       500.00

                       TOTAL SALESMAN NO 21    560.00**

                         11897       160.00
  15          79          7163         5.00

                       TOTAL SALESMAN NO 79    165.00**

                            TOTAL BRANCH NO 15     725.00 ***


                          7163        97.50
              12         11899       200.00

                       TOTAL SALESMAN NO 12    297.50**

                         11147       150.00
                          6432       175.00

                       TOTAL SALESMAN NO 54    325.00**

                            TOTAL BRANCH NO 39     622.50 ***


                       FINAL TOTAL  $  1,347.50 ****
```

EXPLANATION: _____

_____

_____

_____

9.20

PROGRAMMING ASSIGNMENT 1

INSTRUCTIONS

Write the RPG program to produce a Sales Analysis Report listing the Salesman Number and the Items Sold.

INPUT — Sales Analysis Cards

Input is to consist of Sales Analysis Cards containing the Salesman Number, the Item Number, the Item Description, and the Sales Amount.

OUTPUT — Sales Analysis Report

Output is to consist of a Sales Analysis Report listing the Salesman Number, the Item Number, the Item Description, and the Sales Amount. A minor total is to be taken when there is a change in Item Number and an intermediate total is to be taken when there is a change in Salesman Number. A final total is to be printed after all cards have been processed. The Salesman Number and the Item Number should be group indicated as illustrated below.

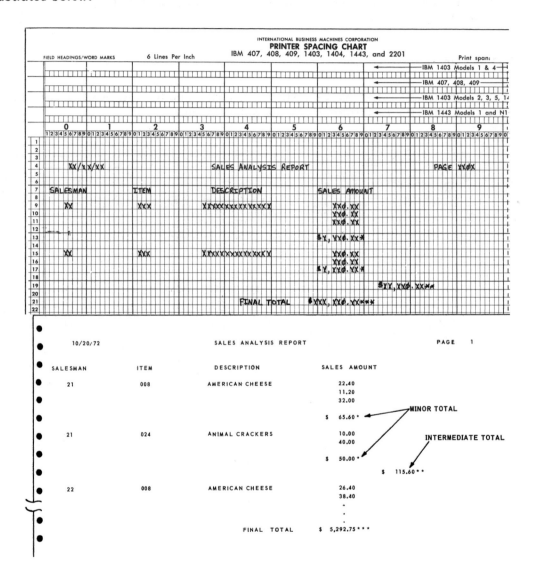

TEST DATA — ASSIGNMENT NO. 1

Item No (col 1-3)	Salesman # (col 4-5)	Description (col 6-20)	Amount (col 21-25)
008	21	American Cheese	02240
008	21	American Cheese	01120
008	21	American Cheese	03200
024	21	Animal Crackers	01000
024	21	Animal Crackers	04000
008	22	American Cheese	02640
008	22	American Cheese	03840
098	25	Broccoli	09750
099	25	Lettuce	12309

DOS JOB CONTROL

// JOB jobname

// OPTION LINK

// EXEC RPG

— Source Deck —

/*

// EXEC LNKEDT

// EXEC

— Test Data —

/*

/&

PROGRAMMING ASSIGNMENT 2

INSTRUCTIONS

A Weekly Service Contract report is to be produced from a file of Sales Cards. Write the RPG program to create this report.

INPUT — Sales Cards

The input is to consist of a file of sales cards which contain the information to be used on the report. The format of the card is illustrated below.

The Code field in the card indicates the type of transaction which is represented by the card. The value ''1'' indicates a Contract Sold and the value ''2'' means a Contract Renewal.

OUTPUT — Weekly Service Contract

The Weekly Service Contract indicates the number and amount of Service Contracts sold and the percent of the Service Contracts charged to PARTS Account and the percent charged to a LABOR Account. The percentage value in the input card is the amount which is to be charged to the LABOR Account. The remainder is charged to the Parts Account.

The format of the report is illustrated below.

INTERNATIONAL BUSINESS MACHINES CORPORATION
PRINTER SPACING CHART
IBM 407, 408, 409, 1403, 1404, 1443, and 2201

FIELD HEADINGS/WORD MARKS   6 Lines Per Inch   Print span:

	DATE 10/20/72			WEEKLY	SERVICE	CONTRACT	REPORT				PAGE 1	

STORE	DEPT	PER CENT	PARTS	CONTRACTS SOLD LABOR	UNITS	AMOUNT	PARTS	RENEWALS LABOR	UNITS	AMOUNT	PARTS	DEPARTMENT TOTALS LABOR	UNITS	AMOUNT
851	9	30%	6.60	15.40	3	22.00					6.60	15.40	3	22.00
	22	20%	6.98	27.92	2	34.90					6.98	27.92	2	34.90
	46	17%	7.62	37.23	3	44.85	4.92	24.03	2	28.95	12.54	61.26	5	73.80
	TOTALS		$ 21.20	$ 80.55	8	$ 101.75	$ 4.92	$ 24.03	2	$ 28.95	$ 26.12	$ 104.58	10	$ 130.70
	FINAL TOTALS		$ 226.46	$ 1,252.75	50	$ 1,479.21	$ 35.71	$ 291.84	19	$ 327.55	$ 262.17	$ 1,549.59	69	$ 1,806.76

The report contains the number and amount of Service Contracts sold and the percent of the Service Contracts charged to a PARTS Account and the percent charged to a LABOR Account. There is one input card for each Service Contract sold and one card for each Renewal. Thus, in the sample report above, there are three cards for Store 851, Department 9. The three service contracts sold (UNITS) were in the amount of $22.00. Thirty percent of the total amount is charged to the Parts Account ($6.60) and the balance is charged to the Labor Account ($15.40). There were no renewals in Department 9. The totals on the right hand side of the report are the sum of the Contracts Sold and Renewals.

Intermediate totals are taken when there is a change in Store Number, and final totals are taken after all cards have been processed. Note that since there is one input card for each contract sold or renewed, the department totals are group-printed. The Store number should be group-indicated.

9.25

TEST DATA — ASSIGNMENT NO. 2

Store (col 15-16)	Dept (col 57-58)	Percent (col 65-66)	Amount (col 70-74)	Code (col 80)
851	09	30	01300	1
851	09	30	00350	1
851	09	30	00550	1
851	22	20	03000	1
851	22	20	00490	1
851	46	17	02100	2
851	46	17	03450	1
851	46	17	00795	2
851	46	17	00435	1
851	46	17	00600	1

DOS JOB CONTROL

// JOB jobname

// OPTION LINK

// EXEC RPG

— Source Deck —

/*

// EXEC LNKEDT

// EXEC

— Test Data —

/*

/&

CHAPTER 10

FIELD-RECORD RELATIONS

MULTIPLE RECORD TYPES

INTRODUCTION

In Chapter 6 it was illustrated that the Record Identifying Indicator can be set to different values dependent upon the code which is punched into a control field in the record. In the example in Chapter 6, the fields within each type of record were the same. In some instances, the fields will vary within input records. The first sample program in this chapter illustrates an application where different fields are in the input records dependent upon the type of record to be processed.

In other applications, records with completely different formats may be read from the same input file. In addition, there may be a prescribed sequence in which the records must appear in order to be processed properly. The second sample program in this chapter illustrates an application of this type.

FIELD-RECORD RELATIONS

The first sample program in this chapter illustrates the RPG coding to produce a Parts Request Listing. The input to the program is a file of cards which may be in one of two formats. The first-card format is designed to indicate which parts are to be produced within a company. This input card contains a Work Order Number. The second card format is designed to indicate which parts are purchased from another company. This input card contains a Purchase Order Number. The format of the two input cards to be processed is illustrated in Figure 10-1.

Input

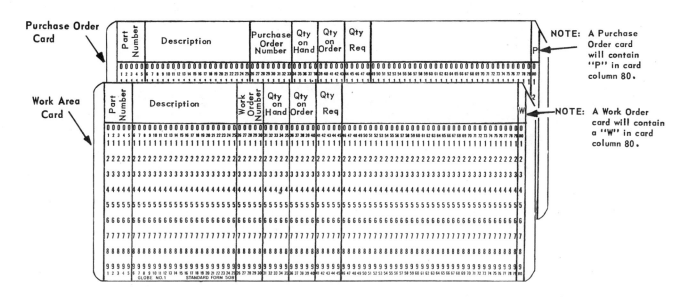

Figure 10-1 Work Order Card and Purchase Order Card

Note from Figure 10-1 that each of the cards contains the Part Number field in columns 1-5, the Description in columns 6-25, and a code ("W" = Work Order, "P" = Purchase Order) in column 80. They also each contain a field for the Quantity on Hand, the Quantity on Order, and Quantity Required. These fields, however, are contained in different columns of the cards. In addition, the Work Order Card contains a Work Order Number in columns 26-30 and the Purchase Order Card contains a Purchase Order Number in columns 26-33. As can be seen, even though the information contained in the Quantity on Hand, the Quantity on Order, and the Quantity Required fields will have the same meaning, the values will be placed in different columns of the card based upon the type of card being processed. The Field Record Relation portion of the Input Specifications are used to specify where each field will be located for the type of input card being processed.

The Parts Request List which is produced by the program lists each part number with its description, work order number or purchase order number, the quantity on hand, the quantity on order, and the quantity required. In addition, if the quantity required is greater than the sum of the quantity on hand and the quantity on order, the number of parts to be ordered is also indicated. The report is illustrated below.

EXAMPLE

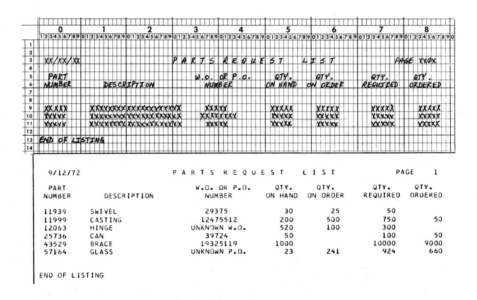

Figure 10-2 Parts Request List

As can be seen from the report in Figure 10-2, if the sum of the quantity on hand and the quantity on order is less than the quantity required, the difference will be ordered so that all requirements for the part may be filled. Note in addition that if the work order is omitted from a Work Order card, the message "UNKNOWN W.O." is placed on the report. The same is true for the Purchase Order number.

In addition, if a part must be ordered, a card is to be punched on the card punch indicating the part number, the purchase order number or the work order number, and the quantity to be ordered. The format of this output card is illustrated below.

Output Card — Work Order

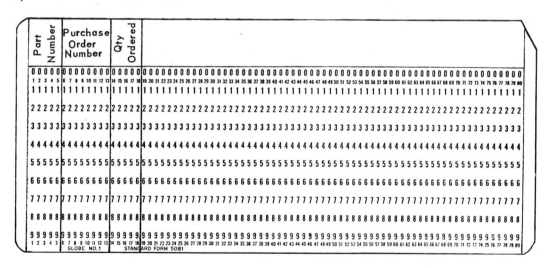

Output Card — Purchase Order

Figure 10-3 Output Cards

INPUT SPECIFICATIONS

In order to define the format of the input records which will be processed by the program, the Input Specifications form is used. The form used for the sample program in order to define the Work Order and Purchase Order cards is illustrated below.

EXAMPLE

RPG INPUT SPECIFICATIONS

Line	Form Type	Filename	Sequence	Number (1-N)	Option (O)	Record Identifying Indicator or **	Position	Not (N)	C/Z/D	Character	Position	Not (N)	C/Z/D	Character	Position	Not (N)	C/Z/D	Character	Stacker Select	P = Packed/B = Binary	From	To	Decimal Positions	Field Name	Control Level (L1-L9)	Matching Fields or Chaining Fields	Field Record Relation	Plus	Minus	Zero or Blank
0 1	0 I	CDFILEI		A	A	01	80		C	W																				
0 2	0 I			O	R	02	80		C	P																				
0 3	0 I																			1	5		PTNO						
0 4	0 I																			6	25		DESCRP						
0 5	0 I																			26	30		WKORD			01		20	
0 6	0 I																			31	35	0	QTYOH			01			
0 7	0 I																			36	40	0	QTYOO			01			
0 8	0 I																			41	45	0	QTYREQ			01			
0 9	0 I																			26	33		PURCH			02		21	
1 0	0 I																			34	38	0	QTYOH			02			
1 1	0 I																			39	43	0	QTYOO			02			
1 2	0 I																			44	48	0	QTYREQ			02			

Figure 10-4 Input Specifications Form

Note in the example above that the filename for the card input is CDFILEI. There are two Record Identifying Indicators which may be turned "on" by the records read from the file. If the code in column 80 is equal to a "W", then the record identifying indicator 01 will be turned "on". If the card is a purchase order card, as identified by the value "P" in column 80, the record identifying indicator 02 will be turned "on".

The field identifications for the input records are specified in the same manner as used previously, that is, the beginning and ending columns in the card are specified together with the field name. As noted previously, however, the Work Order or Purchase Order Number, the Quantity On Hand, the Quantity On Order, and the Quantity Required are in different columns of the input card dependent upon the type of card which was read. In order to identify the columns for each of the types of input cards, the Field Record Identification portion of the form (columns 63-64) are used.

If a field is to be contained in a 01 Record, that is, a record that turns on Record Identifying Indicator 01 (work order record), the value 01 is entered in columns 63-64 to indicate that when the 01 indicator is "on", the field is to be assumed to be in the columns specified in the "Form-To" portion of the form. Thus, in the example in Figure 10-4 it can be seen that when the 01 indicator is "on", the Quantity on Hand field is to be in card columns 31-35 of the input card. When the 02 indicator is "on", the Quantity on Hand field will be in columns 34-38. Thus, whenever the fieldname QTYOH is specified on either the Calculation Specifications or on the Output-Format specifications, the value in columns 31-35 will be used if the 01 indicator is "on" and the value in columns 34-38 will be used if the 02 indicator is "on".

The remainder of the fields are treated in a similar manner. Thus, for the Work Order card, the Quantity on Order field is in columns 36-40 and for the Purchase Order card, the Quantity on Order field is in columns 39-43. It should be noted in the example in Figure 10-4 that the common fields in each card, that is, the Part Number field and the Description field, are specified first on the Input Specification form. These are followed by the fields which will be found in the Work Order card (01 Indicator) and then by the fields which will be found in the Purchase Order cards (02 Indicator). Although it is not required that these fields be placed in any given order, it is more efficient in terms of compiler time if all of the common fields are specified first, followed by all of the 01 fields, followed by all of the 02 fields, etc.

Note also in Figure 10-4 that entries are made in the Field Indicators portion of the Input Specifications form (columns 65-70). This portion of the form is used to specify indicators which will be turned "on" when a numeric field contains either a positive value (columns 65-66), a negative value (columns 67-68) or a value of zero (columns 69-70). For alphanumeric fields, an indicator may be entered in columns 69-70 to indicate that the field contains blanks. In the example it can be seen that indicator 20 is entered in columns 69-70 for the Work Order Number field (WKORD) and indicator 21 is entered in the columns for the purchase order number field (PURCH). Thus, if the WKORD field contains blanks, indicator 20 will be turned "on" and if the PURCH field contains blanks, indicator 21 will be turned "on". These indicators may be tested on the Calculation Specifications or the Output-Format Specifications. They remain "on" or "off" until another card is read and they are reset to reflect the value in the new card.

RESULTING INDICATORS

As noted previously, if the sum of the quantity on hand and the quantity on order is less than the quantity required, then the difference will be the quantity ordered in order to ensure that there are enough parts for the requirements. In addition, if parts must be ordered, a card is to be punched indicating the part number, the purchase order or work order number, and the quantity to be ordered. In order to determine if parts must be ordered, the quantity on hand is added to the quantity on order and this sum is subtracted from the quantity required. If the result is greater than zero, it means parts must be ordered. If the result is negative, there are enough parts for the quantity required. The calculations for this determination are illustrated below.

EXAMPLE

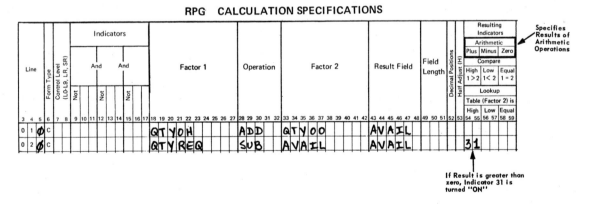

Figure 10-5 Calculation Specifications

Note in the example above that the value in the QTYOH field is added to the value in the QTYOO field and the result is stored in the AVAIL field. After the addition has been performed, the answer which is stored in the AVAIL field is subtracted from the quantity required (QTYREQ). If the result of this subtraction is less than or equal to zero, no parts need be ordered because there are enough parts to satisfy requirements. If, however, the result of the subtraction is greater than zero, that is, if the sum of the quantity on hand and the quantity on order is less than the quantity required, then parts must be ordered. See the examples on the following page.

EXAMPLE 1

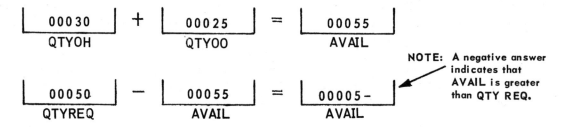

Note in the example above that Quantity Available was 55 and the Quantity Required was 50. Thus, parts need not be ordered.

EXAMPLE 2

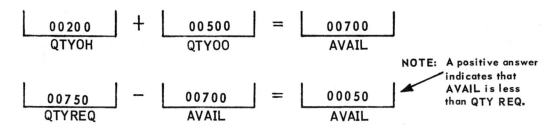

Figure 10-6 Example of Calculations

Note in Example 2 above that the Quantity Available was 700 and the Quantity Required was 750; thus, 50 parts should be ordered.

In order to determine if the result is greater than zero, the Resulting Indicators on the Calculation Specifications are utilized. As a result of arithmetic operations, indicators may be set "on" or "off" dependent upon the value of the results of the operation. An indicator may be set "on" if the result is greater than zero (plus), less than zero (minus), or equal to zero (zero). Note from the example in Figure 10-5 that columns 54-55 are used to name an indicator to be turned "on" if the result is greater than zero, columns 56-57 for an indicator to be turned "on" if the result is less than zero, and columns 58-59 for an indicator to be set "on" if the result is equal to zero. In the example, indicator 31 is specified in columns 54-55. Thus, if the result of the subtraction operation which is stored in the field AVAIL is greater than zero, that is, if it is positive, indicator 31 will be turned "on". If the result is less than zero or equal to zero, indicator 31 will be turned "off".

OUTPUT-FORMAT SPECIFICATIONS

When indicator 31 is turned "on" as a result of the detail calculations, it means that parts must be ordered because the Quantity Required is greater than the Quantity On Hand and the Quantity Ordered. Thus, an entry must be made on the report and a card punched. The entries for the detail lines which are printed on the report are illustrated below.

EXAMPLE

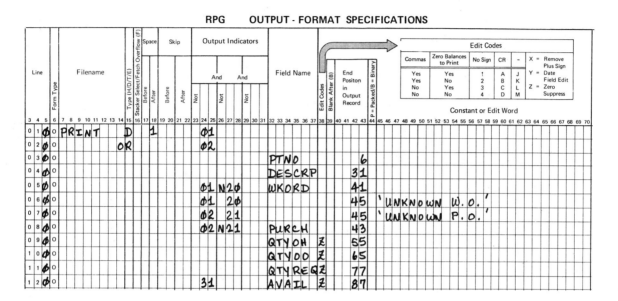

Figure 10-7 Output-Format Specifications

Note in the example above that the detail line will be printed whenever an input card is read, that is, whenever the 01 or 02 Indicator is "on". The Part Number and the Description will always be printed. The Work Order Number will be printed when a Work Order Card is read (01 indicator) and when the Work Order field does not contain blanks (N20). If the Work Order field in the input card contains blanks (indicator 20 "on"), the constant "UNKNOWN W.O." will be printed on the report to indicate that the Work Order field contained blanks. The Purchase Order Number is processed in the same manner, that is, if the Purchase Order field contains blanks, the constant "UNKNOWN P.O." is printed; otherwise, the Purchase Order Number in the card is printed. The Quantity On Hand, the Quantity On Order, and the Quantity Required are all printed each time a card is read. Note that these fields will be in different columns of the input card dependent upon the type of card read but only the field name need be specified on the Output-Format Specifications in order for the field to be printed.

As was noted previously, if the Quantity Required is greater than the sum of the Quantity On Hand and the Quantity On Order, the difference must be the quantity which is to be ordered in order to fill the requirements. If indicator 31 is "on", it means the Quantity Required is greater than the Quantity On Hand and the Quantity On Order (see Figure 10-5). Thus, if indicator 31 is "on", the difference, which is stored in the AVAIL field, will be printed on the report (see Figure 10-7). If indicator 31 is "off", then no value is printed on the report for the quantity ordered field.

If a quantity of parts is to be ordered, a card is punched to reflect this order. The Output-Format Specifications entries for the punched card are illustrated below.

EXAMPLE

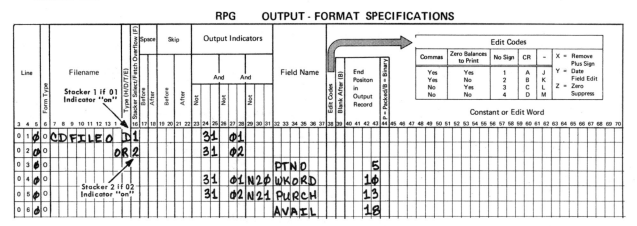

Figure 10-8 Output-Format Specifications

Note in the example above that the card output filename is CDFILEO. It is a detail record which is to be punched and it will be punched if either the 01 and 31 indicators are "on" or if the 02 and 31 indicators are "on". Note the entries in the Stacker Select column (column 16). If the record to be punched is a Work Order Card, the output card will be placed in stacker 1 of the card punch on the 2540. This is indicated by the entry 1 in column 16 on the same coding line as the indicators 31 and 01. The value 2 is entered in column 16 on the same coding line as the indicators 31 and 02. Thus, the Purchase Order Cards, which are identified by the 02 indicator being "on", will be placed in stacker 2 of the 2540 card punch.

The part number will always be punched in the output card, as will the value which is in the AVAIL field. This value is the number of parts which are to be ordered. If the Work Order Number is in the input card, that is, if indicator 20 is not on, the Work Order Number will be punched in the output card. The same is true of the Purchase Order Number.

SAMPLE PROGRAM

The source listing of the program to create the Parts Request List and punch the order card is illustrated below with the output produced.

```
DOS/360*RPG*CL 3-9              CASHMAN              09/12/72           PAGE 0001
           01 010 H                                                    PARTRQ
001        01 020 FCDFILEI IP  F  80  80         READ40 SYSIPT         PARTRQ
002        01 030 FPRINT   O   F 132 132    OF   PRINTERSYSLST         PARTRQ
003        01 040 FCDFILEO O   F  80  80         READ40 SYSPCH         PARTRQ
004        02 010 ICDFILEI AA  01  80 CW                               PARTRQ
005        02 020 I        OR  02  80 CP                               PARTRQ
006        02 030 I                               1   5 PTNO           PARTRQ
007        02 040 I                               6  25 DESCRP         PARTRQ
008        02 050 I                              26  30 WKORD     01  20 PARTRQ
009        02 060 I                              31  35OQTYOH    01    PARTRQ
010        02 070 I                              36  40OQTYOO    01    PARTRQ
011        02 080 I                              41  45OQTYREQ   01    PARTRQ
012        02 090 I                              26  33 PURCH     02  21 PARTRQ
013        02 100 I                              34  38OQTYOH    02    PARTRQ
014        02 110 I                              39  43OQTYOO    02    PARTRQ
015        02 120 I                              44  48OQTYREQ   02    PARTRQ
016        03 010 C         QTYOH    ADD  QTYOO  AVAIL   50            PARTRQ
017        03 020 C         QTYREQ   SUB  AVAIL  AVAIL      31         PARTRQ
018        04 010 OPRINT   H 201     1P                                PARTRQ
019        04 020 O        OR        OF                                PARTRQ
020        04 030 O                      UDATE    9 ' /  / '           PARTRQ
021        04 040 O                              38 'P A R T S'        PARTRQ
022        04 050 O                              53 'R E Q U E S T'    PARTRQ
023        04 060 O                              64 'L I S T'          PARTRQ
024        04 070 O                              81 'PAGE'             PARTRQ
025        04 080 O                      PAGE  Z 86                    PARTRQ
           04 090 O*                                                   PARTRQ
026        04 100 O        H  1      1P                                PARTRQ
027        04 110 O        OR        OF                                PARTRQ
028        04 120 O                               6 'PART'             PARTRQ
029        04 130 O                              46 'W.O. OR P.O.'     PARTRQ
030        04 140 O                              55 'QTY.'             PARTRQ
031        04 150 O                              64 'QTY.'             PARTRQ
032        05 010 O                              76 'QTY.'             PARTRQ
033        05 020 O                              85 'QTY.'             PARTRQ
034        05 030 O        H  2      1P                                PARTRQ
035        05 040 O        OR        OF                                PARTRQ
036        05 050 O                               7 'NUMBER'           PARTRQ
037        05 060 O                              25 'DESCRIPTION'      PARTRQ
038        05 070 O                              42 'NUMBER'           PARTRQ
039        05 080 O                              56 'ON HAND'          PARTRQ
040        05 090 O                              66 'ON ORDER'         PARTRQ
041        05 100 O                              78 'REQUIRED'         PARTRQ
042        05 110 O                              87 'ORDERED'          PARTRQ
           05 120 O*                                                   PARTRQ
043        05 130 O        D  1      01                                PARTRQ
044        05 140 O        OR        02                                PARTRQ
045        05 150 O                      PTNO     6                    PARTRQ
046        06 010 O                      DESCRP  31                    PARTRQ
047        06 020 O              01N20   WKORD   41                    PARTRQ
048        06 030 O              02N21   PURCH   43                    PARTRQ
049        06 040 O              01 20           45 'UNKNOWN W.O.'     PARTRQ
050        06 050 O              02 21           45 'UNKNOWN P.O.'     PARTRQ
051        06 060 O                      QTYOH  Z 55                   PARTRQ
052        06 070 O                      QTYOO  Z 65                   PARTRQ
053        06 080 O                      QTYREQZ  77                   PARTRQ
054        06 090 O              31      AVAIL  Z 87                   PARTRQ
055        06 100 OCDFILEO D1    31 01                                 PARTRQ
056        06 110 O        OR2   31 02                                 PARTRQ
057        06 120 O                      PTNO     5                    PARTRQ
058        06 130 O              31 01N20WKORD   10                    PARTRQ
059        06 140 O              31 02N20PURCH   13                    PARTRQ
060        06 150 O*                     AVAIL  B 18                   PARTRQ
           07 010 O*                                                   PARTRQ
061        07 020 OPRINT   T  2         LR                             PARTRQ
062        07 030 O                              14 'END OF LISTING'   PARTRQ
```

Figure 10-9 Sample Program

10.9

SEQUENCED MULTIPLE RECORD TYPES

In the previous example it was seen how different record types may be read as input from the same file and the processing of these input records may vary dependent upon the type of record which is read. In some applications, there may not only be different record types, but the records must be in a prescribed sequence within a control field. In the sample program to be illustrated, a file of payroll cards are to be read and a Payroll Register report is to be prepared. The file of payroll cards consists of a master card for each employee and one or more timecards indicating the time worked during a week. The format of these two cards is illustrated below.

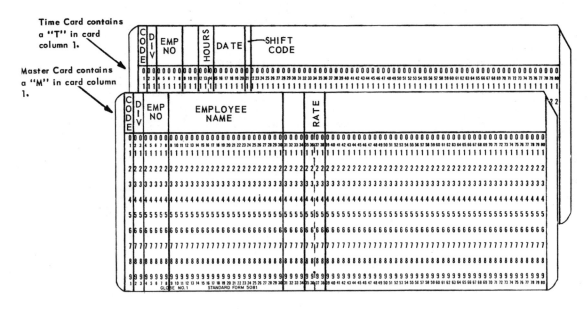

Figure 10-10 Input Card Formats

Note from the card formats illustrated above that the master card contains the code "M" in column 1 and the time card contains the code "T" in column 1. It is these codes which are used to identify the type of card being processed.

Both the master payroll card and the timecard contain the division number (columns 2-3) and the employee number (columns 4-8). The employee number is used as the control field to determine control breaks for the payroll report. The master card also contains the Employee's Name and the Pay Rate of the employee.

The timecard contains, in addition to the fields mentioned above, the hours the employee worked each day, the date, and the shift code. The Payroll Register report which is produced utilizes this information to determine the weekly payroll. The format of the report is illustrated below.

EXAMPLE

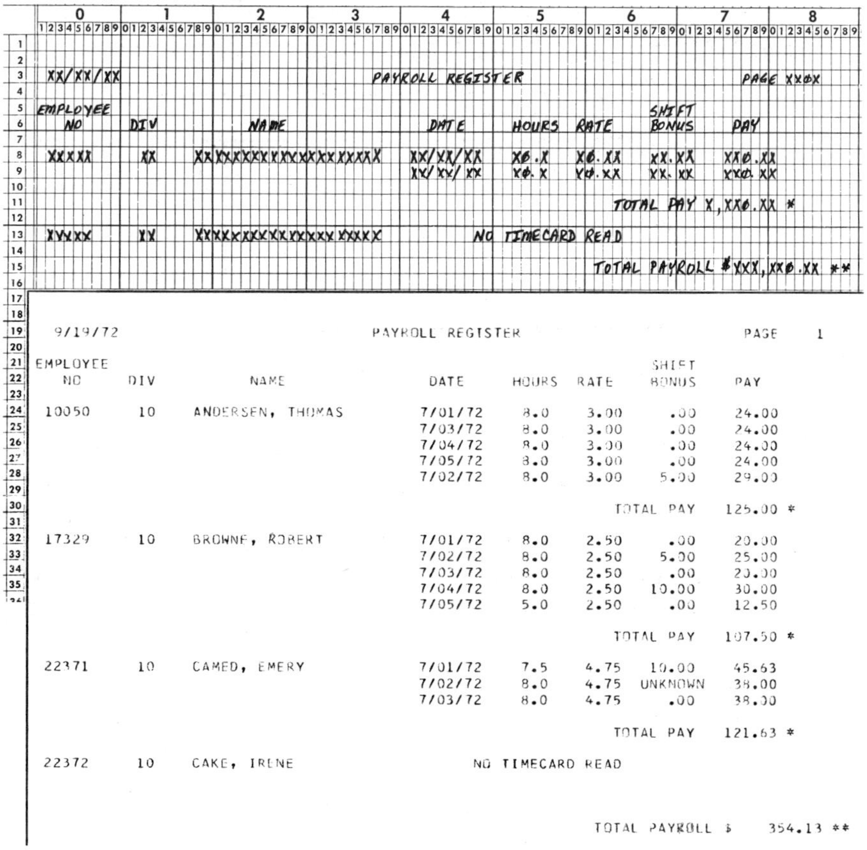

Figure 10-11 Payroll Register Report

Note from the listing illustrated in Figure 10-11 that the Employee Number, Division, and Employee Name, and Rate are printed from the information contained on the master card. The Date and Hours are printed from the Timecard. The pay is calculated by multiplying the hours worked by the pay rate and adding the shift bonus. The shift bonus is 5.00 for the second shift, which is indicated by the value "2" in the Shift Code field in the timecard, and 10.00 for the third shift as indicated by the "3" in the Shift Code field.

Note also that if no timecards are read for a master card which is in the input file, the message "NO TIMECARD READ" is entered on the report for the employee.

INPUT SPECIFICATIONS

In order to process the payroll input cards properly, the cards must be in a specific sequence, that is, each master record must be followed by the timecards for the employee. This sequence is illustrated below.

EXAMPLE

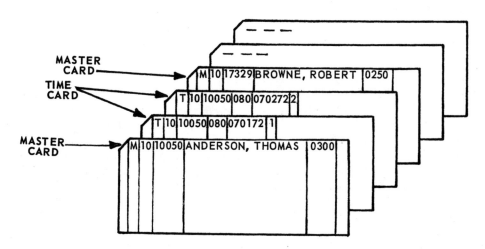

Figure 10-12 Sequence of Input Cards

Note in the example above that the master card for employee 10050 is immediately followed by the timecards for the same employee. After all of the timecards for the employee have been read, the master card for the next employee, 17329, is placed in the input file. Whenever input records must be grouped as illustrated above, the sequence entry on the Input Specifications is used to indicate the sequence of the input records. The Input Specifications used in the sample program are illustrated in Figure 10-13.

EXAMPLE

RPG INPUT SPECIFICATIONS

Line	Form Type	Filename	Sequence	Number (1-N)	Option (O)	Record Identifying Indicator or **	Position (1)	Not (N)	C/Z/D	Character	Position (2)	Not (N)	C/Z/D	Character	Position (3)	Not (N)	C/Z/D	Character	Stacker Select	P = Packed/B = Binary	From	To	Decimal Positions	Field Name	Control Level (L1-L9)	Matching Fields or Chaining Fields	Field Record Relation	Plus	Minus	Zero or Blank
01	I	CARDINP	01	1		01	1		C	M									2											
02	I																				2	3		DIV						
03	I																				4	8		EMPNO	L1					
04	I																				11	30		NAME						
05	I																				35	38	2	RATE						
06	I		02	N		02	1		C	T									1											
07	I																				2	3		DIV						
08	I																				4	8		EMPNO	L1					
09	I																				12	14	1	HOURS						
10	I																				15	20	0	DATE						
11	I																				21	21		SHIFT						

Annotations on form:
- Master identified by "M"
- Place Master cards in Stacker 2
- Master must be first within Control Group
- Only one Master card for each Control Group
- Timecard identified by "T"
- Timecards are optional
- Place Timecards in Stacker 1
- may be 1 or more Timecards

Figure 10-13 Input Specifications

Note from the Input Specifications illustrated above that the filename of the input file which contains the Master Payroll cards and the Timecards is CARDINP. It will be recalled in previous programs that alphabetic values were entered in the Sequence field of the Input Specifications (columns 15-16). In this program, however, numeric values are placed in this field because the Sequence field is used to specify the sequence within a control group where the card must be placed. A control group is considered all of the input records which belong to a given control field within a record. Thus, all input records with the same Employee Number are in the same control group. Note in Figure 10-13 that the Employee Number field (EMPNO) is the field with the control level indicator (L1). As noted in Figure 10-12, within each control group, the Master Payroll card must be first followed by one or more Timecards. Thus, the value 01 is entered in columns 15-16 for the Master Payroll card, which is identified by the character "M" in column 1 (columns 24-27 on Input Specifications form). The value 02 is entered in columns 15-16 for the Timecard because the timecards are to be the second cards within the control group. Whenever a numeric value is entered in the Sequence field on the Input Specifications form, the first value must be equal to 01 and each additional value must be incremented by 1. Thus, if there were four cards within each control group, they would have a Sequence value of 01, 02, 03, and 04. In addition, the record descriptions must be in the same sequence as the Sequence number.

It will be recalled also that when an alphabetic value was entered in the Sequence field, the Number field (column 17) and the Option field (column 18) were left blank. When a numeric value is entered in the Sequence field, that is, when the input records must be in a given sequence within a control group, these two fields must have entries. The Number field (column 17) is used to specify the number of records of the type specified which will be found within a control group. There are two possible values which may be specified — the number "1" is entered in column 17 if there will be only 1 record of the type defined within each control group, or the letter of the alphabet "N", which indicates the possibility of one or more records within the control group. Since, as was mentioned previously, there is only one Payroll Master card for each control group, the value "1" is entered in column 17 for the Master card.

There may be one or more Time cards for each employee which is to be processed, that is, for each master card within a control group, there may be one or more Time cards. Thus, the other valid entry, the letter "N", is placed in column 17 for the timecards. This entry indicates that one or more timecards will be found in the input file for each Master card.

As was noted, there must be a Payroll Master card for each employee. Whenever a card is absolutely required, the Option field (column 18) is left blank on the Input Specifications form. Thus, as can be seen in Figure 10-13, column 18 is blank for the Payroll Master card. The Time cards, on the other hand, need not always be present, that is, if an employee did not work for any given week, there would be a master card for him but no timecards. Whenever an input record is optional within a control group, the alphabetic value "O" is entered in column 18. This indicates that it is possible that a Payroll Master card will be read without any timecards. It must be noted, however, that it is not possible to have timecards without a master card because column 18 is blank for the master card, indicating that one must be present.

The record identifying indicator specified for the master card and the timecard are used in the same manner as has been done previously, that is, the 01 indicator will be turned "on" when a master card is read and the 02 indicator will be turned "on" when a timecard is read. These indicators may, of course, be tested in both the calculation specifications and the output specifications.

Note also in the example in Figure 10-13 that entries have been included in the Stacker Select portion of the form (column 42). The Stacker Select field is used to specify the stacker into which the cards will be placed after they are read. In the example, the master cards will be placed in Stacker 2 and the Time cards will be placed in Stacker 1. This effectively separates the master records from the timecards so that the master records may be retained for the next computer run and the timecards may be placed in a storage area.

CALCULATION SPECIFICATIONS

In order to calculate the weekly pay for an employee, the hours worked on each time-card must be multipled by the pay rate of each employee. This value is added to any bonus pay which is earned by the employee. This daily pay is then added to a counter until all of the timecards for a given employee have been processed. The total of the daily pay is the weekly pay. The entries on the Calculation Specifications to determine the weekly pay of an employee are illustrated below.

EXAMPLE

RPG   CALCULATION SPECIFICATIONS

Line	Form Type	Control Level (L0-L9, LR, SR)	Indicators And Not	And Not	And Not	Factor 1	Operation	Factor 2	Result Field	Field Length	Decimal Positions	Half Adjust (H)	Resulting Indicators Arithmetic Plus High 1>2	Minus Low 1<2 Lookup	Zero Equal 1=2	Comments
0 1	∅ C		02			HOURS	MULT	RATE	DAYPAY	5 2		H				GET BASIC PAY
0 2	∅ C		02			SHIFT	COMP	'2'						30		IF SECOND SHIFT
0 3	∅ C		02	30		DAYPAY	ADD	5.∅∅	DAYPAY							ADD 5.∅∅
0 4	∅ C		02	30			GOTO	OKSHFT								
0 5	∅ C		02			SHIFT	COMP	'3'						31		IF THIRD SHIFT
0 6	∅ C		02	31		DAYPAY	ADD	1∅.∅∅	DAYPAY							ADD 1∅.∅∅
0 7	∅ C		02	31			GOTO	OKSHFT								
0 8	∅ C		02			SHIFT	COMP	'1'					33	33	33	IF NOT = 1,
0 9	∅ C					OKSHFT	TAG									UNKNOWN SHIFT
1 0	∅ C		02			WEKPAY	ADD	DAYPAY	WEKPAY	6 2						ACCUMULATE PAY
1 1	∅ C	L1				TOTPAY	ADD	WEKPAY	TOTPAY	8 2						ADD TO FINAL

Figure 10-14 Calculation Specifications

The first step in the Calculation Specifications illustrated above is to multiply the hours worked, which is found on the Time card, by the pay rate, which is found on the master card. Note that this calculation will be performed when indicator 02 is "on", that is, when a timecard is read. No calculations are performed when a master card is read because all of the data for the calculations has not been read. It should be recalled, however, that the data in the master card for the pay rate will be stored in the input field named RATE and that this data is available until another master card is read. Thus, even though a timecard is read which does not contain the rate, the value is still available in the RATE field and may be used in any calculations and also may be specified on the Output-Format Specifications.

After the basic pay is calculated, the timecard is checked to determine if the employee worked the second or third shift. If he worked the second shift, he is entitled to a $5.00 bonus and if he worked the third shift, he is entitled to a $10.00 bonus. The shift is determined by comparing the value in the SHIFT field on the timecard to the constants "2", "3", and "1". Note on coding line 020 that indicator 30 will be turned "on" if the value in the SHIFT field is equal to '2'. If it is not equal, no indicators will be turned "on". If the shift field does contain the value "2", it means that the employee is entitled to a $5.00 bonus, which must be added to the field DAYPAY. Thus, as can be seen from the coding on line 030, if the indicator 30 is "on", then the value 5.00 is added to the DAYPAY field.

Once it has been determined that the shift code is equal to '2' and the 5.00 bonus has been added to the DAYPAY field, there is no need to check the value in the SHIFT field further. Thus, it is desired to bypass the instructions which test for a code of '3' and a code of '1'. In order to bypass a sequence of instructions on the Calculation Specifications, the GOTO and TAG statements are utilized. The example below illustrates the effect of the GOTO and TAG statements in the example in Figure 10-14.

EXAMPLE

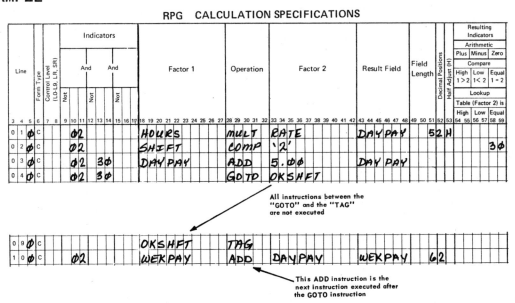

Figure 10-15 Example of the Use of the GOTO and TAG Statements

The GOTO instruction is used to cause a transfer of control from the point at which it is specified to the instruction following the named TAG statement. In the example above it can be seen that the GOTO instruction must have the operation code in columns 28-31. The indicators which are specified are used to determine when the GOTO instruction is to take place. As was noted, the GOTO instruction is to take place only when the 02 and 30 indicators are "on". The name which is entered in the Factor 2 field, OKSHFT, is the name which is associated with a TAG statement somewhere within the calculation specifications.

As can be seen, line 090 contains the name OKSHFT in the Factor 1 field of the form (columns 18-23) and the word TAG in the operation code field. The tag statement is used to identify a point within the calculation specifications where control is to be passed from a GOTO statement. It is not an executable statement, that is, no processing takes place as a result of the TAG statement. It merely serves to identify the point to where control is to be passed. The instruction which will be executed after the GOTO instruction is the ADD instruction on line 100 because it is the instruction which immediately follows the TAG statement.

10.16

The GOTO instruction and TAG statement are normally used when it is desired to bypass a series of instructions which would either have no meaning if executed, such as the subsequent compare instructions in the example in Figure 10-14, or that would cause incorrect results to be produced if they were executed. It will be noted that the proper indicators could be specified in columns 9-17 to indicate which instructions should be executed and which should not be executed depending upon the results of previous instructions. Although this will work properly, it is recommended that, in most instances, the GOTO and TAG statements be used rather than indicators because a more efficient object program will be produced by the RPG compiler. This is especially true when a series of instructions are to be bypassed within the calculation specifications, such as in the example in Figure 10-14.

As noted, the GOTO instruction will take place only when the specified indicators are "on". If the indicator conditions are not satisfied, the GOTO instruction will not take place and the COMP statement on line 050 (Figure 10-14) will take place. This statement is used to determine if the value in the SHIFT field is equal to '3', which indicates the employee worked the third shift. If it is equal to '3', the value 10.00 is added to the DAYPAY field because an employee who works the third shift is entitled to a $10.00 bonus. Note that indicator 31 is turned "on" if the shift code is equal to '3' and this will allow both the addition of the 10.00 to the DAYPAY field and the GOTO statement on line 070 to be executed. If the shift code is not equal to '3', then the GOTO statement on line 070 will not be executed and the COMP statement on line 080 will be executed.

If the shift code is not equal to '3', then the COMP instruction on line 080 will be executed to determine if the shift code is equal to '1'. It will be recalled that the only valid shift codes are 1, 2, or 3. Thus, this comparison will ensure that the value in the SHIFT field is a valid shift code. If the code is equal to '1', indicator 32 will be turned "on". If it is not equal to '1', then indicator 33 will be turned "on". Thus, when indicator 33 is "on", it indicates that an invalid shift code has been punched in the SHIFT field in the timecard. The purpose of the compare instruction on line 080 is merely to ensure that a valid shift code is found. No value is added to the DAYPAY field because an employee working the first shift is not entitled to any bonus.

After the shift code has been checked and the proper processing executed, the value in the DAYPAY field, which contains the daily pay for an employee, is added to the WEKPAY field, which is used to accumulate the daily pay. Also, as can be seen from Figure 10-14, when an L1 control break occurs, the weekly pay for an employee will be added to the TOTPAY field which accumulates all of the salaries paid to be printed at the end of the program.

OUTPUT SPECIFICATIONS

The output specifications define the heading lines of the report, the detail lines, which include the information from the master cards and the timecards, and the total line which prints the weekly pay for each employee. The entries for the detail lines are illustrated below.

EXAMPLE

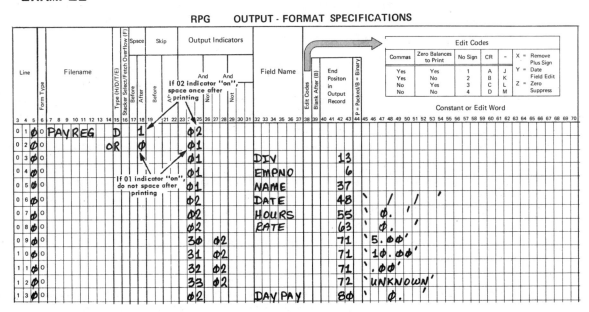

Figure 10-16 Output-Format Specifications

In the example above it can be seen that a detail line will be printed if either the 01 indicator or the 02 indicator are "on", that is, whenever a master card or a timecard are read. The output indicators for each field indicate when the field will be printed. Thus, the DIV field, the EMPNO field, and the NAME field will be printed when the master card is read and the remainder of the fields will be printed when the 02 is "on". The bonus amount which will be printed on the report is dependent upon the results of the Compare instructions executed on the Calculation specifications. Note that if the shift code is not equal to 1, 2, or 3, the constant "UNKNOWN" will be printed for the Shift bonus.

Whenever two different types of records are to be read and processed, such as in the sample program, this must be considered when group indicating the report. As will be recalled, the control break must always be caused by a Master card. Thus, the control break will only occur when the 01 indicator is "on". All of the information which is to be printed on the first detail line after a control break is, however, not all contained in the card which causes the control break, that is, the date, hours, etc. for the first detail line of a new employee is not contained on the master card. Therefore, in order to have the Division, Employee Number and Employee Name on the same print line as the Date, Hours, etc. for the first timecard, the printer should not be spaced one line after printing the Divison, Employee Number, and Name. It should be printed without any spacing. This is illustrated in Figure 10-17.

EXAMPLE

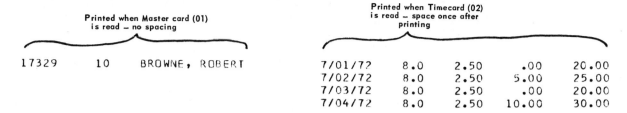

Printed when Master card (01) is read — no spacing

17329   10   BROWNE, ROBERT

Printed when Timecard (02) is read — space once after printing

7/01/72	8.0	2.50	.00	20.00
7/02/72	8.0	2.50	5.00	25.00
7/03/72	8.0	2.50	.00	20.00
7/04/72	8.0	2.50	10.00	30.00

Figure 10-17   Group-Indicated Printout

Note in the example above that Employee Number, the Division, and the Employee Name are on the same print line as the Date, Hours, Pay Rate, Bonus Pay, and Daily Pay which is printed when a timecard is read. Note that if the printer were spaced once after the 01 detail line was printed, these fields would not be on the same print line.

In order to cause different spacing for a detail line dependent upon the indicator which is "on", the number of lines to be spaced is entered in column 18 (Space After) on the same line as the indicator to which it pertains. Thus, as can be seen in Figure 10-16, the value "1" is placed in column 18 on the same coding line as the Output Indicator 02 and the value "0" is placed in column 18 on the same coding line as the Output Indicator 01. The detail line will be printed if either the 01 indicator or the 02 indicator are "on", but the printer will not be spaced if the 01 Indicator is "on" and will be if the 02 indicator is "on".

SETON AND SETOF INSTRUCTIONS

In the previous programs, it has been seen how indicators are used to indicate certain conditions within the program. The indicators have been set "on" and "off" by the types of input records which have been read, the values in certain fields within the input record, the results of compare instructions or arithmetic instructions, and by control breaks encountered in input data. In addition, RPG allows the programmer to turn "on" and turn "off" indicators. This is accomplished through the use of the SETON and SETOF instructions which are specified on the Calculation Specifications form. The use of these two instructions is illustrated below.

EXAMPLE

RPG   CALCULATION SPECIFICATIONS

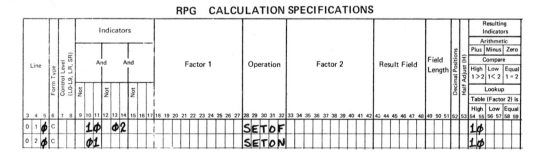

Figure 10-18   Example of SETOF and SETON Instructions

In order to turn an indicator "off", the SETOF instruction is used. As can be seen from the example in Figure 10-18, the operation code SETOF is placed in the Operation portion of the form (columns 28-32). The indicator(s) to be turned off are specified in "Resulting Indicators" portion of the form (columns 54-59). In the example, it can be seen that indicator 10 is specified in columns 54-55. Thus, indicator 10 will be turned "off" when the instruction is executed. It should be noted that one SETOF instruction may be used to turn off a maximum of three indicators (columns 54-55, 56-57, 58-59). The SETOF instruction in Figure 10-18 will be executed only when the indicators 10 and 02 are "on". Thus, the "Indicators" field on the Calculation Specifications (columns 9-17) operate for the SETOF and SETON instructions in the same manner as for all other instructions, that is, they specify when an instruction will be executed.

The SETON instruction is written in the same format of the SETOF instruction but it turns an indicator "on" instead of turning it "off". Thus, as can be seen from the example in Figure 10-18, when the 01 indicator is "on", the SETON instruction will be used to set indicator 10 "on".

It will be recalled that the possibility exists that there may be a master card in the input file without any corresponding time cards. The SETON and SETOF instructions in the sample program are used to indicate this situation. The example in Figure 10-19 illustrates the input file without any timecards for an employee and the indicator settings which would take place as a result of reading the input file and also the SETON and SETOF instructions illustrated in Figure 10-18.

EXAMPLE

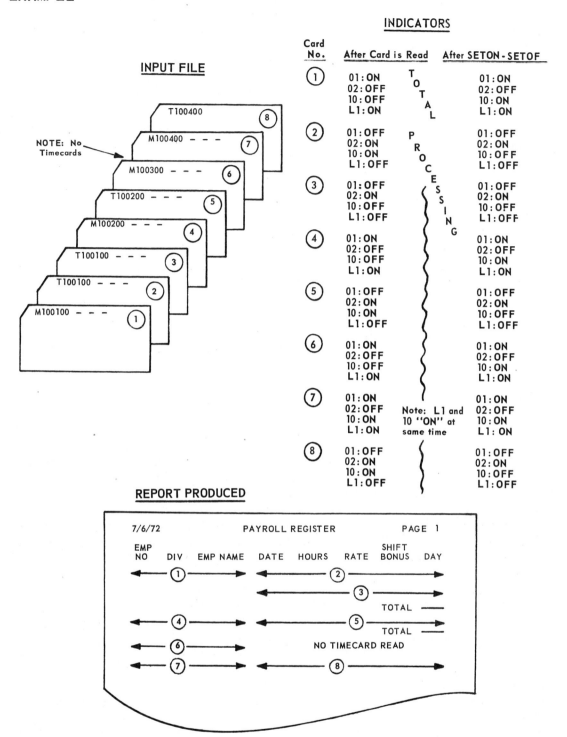

Figure 10-19 Use of SETON and SETOF Instructions

10.21

In the example in Figure 10-19 it can be seen that a portion of the input file is illustrated together with a portion of the output report and the indicator settings both immediately after an input card is read and after the total processing and detail calculations have been performed.

The basic intent of the use of the SETON and SETOF instructions in the example is to determine when two master cards are read without any intervening timecards. Thus, the technique used is to turn on indicator 10 when a master card (01 indicator) is read. When a timecard is read, indicator 10 is turned "off". Since the master card (01) is the only legitimate card which can cause an L1 control break, the absence of a timecard can be indicated by indicator 10 being "on" at L1 control break time.

A step-by-step examination of the example in Figure 10-19 will clarify the use of the SETON and SETOF instructions in indicating the absence of a timecard.

1. When the first master record is read, the 01 indicator is turned "on". The L1 indicator is also turned on when the first card is read but total processing is bypassed on the first card. When the detail calculations are performed, indicator 10 is turned "on" because the 01 indicator is "on" (see Figure 10-18).

2. When the timecard is read, indicator 02 is turned "on" and, of course, indicator 01 is turned "off". Note also that indicator 10 is still "on", as it has not been turned "off". No total processing is performed because the L1 indicator is turned "off" and when the detail calculations are performed, indicator 10 will be turned "off" (see Figure 10-18 line 010).

As can be seen from this example, it is necessary for the programmer to have a basic understanding of the sequences of events which occur within the RPG fixed logic. Again, the basic steps are as follows: A) An input record is read and the corresponding indicator is turned "on"; B) A check for a control break is performed and if one has occurred, the corresponding control level indicator(s) is turned "on"; C) The total time calculations are performed; D) The total time output is performed; E) The detail time calculations performed; F) The detail time output is written. Control is then returned to step A and another card is read. If this basic sequence of operation is kept in mind, the programmer should have little trouble in determining the sequence of processing and when indicators will be turned "on" and turned "off".

3. When the second timecard is read, the 02 indicator is again "on" and, since, indicator 10 was set off in step 2 above, it will remain "off".

4. When the fourth card is read, it is found that it is a master card. Thus, indicator 01 will be turned "on" to indicate that a master card has been read. In addition, the L1 indicator will be turned "on" because a control break occurs when a new master card with a new employee number is read. Thus, when the total output takes place, the L1 and 01 indicators are "on". Note that the 10 indicator is "off" because it was turned "off" when an 02 record was read and will not be turned back "on" until the detail time calculations for the 01 record are performed. Since the total time output is performed before the detail time calculations, the indicator 10 will be "off" when the total time output is written on the report.

After the total time output is written on the report, the detail calculations are performed at which time indicator 10 is turned "on" by the SETON instruction. The detail output is then written without spacing any lines because the 01 indicator is "on".

5. When the timecard is read, no total processing takes place because the timecard will have the same employee number as the master card. Therefore, the detail calculations are performed and indicator 10 will be turned "off" because it is always turned "off" when an 02 record is read. The detail output corresponding to the 02 indicator will then be written on the report.

6. When the master card for employee 100300 is read, indicator 01 will be turned "on" as well as the control level indicator L1 because a control break will occur. Thus, the total time calculations and output will again take place before the detail calculations and the detail output. Note in this situation again that indicator 10 will be "off" during total time processing because it was turned "off" when the timecard (indicator 02) was read and processed. After the total processing indicator 10 is set "on" and the detail output for an 01 record will be written.

7. When the master card for employee 100400 is read, it can be seen that no timecards for employee 100300 were read. In this situation, it is desired to print the message NO TIMECARD READ on the report on the same line as the Employee Number, the Division and the Employee Name which were printed in Step 6.

Since a timecard has not been read, indicator 10, which was set "on" in Step 6 will still be "on" when the total routine for employee 100300 is entered as a result of reading the master card for employee 100400. Thus, as can be seen, if indicator 10 is "on" when the total output routines are processed, it means that no timecards were read for the master record whose totals are to be printed. Therefore, by checking the status of indicator 10 in the total output routine, it can be determined whether or not timecards are read. The entries on the Output-Format Specifications to make this determination are illustrated below.

EXAMPLE

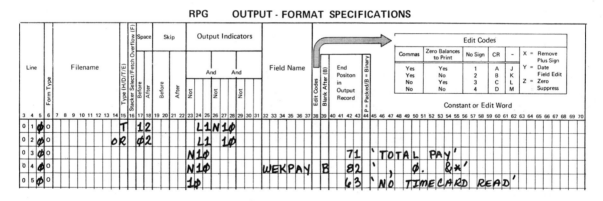

Figure 10-20 Output Specifications for Total Processing

Note in the example above that a total line will be printed if the L1 indicator is "on" and indicator 10 is "off" or if the L1 indicator is "on" and indicator 10 is "on". The spacing for these two conditions is to be different. If indicator 10 is not "on", the printer will be spaced one line before printing and two lines after printing. If indicator 10 is "on", the printer will not be spaced before printing the message "NO TIMECARD READ". This is to ensure that the "no timecard" message is on the same print line as the employee number, employee name, and division which are printed when the master card is read. The printer will be spaced two lines after the message is printed.

After the total printing has been completed, the detail printing of the master record for employee 100400 is accomplished and then the timecard for employee 100400 (card #8) is read and processed as has been illustrated. From this example it can be seen that the SETON and SETOF instructions may be used to indicate various conditions which occur during the processing of the program. In some processing situations, they prove very useful.

COMMENTS

As noted previously, comments may be included on the Calculation Specifications form in order to specify the processing which is to occur. RPG also allows comments on any of the programming forms through the use of the Asterisk (*) entry in column 7 of each form. This is illustrated in the example below.

EXAMPLE

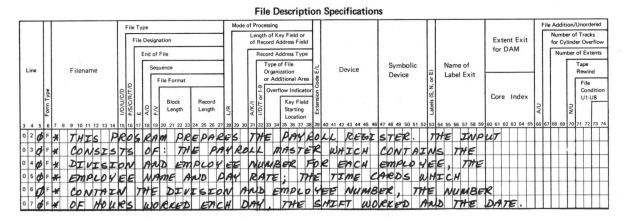

Figure 10-21 Example of the Use of Comment Lines

Note in the example above that each of the comment lines contains an asterisk (*) in column 7. The asterisk indicates to the RPG compiler that the line is to be treated as a comment line and is not to contain any RPG source coding. When a comment line is included on any of the RPG coding forms, it is printed on the source listing created by the RPG compiler but the information on the comment line has no bearing on the program which is generated by the compiler.

SUMMARY

It becomes readily apparent that as programming problems become more complex, the RPG programmer must learn the effective use of the various indicators that may be used to control operations. It is for this reason that the sample programs illustrated in this chapter should be carefully analyzed and thoroughly understood.

Sample Problem

The following is the computer listing of the RPG program to produce the Payroll Register.

```
DOS/360*RPG*CL 3-9              CASHMAN              09/19/72          PAGE 0001

        01 010 H                                                      PAYREG
        01 020 F*                                                     PAYREG
        01 030 F* THIS PROGRAM PREPARES THE PAYROLL REGISTER. THE INPUT    PAYREG
        01 040 F* CONSISTS OF: THE PAYROLL MASTER CARD WHICH CONTAINS THE  PAYREG
        01 050 F* DIVISION AND EMPLOYEE NUMBER FOR EACH EMPLOYEE, THE      PAYREG
        01 060 F* EMPLOYEE NAME AND THE PAY RATE; THE TIME CARDS WHICH     PAYREG
        01 070 F* CONTAIN THE DIVISION AND EMPLOYEE NUMBER, THE NUMBER     PAYREG
        01 080 F* OF HOURS WORKED EACH DAY, THE SHIFT WORKED AND THE DATE. PAYREG
        01 090 F*                                                     PAYREG
        01 100 F*                                                     PAYREG
001     01 110 FCARDINP IP  F  80  80            READ40 SYSIPT        PAYREG
002     01 120 FPAYREG   O   F 132 132      OF    PRINTERSYSLST       PAYREG
003     02 010 ICARDINP  011 01   1 CM          2                    PAYREG
004     02 020 I                                      2   3 DIV      PAYREG
005     02 030 I                                      4   8 EMPNO L1 PAYREG
006     02 040 I                                     11  30 NAME     PAYREG
007     02 050 I                                     35  38 2RATE    PAYREG
        02 060 I*                                                    PAYREG
008     02 070 I            02NO02   1 CT         1                  PAYREG
009     02 080 I                                      2   3 DIV      PAYREG
010     02 090 I                                      4   8 EMPNO L1 PAYREG
011     02 100 I                                     12  14 1HOURS   PAYREG
012     02 110 I                                     15  20 0DATE    PAYREG
013     02 120 I                                     21  21 SHIFT    PAYREG
014     03 010 C   10 02          SETOF                    10        PAYREG
015     03 020 C   01N02          SETON                    10        PAYREG
016     03 030 C   02       HOURS MULT RATE      DAYPAY  52H         PAYREG
017     03 040 C   02       SHIFT COMP '2'                30         PAYREG
018     03 050 C   02 30    DAYPAY ADD 5.00      DAYPAY              PAYREG
019     03 060 C   02 30           GOTO OKSHFT                       PAYREG
020     03 070 C   02       SHIFT COMP '3'                31         PAYREG
021     03 080 C   02 31    DAYPAY ADD 10.00     DAYPAY              PAYREG
022     03 090 C   02 31           GOTO OKSHFT                       PAYREG
023     03 100 C   02       SHIFT COMP '1'                333332     PAYREG
024     03 110 C   02       OKSHFT TAG                                PAYREG
025     03 120 C   02       WEKPAY ADD DAYPAY    WEKPAY  62          PAYREG
026     03 130 CL1          TOTPAY ADD WEKPAY    TOTPAY  82          PAYREG
027     04 010 OPAYREG  H  201        1P                             PAYREG
028     04 020 O        OR            OF                             PAYREG
029     04 030 O                            UDATE    9 ' / / '       PAYREG
030     04 040 O                                    52 'PAYROLL REGISTER'  PAYREG
031     04 050 O                                    80 'PAGE'        PAYREG
032     04 060 O                            PAGE Z  85               PAYREG
033     04 070 O        H  1         1P                              PAYREG
034     04 080 O        OR            OF                             PAYREG
035     04 090 O                                    08 'EMPLOYEE'    PAYREG
036     04 100 O                                    71 'SHIFT'       PAYREG
037     04 110 O        H  2         1P                              PAYREG
038     04 120 O        OR            OF                             PAYREG
039     04 130 O                                    13 'DIV'         PAYREG
040     04 140 O                                    05 'NO'          PAYREG
041     04 150 O                                    27 'NAME'        PAYREG
042     05 010 O                                    46 'DATE'        PAYREG
043     05 020 O                                    55 'HOURS'       PAYREG
044     05 030 O                                    62 'RATE'        PAYREG
045     05 040 O                                    71 'BONUS'       PAYREG
046     05 050 O                                    78 'PAY'         PAYREG
047     05 060 O        D  1         02                              PAYREG
048     05 070 O        OR  0        01                              PAYREG
049     05 080 O                            01  DIV     13           PAYREG
050     05 090 O                            01  EMPNO   06           PAYREG
051     05 100 O                            01  NAME    37           PAYREG
052     05 110 O                            02  DATE    48 ' / / '   PAYREG
053     05 120 O                            02  HOURS   55 ' 0. '    PAYREG
054     05 130 O                            02  RATE    63 ' 0. '    PAYREG
055     05 140 O                            30 02       71 '5.00'    PAYREG
056     05 150 O                            31 02       71 '10.00'   PAYREG
057     06 010 O                            32 02       71 '.00'     PAYREG
058     06 020 O                            33 02       72 'UNKNOWN' PAYREG
059     06 030 O                            02  DAYPAY  80 ' 0. '    PAYREG
        06 040 O*                                                    PAYREG
060     06 050 O        T  12        L1N10                           PAYREG
061     06 060 O        OR 02        L1 10                           PAYREG
062     06 070 O                            L1N10      71 'TOTAL PAY' PAYREG
063     06 080 O                            L1N10 WEKPAY B 82 ',  0. &*' PAYREG
064     06 090 O*                           10         63 'NO TIMECARD READ' PAYREG
        06 100 O*                                                    PAYREG
065     06 110 O        T  2         LR                              PAYREG
066     06 120 O                                       73 'TOTAL PAYROLL' PAYREG
067     06 130 O                            TOTPAY     88 '$  ,  0. &**' PAYREG
```

Figure 10-22 Source Listing

CHAPTER 10

REVIEW QUESTIONS

1. Explain the differences between the Record Identifying Indicators, the Field Record Relation Indicators, and the Field Indicators.

2. If the input records are to be in a specified sequence within control group, what three fields must be used in the Input Specifications? What entries go in each of these fields?

3. Must the TAG statement which is referrenced in a GOTO statement always follow the GOTO statement on the Calculation Specifications coding form? Why?

4. Why are the SETON and SETOF instructions used in a program?

CHAPTER 10

STUDENT EXERCISES

1. Write the Input Specifications to define the two input cards which will be read from the CARDSIN file.

Balance Card: Col 1 — "B"
Col 2-6: Department Number — cannot be blank — is the L1 control level field.
Col 10-15: Balance — format is XXXX.XX — will be used in arithmetic operations — cannot be blank or contain a value of zero.

Transaction Card: Col 1 — "T"
Col 2-6: Department Number — cannot be blank — is the L1 control level field.
Col 25-30: Invoice Amount — format is XXXX.XX — will be used in arithmetic operations — cannot be blank or contain a value of zero.

There will be one Balance card for each department and it will be the first card within the control group. There may be one or more Transaction Cards. There must be at least one transaction card. Any errors which occur, that is, invalid fields in the input, will be printed on the report which is generated by the program.

RPG INPUT SPECIFICATIONS

Line	Form Type	Filename	Sequence	Number (1-N)	Option (O)	Record Identifying Indicator or **	Position 1	Not (N)	C/Z/D	Character	Position 2	Not (N)	C/Z/D	Character	Position 3	Not (N)	C/Z/D	Character	Stacker Select P = Packed/B = Binary	From	To	Decimal Positions	Field Name	Control Level (L1-L9)	Matching Fields or Chaining Fields	Field Record Relation	Plus	Minus	Zero or Blank
0 1	I																												
0 2	I																												
0 3	I																												
0 4	I																												
0 5	I																												
0 6	I																												
0 7	I																												
0 8	I																												
0 9	I																												
1 0	I																												
1 1	I																												
1 2	I																												
1 3	I																												
1 4	I																												
1 5	I																												

2. Write the instructions to set on indicator 45 if indicator 98 is "off" and to set off indicator 98 if it is "on".

RPG   CALCULATION SPECIFICATIONS

Line	Form Type	Control Level (L0-L9, LR, SR)	Indicators And Not	And Not	And Not	Factor 1	Operation	Factor 2	Result Field	Field Length	Decimal Positions	Half Adjust (H)	Resulting Indicators Arithmetic Plus/High 1>2	Minus/Low 1<2	Zero/Equal 1=2
0 1	C														
0 2	C														
0 3	C														
0 4	C														
0 5	C														
0 6	C														
0 7	C														

3. Write the instructions on the Calculation Specifications to bypass the operations in Exercise #2 if indicator 32 is "on" and indicator 87 if "off".

RPG   CALCULATION SPECIFICATIONS

Line	Form Type	Control Level (L0-L9, LR, SR)	Indicators And Not	And Not	And Not	Factor 1	Operation	Factor 2	Result Field	Field Length	Decimal Positions	Half Adjust (H)	Resulting Indicators Arithmetic Plus/High 1>2	Minus/Low 1<2	Zero/Equal 1=2
0 1	C														
0 2	C														
0 3	C														
0 4	C														
0 5	C														
0 6	C														

10.28

Debugging RPG Programs

Problem 1

Instructions: The following RPG program contains an error or errors which have occurred
during compilation. Circle each error and record the corrected entries
directly on the listing. Explain the error and method of correction in the
space provided below.

```
DOS/360*RPG*CL 3-9               CASHMAN                    10/10/72           PAGE 0001

          01 010 H                                                              PARTRQ
001       01 020 FCDFILEI IP  F  80  80          READ40 SYSIPT                  PARTRQ
002       01 030 FPRINT    O  F 132 132    OF    PRINTERSYSLST                  PARTRQ
003       01 040 FCDFILEU O   F  80  80          READ40 SYSPCH                  PARTRQ
004       02 010 ICDFILEI AA  01  80 CW                                         PARTRQ
005       02 020 I          OR 02  80 CP                                        PARTRQ
006       02 030 I                                    1   5 PTNO                PARTRQ
007       02 040 I                                    6  25 DESCRP              PARTRQ
008       02 050 I                                   26  30 WKORD       01   20 PARTRQ
009       02 060 I                                   31  35 0QTYOH      01      PARTRQ
010       02 070 I                                   36  40 0QTYOO      01      PARTRQ
011       02 080 I                                   41  45 0QTYREQ     01      PARTRQ
012       02 090 I                                   26  33 PURCH       02      PARTRQ
013       02 100 I                                   34  38 0QTYOH      02      PARTRQ
014       02 110 I                                   39  43 0QTYOO      02      PARTRQ
015       02 120 I                                   44  48 0QTYREQ     02      PARTRQ
016       03 010 C              QTYOH    ADD  QTYOO   AVAIL   50                 PARTRQ
017       03 020 C              QTYREQ   SUB  AVAIL   AVAIL        31            PARTRQ
018       04 010 OPRINT     H  201     1P                                       PARTRQ
019       04 020 O          OR         OF                                       PARTRQ
020       04 030 O                               UDATE     9 ' / / '            PARTRQ
021       04 040 O                                        38 'P A R T S'        PARTRQ
022       04 050 O                                        53 'R E Q U E S T'    PARTRQ
023       04 060 O                                        64 'L I S T'          PARTRQ
024       04 070 O                                        81 'PAGE'             PARTRQ
025       04 080 O                               PAGE  Z   86 ' '               PARTRQ
                                                                                NOTE 178
          04 090 O*                                                             PARTRQ
026       04 100 O          H  1      1P                                        PARTRQ
027       04 110 O          OR         OF                                       PARTRQ
028       04 120 O                                         6 'PART'             PARTRQ
029       04 130 O                                        46 'W.O. OR P.O.'     PARTRQ
030       04 140 O                                        55 'QTY.'             PARTRQ
031       04 150 O                                        64 'QTY.'             PARTRQ
032       05 010 O                                        76 'QTY.'             PARTRQ
033       05 020 O                                        85 'QTY.'             PARTRQ
034       05 030 O          H  2      1P                                        PARTRQ
035       05 040 O          OR         OF                                       PARTRQ
036       05 050 O                                         7 'NUMBER'           PARTRQ
037       05 060 O                                        25 'DESCRIPTION'      PARTRQ
038       05 070 O                                        42 'NUMBER'           PARTRQ
039       05 080 O                                        56 'ON HAND'          PARTRQ
040       05 090 O                                        66 'ON ORDER'         PARTRQ
041       05 100 O                                        78 'REQUIRED'         PARTRQ
042       05 110 O                                        87 'ORDERED'          PARTRQ
          05 120 O*                                                             PARTRQ
043       05 130 O          D  1      01                                        PARTRQ
044       05 140 O          OR         02                                       PARTRQ
045       05 150 O                               PTNO      6                    PARTRQ
046       06 010 O                               DESCRP   31                    PARTRQ
047       06 020 O                       01N20   WKORD    41                    PARTRQ
048       06 030 O                       02N21   PURCH    43                    PARTRQ
                                                                                NOTE 192
049       06 040 O                       01 20            45 'UNKNOWN W.O.'      PARTRQ
050       06 050 O                       02 21            45 'UNKNOWN P.O.'      PARTRQ
                                                                                NOTE 192
051       06 060 O                               QTYOH  Z 55                    PARTRQ
052       06 070 O                               QTYOO  Z 65                    PARTRQ
053       06 080 O                               QTYREQZ  77                    PARTRQ
054       06 090 O                               31      AVAIL  Z 87            PARTRQ
055       06 100 OCDFILEO 01          31 01                                     PARTRQ
056       06 110 O          OR2       31 02                                     PARTRQ
057       06 120 O                               PTNO      5                    PARTRQ
058       06 130 O                       31 01N20WKORD    10                    PARTRQ
059       06 140 O                       31 02N20PURCH    13                    PARTRQ
060       06 150 O                               AVAIL  B 18                    PARTRQ
          07 010 O*                                                             PARTRQ
061       07 020 OPRINT     T  2      LR                                        PARTRQ
062       07 030 O                                        14 'END OF LISTING'   PARTRQ
```

SYMBOL TABLES

RESULTING INDICATORS

ADDRESS RI	ADDRESS RI	ADDRESS RI	ADDRESS RI	ADDRESS RI	ADDRESS RI	ADDRESS RI
000011 0F	000014 1P	000015 LR	000016 00	000017 01	000018 02	00002A 20
00002B 21	000035 31	00007A L0	000085 H0	000086 H1	000087 H2	000088 H3
000089 H4	00008A H5	00008B H6	00008C H7	00008D H8	00008E H9	

FIELD NAMES

ADDRESS FIELD	ADDRESS FIELD	ADDRESS FIELD	ADDRESS FIELD	ADDRESS FIELD
000123 PTNO	000128 DESCRP	00013C WKORD	000141 QTYOH	000144 QTY00
000147 QTYREQ	00014A PURCH	000152 AVAIL	000155 UDATE	000159 PAGE

LITERALS

ADDRESS LITERAL	ADDRESS LITERAL	ADDRESS LITERAL
00015C ---/--/--	000166 P A R T S	00016F R E Q U E S T
00017C L I S T	000183 PAGE	000187 ---
000188 PART	00018F W.O. OR P.O.	00019B QTY.
00019F NUMBER	0001A5 DESCRIPTION	0001B0 ON HAND
0001B7 ON ORDER	0001BF REQUIRED	0001C7 ORDERED
0001CE UNKNOWN W.O.	0001DA UNKNOWN P.O.	0001E6 END OF LISTING

048	21	NOTE 212
050	21	NOTE 212
025		NOTE 230

NOTE 178   ZERO SUPPRESSION (COLUMN 38) MAY NOT BE SPECIFIED FOR CONSTANTS OR EDIT WORDS.
            ENTRY OF BLANK IN COLUMN 38 IS ASSUMED.

NOTE 192   OUTPUT INDICATOR (COLUMNS 24-25, 27-28, OR 30-31) IS INVALID OR UNDEFINED.
            ENTRY OF L0 IS ASSUMED.

NOTE 212   RESULTING INDICATOR IS INVALID OR UNDEFINED.   ENTRY OF L0 IS ASSUMED.

NOTE 230   FIELD TO BE EDITED IS GREATER THAN THE EDIT WORD.   SIGNIFICANT DIGITS MAY BE
            LOST.

EXPLANATION

CHAPTER 10

Debugging RPG Programs

Problem 2

Instructions: The following RPG program contains an error or errors which occur during execution. Circle each error and record the corrected entries directly on the listing. Explain the error and method of correction in the space provided below.

```
DOS/360*RPG*CL 3-9              CASHMAN                    10/11/72              PAGE 0001

          01 010 H                                                              PARTRQ
001       01 020 FCDFILEI IP  F  80  80          READ40 SYSIPT                  PARTRQ
002       01 030 FPRINT   O   F 132 132    OF    PRINTERSYSLST                  PARTRQ
003       01 040 FCDFILEO O   F  80  80          READ40 SYSPCH                  PARTRQ
004       02 010 ICDFILEI AA   01  80 CW                                        PARTRQ
005       02 020 I        OR   02  80 CP                                        PARTRQ
006       02 030 I                           1    5 PTNO                        PARTRQ
007       02 040 I                           6   25 DESCRP                      PARTRQ
008       02 050 I                          26   30 WKORD    01    20           PARTRQ
009       02 060 I                          31   35QQTYOH    01                 PARTRQ
010       02 070 I                          36   40QQTYOO    01                 PARTRQ
011       02 080 I                          41   45QQTYREQ   01                 PARTRQ
012       02 090 I                          26   33 PURCH    02    21           PARTRQ
013       02 100 I                          34   38QQTYOH    02                 PARTRQ
014       02 110 I                          39   43QQTYOO    02                 PARTRQ
015       02 120 I                          44   48QQTYREQ   02                 PARTRQ
016       03 010 C              QTYOH    ADD QTYOO    AVAIL   50                 PARTRQ
017       03 020 C              QTYREQ   SUB AVAIL    AVAIL   31                 PARTRQ
018       04 010 OPRINT    H 201 1P                                             PARTRQ
019       04 020 O         OR      OF                                           PARTRQ
020       04 030 O                           UDATE    9 ' / / '                 PARTRQ
021       04 040 O                                   38 'P A R T S'             PARTRQ
022       04 050 O                                   53 'R E Q U E S T'         PARTRQ
023       04 060 O                                   64 'L I S T'               PARTRQ
024       04 070 O                                   81 'PAGE'                  PARTRQ
025       04 080 O                           PAGE  Z 86                         PARTRQ
          04 090 O*                                                             PARTRQ
026       04 100 O         H 1    1P                                            PARTRQ
027       04 110 O         OR     OF                                            PARTRQ
028       04 120 O                                    6 'PART'                  PARTRQ
029       04 130 O                                   46 'W.O. OR P.O.'          PARTRQ
030       04 140 O                                   55 'QTY.'                  PARTRQ
031       04 150 O                                   64 'QTY.'                  PARTRQ
032       05 010 O                                   76 'QTY.'                  PARTRQ
033       05 020 O                                   85 'QTY.'                  PARTRQ
034       05 030 O         H 2    1P                                            PARTRQ
035       05 040 O         OR     OF                                            PARTRQ
036       05 050 O                                    7 'NUMBER'                PARTRQ
037       05 060 O                                   25 'DESCRIPTION'           PARTRQ
038       05 070 O                                   42 'NUMBER'                PARTRQ
039       05 080 O                                   56 'ON HAND'               PARTRQ
040       05 090 O                                   66 'ON ORDER'             PARTRQ
041       05 100 O                                   78 'REQUIRED'             PARTRQ
042       05 110 O                                   87 'ORDERED'              PARTRQ
          05 120 O*                                                             PARTRQ
043       05 130 O         D 1    01                                            PARTRQ
044       05 140 O         OR     02                                            PARTRQ
045       05 150 O                           PTNO     6                         PARTRQ
046       06 010 O                           DESCRP  31                         PARTRQ
047       06 020 O                   01 20    WKORD   41                         PARTRQ
048       06 030 O                   02N21    PURCH   43                         PARTRQ
049       06 040 O                   01 20           45 'UNKNOWN W.O.'          PARTRQ
050       06 050 O                   02 21           45 'UNKNOWN P.O.'          PARTRQ
051       06 060 O                           QTYOH  Z 55                         PARTRQ
052       06 070 O                           QTYOO  Z 65                         PARTRQ
053       06 080 O                           QTYREQZ 77                         PARTRQ
054       06 090 O                   31      AVAIL  Z 87                         PARTRQ
055       06 100 OCDFILEO D1         31 01                                      PARTRQ
056       06 110 O         OR2       31 02                                      PARTRQ
057       06 120 O                           PTNO     5                         PARTRQ
058       06 130 O                   31 01N20WKORD   10                         PARTRQ
059       06 140 O                   31 02N20PURCH   13                         PARTRQ
060       06 150 O*                          AVAIL  B 18                         PARTRQ
          07 010 O*                                                             PARTRQ
061       07 020 OPRINT    T 2    LR                                            PARTRQ
062       07 030 O                                   14 'END OF LISTING'        PARTRQ
```

10.31

```
  10/11/72                    P A R T S   R E Q U E S T   L I S T              PAGE    1

     PART                            W.O. OR P.O.      QTY.      QTY.        QTY.      QTY.
    NUMBER      DESCRIPTION            NUMBER         ON HAND   ON ORDER   REQUIRED   ORDERED

     11939      SWIVEL                                   30        25          50
     11999      CASTING              12475512            200       500         750        50
     12063      HINGE                UNKNOWN W.O.        520       100         300
     25736      CAN                                       50                   100        50
     43529      BRACE                19325119           1000                 10000      9000
     57164      GLASS                UNKNOWN P.O.         23       241         924       660

  END OF LISTING


                              NOTE: MISSING WORK ORDER NUMBERS
```

EXPLANATION _____

_____

_____

_____

10.32

PROGRAMMING ASSIGNMENT 1

INSTRUCTIONS

Write the RPG program to produce the Daily Sales Report.

INPUT — Salesman Name Cards and Sales Cards

Input is to consist of two types of cards for each salesman: A Salesman Name Card and a Daily Sales Card reflecting the Amount sold to each customer contacted for the day. There is one Salesman Name Card for each salesman. This card is identified by a "1" control punch in card column 80. There may also be one or more Daily Sales Cards for each salesman. These cards will be identified by a "2" control punch in column 80. The possibility also exists that there will only be a Salesman Name Card and no Daily Sales Card. The format of the cards is illustrated below.

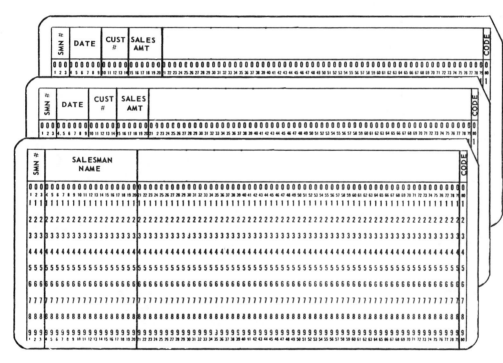

NOTE: A "2" control punch in card column 80 identifies the Daily Sales Cards

A "1" control punch in card column 80 identifies the Salesman Name Cards

10.33

OUTPUT — Daily Sales Report

Output is to consist of a Daily Sales Report listing the Salesman Number and the Salesman Name from the first card. The Date, Customer Number, and Sales Amount are to be printed for each of the Daily Sales Cards. Note that the Date which will be identical for each of the Daily Sales Cards is to be printed only on the first line for each Salesman. If there are no Daily Sales Cards for the Salesman, the message "NO SALES" should be printed adjacent to the Salesman Number and the Salesman Name.

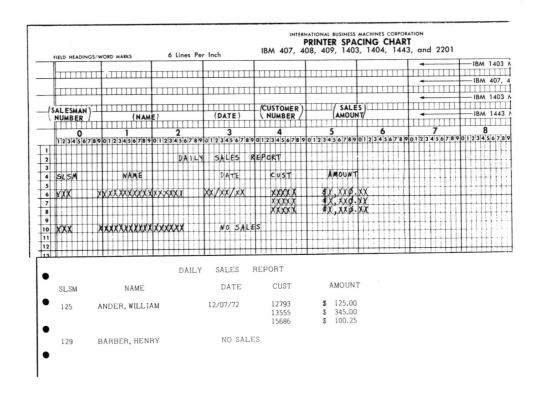

TEST DATA — ASSIGNMENT NO. 1

Salesman # (col 1-3)	Name (col 4-20)	Code (col 80)	Date (col 4-9)	Cust # (col 10-14)	Sales (col 15-20)
125	Ander, William	1			
125		2	120772	12793	012500
125		2	120772	13555	034500
125		2	120772	15686	010025
129	Barber, Harry	1			
146	Clement, Frank	1			
146		2	120772	23476	231987
146		2	120772	53426	008765

DOS JOB CONTROL

// JOB jobname

// OPTION LINK

// EXEC RPG

— Student Source Deck —

/*

// EXEC LNKEDT

// EXEC

— Test Data —

/*

/&

Note: This job stream assumes that there are standard assignments for the card reader and the printer of which the student is aware.

INSTRUCTIONS

Write the RPG program to process Physical Inventory records and create a Physical Inventory Report. A Physical Inventory consists of a count of the number of parts a company currently has. These parts may be in one of three conditions: Raw Material, Work in Process, or Finished Goods. When the part consists merely of Raw Material, then no work has been done to build the part. When a part is in Work in Process, it is in the process of being built. Finished Goods means that the part has been completely built and is ready to be sold to a customer.

INPUT — Physical Inventory Cards

The Physical Inventory Cards consist of three types — one for the Raw Material Count, one for the Work in Process Count, and one for the Finished Goods Count. The format of these cards is illustrated below.

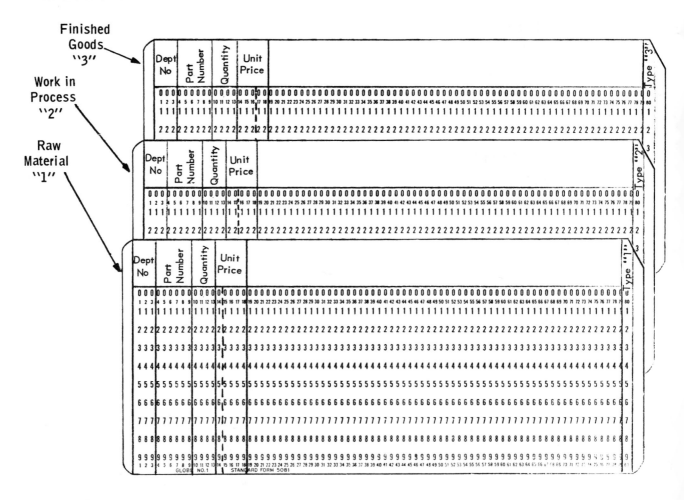

Note from the card formats that each contains a type code in column 80 to identify the type of card being processed. Note also that the number of decimal places to the right of the decimal point in the unit prices is different dependent upon the type of record being processed. For Raw Material, the unit price has the format X.XXXX, for Work in Process the format is XX.XXX, and for Finished Goods, the format is XXX.XX.

OUTPUT – Physical Inventory Report

There is one card per part number for each type. Thus, there would be one raw material card for part number 996543, one Work in Process card for part number 996543, and one Finished Goods card for this part number. Note, however, that there need not be all three cards, that is, one part number may only have a card for Finished Goods.

The report is to have the department number group indicated and the part number group printed. The print line is to have the total amount for each of the three categories. The total amount is determined by multiplying the unit price in the card input by the quantity in the card input. Note that all values on the report are specified as dollars and cents.

INTERNATIONAL BUSINESS MACHINES CORPORATION
PRINTER SPACING CHART
IBM 407, 408, 409, 1403, 1404, 1443, and 2201

	PART	QUANTITY	AMOUNT	QUANTITY	AMOUNT	QUANTITY	AMOUNT	TOTAL
DEPT	NUMBER	R/M	R/M	WIP	WIP	F/G	F/G	AMOUNT

The printed report:

```
    10/16/72                PHYSICAL INVENTORY REPORT                    PAGE    1
                                 ADAMS MFG. CO.

         PART    QUANTITY      AMOUNT    QUANTITY     AMOUNT    QUANTITY     AMOUNT      TOTAL
  DEPT  NUMBER     R/M          R/M        WIP         WIP        F/G         F/G        AMOUNT

   23   279816     400     $  600.00     1,000    $ 20,500.00    2,000   $ 300,000.00   $ 321,100.00
        218760       0     $     .00     7,655    $ 76,550.00       90   $     900.00   $  77,450.00
        776521       0     $     .00         0    $      .00     9,005   $  11,256.25   $  11,256.25

        TOTALS     400     $  600.00     8,655    $ 97,050.00   11,095   $ 312,156.25   $ 409,806.25


  FINAL  TOTALS  23,724    $56,723.40   18,781    $727,299.40   73,284  $1,972,388.56  $2,756,411.36
```

10.37

TEST DATA — ASSIGNMENT NO. 2

Dept No (col 1-3)	Part Number (col 4-9)	Quantity (col 10-13)	Unit Price (col 14-18)	Type (col 80)
250	279816	0400	15000	1
250	279816	1000	20500	2
250	279816	2000	15000	3
250	218760	7655	10000	2
250	218760	0090	01000	3
250	776521	9005	00125	3
543	887656	0095	45327	1
543	667656	8896	00987	3
546	667656	0096	66540	2
668	776549	8600	00675	3

DOS JOB CONTROL

```
// JOB jobname
// OPTION LINK
// EXEC RPG

  — Student Source Deck —

/*
// EXEC LNKEDT
// EXEC

  — Test Data —

/*
/&
```

Note: This job stream assumes that these are standard assignments for the card reader and the printer of which the student is aware.

CHAPTER 11

TABLE LOOK-UP

INTRODUCTION

In the previous examples of programs, the data to be processed and referenced within the program was read from card input files. In many business applications, it is desirable to organize reference data in the form of a "table", store the table in main storage, and retrieve those portions of the table which are needed in the solution of a problem. A table is a series of similar types of information which are stored in consecutive locations within main storage. The elements within the table may be in any desired order to solve a given problem. For example, the first sample program in this chapter is to produce a report listing item numbers of grocery merchandise and the respective description of the merchandise. The chart below illustrates the item numbers and the corresponding descriptions.

ITEM #	DESCRIPTION
008	American Cheese
017	Sweet Butter
024	Asparagus
064	Coffee
069	Dried Peaches
073	Horse Radish
086	Carrots
095	Peas
101	Sweet Potatoes
110	Pineapples
116	Hot Peppers
125	Soda Crackers
137	Rice
138	Tomato Soup
138	Sugar
145	Pears
146	Cocoa
149	Tapioca
152	Nutmeg

Figure 11-1 Items and Descriptions

Note from the table illustrated above that for each item number there is a corresponding description which describes the product involved, that is, item #008 corresponds to American Cheese, item #145 corresponds to Pears, etc.

In order to incorporate this information into the program to be referenced, it can be stored in the form of a table, that is, each item number will be stored in a table in main storage and each corresponding description will be stored in another table. By finding the desired item number in the item number table, the corresponding description may be extracted from the description table. This concept is illustrated below.

EXAMPLE

ITEM NUMBER TABLE (ARGUMENT)

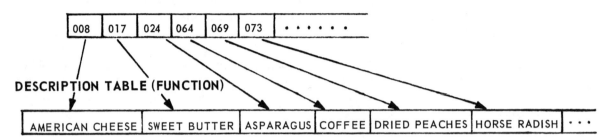

DESCRIPTION TABLE (FUNCTION)

Figure 11-2 Example of Item Number and Description Tables

Note in the example above that the Item Number table consists of the item numbers in consecutive main storage locations. The Description table consists of the descriptions in consecutive main storage locations. Note also that the first entry in the Item Number table, 008, corresponds to the first entry in the description table, American Cheese. Thus, the item numbers in the Item Number table are in the same sequence as the corresponding entries in the Description table.

The Item Numbers within the item number table are called ARGUMENTS. Arguments are the values within the tables which identify the corresponding description. The Descriptions within the description table are called a FUNCTION. The elements stored in the Function table are the elements to be extracted from the "table look-up" operation.

In the first sample program presented in this chapter, a file of cards containing the item number and a sales amount are read. The item number in the card is to be used to extract the appropriate description from the Description table and a report is to be created. The input and the report are illustrated in Figure 11-3.

Input

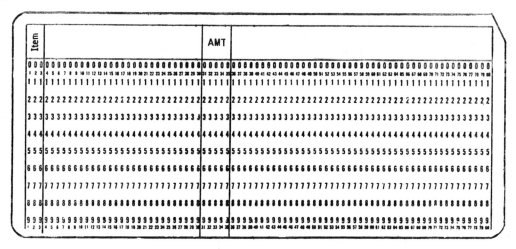

Output

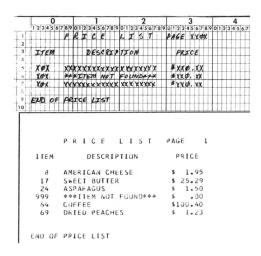

```
              P R I C E   L I S T       PAGE       1

    ITEM          DESCRIPTION           PRICE

      8      AMERICAN CHEESE        $   1.95
     17      SWEET BUTTER           $  25.29
     24      ASPARAGUS              $   1.50
    999      ***ITEM NOT FOUND***   $    .00
     64      COFFEE                 $100.40
     69      DRIED PEACHES          $   1.23


  END OF PRICE LIST
```

Figure 11-3 Input and Output

Note in the example above that the input data to the sample program consists of cards which contain an item number and a sales amount. The report contains the item number and the sales amount from the input card and also the description of the item which is found in the Description table. Thus, the item number which is found on the input card is used to "search" the Description table in order to find the corresponding description to be placed on the report.

11.3

FILE DESCRIPTION SPECIFICATIONS

In order to process data stored in a table, the data which is to be in the table must be read from a card file. Thus input in the problem will consist of a series of cards comprising the table followed by the data card to be processed. See Figure 11-4.

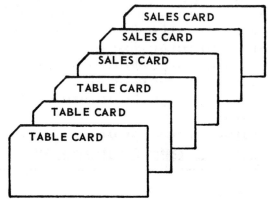

Figure 11-4 Input

In order for this to occur, the file which contains the table information must be defined on the File Description Specifications and also on the File Extension Specifications. The entries on the File Description Specifications for the files to be used in the sample program are illustrated below.

EXAMPLE

RPG   FILE DESCRIPTION SPECIFICATIONS

Line	Form Type	Filename	I/O/U/C/D P/S/C/R/T/D	E	A/D	F/V	Block Length	Record Length	L/R	A/K/I	I/D/T or 1-9	Key Field Starting Location	Extension Code E/L	Device	Symbolic Device
0 2 0	F	CARDTBL	IT			F	80	80					E	READ40	SYSIPT
0 3 0	F	PRCECDS	IP			F	80	80						READ40	SYSIPT
0 4 0	F	PRCELST	O			F	132	132		OF				PRINTER	SYSLST

Figure 11-5 File Description Specifications for Table Input File

Note in the example that the first file defined contains the filename CARDTBL. This file is to be the Table file, that is, the file from which the data which is to be placed in the table is to be read. Note in column 15 that the "I" entry specifies that the file is an input file. The entry of "T" in column 16 indicates that the file is to be a table file, that is, it is to contain the data which is to be placed in a table in main storage.

It can be seen that the file format, record length, and block length are defined as all other card files which have been input to other programs. The card file which contains the data for the table will be read from a 2540 Card Reader (READ40) which is assigned to SYSIPT. The entry in column 39, "E", is used to indicate that further entries to define the table file will be contained on the File Extension Specifications.

When a table file is to be read into main storage and stored in a table, the data in the input cards must be punched in a specified order and defined on the File Extension specifications form. The input cards containing the data to be placed in the table are shown in Figure 11-6.

EXAMPLE

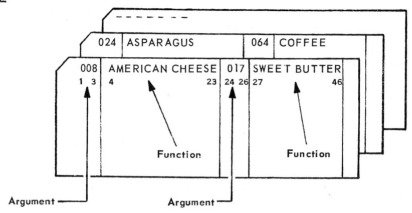

Figure 11-6 Example of Input Data to Build Tables

Note in the example in Figure 11-6 that the Item Number, that is, the first element within the Argument Table, is placed in columns 1-3 of the first input card containing data for the tables. The Description, that is, the first element of the Function table is punched in columns 4-23. The second item number to be placed in the Argument table is then punched in columns 24-26 and the 20 character description immediately follows the second item number. Thus, as can be seen from this example, the data which is to be placed in the tables is in a specific sequence, that is, the first item number, which is to be the first element in the Argument table, is the first entry in the input card followed immediately by the first description, which is to be the first element in the Function table. This arrangement of the table items within the input data is termed the alternating argument-function format. In order to define the input data which is to be placed in a table, the File Extension specifications are utilized. The entries on the File Extension specifications which are used for the table illustrated in Figure 11-1 are shown in the following example.

EXAMPLE

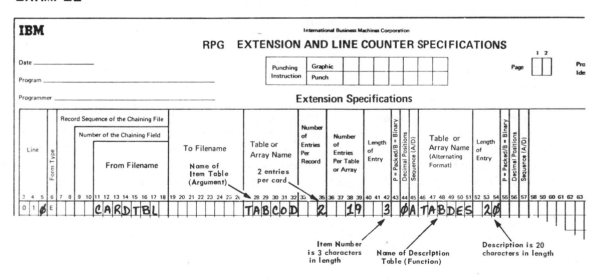

Figure 11-7 File Extension Specifications Entries

Note from the example above that the file extension form contains a Form Type ("E") in column 6 to identify it in the same manner as the other RPG programming forms. The "From Filename" which is specified in columns 11-18 (CARDTBL) must be the same filename which is used on the File Description Specifications (see Figure 11-5). The "TO Filename" entry (columns 19-26) is not used for this application.

When the input data which is placed in the table is in the Alternating Argument - Function format, such as in the example, both the argument table and the function table must be defined for the same input file on the same coding line on the File Extension specifications. The table name entered in the TABLE or ARRAY NAME field (columns 27 - 32) must be the name of the Argument table, that is, the table whose data is the first of the two values entered for each table element on the input data. Thus, the name of the table which will contain the item numbers is TABCOD, as can be seen from Figure 11 - 7. Table names which are used in RPG programs must be four to six characters in length and must begin with the letters TAB. This table name is then used on the Calculation Specifications and the Output Specifications in order to reference data within the table.

The Number of Entries Per Record field (columns 33 - 35) is used to specify the number of "entries" which are contained on each input record in the CARDTBL file. When the Alternating Argument - Function format is used, an "entry" is defined as both an argument value and a function value. As can be seen from Figure 11 - 6, there are two arguments and two functions in each input card. Thus, there are two "entries" for each card and the value "2" is entered in column 35 to indicate this. Note that the number which is placed in this field is right - justified with no required leading zeros.

The Number of Entries per Table or Array field (columns 36 - 39) is used to indicate the number of arguments and the number of functions which are to be placed in the tables. In the example it can be seen that the value placed in this field is "19". As will be noted from Figure 11 - 1, this is the number of item numbers and corresponding descriptions which will be in the table. Again, in this field, the term "entry" refers to an argument and a function value.

The Length of Entry field in columns 40 - 42 is used to specify the length of the elements in the argument table, which are the first values specified for each "entry", that is, for each group of arguments and functions. In the example, it can be seen that the value "3" is specified in column 42. This value indicates that each item number is 3 - digits in length. Thus, when the input data in the CARDTBL file is read, the first three digits are assumed to be the arguments which are to be placed in the TABCOD table. The Decimal Positions field (column 44) is used to indicate the number of positions to the right of the decimal place when a numeric field is being defined. This field functions is the same manner as on the Input Specifications and the Calculation Specifications.

The Sequence field (column 45) is used to specify if the Argument table is in an ascending (A) or descending (D) sequence. In the example in Figure 11 - 7 it can be seen that the value "A" is entered in column 45. This indicates that the values in the Argument table are in an ascending sequence. If the letter "D" were entered, it would indicate the values are in a descending sequence. For the most part, it is more efficient in terms of table look - up time to have the argument table in either an ascending or descending sequence. It should be noted, however, that it is not required that the argument table be in any sequence. When there is no sequence, the Sequence field in column 45 should be left blank.

Columns 46-57 pertain to the Function table, that is, the table which is the second portion of each entry in the input data. In this example, this is the Description Table. The table name is to be TABDES. Note again that the first three characters of any table name must be TAB. The length of Entry field (columns 52-54) is used to indicate the length of each entry within the TABDES table. In the example, the value 20 is specified because each description is 20 characters in length. Note that since the Description is alphanumeric, there are no entries in the Decimal Position field. The description is not necessarily in any sequence, so the sequence field (column 57) is blank.

As can be seen from the previous example, the RPG compiler can generate instructions which will properly read the table data and place it in the defined tables. When an input card is read, the program will place the data which is in the first three columns of the card in the TABCOD table because the elements are specified as three characters in length (column 42). The instructions in the object program will then place the next 20 characters in the TABDES table because each element of the TABDES table is 20 characters in length. Since the compiler knows that there are two entries in each input card (column 35), the next three characters in the input card following the first description are moved to the next element in the TABCOD table. Following the three characters for the item number, the next twenty characters from the input card are moved to the Description table (TABDES). Thus, each input card which is read will contain two elements for each table. The object program will continue to read the input cards containing data to be placed in the tables until the nineteen entries in each of the tables have been filled. Thus, nine cards with two entries for each table will be read (18 entries) and the last table card will contain one entry for each table. This, of course, is a total of 19 entries for the tables as indicated by the entry in columns 38-39.

It should again be noted that when the program is executed, the data which is to be placed in a table is placed in the input stream immediately in front of the detail data which is to be processed within the program. This is illustrated below.

EXAMPLE

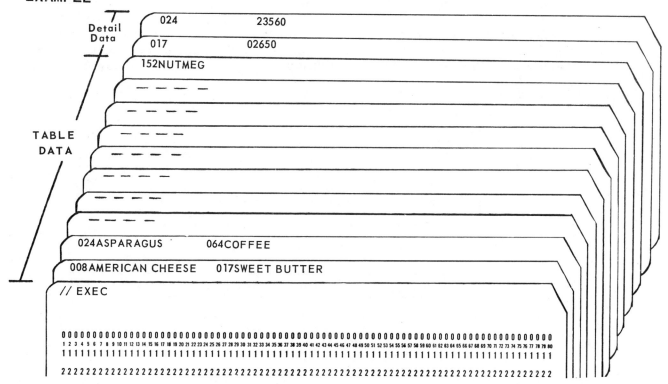

Figure 11-8 Table Data in Input Stream

11.7

CALCULATION SPECIFICATIONS

When the table is defined on the File Description Specifications and the File Extension Specifications, it will be stored in main storage to be processed. In order to "search" the table, the LOKUP instruction is used. This instruction is placed on the Calculation Specifications as illustrated below.

EXAMPLE

RPG   CALCULATION SPECIFICATIONS

Line	Form Type	Control Level (L0-L9, LR, SR)	Indicators And Not	Not	And Not	Factor 1	Operation	Factor 2	Result Field	Field Length	Decimal Positions	Half Adjust (H)	Resulting Indicators Arithmetic Plus / Minus / Zero; Compare High 1>2 / Low 1<2 / Equal 1=2; Lookup Table (Factor 2) is High / Low / Equal
3 4 5	6	7 8	9 10 11	12 13 14	15 16 17	18 19 20 21 22 23 24 25 26 27	28 29 30 31 32	33 34 35 36 37 38 39 40 41 42	43 44 45 46 47 48	49 50 51	52	53	54 55 / 56 57 / 58 59
0 1 Ø	C		Ø1			ITEM	LOKUP	TABCOD	TABDES				5Ø

Figure 11-9 Example of LOKUP Operation

In the example of the entry on the Calculation Specifications illustrated above, it can be seen that the table look-up operation will take place when the 01 indicator is "on". The operation code used to cause a "search argument" to be compared to the elements within the "argument table" and the corresponding element extracted from the "function" table is the LOKUP operation code. The LOKUP operation code causes the value contained in the field specified in the Factor 1 columns (ITEM) to be compared to each element within the argument table specified in the Factor 2 columns (TABCOD), and, when the desired relationship as determined by the Result Indicators is found, the corresponding value in the function table specified in Result Field (TABDES) is made available for processing. Note in the LOKUP operation illustrated in Figure 11-9, that the indicator 50 is specified in columns 58-59. This means that the table look-up operation is to procede until an element in the TABCOD field is found to be equal to the value in the ITEM field. At that time, the corresponding element in the TABDES table will be made available and indicator 50 will be turned "on". This is illustrated in the example below.

EXAMPLE

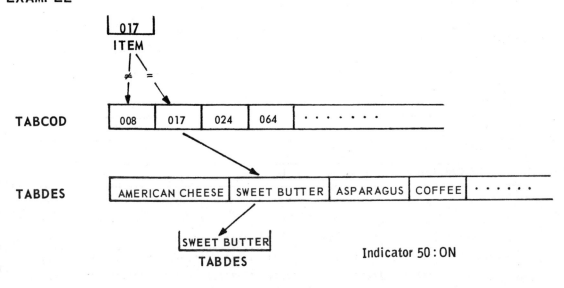

Figure 11-10 Example of LOKUP Operation

11.8

Note from the example in Figure 11-10 that the value in the field specified in the Factor 1 portion of the form (ITEM) is compared to the values contained in the table specified in the Factor 2 portion of the form (TABCOD). When an equal condition is found, that is, when the item number in the ITEM field is equal to an item number in the TABCOD table, the corresponding description in the TABDES table is extracted and placed in a field with the name TABDES. Thus, as can be seen, since the value 017 in the ITEM field is equal to the second item number in the TABCOD table, the second description (SWEET BUTTER) is extracted from the TABDES table and placed in a field with the same name. Note also that since an equal condition was found, indicator 50 is turned "on". If an equal condition were not found, that is, if the value in the ITEM field was compared to all of the item numbers in the TABCOD field and none of them were equal, then indicator 50 would not be turned "on" and no new description would be moved to the TABDES field. It should be noted also from Figure 11-9 that indicators may be placed in columns 54-55 to indicate that the search is to stop when the value in the Factor 2 table is greater than the value in the Factor 1 field or in columns 56-57 to indicate that the table value is less than the Factor 1 value.

OUTPUT-FORMAT SPECIFICATIONS

After the table look-up operation has taken place in the detail calculations, it is desired to print the item number from the input card, the corresponding description which was taken from the TABDES table, and the price which was contained on the input card. The detail specifications on the Output-Format Specifications form to accomplish this are illustrated below.

EXAMPLE

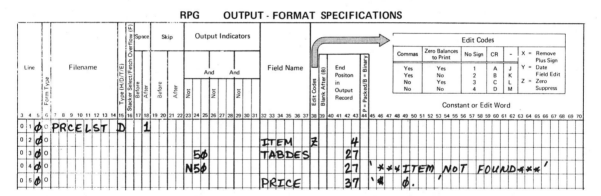

Figure 11-11 Output-Format Specifications

Note in the example above that the value in the ITEM field will be printed each time a detail record is processed. If indicator 50 is "on", the description extracted from the TABDES table and stored in the TABDES field will be printed. If indicator 50 is not "on", it means that an equal condition did not occur, that is, a corresponding item number in the TABCOD table was not found for the item number in the ITEM field. Therefore, the error message is printed in place of the description which is not available. The PRICE field contains the price which was read from the input card (see Figure 11-3).

SAMPLE PROGRAM

The source listing of the program to build the tables and process the input cards illustrated in Figure 11-3 and to produce the report is illustrated below.

```
DOS/360*RPG*CL 3-9                    CASHMAN                    09/15/72            PAGE 0001

       01 010 H                                                              PRICES
001    01 020 FCARDTBL IT  F  80  80              EREAD40 SYSIPT             PRICES
002    01 030 FPRCECDS IP  F  80  80              READ40 SYSIPT             PRICES
003    01 040 FPRCELST O   F 132 132      OF      PRINTERSYSLST             PRICES
004    01 050 E      CARDTBL           TABCOD  2  10  3 DATABLES 20          PRICES
005    02 010 IPRCECDS AA  01                                               PRICES
006    02 020 I                                          1    30ITEM         PRICES
007    02 030 I                                         31    352PRICE       PRICES
008.   03 010 C   01      ITEM      LOKUPTABCOD    TABDES         50         PRICES
009    04 010 OPRCELST H  201      1P                                       PRICES
010    04 020 O          OR        OF                                       PRICES
011    04 030 O                                        26 'P R I C E  L I S T'  PRICES
012    04 040 O                                        33 'PAGE'             PRICES
013    04 050 O                              PAGE  Z   38                    PRICES
014    04 060 O          H  2      1P                                       PRICES
015    04 070 O          OR        OF                                       PRICES
016    04 080 O                                         5 'ITEM'            PRICES
017    04 090 O                                        23 'DESCRIPTION'      PRICES
018    04 100 O                                        36 'PRICE'           PRICES
019    04 110 O          D  1      01                                       PRICES
020    04 120 O                              ITEM  Z    4                    PRICES
021    04 130 O                        50    TABDES    27                    PRICES
022    04 140 O                       N50               27 '***ITEM NOT FOUND***' PRICES
023    04 150 O                              PRICE     37 '$  0. '           PRICES
024    05 010 O          T  2      LR                                       PRICES
025    05 020 O                                        17 'END OF PRICE LIST'  PRICES
```

Figure 11-12 Source Listing

11.10

MULTIPLE TABLE PROCESSING

In the previous sample program, it was illustrated how an "argument" table and a "function" table can be defined and the use of the LOKUP operation to extract a value from the function table illustrated. The input data which was placed in the table was in the alternating argument-function format. The input data which is used to build a table may be organized in other formats. In addition, multiple tables may be used within a program to contain various types of information.

The second sample program in this chapter illustrates the use of multiple tables within a program and also the different formats which may be used to load a table. The program is to read a file of sales cards and create an annual sales report. The format of the input cards is illustrated below.

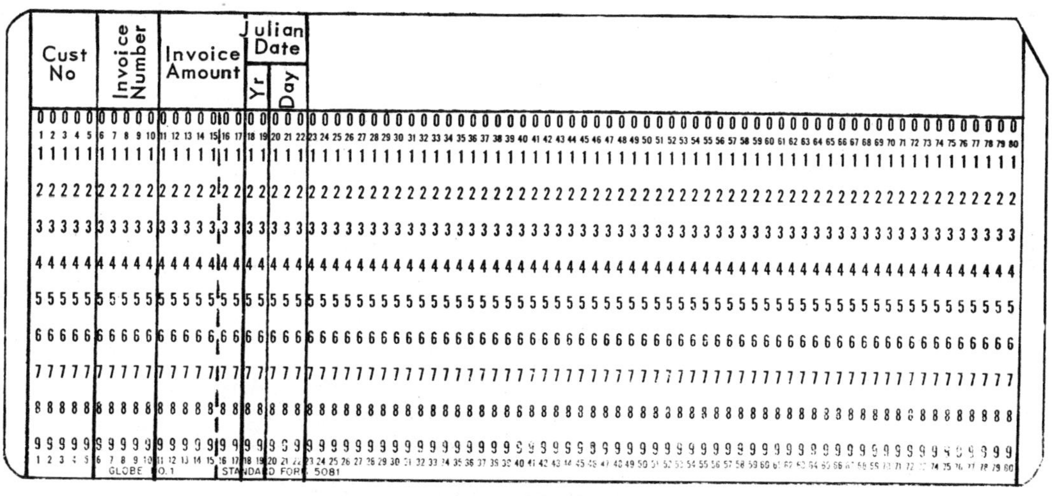

Figure 11-13 Input Card

Note from the format of the input card illustrated above that it contains a Customer Number in card columns 1-5, an Invoice Number in columns 6-10, an Invoice Amount in columns 11-17, and the Julian Date in columns 18-22. The Julian Date is a date based upon the year and the number of the day within a year. For example, the Julian Date of of January 1, 1972 is 72001. The first two digits of the Julian Date are the year and the next three digits are the day of the year. Thus, since January 1 is the first day of the year, the value specified is 001. The Julian Date for February 1, 1972 is 72032 because the year is 1972 and February 1 is the 32nd day of the year. The Julian Date format of expressing a date is commonly used in data processing applications because it is quite easily sorted into a year, day of the year sequence.

11.11

The format of the Annual Sales Report which is produced from the program is illustrated below.

Output

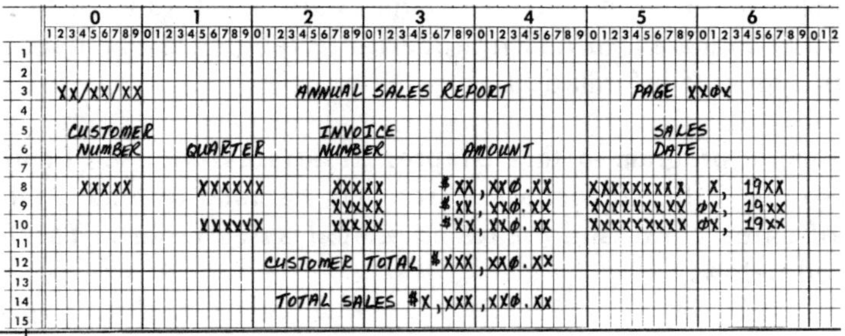

```
9/15/72              ANNUAL SALES REPORT              PAGE    1

CUSTOMER                INVOICE                        SALES
NUMBER      QUARTER     NUMBER       AMOUNT            DATE

12793       FIRST       10000     $    525.00    JANUARY     2,  1972
                        10110     $    400.00    JANUARY    20,  1972
                        13500     $    125.95    JANUARY    31,  1972
                        10725     $    993.23    FEBUARY    24,  1972
            SECOND      12079     $  1,029.35    APRIL      25,  1972
            THIRD       15036     $    250.00    JULY       24,  1972
            FOURTH      16631     $    100.25    DECEMBER   30,  1972
            UNKNOWN     16639     $    500.00    DATE UNKNOWN

                    CUSTOMER TOTAL $  3,923.78


15000       FIRST       10050     $    500.00    JANUARY    30,  1972
            SECOND      12080     $    595.00    APRIL       5,  1972
            FOURTH      16000     $  1,005.00    NOVEMBER   30,  1972

                    CUSTOMER TOTAL $  2,100.00


15001       SECOND      50950     $  2,500.07    MAY        30,  1922

                    CUSTOMER TOTAL $  2,500.07


                    TOTAL SALES $     8,523.85
```

Figure 11-14 Format of Output Report

Note in the example of the report above that the report is group-indicated by Customer Number. The Invoice Number and the Invoice Amount are printed from each input card which is read. Note, however, that the Quarter field and the Sales Date field contain information which is not on the input cards, that is, in which quarter of the year the sale took place and the date of the sale. The quarter and the actual date of the sale are calculated using data which is stored in tables which are loaded in the program.

As will be noted from the format of the Julian Date, the year is available as the first two digits. In order to find the quarter, the month, and the day of the month, however, it is necessary to use tables in order to convert the day of the year to a month-day format. Three tables are utilized in the sample program to convert the Julian Date to the Month-Day format and to determine the quarter. These tables are illustrated below.

TABLES

	TABJUL	TABDTE	TABDAY
1.	031	JANUARY FIRST	000
2.	059	FEBRUARY FIRST	031
3.	090	MARCH FIRST	059
4.	120	APRIL SECOND	090
5.	151	MAY SECOND	120
6.	181	JUNE SECOND	151
7.	212	JULY THIRD	181
8.	243	AUGUST THIRD	212
9.	273	SEPTEMBERTHIRD	243
10.	304	OCTOBER FOURTH	273
11.	334	NOVEMBER FOURTH	304
12.	365	DECEMBER FOURTH	334

Figure 11-15 Table Entries for Julian Date Conversion

Note in the example in Figure 11-15 that the names of the three tables are TABJUL, TABDTE, and TABDAY. As was noted previously, table names in an RPG program must begin with the three letters "TAB" and may be from four to six characters in length. The TABJUL table contains the total number of days which has past for each month of the year. For example, the first entry is 031, meaning that there are a total of 31 days past in the year at the end of the month of January. The second entry, 059, specifies that there have been a total of 59 days past (31 + 28) at the end of the month of February. The last entry in the table, 365, indicates that there are a total of 365 days in the year. Note that the possibility of a leap year is not included in this table.

The table TABDTE contains the month of the year and the quarter of the year corresponding to the entries in the TABJUL table. Thus, for up to 31 days of the year, the month is January and the quarter is the First quarter. Between 31 days and 59 days of the year, the month is February and the first quarter, etc. The TABDAY table indicates the number of days which have passed in all of the previous months. For example, at the conclusion of the month of April, 120 days of the year have passed. The value in this table is used to calculate the day of the month.

In order to convert the Julian Date to a Calendar Date, the tables are utilized in the following manner:

1. Assume the Julian Date in the input card is 72219. The "day" portion of the Julian Date is used in a LOKUP operation to find a condition where the day in the Julian Date is less than or equal to the values in the TABJUL table.

As can be seen from the table in Figure 11-15, the day 219 is less than the eighth entry in the TABJUL table. Therefore, the eighth entries in both the TABDTE table and the TABDAY table will be utilized.

2. The TABDTE table contains both the Month and the corresponding Quarter. Thus, as can be seen from Figure 11-15, the 219th day of the year falls in the month of August and is in the third quarter of the year.

3. In order to calculate the day within the month, the number of days which are in all of the previous months must be subtracted from the day in the Julian Date. The difference is the day of the month. Thus, the value 212, which is the eighth entry in the TABDAY table, would be subtracted from the value 219, which is the day in the Julian Date. The difference, "7", is the day of the month. Thus, the Julian Date 62219 corresponds to the calendar date August 7, 1972.

FILE DESCRIPTION SPECIFICATIONS

In order to load the tables, the file for the tables must be defined on the File Description Specifications in the same manner as used in the previous example. The entries for the table to convert the Julian Date to a Calendar Date are illustrated below.

EXAMPLE

RPG FILE DESCRIPTION SPECIFICATIONS

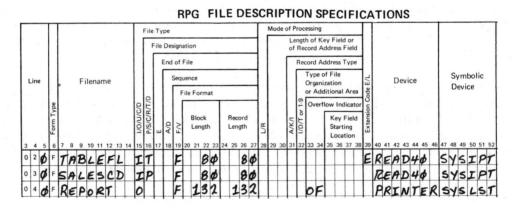

Line	Form Type	Filename	I/O/U/C/D	P/S/C/R/T/D	E	A/D	F/V	Block Length	Record Length	L/R	A/K/I	I/D/T or 1-9	Key Field Starting Location	Extension Code E/L	Device	Symbolic Device
0 2 0	F	TABLEFL	IT		F			80	80					E	READ40	SYSIPT
0 3 0	F	SALESCD	IP		F			80	80						READ40	SYSIPT
0 4 0	F	REPORT	O		F			132	132		OF				PRINTER	SYSLST

Figure 11-16 File Description Specifications

Note from the example in Figure 11-16 that the file which will be used as input to load the table, TABLEFL, is defined in the same manner as in the previous program, that is, it is specified as an input file (column 15), as a table file (column 16) and it is indicated that further entries for the file are contained on the File Extension Specifications (column 39). The card input and printer output files are defined in the same manner as in previous examples.

FILE EXTENSION SPECIFICATIONS

Even though, as illustrated in Figure 11-16, there is no difference in the File Description Specifications when defining a file to be used for more than one table, there are differences on the File Extension Specifications. The entries for the sample program are illustrated below.

EXAMPLE

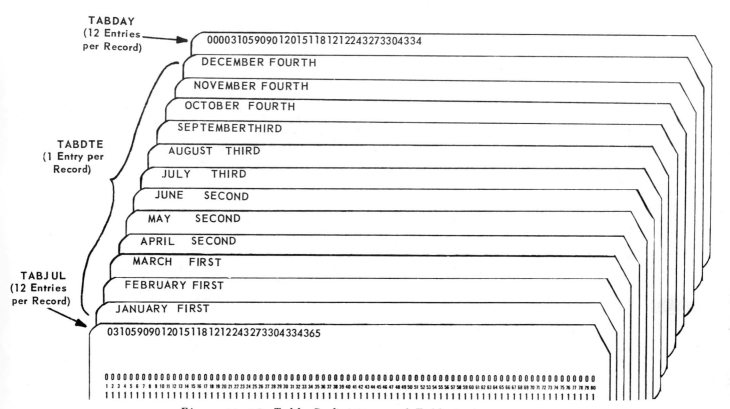

Figure 11-17 Table Definitions and Table Input

In the example in Figure 11-17, both the File Extension Specifications for the tables are illustrated together with the data which will be used to load the tables. Note that all three tables will be loaded from the file named TABLEFL because this is the file defined on the File Description Specifications from which the data for the table will be read. The table names in columns 27-32 are used in the same manner as illustrated previously, that is, each table which is to be loaded is given a unique name which must begin with the letters TAB. In the example, it can be seen that the table names are TABJUL, TABDTE, and TABDAY.

The "Number of Entries per Record" field on the File Extension Specifications is used to indicate the number of table elements which will be placed on each input card. Note in the example that the value "12" is specified for the TABJUL table, and, as can be seen from the TABLEFL input data, the first card contains twelve entries, each of which are three digits in length. The "3" in column 42 indicates that each entry for the table is three characters in length. The data is to be considered numeric because of the zero entry in column 44 and the entries are in an ascending sequence (column 45). Note that no alternate table name is placed in columns 46-51 of the File Extension form. This is because the input data is not in the alternating argument-function format. The data in the card which contains the entries for the TABJUL table are consecutive entries for that table only. Thus, as can be seen, it is not necessary that an alternating format be used — each table may be loaded individually from the input data.

The second table defined on the File Extension specifications is the TABDTE table. Note that the specifications for this table indicate that there are to be twelve entries for the table but that only one entry will be contained on each input record which is read. Thus, as can be seen in the data illustrated in Figure 11-17, there are twelve cards which are input to the TABDTE table, each card containing one 15 character entry which will be placed in the table. Again, there is no second table defined in the second Table Name field because the alternating format is not used.

The third table is defined on the File Extension specifications in the same manner as the TABJUL table, that is, there are twelve elements in the table and all twelve are contained on one input card. As will be noted, the entries in the input data correspond to the values placed in the table as illustrated in Figure 11-15. Thus, when the tables are loaded, all of the necessary data to convert the Julian Date to a Calendar Date will be available in the tables.

CALCULATION SPECIFICATIONS

After the tables have been defined on the File Extension Specifications, it is necessary to specify the look-up operations which must take place in order to extract the required information to convert the dates. These operations are defined as detail operations on the Calculation Specifications. The entries to cause the conversion of the dates are illustrated in Figure 11-18.

EXAMPLE

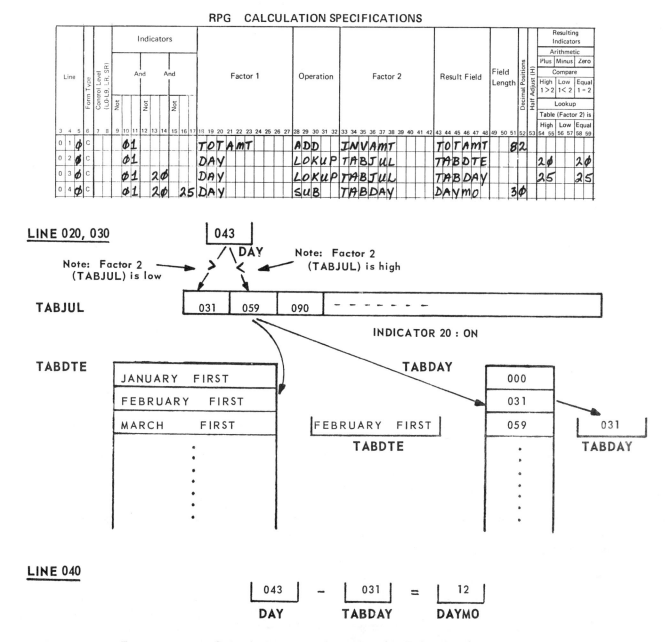

Figure 11-18 Calculation Specifications for Table Look-Up

Note in the Calculation Specifications illustrated above that the value in the INVAMT field, which contains the invoice amount, is added to the TOTAMT field. This is done so that a total for each customer may be printed when a control break occurs. The value in the DAY field is then used as the Search Argument in order to search the TABJUL table. The value in the DAY field is the day of the year which is a part of the Julian Date submitted on each input card. Note in the example above that this value is 043, meaning that the date is the 43rd day of the year.

11.17

When the value in the DAY field is used to search the TABJUL table, the search will stop and indicator 20 will be turned "on" whenever the value in TABJUL is greater than or equal to the value in the DAY field. This is because indicator 20 is specified both in columns 54-55 and columns 58-59. It should be noted that the Resulting Indicators are set according to whether the value in the table specified in the Factor 2 field is greater than, less than, or equal to the value in the field specified in the Factor 1 field. In addition to turning "on" indicator 20 when the value in the table TABJUL is greater than or equal to the value in the DAY field, the corresponding element in the TABDTE table will be moved to the TABDTE field. Thus, as can be seen from the example in Figure 11-18, since the value in the DAY field, 043, is less than the second entry in the TABJUL table, 059, indicator 20 is turned "on" and the second entry in the TABDTE table is moved to the TABDTE field. As will be noted, the table TABJUL is the Argument Table and the TABDTE table is the Function Table because a value is extracted from the TABDTE table.

Coding line 030 contains the LOKUP instruction which is used to extract the number of days which must be subtracted from the value in the DAY field in order to find the day of the month. Again, the DAY field from the detail input card is used as the Search Argument and the TABJUL table is the Argument Table. When the day in the TABJUL table is greater than or equal to the value in the DAY field, indicator 25 is turned "on" and the corresponding entry in the table TABDAY is moved to the TABDAY field in main storage. Thus, as can be seen from the example, the value 031 is extracted from the TABDAY table and is placed in the TABDAY field.

Line 040 contains the SUBtract instruction which is used to subtract the value extracted from the TABDAY table from the value in the DAY field. The difference is the day of the month and will be stored in the DAYMO field. Note from the example that the difference is 12. Thus, Julian Day 043 corresponds to calendar date February 12.

It will be noted from the example in Figure 11-18 that the TABDTE table contains, in fact, two function entries – the Month and the Quarter. It is perfectly allowable to have a single table contain more than one desired function element. The only requirement is that the table be defined in such a way that each element, regardless of the number of functions, appears to the RPG compiler as a single function. Thus, as can be seen from this example, the table is defined on the File Extension Specifications as a table containing entries each of which are fifteen characters in length when actually the entries consist of a nine character function (Month) and a six character function (Quarter). When more than one function is included as an element within a table, it is always necessary to extract the functions from the field in which they are stored after the table look-up operation takes place. Thus, in this example, it is necessary to extract the Month and the Quarter from the field TABDTE. In order to place portions of a field into another field, the MOVE and MOVEL instructions may be used. These instructions are illustrated in Figure 11-19.

EXAMPLE

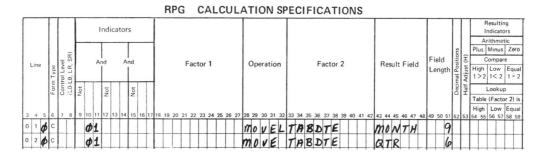

RPG CALCULATION SPECIFICATIONS

Line	Form Type	Control Level (L0-L9, LR, SR)	Indicators						Factor 1	Operation	Factor 2	Result Field	Field Length	Decimal Positions	Half Adjust (H)	Resulting Indicators
0 1	C		Ø1							MOVEL	TABDTE	MONTH	9			
0 2	C		Ø1							MOVE	TABDTE	QTR	6			

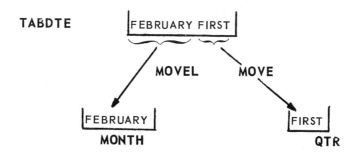

Figure 11-19 Example of MOVEL and MOVE Instructions

In the example above it can be seen that both the MOVEL and MOVE operation codes must be specified in the Operation field on the Calculation Specifications (columns 28-32). Both instructions are used to move data from the field specified in the Factor 2 portion of the form to the field specified in the Result Field portion of the form. The difference is that the MOVEL instruction causes the data in the Factor 2 field to be moved to the field in the Result Field beginning with the leftmost character in the field and proceeding to the right. The length of the field in the Result Field portion of the form determines how many characters are moved. Thus, from the example above, it can be seen that when the MOVEL instruction is executed, the data from the TABDTE field is moved to the field MONTH beginning with the leftmost character in the TABDTE field and continuing to the right until nine characters have been moved to the MONTH field. Nine characters are moved because this is the length of the MONTH field as defined on the Calculation Specifications.

The MOVE instruction, on the other hand, begins with the rightmost character in the field specified in the Factor 2 portion of the form and continues to the left for as many characters as are defined for the field specified in the Result Field portion of the form. Thus, when the MOVE instruction in Figure 11-19 is executed, six characters will be moved from the TABDTE field to the QTR field because the QTR field is six characters in length, as defined on the Calculation Specifications. The six characters moved will begin with the rightmost character in the TABDTE field and will continue to the left. As can be seen from Figure 11-18, these six characters are the Quarter of the year as extracted from the TABDTE table.

The MOVE and MOVEL instructions may be used to move data from any field defined on either the input specifications or the calculations specifications to any other field defined on these specifications. In addition, literal values may be specified in the Factor 2 portion of the Calculation Specifications to allow constants to be moved to defined fields.

GROUP INDICATION

In previous examples, it has been seen how reports may be group indicated by using the Control Break indicators to specify when group indication is to take place. In this sample program, for example, the report is group indicated by customer number, which is the field defined by an L1 control break. It will be noted in Figure 11-14, however, that the Quarter field on the output report is also group indicated, that is, each quarter is printed only once for each Customer Number regardless of the number of invoices for each quarter. As will be recalled, the Quarter is extracted from the TABDTE table and, therefore, may not be identified by a Control Break Indicator. When this situation occurs, the program, through the use of indicators, must indicate its own control break.

In order to cause a control break, indicators must be set "on" and set "off" in the detail and total calculations. The entries used in the sample program are illustrated below.

EXAMPLE

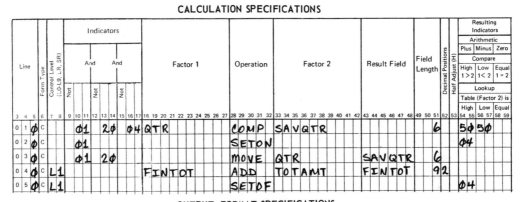

Figure 11-20 Specifications for Program Generated Group Indication

Note from the example in Figure 11-20 that indicators are used on both the Calculation Specifications and the Output-Format Specifications in order to cause a program-generated group indication on the report. The following example illustrates the settings of the indicators at various steps within the detail and total processing.

EXAMPLE

Step 1: The first card is read and the table look-up takes place.

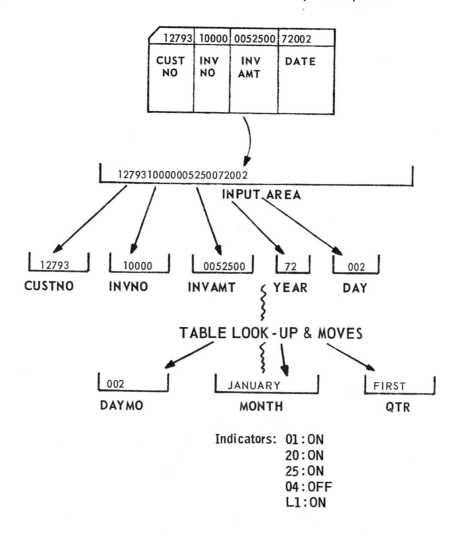

Indicators: 01:ON
20:ON
25:ON
04:OFF
L1:ON

Figure 11-21 First Card is Processed

Note from the example in Figure 11-21 that the first card will be read into the input area and the data will be moved to the input fields. After the table look-up operations and the MOVE and MOVEL statements have been executed, the day of the month (DAYMO), the month (MONTH), and the quarter (QTR) have been determined. Note also that indicator 01 is "on" because the detail card was read, indicator 20 is "on" because a valid date has been found in the table, Control Break indicator L1 is "on" because a new customer has been read, and indicator 04 is "off". As was noted in previous examples, even though the L1 indicator is "on" when the first card is read, total processing will be bypassed. The 04 indicator is "off" because it has not yet been turned on through the use of the SETON instruction as illustrated in Figure 11-20.

Step 2: The Compare operation is bypassed because indicator 04 is not "on". Indicator 04 is then set on and the quarter is moved to a compare area.

RPG   CALCULATION SPECIFICATIONS

Line	Form Type	Control Level (L0-L9, LR, SR)	Indicators And Not	And Not	And Not	Factor 1	Operation	Factor 2	Result Field	Field Length	Decimal Positions	Half Adjust (H)	Resulting Indicators Arithmetic / Compare / Lookup High 1>2 / High	Low 1<2 / Low	Equal 1=2 / Equal
0 1	Ø C		Ø1	2Ø	Ø4	QTR	COMP	SAVQTR		6			5Ø	5Ø	
0 2	Ø C		Ø1				SETON						Ø4		
0 3	Ø C		Ø1	2Ø			MOVE	QTR	SAVQTR	6					

Before Execution:

FIRST
QTR

_____
SAVQTR

Indicators: 01 : ON
20 : ON
25 : ON
04 : OFF
L1 : ON
50 : OFF

After Execution:

FIRST
QTR

FIRST
SAVQTR

Indicators: 01 : ON
20 : ON
25 : ON
04 : ON
L1 : ON
50 : OFF

Figure 11-22 Detail Calculation Processing

In the example above it can be seen that the comparison between the value in the QTR field and the value in the SAVQTR field will not take place for the first card because indicator 04 is "off". After bypassing the comparison, indicator 04 is turned "on" by the SETON instruction. This means that on subsequent input cards, the comparison will take place because indicator 04 will be "on". It is this comparison between the value in the QTR field and the value in the SAVQTR field which will turn "on" indicator 50 and cause the group indication to take place. As can be seen from Figure 11-22, indicator 50 will be turned "on" when the values in QTR and SAVQTR are not equal. This will, in turn, cause the Quarter to print on the report as is illustrated in Figure 11-23.

Step 3: The detail output line is printed.

RPG   OUTPUT - FORMAT SPECIFICATIONS

Line	Form Type	Filename	Type (H/D/T/E)	Stacker Select/Fetch Overflow (F)	Space Before	Space After	Skip Before	Skip After	Output Indicators Not	And	Not	And	Not	Field Name	Edit Codes	Blank After (B)	End Position in Output Record	P = Packed/B = Binary	Constant or Edit Word
01	Ø	O	REPORT		D		1			01										
02	Ø	O								L1					CUSTNO			8		
03	Ø	O								5Ø	2Ø				QTR			2Ø		
04	Ø	O								L1	2Ø				QTR			2Ø		
05	Ø	O								5Ø	N2Ø							21		`UNKNOWN`
06	Ø	O								L1	N2Ø							21		`UNKNOWN`
07	Ø	O													INVNO			31		
08	Ø	O													INVAMT			46		`$    ,   Ø.    `
09	Ø	O								2Ø					MONTH			58		
10	Ø	O								2Ø					DAYMO	Z		61		
11	Ø	O								2Ø								62		`,`
12	Ø	O								2Ø								65		`19`
13	Ø	O								2Ø					YEAR			67		
14	Ø	O								N2Ø								61		`DATE UNKNOWN`

Edit Codes:

Commas	Zero Balances to Print	No Sign	CR	–	X = Remove Plus Sign
Yes	Yes	1	A	J	Y = Date Field Edit
Yes	No	2	B	K	
No	Yes	3	C	L	Z = Zero Suppress
No	No	4	D	M	

Indicators: 01:ON   04:ON
                   20:ON   L1:ON
                   25:ON   50:OFF

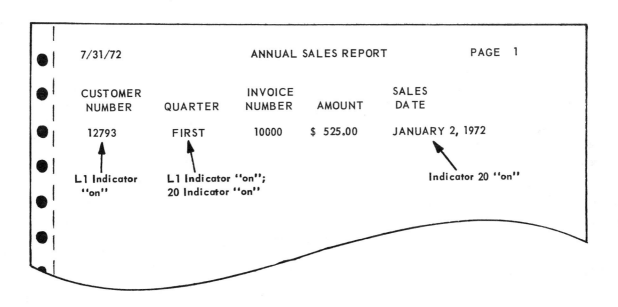

Figure 11-23 Detail Output is Written

As can be seen from Figure 11-23, the detail line will be printed because the 01 indicator is "on". Within the detail line, the Customer Number will be printed because the L1 indicator is "on", the Quarter is printed because both the L1 and 20 indicators are "on", and the date will be printed because indicator 20 is "on". Note that there are two sets of indicators which will cause the Quarter to print — 50 and 20; and L1 and 20. When indicator 20 is "on" it means that a valid date has been found in the table look-up operation. When L1 is "on", it indicates that a new customer number has been read. Whenever this occurs, it is always desired to print the Quarter together with the new customer number. When indicator 50 is "on", it means that an unequal condition has occurred in the comparison between the value in the QTR field in the input record and the value in the SAVQTR field which contains the quarter of the previous record. Thus, as can be seen, whenever a different quarter is found in the input record, a "control break" will occur, that is, the quarter will be printed on the report as a group indicated value. It is this ability to set indicators and to test them which allows a great deal of flexibility in the processing of data in an RPG program.

SAMPLE PROGRAM

The source listing of the sample problem to create the Annual Sales Report is illustrated below.

```
DOS/360*RPG*CL 3-9                  CASHMAN                     09/15/72           PAGE 0001

         01 010 H                                                                    SALRPT
001      01 020 FTABLEFL IT  F  80  80              EREAD40 SYSIPT                   SALRPT
002      01 030 FSALESCD IP  F  80  80              READ40 SYSIPT                    SALRPT
003      01 040 FREPORT   O  F 132 132        OF    PRINTER SYSLST                   SALRPT
004      01 050 E    TABLEFL           TABJUL 12  12  3 0A                           SALRPT
005      01 060 E    TABLEFL           TABDTE  1  12 15                              SALRPT
006      01 070 E    TABLEFL           TABDAY 12  12  3 0                            SALRPT
007      02 010 ISALESCD AA  01                                                      SALRPT
008      02 020 I                                          1    5 CUSTNOL1           SALRPT
009      02 030 I                                          6   10 INVNO              SALRPT
010      02 040 I                                         11  172INVAMT              SALRPT
011      02 050 I                                         18   19 YEAR               SALRPT
012      02 060 I                                         20  220DAY                 SALRPT
013      03 010 C   01        TOTAMT    ADD  INVAMT   TOTAMT  82                      SALRPT
014      03 020 C   01        DAY       LOKUPTABJUL   TABDTE     20   20              SALRPT
015      03 030 C   01 20     DAY       LOKUPTABJUL   TABDAY     25   25              SALRPT
016      03 040 C   01 20 250AY         SUB  TABDAY   DAYMO   30                      SALRPT
017      03 050 C   01                  MOVELTABDTE   MONTH    9                      SALRPT
018      03 060 C   01                  MOVE TABDTE   QTR      6                      SALRPT
019      03 070 C   01 20 04QTR         COMP SAVQTR             6  5050              SALRPT
020      03 080 C   01                  SETON                      04                SALRPT
021      03 090 C   01 20               MOVE QTR      SAVQTR   6                      SALRPT
022      03 100 CL1           FINTOT    ADD  TOTAMT   FINTOT  92                      SALRPT
023      03 110 CL1           SETOF                              04                  SALRPT
024      04 010 OREPORT   H  201   1P                                                SALRPT
025      04 020 O          OR        OF                                              SALRPT
026      04 030 O                            UDATE     9 ' / / '                      SALRPT
027      04 040 O                                     42 'ANNUAL SALES REPORT'       SALRPT
028      04 050 O                                     57 'PAGE'                      SALRPT
029      04 060 O                            PAGE  Z  62                             SALRPT
030      04 070 O          H   1    1P                                               SALRPT
031      04 080 O          OR        OF                                              SALRPT
032      04 090 O                                     10 'CUSTOMER'                  SALRPT
033      04 100 O                                     32 'INVOICE'                   SALRPT
034      04 110 O                                     60 'SALES'                     SALRPT
035      04 120 O          H   2    1P                                               SALRPT
036      04 130 O          OR        OF                                              SALRPT
037      04 140 O                                      9 'NUMBER'                    SALRPT
038      04 150 O                                     20 'QUARTER'                   SALRPT
039      05 010 O                                     31 'NUMBER'                    SALRPT
040      05 020 O                                     44 'AMOUNT'                     SALRPT
041      05 030 O                                     59 'DATE'                      SALRPT
042      05 040 O          D   1    01                                               SALRPT
043      05 050 O                            L1  CUSTNO   8                           SALRPT
044      05 060 O                            50 20  QTR    20                         SALRPT
045      05 070 O                            L1 20  QTR    20                         SALRPT
046      05 080 O                            50N20        21 'UNKNOWN'                SALRPT
047      05 090 O                            L1N20        21 'UNKNOWN'                SALRPT
048      05 100 O                            INVNO       31                           SALRPT
049      05 110 O                            INVAMT      46 '$ , 0. '                 SALRPT
050      05 120 O                       20   MONTH       58                           SALRPT
051      05 130 O                       20   DAYMO Z    61                            SALRPT
052      05 140 O                       20              62 ','                        SALRPT
053      05 150 O                       20              65 '19'                       SALRPT
054      06 010 O                       20   YEAR       67                            SALRPT
055      06 020 O                       N20             61 'DATE UNKNOWN'             SALRPT
056      06 030 O          T  13    L1                                               SALRPT
057      06 040 O                                       34 'CUSTOMER TOTAL'          SALRPT
058      06 050 O                            TOTAMT B   46 '$ , 0. '                  SALRPT
         06 060 O*                                                                   SALRPT
059      06 070 O          T   3    LR                                               SALRPT
060      06 080 O                                       32 'TOTAL SALES'             SALRPT
061      06 090 O                            FINTOT     46 '$ , , 0. '                SALRPT
```

Figure 11-24 Source Listing

11.25

CHAPTER 11

REVIEW QUESTIONS

1. What are the advantages, if any, of including the information in the first sample program in a table rather than punching the description on the actual input card which contains the item number and the amount?

2. How is it determined by the object program when the table cards have been completely read and the data input card begins?

3. Define the term Argument and the term Function.

4. Why must a LOKUP operation be performed rather than using a COMP operation when the elements within a table are being compared to an item specified in Factor 1?

CHAPTER 11

STUDENT EXERCISES

1. Write the entries required on the File Description Specifications and the File Extension Specifications to define the table illustrated below.

Part Number	Unit Cost
76481	.072
77926	.082
78273	.004
80541	.013
86924	.272
86938	.891
88092	.003
89173	.926
89476	.557
90291	.204
91763	.772
91955	.656

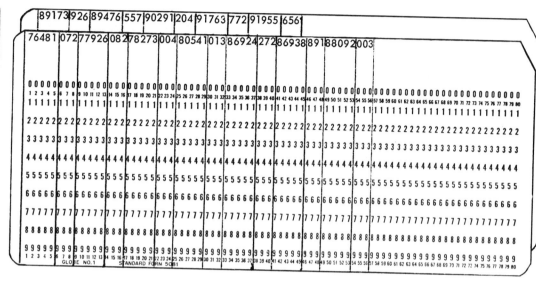

FILE DESCRIPTION SPECIFICATIONS

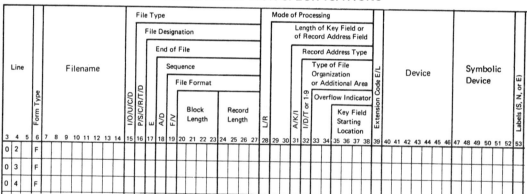

RPG EXTENSION SPECIFICATIONS

2. Write the entries on the Calculation Specifications required to find the corresponding part number in the table as is in the field PTNO. If a corresponding part number is found, multiply the quantity in the field QTY by the corresponding unit cost in the table and store the answer in dollars and cents in the TOTCOST field. If an equal part number is not found, an indicator must be set so that an error message can be written on a report.

RPG CALCULATION SPECIFICATIONS

Line	Form Type	Control Level (L0-L9, LR, SR)	Indicators And Not	And Not	And Not	Factor 1	Operation	Factor 2	Result Field	Field Length	Decimal Positions	Half Adjust (H)	Resulting Indicators Arithmetic Plus High 1>2	Minus Low 1<2	Zero Equal 1=2
0 1	C														
0 2	C														
0 3	C														
0 4	C														
0 5	C														
0 6	C														

11.28

Instructions: The following RPG program contains an error or errors which have occurred during compilation. Circle each error and record the corrected entries directly on the listing. Explain the error and method of correction in the space provided below.

```
DOS/360*RPG*CL 3-9              CASHMAN                    10/13/72        PAGE 0001
                                                                          PRICES
        01 010 H                                                          NOTE 201
                                                                          NOTE 203
        01 050 F   CARDTBL        TABCOD  2  10  3 OATABDES 20            PRICES
                                                                          NOTE 031
      S 01 020 FCARDTBL IT  F  80  80       EREAD40 SYSIPT                PRICES
                                                                          NOTE 200
        01 030 FPRCECDS IP  F  80  80       READ40 SYSIPT                 PRICES
                                                                          NOTE 200
        01 040 FPRCELST O   F 132 132    OF PRINTERSYSLST                 PRICES
                                                                          NOTE 200
        02 010 IPRCECDS AA  01                                           PRICES
                                                                          NOTE 111
        02 020 I                            1    30ITEM                   PRICES
                                                                          NOTE 130
        02 030 I                            31   352PPICE                 PRICES
                                                                          NOTE 130
                                                                          NOTE 077
        03 010 C   01    ITEM     LOKUPTABCOD  TABDES      50             PRICES
                                                                          NOTE 072
                                                                          NOTE 072
  001   04 010 OPRCELST H  201   1P                                      PRICES
  002   04 020 O          OR     OF                                      PRICES
                                                                          NOTE 192
  003   04 030 O                            26 'P R I C E   L I S T'     PRICES
  004   04 040 O                            33 'PAGE'                    PRICES
  005   04 050 O                    PAGE Z  38                           PPICES
  006   04 060 O          H  2    1P                                     PRICES
  007   04 070 O          OR     OF                                      PRICES
                                                                          NOTE 192
  008   04 080 O                            5 'ITEM'                     PRICES
  009   04 090 O                            23 'DESCRIPTION'             PRICFS
  010   04 100 O                            36 'PRICE'                   PRICES
  011   04 110 O          D  1    01                                     PRICES
                                                                          NOTE 192
        04 120 O                    ITEM Z  4                            PRICFS
                                                                          NOTE 179
        04 130 O                      50 TABDES  27                      PRICES
                                                                          NOTE 179
  012   04 140 O                    N50      27 '***ITEM NOT FOUND***'   PRICES
        04 150 O                    PRICE    37 '$  0. '                 PRICES
                                                                          NOTE 179
  013   05 010 O          T  2    LR                                     PRICES
  014   05 020 O                            17 'END OF PRICE LIST'       PRICES
```

SYMBOL TABLES

RESULTING INDICATORS

ADDRESS RI	ADDRESS RI	ADDRESS RI	ADDRESS RI	ADDRESS RI	ADDRESS RI	ADDRESS RI
000011 0F	000014 1P	000015 LR	000016 00	000017 01	000048 50	00007A L0
000085 H0	000086 H1	000087 H2	000088 H3	000089 H4	00008A H5	00008B H6
00008C H7	00008D H8	00008E H9				

FIELD NAMES

ADDRESS FIELD	ADDRESS FIELD	ADDRESS FIELD	ADDRESS FIELD	ADDRESS FIELD
000123 PAGE				

LITERALS

ADDRESS LITERAL	ADDRESS LITERAL	ADDRESS LITERAL
000126 PRICE LIST	000139 PAGE	000130 ITEM
000141 DESCRIPTION	00014C PRICE	000151 ***ITEM NOT FOUND***
000165 END OF PRICE LIST		

```
          002                        0F          NOTE 212
          007                        0F          NOTE 212
          011                        01          NOTE 212
          001                                    NOTE 220
          006                                    NOTE 220
          011                                    NOTE 220
          013                                    NOTE 220
                                                 NOTE 222
```

NOTE 031   'FROM FILENAME' (COLUMNS 11-18) IS NOT SPECIFIED AS ON FILE DESCRIPTION
           SPECIFICATION. SPECIFICATION IS NOT PROCESSED.

NOTE 072   UNDEFINED TABLE SPECIFIED IN LOKUP OPERATION. SPECIFICATION IS NOT PROCESSED.

NOTE 077   THERE ARE NO VALID INPUT SPECIFICATIONS IN THIS PROGRAM. EXECUTION IS DELETED.

NOTE 111   UNDEFINED FILENAME. SPECIFICATION IS NOT PROCESSED.

NOTE 130   RECORD IDENTIFICATION IS OUT OF SEQUENCE - I.E., FIRST INPUT SPECIFICATION OR
           FOLLOWING AN INVALID 'OR', 'AND', OR FILE NAME. SPECIFICATION IS NOT
           PROCESSED.

NOTE 179   FIELD NAME (COLUMNS 32-37) IS UNDEFINED. SPECIFICATION IS NOT PROCESSED.

NOTE 192   OUTPUT INDICATOR (COLUMNS 24-25, 27-28, OR 30-31) IS INVALID OR UNDEFINED.
           ENTRY OF L0 IS ASSUMED.

NOTE 200   FORM TYPE (COLUMN 6) IS INVALID OR OUT OF SEQUENCE. SPECIFICATION IS NOT
           PROCESSED.

NOTE 201   FILE DESCRIPTION SPECIFICATIONS ARE MISSING. EXECUTION IS DELETED.

NOTE 203   WARNING - PRIMARY FILE IS NOT SPECIFIED.

NOTE 212   RESULTING INDICATOR IS INVALID OR UNDEFINED. ENTRY OF L0 IS ASSUMED.

NOTE 220   FILE SPECIFIED ON OUTPUT FORMAT SPECIFICATIONS IS UNDEFINED OR NOT AN OUTPUT
           FILE (U, C, OR O). ENTIRE FILE IS DELETED FROM PROCESSING.

NOTE 222   NO VALID OUTPUT SPECIFICATIONS ARE PRESENT. EXECUTION IS DELETED.

'END OF COMPILATION'

EXPLANATION

Debugging RPG Programs

Problem 2

Instructions: The following RPG program contains an error or errors which occur during execution. Circle each error and record the corrected entries directly on the listing. Explain the error and method of correction in the space provided below.

```
DOS/360*RPG*CL 3-9              CASHMAN              10/13/72        PAGE 0001
        01 010 H                                              PRICES
001     01 020 FCARDTBL IT  F  80  80          EREAD40 SYSIPT  PRICES
002     01 030 FPRCECDS IP  F  80  80          READ40 SYSIPT   PRICES
003     01 040 FPRCELST O   F 132 132     OF   PRINTERSYSLST   PRICES
004     01 050 E   CARDTBL       TABCOD  2  10  3 DATABDES 20  PRICES
005     02 010 IPRCECDS AA  01                                 PRICES
006     02 020 I                          1    30ITEM          PRICES
007     02 030 I                          31   352PRICE        PRICES
008     03 010 C   01      ITEM    LOKUPTABCOD  TABDES    50   PRICES
009     04 010 OPRCELST H  201  1F                             PRICES
010     04 020 O          OR     OF                            PRICES
011     04 030 O                               26 'P R I C E   L I S T'  PRICES
012     04 040 O                               33 'PAGE'       PRICES
013     04 050 O                        PAGE Z 38              PRICES
014     04 060 O          H  2  1P                             PRICES
015     04 070 O          OR     OF                            PRICES
016     04 080 O                                5 'ITEM'       PRICES
017     04 090 O                               23 'DESCRIPTION' PRICES
018     04 100 O                               36 'PRICE'      PRICES
019     04 110 O          D  1  01                             PRICES
020     04 120 O                     ITEM  Z   4               PRICES
021     04 130 O                       50 TABDES    27         PRICES
022     04 140 O                       50         27 '***ITEM NOT FOUND***' PRICES
023     04 150 O                     PRICE     37 '$   0.  '   PRICES
024     05 010 O          T  2  LR                             PRICES
025     05 020 O                               17 'END OF PRICE LIST' PRICES
```

```
          P R I C E   L I S T   PAGE   1

ITEM        DESCRIPTION        PRICE

    8   ***ITEM NOT FOUND***   $   1.95
   17   ***ITEM NOT FOUND***   $  25.29
   24   ***ITEM NOT FOUND***   $   1.50
  999                          $    .00
   64   ***ITEM NOT FOUND***   $100.40
   69   ***ITEM NOT FOUND***   $   1.23

END OF PRICE LIST
```

EXPLANATION _____

_____

_____

_____

CHAPTER 11

PROGRAMMING ASSIGNMENT 1

INSTRUCTIONS

Write the RPG program to produce a listing of employees of a company with a description of their Job Type and Job Class. The Job Type and Job Class are to be extracted from tables.

INPUT — Employee Cards

Input is to consist of Employee Cards that contain the Employee Number, the Employee Name, the Job Type Code, and the Job Class Code. The Job Type Code field will contain codes 01-10 and the Job Class Code field will contain codes from 01-05. For example, a Job Type of "01" could indicate an accountant and a Job Class Code of "01" could indicate a part-time employee.

TABLES

The tables are to contain the Job Type Code and a corresponding Job Type and also the Job Class Code and a corresponding Job Classification. The data for the tables to be used in the assignment are illustrated below. The student can design the tables within his program in any manner desired.

Job Type Code	Job Type
01	ACCOUNTANT
02	BUYER
03	CLERK
04	TYPIST
05	SECRETARY
06	KEYPUNCHER
07	OPERATOR
08	PROGRAMMER
09	ANALYST
10	CODER

Job Class Code	Job Class
01	Part-Time
02	Trainee
03	Permanent
04	Probation
05	Consultant

OUTPUT — Employee Listing

The output consists of an Employee Listing with their job type and job class. A portion of the report which could be produced is illustrated below. The student may use the format below or design his own report format. If one of the type or class codes is not found in one of the tables, an error message should be printed on the report to identify the card in error.

```
                        EMPLOYEE LISTING

    EMP. NO.           NAME              JOB TYPE        JOB CLASS

      100         BALLOU, RALEIGH         CLERK          TRAINEE
      105         DANDER, STEVEN          BUYER          PERMANENT
```

TEST DATA — ASSIGNMENT NO. 1

Emp No (col 1-3)	Name (col 4-20)	Type (col 21-22)	Class (col 23-24)
100	Ballou, Raleigh	03	02
105	Dander, Steven	02	03
110	Ellison, George	09	05
198	Fromm, Yul	11	04
285	Krantz, Otto	05	08
534	Mason, Tommy	08	01

DOS JOB CONTROL

```
// JOB jobname
// OPTION LINK
// EXEC RPG
  — Student Source Deck —
/*
// EXEC LNKEDT
// EXEC
  — Test Data —
/*
/&
```

Note: This job stream assumes that there are standard assignments for the card reader and the printer of which the student is aware.

PROGRAMMING ASSIGNMENT 2

INSTRUCTIONS

Write the RPG program to produce a Shipping Report. Two tables are to be used to determine the Metal Cost, Shipping Weight, Shipping Charges, and Total Cost of specific metal types which have been ordered from a company.

INPUT — Sales Cards

Input is to consist of Sales Cards that contain the Part Number (which indicates a type of metal), and the size (length and width) of products ordered. The input cards are illustrated below.

The following charts are to be used in the calculations within the program.

CHART I

WEIGHT/COST PER SQUARE FOOT

PART NUMBER	DESCRIPTION	WEIGHT SQ/FT	COST SQ/FT
100	¼ ALUMINUM ALLOY	3 lb.	1.25
101	½ ALUMINUM ALLOY	2 lb.	2.00
102	¾ ALUMINUM ALLOY	3 lb.	2.80
120	¼ MAGNESIUM	1 lb.	3.75
121	½ MAGNESIUM	2 lb.	7.00
122	¾ MAGNESIUM	3 lb.	11.00

CHART II

SHIPPING CHARGES

AREA I

POUNDS	SHIPPING CHARGES
0-5	10.00
50-100	20.00
100-200	45.00
200-300	85.00
300-400	120.00
400-500	150.00

NOTE: MAXIMUM POUNDAGE 500 LBS.

OUTPUT — Shipping Report

The output that is to be obtained is illustrated below. Note that the Metal Cost is obtained by: (1) determining the number of square feet of the metal type desired by multiplying the length field by the width field on the input data cards; (2) determining the Cost Per Square Foot from Chart I; (3) multiplying the number of square feet by the Cost Per Square Foot. For example in the report below Part Number 100 is 2 feet in length and 2 feet in width for a total of 4 square feet. From Chart I it is determined that the Cost Per Square Foot is $1.25. By multiplying the number of square feet (4) by the Cost Per Square Foot ($1.25), the Metal Cost is obtained.

In addition the Shipping Weight and the Shipping Charges are to be determined from Charts I and II.

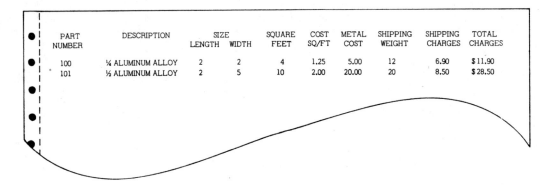

PART NUMBER	DESCRIPTION	SIZE LENGTH	WIDTH	SQUARE FEET	COST SQ/FT	METAL COST	SHIPPING WEIGHT	SHIPPING CHARGES	TOTAL CHARGES
100	¼ ALUMINUM ALLOY	2	2	4	1.25	5.00	12	6.90	$11.90
101	½ ALUMINUM ALLOY	2	5	10	2.00	20.00	20	8.50	$28.50

The student should design and define the tables which are to be used in the program. The format of the report should be designed by the student but should contain the information as illustrated above.

TEST DATA – ASSIGNMENT NO. 2

Part No (col 1-3)	Length (col 4-6)	Width (col 7-9)
100	002	002
101	002	005
120	008	020
121	010	020
122	003	050

DOS JOB CONTROL

```
// JOB jobname
// OPTION LINK
// EXEC RPG
  – Student Source Deck –
/*
// EXEC LNKEDT
// EXEC
  – Test Data –
/*
/&
```

Note: This job stream assumes that there are standard assignments for the card reader and the printer of which the student is aware.

CHAPTER 12

MATCHING RECORDS

MAGNETIC TAPE

INTRODUCTION

The System/360 may utilize many types of "peripheral devices", that is, devices which are connected to the Central Processing Unit, to input data to the system and receive output. In previous chapters, the use of the card reader, the card punch, and the printer have been illustrated. In addition to these devices, magnetic tape drives play a vital role in the complete System/360 or System/370.

Information is stored on the magnetic tape, which is similar to tape used in audio tape recorders, as a series of small spots. The "spots" may represent any of the 256 possible hexadecimal values which can be stored in main storage. In addition, data may be stored in the packed decimal or binary format. One of the important advantages of the use of magnetic tape is the density of recording, that is, the number of small magnetic spots which make up a character, which can be recorded per inch of tape. Although the density of magnetic tape varies, the IBM 2400 series of magnetic tape units may record or read data with a density of 800 characters or 1600 characters per inch. This means that on a full 2400 foot reel of tape, data equivalent to that in 480,000 cards punched in all 80 columns may be stored.

SEQUENTIAL FILE PROCESSING

Although tape drives operate in different modes with different densities and speeds of operation, they all process data in a sequential access method. Sequential processing means that records are read or written one after another. In addition, the records stored on magnetic tape are normally arranged sequentially on the basis of some control field or "key" such as the item number of individual records, the salesman number, etc.

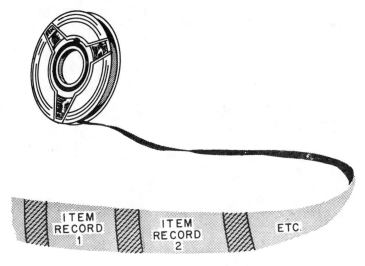

Figure 12-1 Illustration of records arranged sequentially on Magnetic Tape

After each record is written sequentially on a magnetic tape, there is an inter-block-gap (IBG) created (also called an IRG or inter-record-gap). This inter-block or inter-record-gap is a blank space on the tape approximately .6 inch long and indicates to the magnetic tape drive that the end of the record has been reached. This inter-block-gap is necessary to allow for the starting and stopping, acceleration and deceleration, of the magnetic tape unit, and is required for correct reading and writing of records. Data to be read begins with the first character after an inter-block-gap and continues to the next inter-block-gap.

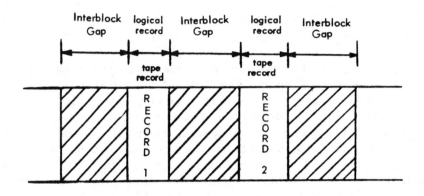

Figure 12-2 Illustration of Records Stored on Magnetic Tape

When writing on tape, the records are written sequentially with inter-block-gaps between each record. During writing, the gap is automatically produced at the end of each record or block of records.

When all of the records of the FILE (that is, the group of related records on the tape) have been written by the program, a special character called a TAPE MARK is written. When a tape mark is written on the tape, it signifies that the file has been completely written. Thus, when the tape is read by another program, the tape mark will indicate the end of the file (similar to the way the /* card indicates the end of data when reading cards).

BLOCKING

In Figure 12-2, the records are shown to be written one by one in a sequential manner with inter-block-gaps between each record. In many instances, it is advantageous to BLOCK records. BLOCKING refers to the process in which two or more individual records (referred to as "logical records") are grouped together and written on a magnetic tape creating a "physical record" or "block". (See Figure 12-3).

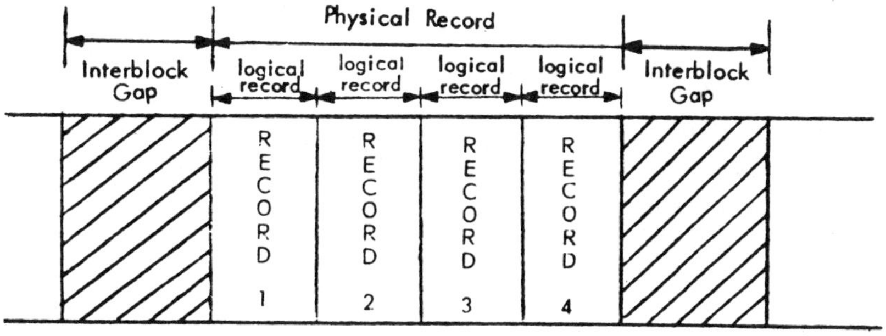

Figure 12-3 Illustration of Blocked Records

Blocking has two major advantages: (1) More records can be written on the tape because a number of records are recorded between each inter-block-gap, thus reducing the number of gaps on the tape; (2) The records can be read faster because two or more records can be read before the read operation is stopped by the inter-block-gap. The limiting factor in blocking records is the amount of core storage available for input/output operations, as there must be enough room in core to store the complete block of data to be processed. Thus, the larger the block of records, the more core storage that must be allocated for storing the block. For example, if fifty 80 character records comprise a physical record, then 4,000 characters in main storage are required when the physical record is transferred from magnetic tape to core or from core to magnetic tape. The programmer or analyst must make the determination as to what size block can be used so that there is enough core storage available and the blocking is efficient as possible.

The number of logical records comprising the "physical record" is called the BLOCKING FACTOR.

TAPE LABELING

Installations utilizing magnetic tape as a form of input normally maintain a tape "library". This library may consist of hundreds and even thousands of reels of tape containing data to be processed. It is essential, therefore, that an effective means of identifying the individual reels of tape be developed. To identify the individual reels of tape, techniques of tape "labeling" have been developed. These techniques consist of recording as the first records on each reel, information that uniquely identifies the reel. The label at the beginning of the reel is called a Volume Label. Each file which is recorded on the tape is further identified through the use of a Header Label at the beginning of the file and a Trailer Label at the end of the file.

Standard Labels

With the Disk Operating System, information for the recording of labels on magnetic tape is obtained from the Job Control cards utilized with the problem program. In actual practice, the three standard labels which are normally used are the Volume Label, the Header Label, and the Trailer Label.

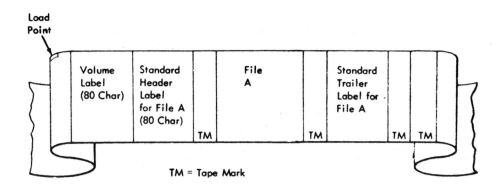

Figure 12-4 Standard Tape Labels

The Volume Label identifies the tape volume with the volume number assigned to it. This volume number is usually unique to the reel of tape and is used to ensure the proper volume is being used in tape processing.

The header label immediately follows the volume label with only an IBG between them. The header label is, like the volume label, 80 characters in length.

When tape is used as input to a program, the header label is checked to ensure that the proper magnetic tape file is being used. A header label normally contains the following fields:

1. LABEL IDENTIFIER – Identifies Header Labels.
2. TAPE SERIAL NUMBER – Identifies a particular reel of tape.
3. FILE SERIAL NUMBER – Identifies a tape file. This number may often be the same as the tape serial number of the first reel of tape in the file.
4. SEQUENCE NUMBER – Ensures that reels within a file enter the system in sequence.
5. FILE IDENTIFICATION – Identifies the name of the file.
6. CREATION DATE – Dates the creation of the file.
7. RETENTION CYCLE – Indicates the obsolescence data concerning a file.

These fields are basic to a header label. Additional control information may be desired in a particular application.

A trailer label is used by the program to ensure that the entire reel has been accurately processed. A trailer label may contain the following fields:

1. LABEL IDENTIFIER – Identifies the trailer label.
2. BLOCK COUNT – Is used by the program to ensure that the indicated number of blocks has been processed.
3. TAPE DATA RECORD COUNT – Is used by the program to ensure that the indicated number of tape records has been processed.

Trailer labels may contain additional information necessary to a particular application.

MASTER FILES

Magnetic tape is commonly used to store sequential master files. A Master File is a file consisting of records which contain up-to-date information relating the status of a system of which a master record is a part. For example, in a customer sales system, the master file could contain a record for each customer reflecting year-to-date sales.

Two steps are normally required in order to process a master file – it must first be created and, after it is created, it must be periodically updated with current information so that the file always contains the most recent data. The two sample programs in this chapter will illustrate first the loading or creating of the master file and then the updating of the master file.

The first sample program is used to load the master file on magnetic tape from a card input file. The format of the input records is illustrated below.

Input Records

"Name" Card

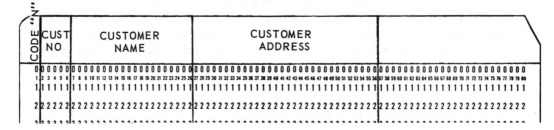

"Sales" Card

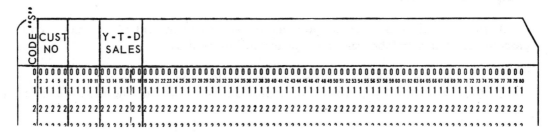

Figure 12-5 Card Input

Note from Figure 12-5 that there are two formats for the input records. The "Name" card contains the Customer Number, the Customer Name, and the Customer Address. It is identified by the letter "N" punched in column 1. The "Sales" card contains the Customer Number and the Year-To-Date sales. It is identified by the letter of the alphabet "S" in column 1. A "Name" card is required for each customer but a "Sales" card is optional. If there is no sales card, the year-to-date sales in the master record will be zero. In addition, there will be only one of each type for each customer.

The output from the program is the Master File stored on Magnetic Tape. The format of the record stored in the master file is illustrated below.

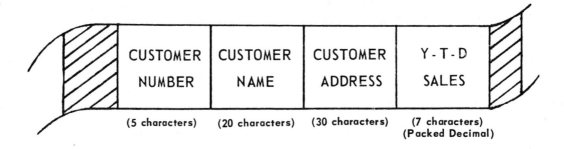

Figure 12-6 Master Record Format

Note from the example in Figure 12-6 that the data in the master record is taken from both the Name card and the Sales card. Note also that the Year-To-Date Sales will be stored in a packed-decimal format in the master record. When processing data on tape, it is many times desirable to store numeric data in a packed-decimal format to save space on the tape.

FILE DESCRIPTION SPECIFICATIONS

The file which is to be stored on magnetic tape must be defined on the File Description Specifications in much the same manner as the card and printer files illustrated previously. The entries for the sample program are illustrated below.

EXAMPLE

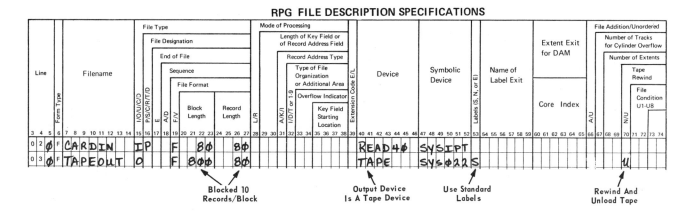

Figure 12-7 File Description Specifications

In Figure 12-7 it can be seen that the card input file is defined in the same manner as in previous examples. The tape output file, TAPEOUT, however, has several different entries. Note that the filename and the File Type, however, are the same as any output file. The File Format, as illustrated by the "F" in column 19, is fixed-length records.

As noted previously, when records are recorded on magnetic tape, it is possible to write more than one logical record in a physical record or block. The block length entry on the File Description Specifications (columns 20-23) is used to specify the size of the physical record or block which is to be written on the file. Thus, as can be seen from Figure 12-7, the block length for the TAPEOUT file is 800 characters. The record length field (columns 24-27) is used to specify the length of the logical record which will be written as a part of the physical record. The logical record length in this example is 80 characters. Thus, the file is blocked 10 logical records per physical record or block. The blocking factor, therefore, is ten.

Whenever a file which is stored on magnetic tape is defined on the File Description Specifications, the entry in the Device field (columns 40-46) must be TAPE. This indicates to the RPG compiler that the file is stored on a magnetic tape device. The symbolic device number entered in columns 47-52 is one of a series of "programmer logical units" which may be assigned to a magnetic tape device. All of these programmer logical units begin with the letters of the alphabet "SYS". The next three numbers are used to identify the particular device which is to be used. These devices and the associated programmer logical unit are assigned through the use of job control statements. Which "SYS" number is used is normally dependent upon the installation where the program is to be executed.

As was noted previously, most installations utilizing magnetic tape place standard labels on the tapes. When standard labels are to be used, the letter "S" must be placed in the Labels column (column 53). This indicates to the RPG compiler that the tape labels must be checked prior to processing the tape file. It is possible, however, that other types of labels may be used on magnetic tape. If standard labels are to be used together with special "user standard labels", the value "E" is placed in column 53. If non-standard labels are used, the value "N" is placed in this field. If the field is left blank, it indicates that there are no labels on the magnetic tape and the first record on the tape is a data record, not a label record.

If non-standard labels or user standard labels are to be utilized on a magnetic tape, special label processing routines must be written in Assembler Language and be included in the program to process these labels. The field in columns 54-59 is used to indicate the name of the routine which will process these labels. This name must be left-justified and be six characters or less. In the example in Figure 12-7, only standard labels are used so there is no need to specify the name of a label-processing routine.

The entry in column 70 is used to specify the disposition of the tape both before and after the file has been processed. There are six possible entries in this column of which the two most common are the entries R and U. If the value "U" is placed in column 70, the tape will be rewound to the load point prior to processing and will be rewound and unloaded after the file is processed. Unloading refers to the process which takes the tape out of the "ready" status and allows the computer operator to remove the tape from the tape drive. The entry "R" specifies that the tape should be rewound both before and after the file is processed. Thus, after the file has been processed, it is rewound to the load point and is ready for further processing. The meanings of all of the possible entries are illustrated in the following table.

Tape Positioning Option	Meaning		With Alternate Assigned	No Alternate Assigned
	Open	Close		
R	RWD	RWD	RWD--At EOV RWD--Begin next Vol.	UNLD--At EOV RWD--Begin next Vol.
U	RWD	UNLD	UNLD--At EOV RWD--Begin next Vol.	UNLD--At EOV RWD--Begin next Vol.
N	NORWD	NORWD	NORWD--At EOV NORWD--Begin next Vol.	UNLD--At EOV NORWD--Begin next Vol.
K	RWD	NORWD	NORWD--At EOV NORWD--Begin next Vol.	UNLD--At EOV NORWD--Begin next Vol.
L	NORWD	RWD	RWD--At EOV RWD--Begin next Vol.	UNLD--At EOV RWD--Begin next Vol.
M	NORWD	UNLD	UNLD--At EOV RWD--Begin next Vol.	UNLD--At EOV RWD--Begin next Vol.

Figure 12-8 Rewind Codes

INPUT SPECIFICATIONS

As noted previously, the input to the program consists of Name cards and Sales cards (see Figure 12-5). The entries on the Input Specifications to define these cards are illustrated below.

EXAMPLE

RPG   INPUT SPECIFICATIONS

Line	Form Type	Filename	Sequence	Number (1-N)	Option (O)	Record Identifying Indicator or **	Position (1)	Not (N)	C/Z/D	Character	Position (2)	Not (N)	C/Z/D	Character	Position (3)	Not (N)	C/Z/D	Character	Stacker Select	P=Packed/B=Binary	From	To	Decimal Positions	Field Name	Control Level (L1-L9)
0 1	Ø	I	CARDIN	Ø11		Ø1		1		C	N															
0 2	Ø	I																				2	6		CUSTNO	L1
0 3	Ø	I																				7	26		NAME	
0 4	Ø	I																				27	56		ADDR	
0 5	Ø	I		Ø21	Ø2			1		C	S															
0 6	Ø	I																				2	6		CUSTNO	L1
0 7	Ø	I																				12	18	2	YTDSLS	

Figure 12-9 Input Specifications

Note in the example above that two formats are defined for the input cards — a format for the Name card and a format for the Sales card. These cards must be in sequence within Customer Number, so entries are made in the Sequence field in columns 15-16. The Name card, as defined by the character "N" in column 1, must always be the first card in the group. Thus, it is given the sequence number 01. There will only be one card per group (column 17) and the card is required (blank in column 18). The Name card is identified by the Record Identifying Indicator 01.

The Sales card, which is identified by the entry "S" in column 1, must be the second card in the group. Since there may be only one Sales card, the value "1" is entered in column 17. The Sales card is optional so the alphabetic value "O" is entered in column 18. If the Sales card is not present, the sales amount will be written in the master output record as zero.

As can also be seen from the example above, the Customer Number (CUSTNO) field will cause a control break to occur. This is done so that both the Name Card and the Sales Card will be written in the tape output file.

OUTPUT SPECIFICATIONS

The only output from the card-to-tape program is the master output file. The output specifications for the master output file are illustrated in Figure 12-10.

EXAMPLE

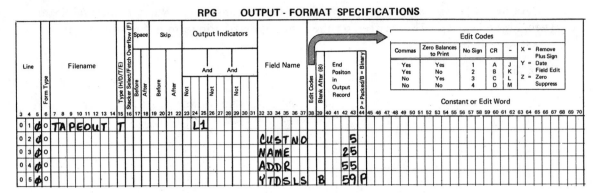

Figure 12-10 Output Specifications for Tape Output File

In the example above it can be seen that the tape master file TAPEOUT is to be written at total time, that is, when an L1 control break occurs. As noted previously, a control break will occur when the customer number in the input records changes. This will occur either after a Name card has been read if there is no Sales card, or after a Sales card has been read.

It will be noted in the Output Specifications illustrated in Figure 12-10 that the Year-To-Date Sales field (YTDSLS) is defined as a packed-decimal field ("P" in column 44). When an output field is defined as a packed-decimal field, the numeric data will be written in a packed-decimal format on the output tape. This results in saving space on the output tape as illustrated below.

EXAMPLE

Zoned Decimal   Packed Decimal

Figure 12-11 Illustration of Packed Decimal Format

Note in the example that when the Year-To-Date sales is stored in the zoned-decimal format, that is, one number per byte in main storage, it requires six characters in core storage. When it is stored in the packed-decimal format, however, it requires only four bytes of main storage. This is because the zone portion of each numeric digit is removed from all digits except the low-order digit, which contains the sign of the field. Thus, as can be seen from the example, two bytes are saved in each record which is written on the tape. This may constitute a considerable savings of storage space on the tape when many records are written in the master file. Again, the only entry required to cause a numeric field to be written in the packed-decimal format is the entry "P" in column 44 of the Output Specifications.

SAMPLE PROGRAM

The sample program to load the master file is illustrated below.

```
DOS/360*RPG*CL 3-9              CASHMAN                    09/27/72          PAGE 0001

           01 010 H                                                         CDTAPE
001        01 020 FCARDIN  IP  F  80  80        READ40 SYSIPT               CDTAPE
002        01 030 FTAPEOUT O   F 800  80        TAPE   SYS022S         U    CDTAPE
003        02 010 ICARDIN  011 01   1 CN                                    CDTAPE
004        02 020 I                                 2   6 CUSTNOL1          CDTAPE
005        02 030 I                                 7  26 NAME              CDTAPE
006        02 040 I                                27  56 ADDR              CDTAPE
007        02 050 I         021002   1 CS                                   CDTAPE
008        02 060 I                                 2   6 CUSTNOL1          CDTAPE
009        02 070 I                                12 182YTDSLS             CDTAPE
010        03 010 OTAPEOUT T        L1                                      CDTAPE
011        03 020 O                       CUSTNO     5                      CDTAPE
012        03 030 O                       NAME      25                      CDTAPE
013        03 040 O                       ADDR      55                      CDTAPE
014        03 050 O                       YTDSLS B  59P                     CDTAPE
```

Figure 12-12 Source Listing

SEQUENTIAL FILE UPDATING

Once a master file has been created, it is periodically necessary to update this file with current information so that the file always contains the most recent data. Typically, file updating procedures take three forms: additions, deletions, and changes.

An addition takes place when a new record is added to an already established master file. For example, in a customer sales system, if a new customer is acquired, it would be necessary to add a record to the master file reflecting the acquisition of the new customer.

A deletion becomes necessary when data currently stored on the master file is to be removed. For example, if a customer no longer purchases from the company, it would be necessary to delete the corresponding master record from the file.

A change must be made to the master file whenever the data on the master file no longer contains accurate, up-to-date information. For example, in a customer sales system, when a new sale is made, the sales amount must be added to the year-to-date sales amount in the master record to reflect a sale to the customer.

Sequential updating involves the reading of a sequential master file, the reading of a sorted sequential transaction file, and the creation of a new, updated master file. Normally, an exception report which lists transaction errors, such as invalid transaction codes, is also created.

An example of a sequential file update is illustrated in Figure 12-13.

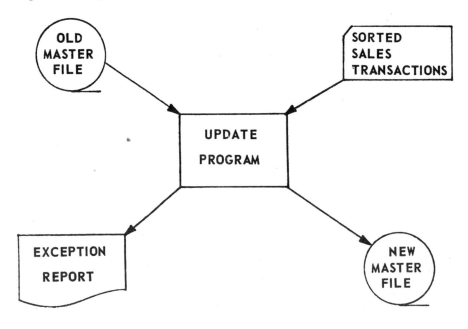

Figure 12-13 Sequential File Update

In the example in Figure 12-13 it can be seen that a master file stored on magnetic tape is to be updated by a sorted sales transaction file stored on punched cards. Output is to consist of the new updated magnetic tape master file and an Exception Report. The Exception Report lists transaction records in error such as cards containing invalid codes, cards with no related master records, etc.

The second sample program in this chapter illustrates a technique to sequentially update the master file created in the first sample program. As noted, the master file contains the year-to-date sales amounts for customers. This master file is to be updated with the new sales figures for the month. In addition, the update program will add customers or delete customers from the master file as needed. An error listing will also be produced which contains a list of any transaction records with errors such as invalid transaction codes.

The format of the master record is illustrated in Figure 12-6. The format of the transaction records to be used to update the master file are illustrated below.

TRANSACTION FILE - INPUT

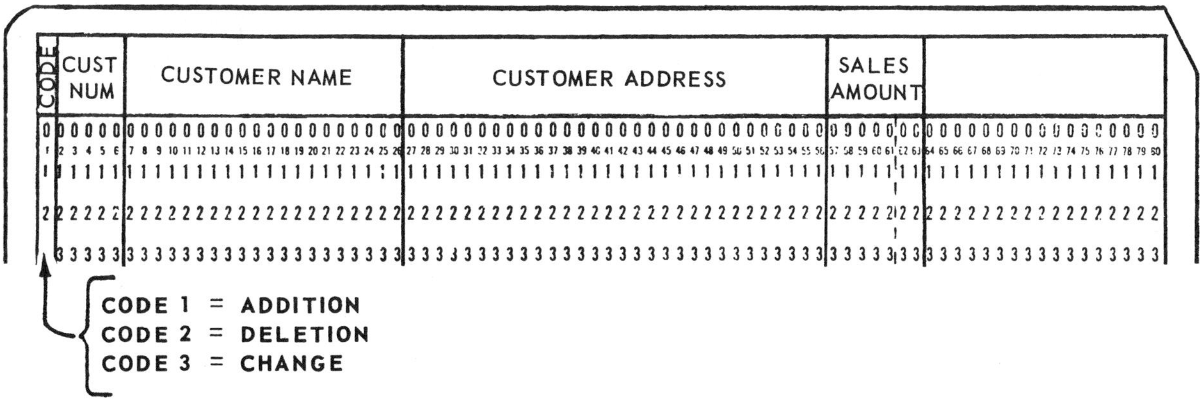

CODE 1 = ADDITION
CODE 2 = DELETION
CODE 3 = CHANGE

Figure 12-14 Transaction Card

The transaction record contains the same fields as the master record. In addition, it contains a transaction code which is used to indicate the type of processing which is to occur. A "1" in the Transaction Code field indicates that the transaction record is an addition to the master file; a "2" indicates a deletion, and a "3" indicates a change to the Sales Amount field in a master record currently on the master file.

Before examining the RPG entries which are required to process two input files, it is necessary to understand the processing which is to take place. Basically, the procedure is as follows: 1) A transaction record is read; 2) A Master Record is read; 3) the Customer Number in the master record and the transaction record are compared to determine if the master record is equal to, less than, or greater than the transaction record; 4) the required processing is performed based upon the comparison.

In order to illustrate this processing, the data in the master file and the transaction file in Figure 12-15 will be used in a step-by-step analysis of the processing.

Test Data

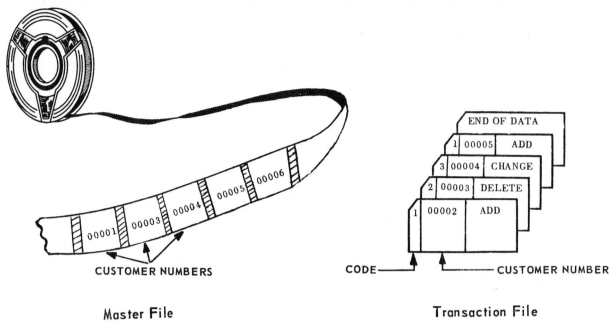

Master File   Transaction File

Figure 12-15 Test Data

Note in the data illustrated above that only the customer numbers on the master file and the transaction codes and customer numbers in the transaction file are illustrated. In actual practice, these records may also contain the Name and Address fields.

The following steps illustrate the processing of the data shown in Figure 12-15.

Step 1:   A transaction record and a master record are read.

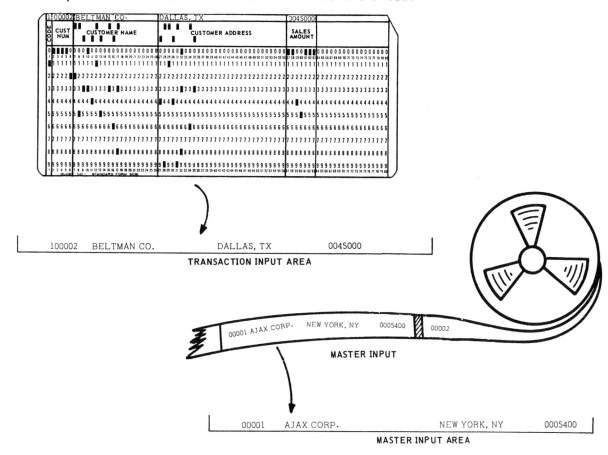

Figure 12-16 Master and Transaction Records are Read

In the example above it can be seen that the first record on the transaction file and the first record in the master file are read into main storage. The transaction record contains a customer number 00002 and the master record contains the customer number 00001. An important fact to recall is that both of these input files must be sorted into an ascending sequence, that is, each subsequent record in the master file and in the transaction file contains a customer number which is higher than the previous customer number. It should also be seen that in order to change or delete a master record, there must be a corresponding transaction record, that is, the customer numbers must be the same. In the example above it can be seen that the customer number in the master file (00001) is less than the customer number in the master file (00002). Therefore; since the transaction file is in an ascending sequence, there will never be a transaction record with the customer number 00001. When this occurs, there is no processing to be performed on the master record so it is merely rewritten on the new master file. This is illustrated in Figure 12-17.

Step 2: The "old" master record is written on the "new" master output tape.

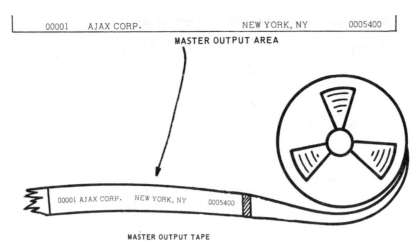

Figure 12-17 Master Output Record is Written

In the example above it can be seen that the record which was stored in the master input area is written on the output tape from the master output area. It will be recalled that RPG moves the data from the input area to the individual fields which are defined on the Input Specifications. In this example, that move will not be shown.

After the first master record is written on the new master file, another master input record must be read to continue the processing. This is illustrated below.

Step 3: Another master record is read.

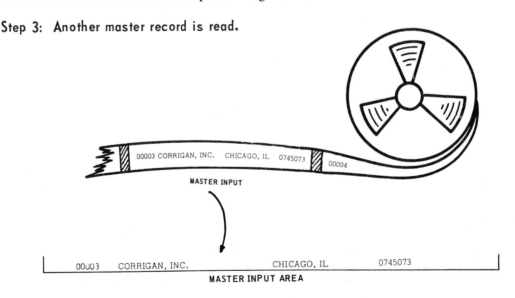

Figure 12-18 Master Record is Read

12.16

In Figure 12-18 it can be seen that the second record on the "old" master file is read into the master input area. The customer number on this master record is equal to 00003. As will be noted, this customer number is greater than the customer number in the transaction record which is in main storage (customer number is 00002). Again, since both the transaction and master records are sorted in an ascending sequence, there will never be a master record with a customer number equal to the customer number in the transaction record which was read in Figure 12-16. Thus, the transaction record will never be able to delete or change an existing master record. The only valid function of a transaction record which does not have a matching customer number in a master record is to add the transaction record to the master file as a new customer. As was noted previously, this process of adding a record to the master file will occur when a new customer is acquired.

As noted, when the customer number in the transaction record is less than the customer number in the master record, the transaction record may only be added to the master file. Whenever a transaction record is to be added to the master file, the transaction code in the transaction record must be equal to "1". If it is not equal to "1", the transaction record is in error because an add is the only valid operation to be performed. When a transaction record with a low customer number is found without a transaction code of "1", an error message is written on the exception report created in the program. In this example, it can be seen in Figure 12-16 that the transaction code is equal to "1". Therefore, the transaction record is added to the new master file.

Step 4: The transaction record is added to the new master file.

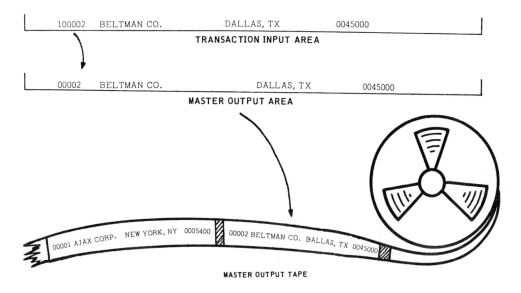

Figure 12-19 Transaction record is added to Master File

Note from the example above that the data in the transaction input area is moved to the master output area and then the data in the master output area is written on the new master output file. As with the previous example, RPG would move the data in the transaction input area to the input fields for processing and then from the input fields to the output area to be written. This step is bypassed in this example and all examples of the sequential update.

Since the transaction record has been processed by being added to the new master file, another transaction record must be read. This is illustrated below.

Step 5: Another transaction record is read.

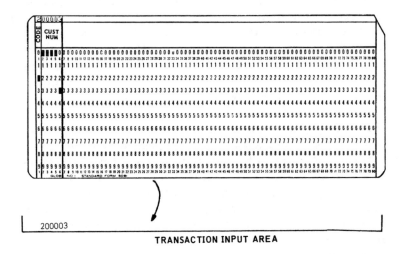

Figure 12-20 Transaction Record is Read

Note in Figure 12-20 that the next transaction record is read and placed in the transaction input area. Then, as with the previous examples, the customer number in the transaction record is compared to the customer number in the master record, which is in the master input area, to determine whether it is higher, lower than, or equal to the master customer number. In this case, it will be noted that customer number 00003, which is contained in the transaction record read in Figure 12-20, is equal to the customer number in the master input area (Figure 12-18).

When the customer number in the transaction record is equal to the customer number in the master record, one of two types of processing may take place — the transaction record may specify that the master record is to be deleted from the new master file or it may specify that the sales amount in the transaction record is to be added to the sales amount in the old master record. The transaction code to cause the master record to be deleted is a "2" and the transaction code to cause the sales amount to be updated is a "3". In Figure 12-20, it can be seen that the transaction code is equal to the value "2", which indicates that the corresponding master record is to be deleted from the new master file. It should be noted also that a transaction code other than "2" or "3" when the customer numbers are equal is invalid and an entry will be made on the Exception Report.

The process used to delete a master record from the new master file is to merely not write it on the new master file. This may be accomplished by reading a new transaction record and reading a master record from the old master file without writing the old master record which is in the master input area on the new master file. Thus, when a master record is to be deleted, the next step is to read another transaction record and another master record. This is illustrated in Figure 12-21.

Step 6: A transaction record and a master record are read.

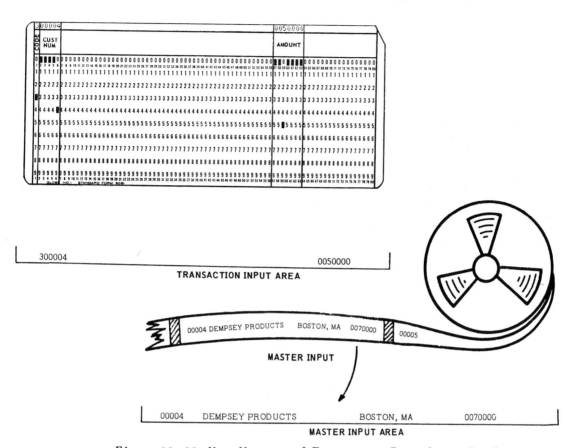

Figure 12-21 New Master and Transaction Records are Read

Note from the example above that after a delete transaction record is found, a new transaction and master record are read without writing the master record on the new master file. Thus, the master record is effectively deleted because it is not written on the new master file.

After the records are read, the comparison between the customer numbers in the transaction and master records again takes place. In the example in Figure 12-21 it can be seen that they are equal, that is, the customer number in both the transaction record and the customer record is equal to 00004. Thus, the valid operations are to delete the master record or to add the sales amount in the transaction record to the sales amount in the master record. The transaction code "2" indicates a deletion and the code "3" indicates a change or update to the sales amount. In the example, the transaction code is equal to "3", so the sales amount in the transaction record is to be added to the sales amount in the master record. This is illustrated in Figure 12-22.

Step 7: The amount field in the master record is incremented by the amount field in the transaction record.

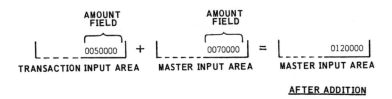

Figure 12-22 Amount is Incremented

Note in the example above that the value which is in the Amount field in the transaction input area is added to the value which is in the Amount field in the master input area. Thus, the sales amount in the master record is updated by the sales amount in the transaction record.

After the master sales amount has been updated by the transaction sales amount, the updated master record must be written on the new master file. This is illustrated in Figure 12-23.

Step 8: The updated master record is written on the new master file.

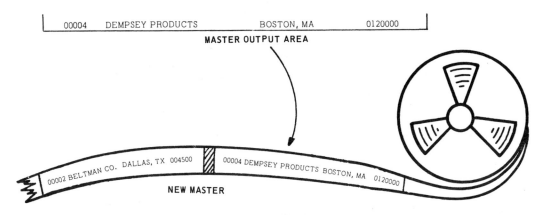

Figure 12-23 Updated Master Record is Written on New Master File

Note from the example above that the updated master record with the new sales amount is written on the new master file. Thus, the "change" transaction has accomplished its function because the sales amount field has been incremented to reflect the new year-to-date sales amount.

After the change transaction has been processed, a new transaction record must be read to be processed against a master record.

Step 9: Another transaction record is read.

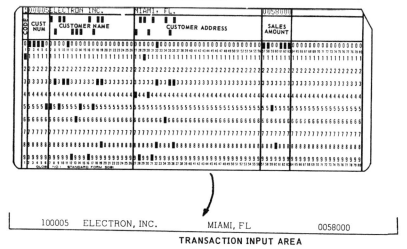

TRANSACTION INPUT AREA

100005   ELECTRON, INC.   MIAMI, FL   0058000

Figure 12-24 Transaction Record is Read

When the updated master record is written on the new master file, there is no more processing to be performed on the master record which is in the master input area. Therefore, another master record must also be read from the old master.

Step 10: Another master record is read.

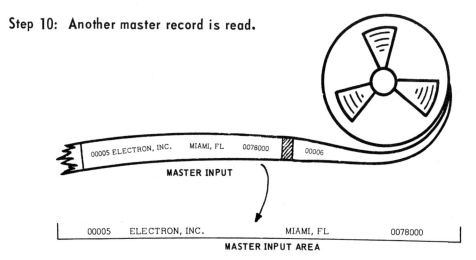

MASTER INPUT

00005   ELECTRON, INC.   MIAMI, FL   0078000

MASTER INPUT AREA

Figure 12-25 A Master Record is Read

Note from Figure 12-25 that a master record with a customer number 00005 is read from the master input file. As when any record is read, the customer number in the master input record is compared to the customer number in the transaction input area (see Figure 12-24). As can be seen, the customer numbers are equal.

It will be recalled that when the customer numbers in the master record and the transaction record are equal, there are two valid types of processing which may take place — the deletion of the master record or the updating of the Sales Amount field. Therefore, the transaction code in the transaction record must be checked to verify that it specifies either a deletion or an update. As can be seen from Figure 12-24, the transaction code in the record is a "1", which indicates an addition. Adding the transaction record to the master file is not valid, however, because there is already a record on the master file. Thus, when the transaction code indicates an addition and equal customer numbers are found, the transaction record is in error. When this occurs, an entry must be made on the printed Exception Report as illustrated below.

Step 11: Entry is made on Exception Report.

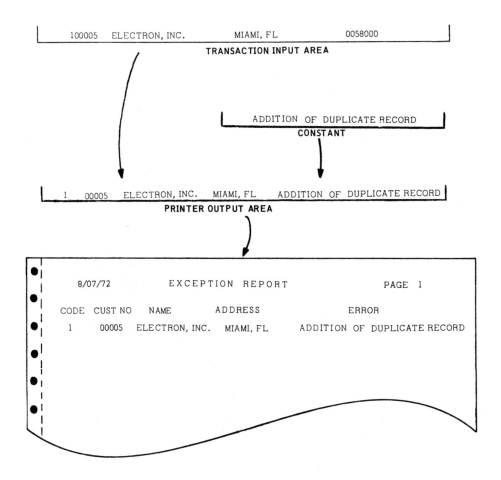

Figure 12-26 Entry is Made on Exception Report

As can be seen from the example above, when the customer numbers are equal but the transaction code indicates an addition, the error message "Addition of Duplicate Record" is placed on the Exception Report together with the information contained in the transaction record so that the record in error may be identified.

After the entry has been made on the Exception Report, another transaction record must be read. As can be seen from Figure 12-15, the transaction record with the customer number 00005 is the last transaction record. Thus, when an attempt is made to read the next transaction record, end-of-file will be indicated. Whenever two input files are being processed, the program is usually not ended when only one of the files has reached end-of-file. Thus, the remainder of the master records must be processed. This processing consists of merely writing the master in main storage on the new master file and then reading the remainder of the records on the master input file and writing them on the master output file. Thus, the master record with the customer number 00005, which is stored in main storage, would be written on the new master file and then the master record with the customer number 00006 (see Figure 12-15) would be read and written on the new master file. The program would then be ended.

FILE DESCRIPTION SPECIFICATIONS

The four files which are used for the Sequential Update program are the transaction file, the old master file, the new master file, and the printer file for the Exception Report. The File Description Specifications for these files are illustrated below.

EXAMPLE

RPG FILE DESCRIPTION SPECIFICATIONS

Line (3-5)	Form Type (6)	Filename (7-14)	File Type I/O/U/C/D (15)	File Designation P/S/C/R/T/D (16)	End of File E (17)	Sequence A/D (18)	File Format F/V (19)	Block Length (20-23)	Record Length (24-27)	L/R (28)	Length of Key Field or of Record Address Field (29-30)	Record Address Type A/K/I (31)	Type of File Organization or Additional Area I/D/T or 1-9 (32)	Overflow Indicator (33-34)	Key Field Starting Location (35-38)	Extension Code E/L (39)	Device (40-46)	Symbolic Device (47-52)	Labels (S, N, or E) (53)	Name of Label Exit (54-59)	Extent Exit for DAM / Core Index (60-65)	A/U (66)	File Addition/Unordered (66)	Number of Tracks for Cylinder Overflow (67-69)	Number of Extents	N/U (70)	Tape Rewind (71)	File Condition U1-U8 (72-74)
02Ø	F	MSTRIN	I	P		A	F	8ØØ	8Ø								TAPE	SYSØ22	S									
03Ø	F	TRANSIN	I	S		A	F	8Ø	8Ø								READ4Ø	SYSIPT										
04Ø	F	MSTROUT	O				F	8ØØ	8Ø								TAPE	SYSØ23	S									
05Ø	F	EXCPRPT	O				F	132	132					OF			PRINTER	SYSLST										

Figure 12-27 File Description Specifications

As noted, the master input and output files are stored on magnetic tape. Thus, the entries for the Device field (columns 40-46) must be the word TAPE. As can be seen, the input file (MSTRIN) will be stored on SYS022 with standard labels and the output file (MSTROUT) will be stored on SYS023 with standard labels.

When a sequential updating process is to take place, an RPG feature called MATCHING RECORDS is utilized. The Matching Records feature provides for the comparisons of control fields such as the Customer Number in the previous examples. When Matching Records are to be used, one of the input files must be defined as the Primary file ("P" in column 16) and the second and subsequent files must be defined as Secondary files ("S" in column 16). Note from Figure 12-27 that the master input file is defined as the Primary file and the transaction file is defined as the Secondary file. In most situations, master files are the primary files in an RPG program.

As was noted previously, whenever two files are to be matched against one another, such as the master file and the transaction, they must be in sequence by the control field. In this example, both of the files are in an ascending sequence by customer number. The RPG compiler must be informed of this fact by placing the letter of the alphabet "A" in column 18. This signifies that the files are in an ascending sequence. The letter "D" in column 18 would indicate that the files are in a descending sequence. Again, when files are to be matched against one another, they must both be in either an ascending or a descending sequence. As can also be seen from Figure 12-27, the tape files (MSTRIN and MSTROUT) have the same block lengths and record lengths as the master file which was created in the first sample program in this chapter. Whenever a tape file is to be used as an input file, the blocking factor and record length must be the same as was specified in the program which created the file.

INPUT SPECIFICATIONS

As noted, the Matching Record feature of RPG is used when two sequential files are processed against one another. The field to be used in the matching of the records in the files must be specified on the Input Specifications as illustrated below.

EXAMPLE

RPG INPUT SPECIFICATIONS

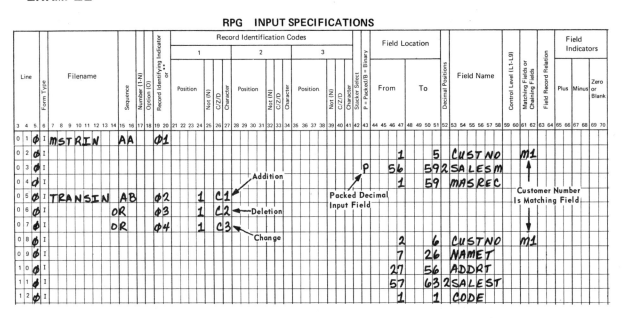

Figure 12-28 Input Specifications

In the example above it can be seen that the two input files, MSTRIN and TRANSIN, are defined in the same manner as has been used in previous programs. The Record Identifying Indicator 01 will be "on" when a master record is read. The Record Identifying Indicator 02 will be "on" when an add record (transaction code = 1) is read, indicator 03 will be a delete record (transaction code = 2) and indicator 04 will be a change (transaction code = 3).

The input fields for the master record are defined as in previous examples, that is, the "From" and "To" fields express the columns in the record where the fields appear and the Field Name columns are used to give the fields a name. Note that the definitions of the fields in the input record correspond to the fields in the output records in the first sample program of this chapter. Whenever a file is to be used as input to a program, the field definitions must be the same as those used when the file is created. It will be recalled also that the Sales Amount in the master record is stored in the packed-decimal format (see Figure 12-11). Thus, when the field is input to the update program, it must be defined as a packed-decimal field by specifying the value "P" in column 43 of the Input Specifications. This indicates to the compiler that the field will be in a packed-decimal format when it is read from the master file. Note also on coding line 040 that the first 59 characters of the master record are given the name MASREC. This name refers to the portion of the master record which contains actual data and will be used on the output specifications to cause the entire record to be rewritten on the new master file.

The entry "M1" in columns 61-62 on the same coding line as the CUSTNO field (coding line 020 and 080) specifies that this field is to be used in the "matching" operation when the two records are read, that is, it specifies that the Customer Number field in columns 1-5 of the Master Record is to be compared to the Customer Number field in the Transaction Record in order to determine which record is to be processed next. The value "M1" states that the field is the first or only field to be used in the comparison. It is possible to have up to nine different fields which would form the single value to be compared. The indicators would be numbered M1 — M9. When more than one field is to be used for matching records, the highest numbered field is considered the major field, that is, if three fields are numbered M1, M2, and M3, then the M3 field is the high-order field, the M2 field is in the center, and the M1 field is in the low-order positions.

MR INDICATOR

Whenever matching fields are found, that is, whenever the data in the fields identified in the input specifications as matching fields by the M1, M2, etc. indicators contains equal data, the MR indicator is turned "on". When the MR indicator is "on", it means that a record in the primary file has a value in its control field which is equal to the value in the control field of a record in the secondary file. Thus, it is through the use of the MR indicator that an equal condition as illustrated in the previous examples may be detected.

When the MR indicator is used in a sequential update, it is the combination of the MR indicator and the Record Identifying Indicator which dictates the status of the update operation and which records are to be processed. The indicators used in the sample program and their meanings are illustrated below.

INDICATORS	MEANING
MR,01	Master Record with matching secondary record is to be processed.
MR,02	An Add Record with a Matching Master Record has been read.
MR,03	A Delete Record with a Matching Master Record is ready for processing.
MR,04	A Change Record with a Matching Master Record is ready for processing.
NMR,01	A Master Record without a Matching Master Record is ready for processing.
NMR,02	An Add Transaction Record without a Matching Master Record is ready for processing.
NMR,03	A Delete Transaction Record without a Matching Master Record is ready for processing.
NMR,04	A Change Transaction Record without a Matching Master Record is ready for processing.

In the list above it can be seen that the combination of the Matching Record Indicator and the Record Identifying Indicator can be used to determine the processing of each record. Based upon the meanings of the indicators illustrated above and the processing illustrated in the example of processing the files, the following action would be taken when these combinations are found.

INDICATORS	ACTION TAKEN
MR,01	No action taken — a transaction record must be read.
MR,02	This is an error — an attempted addition of a record already on the master file. An entry will be made on the exception report and the old master record will be written on the new master file.
MR,03	Another master record and transaction record will be read. No output processing takes place because the old master record is not to be written on the new master file.

INDICATORS	ACTION TAKEN
MR,04	The sales amount in the transaction record is added to the sales amount in the master record and the master record is written on the new master file.
NMR,01	The old master record is written on the new master file because there is no transaction record to update the master record.
NMR,02	A valid addition — the data in the transaction record is moved to the master output area and the data is written as a new master record in the new master file.
NMR,03	This is an error — attempting to delete a master record which is not on the master file. An entry will be made on the exception report.
NMR,04	This is an error — attempting to change a master record which is not on the master file. An entry will be made on the exception report.

As can be seen, these combinations illustrated above are those which may occur when updating the master file. The calculation and output specifications to cause the above processing to take place are illustrated in Figure 12-29.

EXAMPLE

Calculation Specifications

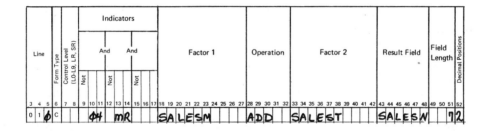

Output Specifications

Line	Form Type	Filename	Type (H/D/T/E)	Stacker Select/Fetch Overflow (F)	Space Before	Space After	Skip Before	Skip After	Output Indicators Not		Not		Not	Field Name	Edit Codes	Blank After (B)	End Position in Output Record	P = Packed/B = Binary	Constant or Edit Word
010	O	EXCPRPT	D		1				NMR	N01	N02								
020	O	OR							MR		02								
030	O													CODE			4		
040	O													CUSTNO			15		
050	O													NAMET			39		
060	O													ADDRT			72		
070	O								NMR		03						95		'MASTER NOT ON FILE'
080	O								NMR		04						95		'MASTER NOT ON FILE'
090	O								MR		02						95		'ADDITION OF DUPLICATE'
100	O								MR		02						103		'RECORD'
110	O	MSTROUT	D		1				NMR		01								
120	O	OR							MR		02								
130	O													MASREC			59		
140	O		D						NMR		02								
150	O													CUSTNO			5		
010	O													NAMET			26		
020	O													ADDRT			55		
030	O													SALEST			59	P	
040	O		D						MR		04								
050	O													MASREC			59		
060	O													SALESN			59	P	

Edit Codes

Commas	Zero Balances to Print	No Sign	CR	–	
Yes	Yes	1	A	J	X = Remove Plus Sign
Yes	No	2	B	K	Y = Date Field Edit
No	Yes	3	C	L	Z = Zero Suppress
No	No	4	D	M	

Figure 12-29 Output Processing

Note in the Calculation Specifications illustrated in Figure 12-29 that the sales amount in the transaction record and the sales amount in the master record are added and stored in the SALESN field when the indicators MR and 04 are "on", which indicates a change record with a matching master record. The updated record is then written on the new master file. Note on coding lines 050 and 060 of the second page of the Output Specifications that the entry MASREC is made followed by the entry SALESN. The MASREC field references the entire master record containing valid data (see Figure 12-28). The SALESN field is the field which contains the updated sales amount. This technique of specifying the entire record and then the fields which are to be changed is used to minimize the number of move statements in the object coding which must be used in order to move the data from the input fields to the output area. Note that two moves will be used in this example — one to move the entire master record to the output area and one to move the SALESN field to the proper portion of the output area. If each individual field in the master record were specified, additional moves would be required. It is important to note in this technique that the field MASREC is specified before the field SALESN on the coding form. This is done because the fields are moved to the output area in the same sequence as they are specified on the form. Thus, the MASREC field is moved to the output field and then the SALESN field is moved to the output area. Thus, the data in the SALESN field is moved over data which is in the SALESM field in the master record and replaces that data, which is the desired result. If the SALESN field were specified first, it would be moved to the output area and then the MASREC data would be moved to the output area. If this happened, the data which was in the output area from the SALESN field would be replaced by the data which was in the SALESM portion of the MASREC field. Thus, the updated sales amount would not be stored in the new master record.

The Output Indicators NMR and N01 and N02 or the indicators MR and 02 must be satisfied in order to cause a line to be printed on the Exception Report. The NMR, N01, and N02 combination occurs when a delete record (03) or an update record (04) is read without a corresponding master record. This combination will cause the message "Master Not On File" to be printed on the report. The MR and 02 combination means that an addition record attempted an add operation when a master was already on the master file and the message "Addition of Duplicate Record" will be printed. Note that in addition to the messages, the Code, Customer Number, Name, and Address of the transaction record are printed so that the transaction record in error may be identified and corrected.

SEQUENTIAL DISK PROCESSING

The previous example of processing the sequential files assumed that the files were stored on magnetic tape. Sequential file processing may also take place on Direct Access Storage Devices. Direct Access Storage Devices include 2311 Disk Drives, 2314 Disk Drives, 2321 Data Cells and other devices. In order to process sequential files on direct access devices, the type of device to be used must be defined in the "Device" portion of the File Description Specifications. The entries to define the files used in the sample program for 2311 Disk Drives is illustrated below.

EXAMPLE

RPG FILE DESCRIPTION SPECIFICATIONS

Line (3-5)	Form Type (6)	Filename (7-14)	File Type I/O/U/C/D (15)	File Designation P/S/C/R/T/D (16)	End of File E (17)	Sequence A/D (18)	File Format F/V (19)	Block Length (20-23)	Record Length (24-27)	L/R (28)	Length of Key Field or of Record Address Field (29-30)	Record Address Type A/K/I (31)	Type of File Organization or Additional Area I/D/T or 1-9 (32)	Overflow Indicator (33-34)	Key Field Starting Location (35-38)	Extension Code E/L (39)	Device (40-46)	Symbolic Device (47-52)	Labels (S, N, or E) (53)
020	F	MSTRIN	I	P		A	F	800	80								DISK11	SYS016	S
030	F	TRANSIN	I	S		A	F	80	80								READ40	SYSIPT	
040	F	MSTROUT	O				F	800	80								DISK11	SYS017	S
050	F	EXCPRPT	O				F	132	132					OF			PRINTER	SYSLST	

Figure 12-30 Definition of Sequential Direct Access Files

Note in the example above that the file definitions for the master input and master output files are identical to those for the files on tape (see Figure 12-27) except that the device is specified as a DISK11 instead of TAPE. In addition, the "SYS" number is different indicating that a different device is to be used. The other "device" entries which may be made are DISK14 for a 2314 Disk Drive and CEL01 for a 2321 Data Cell.

SAMPLE PROGRAM

The source listing of the sample program is illustrated below.

```
DOS/360*RPG*CL 3-9                    CASHMAN                      09/27/72              PAGE 0001

             01 010 H                                                              SEQUDP
001          01 020 FMSTRIN  IP AF 800   80              TAPE   SYS022S            SEQUDP
002          01 030 FTRANSIN IS AF  80   80              READ40 SYS1PT             SEQUDP
003          01 040 FMSTROUT O   F 800   80              TAPE   SYS023S            SEQUDP
004          01 050 FEXCPRPT O   F 132  132        OF    PRINTER SYSLST            SEQUDP
005          02 010 IMSTRIN  AA  01                                                SEQUDP
006          02 020 I                                  1     5 CUSTNO  M1          SEQUDP
007          02 030 I                                P 56   592SALESM              SEQUDP
008          02 040 I                                  1    59 MASREC              SEQUDP
009          02 050 ITRANSIN AB  02    1 C1                                        SEQUDP
010          02 060 I        OR  03    1 C2                                        SEQUDP
011          02 070 I        OR  04    1 C3                                        SEQUDP
012          02 080 I                                  2     6 CUSTNO  M1          SEQUDP
013          02 090 I                                  7    26 NAMET               SEQUDP
014          02 100 I                                 27    56 ADDRT               SEQUDP
015          02 110 I                                 57   632SALEST              SEQUDP
016          02 120 I                                  1     1 CODE                SEQUDP
017          03 010 C    04 MR     SALESM    ADD  SALEST   SALESN  72              SEQUDP
018          04 010 OEXCPRPT H  201    1P                                          SEQUDP
019          04 020 O        OR      OF                                            SEQUDP
020          04 030 O                        UDATE     9 '  /  /  '                SEQUDP
021          04 040 O                                 40 'E X C E P T I O N'       SEQUDP
022          04 050 O                                 54 'R E P O R T'             SEQUDP
023          04 060 O                                 73 'PAGE'                    SEQUDP
024          04 070 O                        PAGE  Z  88                           SEQUDP
025          04 080 O        H  2    1P                                            SEQUDP
026          04 090 O        OR      OF                                            SEQUDP
027          04 100 O                                  6 'CODE'                    SEQUDP
028          04 110 O                                 16 'CUST NO'                 SEQUDP
029          04 120 O                                 29 'NAME'                    SEQUDP
030          04 130 O                                 57 'ADRESS'                  SEQUDP
031          04 140 O                                 85 'ERROR'                   SEQUDP
032          04 150 O        D  1    N01N01N02                                     SEQUDP
033          05 010 O        OR      MR 02                                         SEQUDP
034          05 020 O                        CODE      4                           SEQUDP
035          05 030 O                        CUSTNO   15                           SEQUDP
036          05 040 O                        NAMET    39                           SEQUDP
037          05 050 O                        ADDRT    72                           SEQUDP
038          05 060 O               NMR 03             95 'MASTER NOT ON FILE'     SEQUDP
039          05 070 O               NMR 04             95 'MASTER NOT ON FILE  '   SEQUDP
040          05 080 O                MR 02             95 'ADDITION OF DUPLICATE'  SEQUDP
041          05 090 O                MR 02            103 'RECORD'                 SEQUDP
042          05 100 OMSTROUT D      NMR 01                                         SEQUDP
043          05 110 O        OR      MR 02                                         SEQUDP
044          05 120 O                        MASREC   59                           SEQUDP
045          05 130 O        D      NMR 02                                         SEQUDP
046          05 140 O                        CUSTNO    5                           SEQUDP
047          05 150 O                        NAMET    25                           SEQUDP
048          06 010 O                        ADDRT    55                           SEQUDP
049          06 020 O                        SALEST   59P                          SEQUDP
050          06 030 O        D       MR 04                                         SEQUDP
051          06 040 O                        MASREC   59                           SEQUDP
052          06 050 O                        SALESN   59P                          SEQUDP
```

CHAPTER 12

REVIEW QUESTIONS

1. What are the advantages and disadvantages of blocking records on a magnetic tape file?

2. State several reasons why a numeric field should be stored in the packed-decimal format in a magnetic tape file.

3. What are the valid operations when the control field in a transaction record is equal to a control field in a master record? When the transaction record control field is less than the master record? When the transaction record control field is greater than the master record?

4. What is the difference between the M1, M2, etc. indicators used on the Input Specifications and the MR indicator used on the Calculation Specifications and the Output Specifications?

CHAPTER 12

STUDENT EXERCISES

1. Write the entries for the Input Specifications to define the following tape record:

Columns 1-3: Division
Columns 4-10: Part Number
Columns 11-30: Description
Columns 31-35: Manufacture Date (Julian Date)
Columns 36-40: Quantity

The following fields in the master record defined above are to be matched with fields in transaction records: High-order — Division; Intermediate — Part Number; Low-order — Manufacture Date. The filename for the file is TPMAST.

RPG   INPUT SPECIFICATIONS

Line	Form Type	Filename	Sequence	Number (1-N)	Option (O)	Record Identifying Indicator or **	Record Identification Codes 1 Position	Not (N)	C/Z/D	Character	2 Position	Not (N)	C/Z/D	Character	3 Position	Not (N)	C/Z/D	Character	Stacker Select	P = Packed/B = Binary	Field Location From	To	Decimal Positions	Field Name	Control Level (L1-L9)	Matching Fields or Chaining Fields	Field Record Relation	Plus	Minus	Zero or Blank
0 1	I																													
0 2	I																													
0 3	I																													
0 4	I																													
0 5	I																													
0 6	I																													

2. Write the corresponding entries for the transaction file records which have the following format:

Columns 1-7: Part Number
Columns 11-30: Description
Columns 40-42: Division
Columns 56-60: Quantity
Columns 76-80: Manufacture Date (Julian Date)

The filename is TRANSIN and is stored on punched cards. The transaction codes are "1" for additions, "2" for deletions, and "3" for changes to the Quantity field.

RPG   INPUT SPECIFICATIONS

Line	Form Type	Filename	Sequence	Number (1-N)	Option (O)	Record Identifying Indicator or **	Record Identification Codes 1 Position	Not (N)	C/Z/D	Character	2 Position	Not (N)	C/Z/D	Character	3 Position	Not (N)	C/Z/D	Character	Stacker Select	P = Packed/B = Binary	Field Location From	To	Decimal Positions	Field Name	Control Level (L1-L9)	Matching Fields or Chaining Fields	Field Record Relation	Plus	Minus	Zero or Blank
0 1	I																													
0 2	I																													
0 3	I																													
0 4	I																													
0 5	I																													
0 6	I																													

12.32

3. Assuming that the proper processing has been accomplished on the Calculation Specifications to update the Quantity field, write the entries on the Output Specifications to rewrite the new master file which has a filename NEWMAST.

RPG   OUTPUT - FORMAT SPECIFICATIONS

Line	Form Type	Filename	Type (H/D/T/E)	Stacker Select/Fetch Overflow (F)	Space Before	Space After	Skip Before	Skip After	Output Indicators Not	Output Indicators And Not	Output Indicators And Not	Field Name	Edit Codes	Blank After (B)	End Positon in Output Record	P = Packed/B = Binary	Constant or Edit Word
0 1	O																
0 2	O																
0 3	O																
0 4	O																
0 5	O																
0 6	O																
0 7	O																
0 8	O																
0 9	O																
1 0	O																
1 1	O																
1 2	O																
1 3	O																
1 4	O																
1 5	O																

Edit Codes

Commas	Zero Balances to Print	No Sign	CR	-
Yes	Yes	1	A	J
Yes	No	2	B	K
No	Yes	3	C	L
No	No	4	D	M

X = Remove Plus Sign
Y = Date Field Edit
Z = Zero Suppress

CHAPTER 12

Debugging RPG Programs

Problem 1

Instructions: The following RPG program contains an error or errors which occur during execution. Circle each error and record the corrected entries directly on the listing. Explain the error and method of correction in the space provided below.

```
DOS/360*RPG*CL 3-9              CASHMAN                    10/25/72          PAGE 0001
        01 010 H                                                            SEQUDP
001     01 020 FMSTRIN  IP AF 800  80         TAPE    SYS022S               SEQUDP
002     01 030 FTRANSIN IS AF  80  80         READ40 SYSIPT                 SEQUDP
003     01 040 FMSTROUT O  F 800  80          TAPE    SYS023S               SEQUDP
004     01 050 FEXCPRPT O  F 132 132     OF   PRINTERSYSLST                 SEQUDP
005     02 010 IMSTRIN  AA  01                                              SEQUDP
006     02 020 I                             1   5 CUSTNO  M1               SEQUDP
007     02 030 I                          P 56  592SALESM                   SEQUDP
008     02 040 I                            1  59 MASREC                    SEQUDP
009     02 050 ITRANSIN AB  02    1 C1                                      SEQUDP
010     02 060 I        OR  03    1 C2                                      SEQUDP
011     02 070 I        OR  04    1 C3                                      SEQUDP
012     02 080 I                             2   6 CUSTNO  M1               SEQUDP
013     02 090 I                             7  26 NAMET                    SEQUDP
014     02 100 I                            27  56 ADDRT                    SEQUDP
015     02 110 I                            57 632SALEST                    SEQUDP
016     02 120 I                             1   1 CODE                     SEQUDP
017     03 010 C    04 MR . SALESM    ADD SALEST   SALESN  72               SEQUDP
018     04 010 OEXCPRPT H  201   1P                                         SEQUDP
019     04 020 O        OR        OF                                        SEQUDP
020     04 030 O                        UDATE    9 ' / / '                  SEQUDP
021     04 040 O                                40 'E X C E P T I O N'       SEQUDP
022     04 050 O                                54 'R E P O R T'            SEQUDP
023     04 060 O                                73 'PAGE'                   SEQUDP
024     04 070 O                        PAGE  Z 88                          SEQUDP
025     04 080 O        H  2    1P                                          SEQUDP
026     04 090 O        OR        OF                                        SEQUDP
027     04 100 O                                 6 'CODE'                   SEQUDP
028     04 110 O                                16 'CUST NO'                SEQUDP
029     04 120 O                                29 'NAME'                   SEQUDP
030     04 130 O                                57 'ADRESS'                 SEQUDP
031     04 140 O                                85 'ERROR'                  SEQUDP
032     04 150 O        D  1    MRN01N02                                    SEQUDP
033     05 010 O        OR    MR 02                                         SEQUDP
034     05 020 O                        CODE     4                          SEQUDP
035     05 030 O                        CUSTNO  15                          SEQUDP
036     05 040 O                        NAMET   39                          SEQUDP
037     05 050 O                        ADDRT   72                          SEQUDP
038     05 060 O              NMR 03                95 'MASTER NOT ON FILE'  SEQUDP
039     05 070 O              NMR 04                95 'MASTER NOT ON FILE ' SEQUDP
040     05 080 O              MR 02                 95 'ADDITION OF DUPLICATE' SEQUDP
041     05 090 O              MR 02                103 'RECORD'             SEQUDP
042     05 100 OMSTROUT D     NMR 01                                        SEQUDP
043     05 110 O        OR    MR 02                                         SEQUDP
044     05 120 O                        MASREC  59                          SEQUDP
045     05 130 O        D     NMR 02                                        SEQUDP
046     05 140 O                        CUSTNO   5                          SEQUDP
047     05 150 O                        NAMET   25                          SEQUDP
048     06 010 O                        ADDRT   55                          SEQUDP
049     06 020 O                        SALEST  59P                         SEQUDP
050     06 030 O        D     MR 04                                         SEQUDP
051     06 040 O                        MASREC  59                          SEQUDP
052     06 050 O                        SALESN  59P                         SEQUDP
```

12.34

```
10/25/72          E X C E P T I O N   R E P O R T          PAGE

CODE   CUST NO        NAME              ADRESS              ERROR
 3     23456  ◄───────────── Note: These records are valid
 2     28798  ◄─────────────       update records
 1     30179   OBLIN INC.        PASADENA, CA.      ADDITION OF DUPLICATE  RECORD
```

EXPLANATION

12.35

CHAPTER 12

PROGRAMMING ASSIGNMENT 1

INSTRUCTIONS

Write the RPG program to load a Master Employee File with the input data illustrated below.

INPUT — Load Data

The following data is to be loaded on a Master Employee File to be stored on magnetic tape.

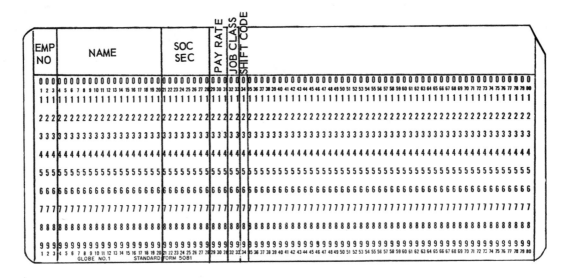

The Employee Number field (columns 1-3) is the control field for the master output file. The format of the Master Employee File may be any desired by the programmer, but the Social Security Number and the Pay Rate should be stored as packed-decimal fields.

TEST DATA – ASSIGNMENT NO. 1

EMP NO (col 1-3)	NAME (col 4-20	SOC SEC (col 21-28)	PAY RATE (col 29-31)	CLASS (col 32-33)	SHIFT (col 34)
096	Allen, Allan	65498754	540	09	1
145	Bebit, Harold	67583439	275	05	2
236	Cloter, James	86530983	550	09	3
540	Heath, Kit	99876547	450	03	2
663	Numb, Ian	88765452	600	10	1
785	Vergen, Mary	76545671	690	12	2

DOS JOB CONTROL

// JOB jobname

// OPTION LINK

// EXEC RPG

– Student Source Deck –

/*

// LBLTYP TAPE

// EXEC LNKEDT

// ASSGN SYS021,X'180'

// TLBL filename,'EMP MASTER',71/001

// EXEC

– Test Data –

/*

/&

Note: This job stream assumes that there is a standard assignment for the card reader. It also assumes that the tape to be used will be mounted on tape drive X'180' assigned to SYS021 and that the tape contains standard labels. Thus, some of the job control statements in the job stream above may need to be changed to conform to the installation where the job is to be run.

PROGRAMMING ASSIGNMENT 2

INSTRUCTIONS

Write an RPG program to update the Employee Master File created in Assignment #1. The transaction records will contain Additions, Deletions, and Changes.

INPUT

The input consists of the Master Employee File created in Assignment #1 and is stored on magnetic tape, and Transaction Records which are stored on punched cards. Both files are sorted in an ascending sequence by Employee Number. The format of the records on tape are whatever was used by the programmer in Assignment #1. The format of the cards in the Transaction File are illustrated below.

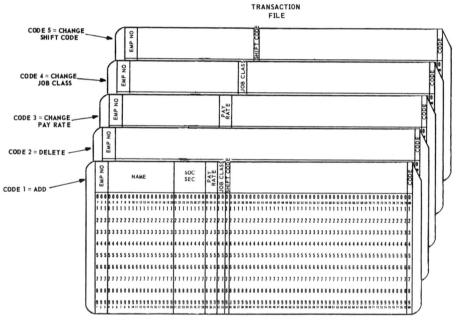

OUTPUT

Output is to consist of an updated master file in the same format as the input master file and an Exception Report listing any invalid transaction records.

TEST DATA – ASSIGNMENT NO. 2

Emp No (col 1-3)	Name (col 4-20)	Soc Sec (col 21-28)	Pay Rate (col 29-31)	Class (col 32-33)	Shift (col 34)	Code (col 80)
086	Abbot, Bud	09876598	900	17	1	1
145						2
236			600			3
240	Dumdum, Eddie	87678531	200	01	3	1
540	Health, Jim	64532780	500	05	2	1
650						2
663				12		4
754			700			3
785					3	5
987	Zilch, Zelda	69887674	250	04	1	1

DOS JOB CONTROL

The following job stream could be used to both load the master file in Assignment #1 and to update the file in Assignment #2.

```
// JOB jobname
// OPTION LINK
// EXEC RPG
  – Source Deck - Assignment #1 –
/*
// LBLTYP TAPE
// EXEC LNKEDT
// ASSGN SYS021,X'180'
// TLBL filename,'EMP MASTER',71/001
// EXEC
  – Test Data - Assignment #1 –
/*
// OPTION LINK
// EXEC RPG
  – Source Deck - Assignment #2 –
/*
// LBLTYP TAPE
// EXEC LNKEDT
// ASSGN SYS022,X'181'
// TLBL filename-input,'EMPMASTER'
// TLBL filename-output,'EMPMASTER',71/001
// EXEC
  – Test Data - Assignment #2 –
/*
/&
```

CHAPTER 13

INDEXED SEQUENTIAL ACCESS METHOD

DIRECT ACCESS STORAGE DEVICES

Another type of input/output device which is an effective storage media for many applications is a DIRECT ACCESS STORAGE DEVICE (DASD). Direct access storage devices may process files organized sequentially as with magnetic tape but also offer the advantage of "random" retrieval of individual records from a file. Although a number of direct access devices are currently available, the IBM 2311 disk drive is one of the most widely used direct access storage devices and serves as a general example for similar units. The 2311 disk storage drive is illustrated below.

Figure 13-1 2311 Disk Drive

The 2311 disk drive is a single unit which allows the mounting of removable disk "packs" (2316 disk packs). The packs when removed from the drive are enclosed in protective covers. Each pack consists of six disks mounted on a vertical shaft. The disks are 14 inches in diameter and are made of metal with a magnetic oxide coating on both sides of the disk. There are ten recording surfaces on each pack. The top surface of the upper disk and the bottom surface of the lower disk are not used for recording data.

Figure 13-2 illustrates a schematic of the disk unit.

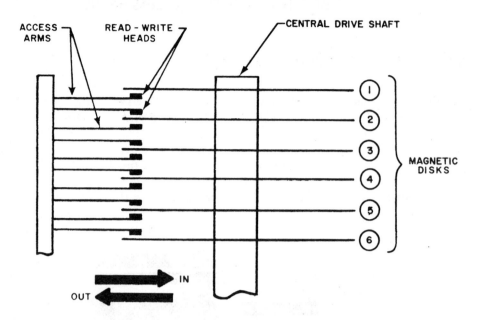

Figure 13-2 Schematic of Disk Unit

The disks rotate at 2400 revolutions per minute. To transfer data to or from the recording surface requires some type of "access" mechanism. On the 2311 disk drive the access mechanism consists of a group of access arms consisting of read/write heads that move together as a unit in and out between the recording surfaces of the disk pack. These comb-type access arms can move to 203 different positions on the surface of the disk as there are 203 discrete recording positions within a disk surface. It should be noted that only 200 positions are normally used for recording data. Three alternate areas are supplied if any of the first 200 positions are defective.

Recording of Data

Data is recorded on the surface of the disks in the form of magnetic spots along a series of concentric circular recording positions on each disk recording surface. The recording surface of each disk pack is divided into many tracks. It should be noted that the tracks are concentric, not spiral like a phonograph record. Data is recorded serially bit-by-bit, eight bits per byte, along a track. On the 2311 disk drive there are 200 tracks per surface (plus 3 alternates) with each track capable of storing a maximum of 3,625 bytes.

The following is a schematic drawing illustrating the 200 tracks on a recording surface.

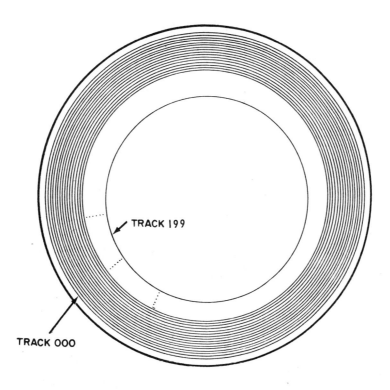

Figure 13-3 Schematic of Disk Recording Track Position

It should be noted that only 200 tracks can be defined for use by the programmer and that the 3 alternate tracks are used if any of the 200 tracks are defective.

Cylinder Concept

Each concentric circle as one looks "three dimensionally" from the top of the disk pack is called a CYLINDER. A "cylinder of data" is defined as the amount of data that is accessible with one positioning of the access mechanism. This is an important concept since movement of the access mechanism represents a significant portion of the time required to access and transfer data.

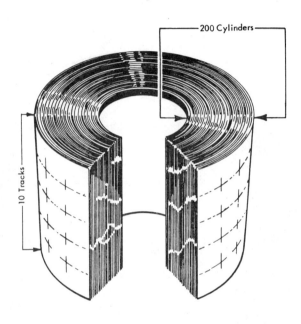

Figure 13-4 Cylinder Concepts

Each 2316 disk pack has 200 cylinders which is equal to the number of positions to which the access mechanism can move. Each cylinder has ten tracks, which is equal to the number of recording surfaces. Thus, a cylinder has a maximum capacity of 36,250 bytes (3,625 bytes per track, 10 tracks per cylinder). A pack has a maximum capacity of 7.25 million bytes (36,250 bytes per cylinder, 200 cylinders per pack).

Each track can hold a maximum of 3,625 characters. Of course, every record which is recorded on the disk is not 3,625 characters long. Therefore, more than one record can be recorded on a track. These records are separated by a gap similar in function to the inter-block-gap on tape. One method of referencing a particular record on a track is by a "record number". The first record on a track is called record "0". Record zero is used for a special purpose by the programming system. The first user record is normally record "1".

In order to develop an address for a record on a disk pack, the program specifies the cylinder number, the track number and the record number.

The "track number" when used in referencing records stored on the disk refers to the number of the disk surface. The first recording surface is called track 0, the second recording track 1, etc. See the illustration below.

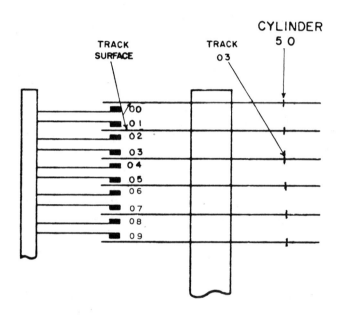

Figure 13-5 Data Record Recorded on Disk

In the example above, if data is recorded beginning on cylinder 50, track 3, one could specify the address of "RECORD2" by indicating that it resides on cylinder 50, track 3, record 2.

INDEXED SEQUENTIAL ACCESS METHOD

Sequential processing, as illustrated in Chapter 11, involves processing records one after another. Due to the addressing scheme used on direct access devices, another type of processing called RANDOM PROCESSING is possible. Random processing is a means by which non-sequential records may be read, written, and processed. Devices such as card readers and tape drives cannot process records randomly because there is no way, for example, to read the fourth record in an input stream and then read the first record because the first record must be read first, followed by the second, third, fourth, etc.

Direct-access devices, however, offer the opportunity to read and retrieve the fourth record in a file and then the first record in a file because each record which is stored on a direct-access device has a unique record address which indicates the exact location on the disk pack where the record is stored.

The Indexed Sequential Access Method allows BOTH sequential and random access to a file.

FILE STRUCTURE

The records of an indexed sequential file are organized on the basis of a collating sequence determined by a specific control field or "key" within the record. An indexed sequential file exists in space allocated on the disk called the PRIME DATA area, the OVERFLOW areas, and the INDEX areas.

When an indexed sequential file is initially established on the disk, all data records are loaded into an area called the PRIME DATA AREA. The data in this area is available to be processed by both sequential and random access methods. Figure 13-6 illustrates this concept.

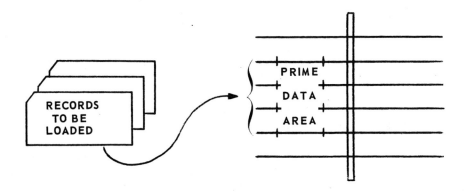

Figure 13-6 Records loaded in Prime Data Area

After the file is established, the user can ADD records without reorganizing the entire file as in sequential file organization. A new record added to an indexed sequential file is placed into a location on a track determined by the value of a "key" or control field in each record. To handle additions, an OVERFLOW AREA exists.

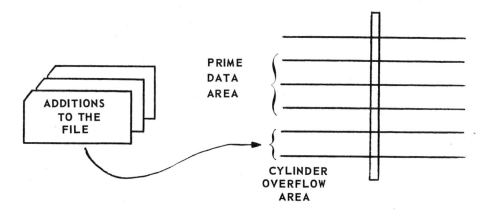

Figure 13-7 Records Added to the File

Two types of overflow areas may be used either separately or together — the cylinder overflow area and the independent overflow area. A CYLINDER OVERFLOW AREA is a track or tracks located on each cylinder within the storage area defined for the prime data area. The number of tracks to be allocated to the Cylinder Overflow Area is determined by an entry made on the File Description Specifications. The INDEPENDENT OVERFLOW AREA is a separate area outside of the prime data area and is used strictly as an overflow area.

The following diagram illustrates the concept of the prime data area, the cylinder overflow area, and the independent overflow area as they appear on the disk.

EXAMPLE

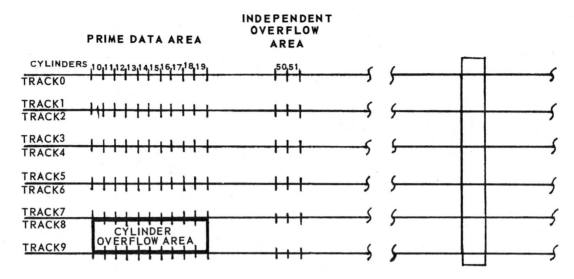

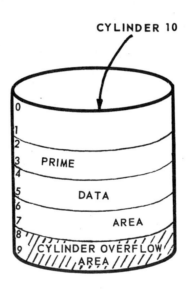

Figure 13-8 Prime Data Area and Overflow Areas

In the drawing in Figure 13-8, Cylinders 10-19 are assigned to the prime data area. Within the prime data area, track 8 and 9 are used as the Cylinder Overflow Area. When an indexed sequential file is loaded using an RPG program, the number of tracks to be reserved for the Cylinder Overflow area is specified on the File Description Specifications. The Independent Overflow Area is an optional area which is used exclusively for overflow records. In the drawing above, Cylinders 50 and 51 are used as the independent overflow area. All ten tracks will be used for overflow records. Records will be placed in the independent overflow area when the Cylinder Overflow area is full.

KEYS AND INDEXES

The indexed sequential access method allows both sequential and random access to data through the use of KEYS and INDEXES. A KEY is a means by which a record may be identified. The Key is normally a part of the record which will uniquely identify the record. For example, a customer sales file may be composed of a series of individual records, with each record representing a customer which purchases from the company. Each record contains a unique customer number. Thus, the customer number acts as the key to the record and always uniquely identifies the record.

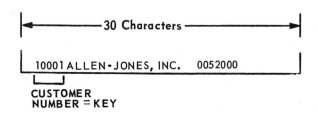

Figure 13-9 Customer Sales Record with Customer Number as Key

It should be noted that the key could be anywhere within the record — it does not have to be the first digits in the record. The key can also be numeric or alphanumeric. The minimum key length is one byte and the maximum is 255 bytes. Within one file, all keys must have the same length. Duplicate keys can never be used on an indexed sequential file. The key must consist of consecutive bytes within the record, that is, the key cannot be scattered throughout the record.

In addition to keys, the Indexed Sequential Access Method (ISAM) utilizes INDEXES. An INDEX is a pointer which is used by ISAM to point to the disk location of a record within the file. Thus, by assigning a particular cylinder, track, and record location to a record and associating the key of the record with that address and placing this information in an index, any record for which the key is known can be located and processed.

Three types of indexes are used by ISAM — a track index, a cylinder index, and a master index. The first two indexes are required and the master index is optional.

TRACK INDEX

The lowest level index is the TRACK INDEX. A track index is built on every CYLINDER which is used in the prime data area of the indexed sequential file. Thus, if there were 10 cylinders in the prime data area, there would be 10 track indexes. The track index is built on the first track of each cylinder in the prime data area. Therefore, if the area reserved for the prime data area of the file were Cylinder 10 Track 0, through Cylinder 19 Track 9, each cylinder (10, 11, 12, etc) would have a track index on its track 0. The track index always is contained on the cylinder for which it is the index and it contains index entries for only the cylinder on which it resides.

The following is a schematic diagram of records stored on disk. Note in the example that the Track Index is stored on Cylinder 10 Track 0. On Cylinder 10, Track 1 the first record has a key of 1. The highest numbered record stored on Cylinder 10, Track 1 is a record with a key of 50. On Cylinder 10 Track 2 the first record has a key of 51 and the highest numbered record on Cylinder 10, Track 2 has a key of 125. The highest numbered record illustrated in the example has a key of 1255 and is stored on Cylinder 10, Track 7.

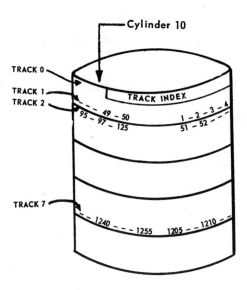

Figure 13-10 Records Stored on Disk

To randomly retrieve records from the file the Track Index must be referenced. A segment of the Track Index is illustrated in Figure 13-11.

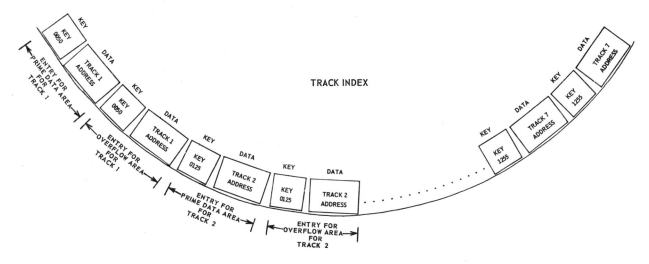

TRACK INDEX

Figure 13 - 11 Track Index

The Track Index consists of a series of entries for the Prime Data Area and the Overflow Area for each track. Each of the entries for each track contains what is called a KEY entry and a DATA entry. The track index consists of two parts: (1) For the Prime Data Area, the KEY entry in the track index specifies the HIGHEST KEY of a record on the track and the DATA entry specifies the ADDRESS of the LOWEST RECORD on that track. From the example in Figure 13-11 it can be seen that the first entry in the Track Index, the KEY entry, contains 0050, and the DATA entry specifies the Track 1 Address. This address would specify the cylinder number containing the records. In the example Cylinder 10 would be specified; therefore, this entry in the Track Index specifies that the highest numbered record on Cylinder 10, Track 1 is a record with a key of 50.

Thus, by examining the Track Index it can be determined that any record with a key of from 1 to 50 will be found on Cylinder 10 Track 1.

13.11

(2) For the overflow area, the KEY entry specifies the HIGHEST KEY associated with that track and the DATA entry specifies the address of the LOWEST RECORD in the overflow area. If no overflow entry has been made, the second entry is the same as the first entry.

In the previous example, it can be seen that the track index resides on Track 0 of a cylinder and the data area begins on Track 1. The highest key on Cylinder 10 Track 1 is 0050 and this is indicated by the KEY entry in the prime data area for Track 1. The overflow entry for Track 1 is the same as the prime data entry which indicates that no records have been placed in the overflow area. Similarly, the highest key on Cylinder 10 Track 2 is 0125 and the highest key on Cylinder 10 Track 7 is 1255.

As can be seen from the example, the keys are in ascending order. It is, therefore, one of the requirements of an indexed sequential file that all records which are used to build the file be sorted by key so that the incoming keys are in ascending order.

Note, that when a record is to be found, the index can be searched to find a key higher than the given key. When the higher key is found, its associated track address points to the track which contains the record having the given key. See the illustration below.

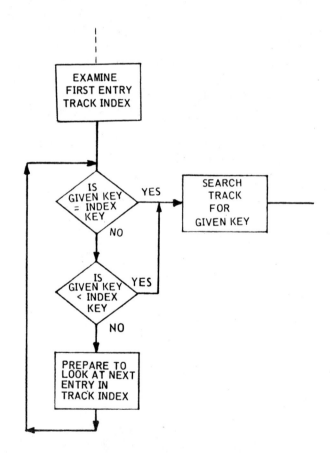

Figure 13-11 Logic for finding key in track index

The example in Figure 13-11 illustrates the steps which occur in retrieving a record from an indexed sequential file.

In the example below, the record to be found has a key of 0095. Since the highest key on track 1 is 0050, the next entry in the index is checked. It shows that the highest key on track 2 is 0125. Therefore, the desired record resides on track 2. The track is then read for the proper key and the record can then be retrieved.

KEY

TRACK INDEX

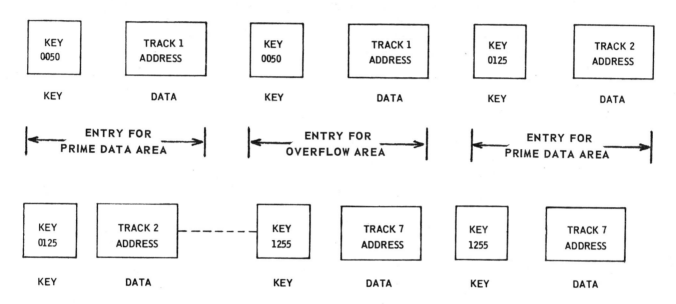

Dummy Entry

Figure 13-12 Record and Track Index

Note in the example that the last record in the track index is a dummy record which indicates the end of the track index——it is a record of all 1 bits. Therefore, to avoid any problems, a key should never be all 1 bits.

Note also that track 7 is the last entry in the index when the file is organized——this is because of the cylinder overflow feature.

CYLINDER INDEX

The CYLINDER INDEX is the intermediate index used by the Indexed Sequential Access Method. It has a function similar to that of the track index, except that it points to the cylinders in the file rather than the tracks within the cylinder. The cylinder index is built on a separate area of the disk from the prime data and overflow areas. Job control is used to specify the cylinder(s) to be used for the cylinder index. The cylinder index cannot be on the same cylinder as the prime data record area and it must be located on one or more consecutive cylinders.

The cylinder index has one entry in it for each cylinder in the prime data area of the file. Thus, if there were 100 cylinders for the prime data area, there would be 100 entries in the cylinder index. The format of the cylinder index is similar to the format of the track index but there is only one entry for each cylinder. The following diagram illustrates the entries in the cylinder index.

CYLINDER INDEX

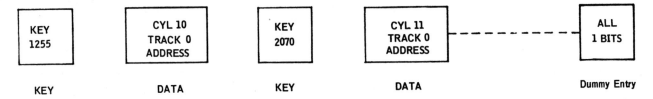

Figure 13-13 Cylinder Index

The entries in the cylinder index consist of the **HIGHEST KEY OF A RECORD** on the entire cylinder and the **ADDRESS OF THE TRACK INDEX** for that cylinder. The key area contains the highest key associated with the given cylinder. The data area contains the address of the associated track index. Thus, in the example, the highest key on cylinder 10 is 1255 and the address of the track index is cylinder 10, track 0. The track index for cylinder 10 is contained in Figure 13-10. The highest key on cylinder 11 is 2070 and the address of the track index is cylinder 11, track 0. This example assumes the prime data area begins on cylinder 10.

To retrieve record 95 the cylinder index is searched using the same logic as illustrated in Figure 13-11. In the example, record 95 would be compared to the first KEY entry in the cylinder index. Since record 95 is less than 1255, the associated track index whose address is specified in the DATA portion of the first entry is searched in the manner shown previously. In this example, the track index would be found on cylinder 10, track 0.

13.14

MASTER INDEX

The master index is an optional index which can be used if desired by the programmer. It contains the track address of each track in the cylinder index and the highest key referenced by the corresponding track. Its use is not recommended unless the cylinder index is more than four tracks. This is because it is more efficient, time-wise, to search a 4 track cylinder index than it is to search a master index and then the 4 track cylinder index.

The master index is built within the extents specified by the job control EXTENT statement. The master index must immediately precede the cylinder index on the disk volume. It may be more than one cylinder long.

MASTER INDEX

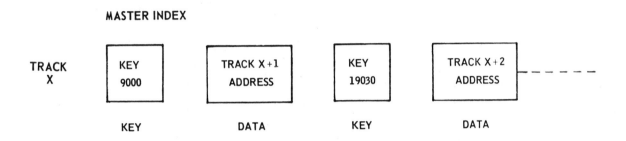

Figure 13-14 Master Index

In the example, the master index is located on track X. The data portion of the master index contains the address of the first track of the cylinder index, which must immediately follow the master index. Thus, in the example, it is assumed the master index takes one track and, since the cylinder index must immediately follow the master index, the first track of the cylinder index would be track (X + 1).

Thus, by using these indexes, the indexed sequential access method can randomly retrieve any record for which the key is known. It can also process the records sequentially by beginning anywhere in the file (determined by key) and sequentially process the records by just reading the prime data and overflow areas. This flexibility of indexed sequential files makes it an extremely useful tool in many applications requiring diversified usage of the data on the file.

SAMPLE PROGRAM

The sample programs in this chapter illustrate an application in which a customer sales file is built as an indexed sequential file and then is sequentially retrieved and randomly updated. The first program is used to build or "load" the indexed sequential file. The input to the program is a file of sorted customer sales cards. The card format is illustrated below.

Input

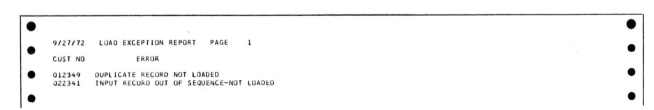

Figure 13-15   Card Input

As can be seen from the example above, the input card contains a Customer Number, a Customer Name, and Customer Sales. The master record which is to be written in the Indexed Sequential Master File contains the same data as is in the input card. The Sales Amount will be in a packed-decimal format and the Customer Number is the key of the record.

In addition to the master output file, an Exception Report will be created in the program to list two types of errors — input records with duplicate keys and input records which are out of sequence. As noted previously, all input records to load an indexed sequential file must be in an ascending sequence by key and there may be no records with duplicate keys loaded on the file. If an input record is out of sequence or if a record with a duplicate key is read, then an entry is made on the Exception Report. A sample of the report is illustrated in Figure 13-16.

```
  9/27/72   LOAD EXCEPTION REPORT    PAGE    1

  CUST NO           ERROR

  012349   DUPLICATE RECORD NOT LOADED
  022341   INPUT RECORD OUT OF SEQUENCE-NOT LOADED
```

Figure 13-16   Exception Report

FILE DESCRIPTION SPECIFICATIONS

The definition of an indexed sequential file differs somewhat from the definitions of sequential files. The entries to define the card input file and the customer sales indexed sequential file are illustrated below.

EXAMPLE

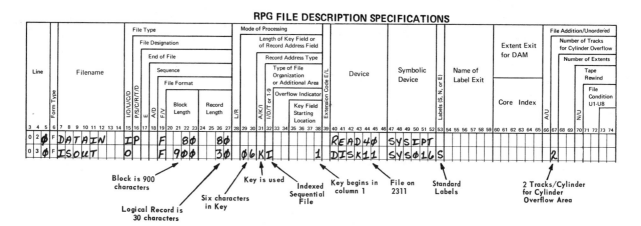

Figure 13-17 File Description Entries for Indexed Sequential File

In the example above it can be seen that the card input file DATAIN is defined in the same manner as used in previous programs. The indexed sequential file ISOUT, however, has some new entries.

When an indexed sequential file is being created for the first time, such as in this example, it must always be specified as an Output file (column 15). Indexed Sequential files will always contain fixed-length records, so the entry "F" in column 19 is required. The block length may be any desired up to a maximum of 3600 for a 2311. In the example it can be seen that the block length is 900 characters. The record length may be any desirable length also but the block length must be evenly divisible by the record length. In the example in Figure 13-17 it can be seen that the block length of 900 is evenly divisible by the record length of 30. The blocking factor for the indexed sequential file is 30. The record length of the Indexed Sequential File is specified as 30, that is, 6 positions will be required for the Customer Number, 20 positions for the Customer Name, and the 7 position Sales field on the card which is to be stored in a packed-decimal format on the disk will require 4 positions.

As was noted previously, every indexed sequential file must contain a key within the data. The entry in columns 29-30 specify the length of the key. In this example, the length of the customer number is 6 characters and, therefore, the length of the key is 6 characters. The entry in columns 29-30 must always specify the length of the key which is used in the indexed sequential file. The entry "K" in column 31 specifies that a key will be used to identify the records in the file and must always be included for an indexed sequential file. The entry "I" in column 32 states that the output file is an indexed sequential file and is also required for all indexed sequential files. The entry "1" in column 38 specifies that the key begins in column 1 of the record to be stored in the indexed sequential file.

The indexed sequential file will be stored on a 2311 (DISK11) and the symbolic device assigned to the 2311 is SYS016. This file, like all files which are stored on a direct-access device, must have standard labels as specified by the entry "S" in column 53. The entry "2" in column 67 states that two tracks on each cylinder within the prime data area will be used as the Cylinder Overflow area. Although the number of tracks to be used is determined by the programmer, two tracks is normally the most efficient.

13.17

INPUT SPECIFICATIONS AND CALCULATION SPECIFICATIONS

After the input and output files have been defined, the description of the input data must be made on the Input Specifications. In the sample program, the input is the card file which will be used to load the indexed sequential file. As was noted previously, the two errors which normally occur when an indexed sequential file is being loaded is that the input data is out of sequence or a duplicate record is entered in the input data. In order to check for these two occurrences, entries are required on both the input specifications and the calculations specifications. The entries on the Input Specifications for the sample program are illustrated below.

Input Specifications

RPG INPUT SPECIFICATIONS

Line	Form Type	Filename	Sequence	Number (1-N)	Option (O)	Record Identifying Indicator or **	Record Identification Codes 1 Position	Not (N)	C/Z/D	Character	Record Identification Codes 2 Position	Not (N)	C/Z/D	Character	Record Identification Codes 3 Position	Not (N)	C/Z/D	Character	Stacker Select	P = Packed/B = Binary	Field Location From	Field Location To	Decimal Positions	Field Name	Control Level (L1-L9)	Matching Fields or Chaining Fields
0 1	Ø I	DATAIN	AA			Ø1																				
0 2	Ø I																				1	6		CUSTNO	L1	M1
0 3	Ø I																				7	26		NAME		
0 4	Ø I																				27	332		SALES		

Figure 13-18 Input Specifications

Note in the example of the Input Specifications above that the fields are defined to correspond to the card input as illustrated in Figure 13-15. Two additional entries are made, however, so that the duplicate record and out of sequence errors may be detected. First, the control level indicator L1 is specified in columns 59-60. Since only one record with the same customer number should be read, the L1 indicator should be turned on each time a new card record is read. If two records with the same customer number are read, the L1 indicator will not be turned on for the second card and it will then be treated as a duplicate record.

The second entry which is included on the Input Specifications is the M1 indicator for the customer number field (columns 61-62). Even though two input files are not processed in this program, the M1 indicator may still be included in order to check the sequence of the input records. As noted in Chapter 12, when matching record indicators are specified for input files, the records within the files must be either in an ascending sequence or a descending sequence. In the example above, since no sequence is specified on the File Description specifications, the data must be in an ascending sequence by customer number. If the records are not in an ascending sequence, the HO indicator will be turned "on". Thus, if a record is read with a customer number which is less than the previous customer number just read, the HO indicator will be turned on.

In order to check the results of the indicator after an input record is read, entries must be made on the calculation specifications. The entries used in the sample program are illustrated below.

EXAMPLE

RPG CALCULATION SPECIFICATIONS

Line	Form Type	Control Level (L0-L9, LR, SR)	Indicators And / And	Factor 1	Operation	Factor 2	Result Field	Field Length	Decimal Positions	Half Adjust (H)	Resulting Indicators Plus/High 1>2	Minus/Low 1<2	Zero/Equal 1=2
01	0	C		01 70		SETON						71		
02	0	C		01		SETON						70		
03	0	C	L1			SETOF						70	71	75
04	0	C	L1	H0		SETON						75		
05	0	C	L1	75		SETOF						H0		

Figure 13-19 Calculation Specifications

Note from Figure 13-19 that the only entries on the Calculation Specifications are SETON and SETOF instructions. This is because the only function of the entries on the Calculation Specifications is to set indicators for duplicate records and out of sequence records. There are no arithmetic or comparison operations to be performed.

As was noted, if two records with the same customer number are read, they will both be detail records, that is, the L1 control break indicator will not be set "on". When this occurs, the second record is in error because it is a duplicate of the first record. The indicators 70 and 71 are used to check this condition. As can be seen from the specifications in Figure 13-19, when the first record is read, only the 01 indicator will be "on". Thus, the SETON instruction on coding line 020 will turn on indicator 70. If the next record contains a different customer number, the total routine will be entered before the detail routine and indicators 70 and 71 will be turned "off" (coding line 030). Thus, when the detail calculations for the second card are entered, only the 01 indicator will be on.

If, however, the second card read contains the same customer number as the first card, the total calculations will not be entered. Instead, only the detail calculations will be processed. When the detail calculations are entered, indicator 70 will be "on" from the first card. Thus, as can be seen on coding line 010, when both the 01 indicator and the 70 indicator are "on", indicator 71 is turned "on". Thus, whenever indicator 71 is "on", it indicates that a record with a duplicate customer number has been read. This can then be tested on the output specifications (Figure 13-20).

The second test which is performed is the "out of sequence" test. As noted, if a record which is read contains a customer number which is less than the previous record, indicator HO will be set on because of the M1 entry in the input specifications. In addition, since the customer numbers will be different, the L1 control break indicator will be turned "on". Thus, on coding line 040 in Figure 13-19 it can be seen that if the HO indicator is "on" when a control break occurs, indicator 75 is turned "on" and, on coding line 050, indicator HO will be turned "off". The HO indicator is turned "off" because it will cause the cancellation of the program if it is left on and this is not desired. Therefore, the HO indicator must be turned "off" to avoid the cancellation of the program. The indicator 75, however, will be "on" and it is this indicator which may be tested on the output specifications to determine if an out of sequence condition has occurred.

13.19

OUTPUT SPECIFICATIONS

The Output Specifications provide the definitions of the heading lines which are to be printed on the Exception Report and also the testing of the indicators to determine when a valid record is to be written in the indexed sequential file and when an error has occurred and an entry must be made on the Exception Report. The entries for the detail lines and the total output in the sample program are illustrated below.

EXAMPLE

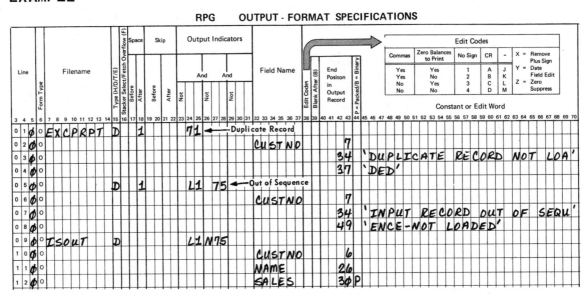

Figure 13-20 Output Specifications

Note from the example above that two possible lines will be written on the Exception Report — one identifying the input record as a duplicate record and one specifying that the input record was out of sequence. The Duplicate Record message will be written on the report when indicator 71 is "on", which means a duplicate record was found as illustrated in Figure 13-19. When the L1 indicator and indicator 75 are both "on", it indicates that a record which was out of sequence was read from the input file. Thus, the "out of sequence" message is written on the Exception Report.

When the L1 indicator is "on" and indicator 75 is not "on", it means that a record with a new customer number that is in an ascending sequence has been read. This is a valid record and will be written in the indexed sequential output file ISOUT. It should be noted that all of the records are detail records on the Output Specifications. This is done so that the record which caused the indicators to be turned "on" or "off" is the record written on either the Exception Report or the Indexed Sequential file. It will be recalled that when total output is written, the data available in the input fields to be moved to the output area is the data which was in the previous record, not the record which caused the control break. Thus, in order to cause the record which caused the control break to occur to be written, the data is specified as detail data rather than total data. The L1 control break indicator will be "on" during detail time processing of the record which caused the control break because it remains on during the first cycle of detail processing following a control break. It is this feature, it will be recalled, which allows group indicated reports.

SAMPLE PROGRAM 1

The source listing of the program to load the Indexed Sequential File is illustrated below.

```
DOS/360*RPG*CL 3-9              CASHMAN                 09/27/72          PAGE 0001

              00 000 H
001    01 010 FDATAIN  IP  F  80  80           READ40 SYSIPT              LOADIS
002    01 020 FISOUT   O   F 900  30 06KI   1 DISK14 SYS016S          2   LOADIS
003    01 030 FEXCPRPT O   F 132 132      OF   PRINTERSYSLST              LOADIS
004    02 010 IDATAIN  AA  01                                             LOADIS
005    02 020 I                                    1   6 CUSTNOL1M1       LOADIS
006    02 030 I                                    7  26 NAME            LOADIS
007    02 040 I                                   27 332SALES            LOADIS
008    03 010 C    01 70          SETON                   71             LOADIS
009    03 020 C    01             SETON                   70             LOADIS
010    03 030 CL1                 SETOF                   717075         LOADIS
011    03 040 CL1 H0              SETON                   75             LOADIS
012    03 050 CL1 75              SETOF                   H0             LOADIS
013    04 010 OEXCPRPT H 201  1P                                         LOADIS
014    04 020 O         OR     OF                                        LOADIS
015    04 030 O                         UDATE     8 ' / / '              LOADIS
016    04 040 O                                  32 'LOAD EXCEPTION REPORT'. LOADIS
017    04 050 O                                  39 'PAGE'               LOADIS
018    04 060 O                         PAGE  Z  44                      LOADIS
019    04 070 O       H  2    1P                                         LOADIS
020    04 080 O         OR     OF                                        LOADIS
021    04 090 O                                   8 'CUST NO'            LOADIS
022    04 100 O                                  24 'ERROR'              LOADIS
       04 110 O*                                                         LOADIS
023    04 120 O       D  1    71                                         LOADIS
024    04 130 O                         CUSTNO    7                      LOADIS
025    04 140 O                                  34 'DUPLICATE RECORD NOT LOA' LOADIS
026    04 150 O                                  37 'DED'                LOADIS
027    05 010 O       D  1    L1 75                                      LOADIS
028    05 020 O                         CUSTNO    7                      LOADIS
029    05 030 O                                  34 'INPUT RECORD OUT OF SEQU' LOADIS
030    05 040 O                                  49 'ENCE-NOT LOADED'    LOADIS
031    05 050 OISOUT   D       L1N75                                     LOADIS
032    05 060 O                         CUSTNO    6                      LOADIS
033    05 070 O                         NAME     26                      LOADIS
034    05 080 O                         SALES    30P                     LOADIS
```

Figure 13-21 Source Listing

SEQUENTIAL RETRIEVAL

After an indexed sequential file has been created, it is normally processed in one of three ways — it may be sequentially retrieved, it may be randomly retrieved, or records may be added to the file. The records in the file may be updated, that is, data in the records may be changed, when the file is retrieved either sequentially or randomly.

The second sample program in this chapter will be used to sequentially retrieve the data in the indexed sequential master file and print a report. The input to the program is the indexed sequential file which was created in the first sample program. The output is a Customer Listing printed report. A portion of the report is illustrated in Figure 13-22.

EXAMPLE

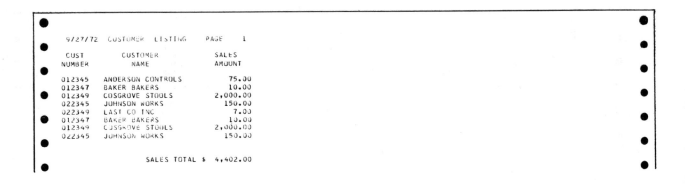

Figure 13-22 Example of Printed Report

In the example above it can be seen that the Customer Number, the Customer Name and the Sales Amount are read from the indexed sequential file and included on the report. It should also be noted that three of the customer numbers are printed twice, that is, customers 012347, 012349, and 022345 are printed on the report twice. The records which are to be retrieved from the file are determined from the entries which are made in a Record Address File which may be used when an indexed sequential file is to be sequentially retrieved.

RECORD ADDRESS FILES

As has been noted, an indexed sequential file is organized on the basis of a control field or "key" which is a part of each record and which must be in an ascending sequence. When the data in an indexed sequential file is to be sequentially retrieved, many applications require that the beginning and ending "key" be specified so that the retrieval will begin with a given key within the file and end with a given key. In order to supply the beginning and ending points of an indexed sequential file to be sequentially retrieved, a RECORD ADDRESS FILE is used. This file must be defined on both the File Description Specifications and the File Extension Specifications. In addition, entries must be made in the definition of the indexed sequential file to specify that a RAF file is to be used. The entries for the sample program are illustrated below.

EXAMPLE

File Description Specifications

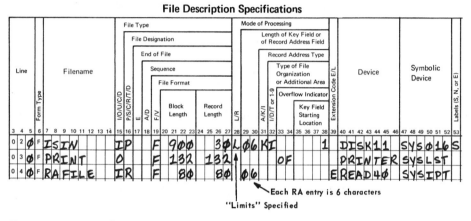

File Extension Specifications

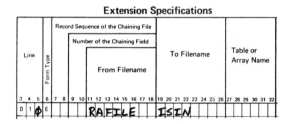

Figure 13-23   Entries for Record Address File

Note in the example above that the indexed sequential file, ISIN, is defined as the primary input file with fixed-length records. The Length of the Key (columns 29-30), the Key address type (column 31), the file organization (column 32) and the key field starting location (column 38) are all specified the same as when the file was created (see Figure 13-18). The file will be on a 2311 Disk Drive (DISK11) assigned to SYS016. This file, as all files which are stored on a direct-access device, will have standard labels.

The entry "L" in column 28 is used to indicate that processing Limits will be supplied via a Record Address file in order to sequentially retrieve the file. Another possible entry in this field, the value "R", is specified when the records in the indexed sequential file will be retrieved randomly, as will be illustrated in the third sample program in this chapter. If the field is left blank, then the entire indexed sequential file will be retrieved sequentially.

Whenever a record address file is to be used to specify the processing limits for an indexed sequential file, it must be defined on the File Description Specifications as well as the File Extension Specifications. As can be seen from Figure 13-23, it is defined as an Input file ("I" in column 15) and as a Record Address file ("R" in column 16). The filename, RAFILE, is not a required name and any filename desired by the programmer may be used. The record format for the RAF is fixed-length because it is stored on punched cards which will be read by the program. The record length, as with all card files, is 80 characters. The entry "06" in columns 29-30 specify that each "limit" entry in the RAF cards will be six characters in length to correspond to the length of the key in the indexed sequential file. The "E" in column 39 of the File Description Specifications for the RAF specifies that an entry is contained on the File Extension Specifications.

Only two entries must be made on the File Extension Specifications — the name of the Record Address File must be specified in columns 11-18 and the name of the indexed sequential file must be specified in columns 19-26.

Each card in a Record Address File which is to be used to specify processing limits must contain two entries — the first entry is the key value which is to be used to begin processing and the second entry is the key value which is to end processing. This is illustrated below.

EXAMPLE

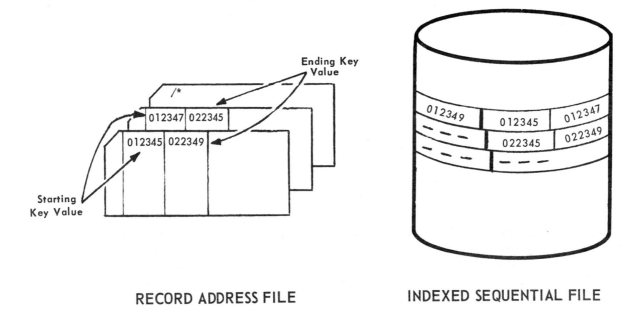

RECORD ADDRESS FILE   INDEXED SEQUENTIAL FILE

Figure 13-24 Example of the Use of a Record Address File

13.24

Note from Figure 13-24 that two cards are contained in the Record Address File. These two cards would produce the report illustrated in Figure 13-22. The first card contains the value 012345 in columns 1-6 and 022349 in columns 7-12. As was noted previously, the key in the indexed sequential file is six characters in length. Thus, each entry in the RAF file must be six characters in length as specified in columns 29-30 of the File Description Specifications (see Figure 13-23). The first six characters in the card specify the key with which processing is to begin. Thus, the sequential retrieval of the indexed sequential file is to begin with the record with the key 012345. The next six characters in the RAF input card specify the key of the last record which is to be processed. Thus, for the first RAF card, sequential retrieval will cease after the record with the key 022349 has been retrieved. Note in the RAF card that there are no blanks between the beginning key and the ending key and that one card is used for each set of keys which are to be retrieved. The second card in the file specifies that the records with key values of 012347 through 022345 are to be retrieved from the indexed sequential file. Thus, as can be seen from the report in Figure 13-22, these records are retrieved and printed on the report. Since there are only two cards in the RAF file, when the /* card is read, the processing of the program will be completed and the program will be ended.

A Record Address File must always be used when specific limits must be specified in order to retrieve the indexed sequential file. If the entire indexed sequential file is to be retrieved for sequential processing, a Record Address File is not necessary. Instead, the indexed sequential file is defined as an input file without any limits, that is, the entry in column 28 is left blank. When column 28 is blank, the compiler assumes that the entire indexed sequential file is to be sequentially retrieved for processing.

The Input Specifications, the Calculation Specifications, and the Output Specifications are written in the same manner as if a tape or card file were being retrieved and printed. The input record from the indexed sequential file may be given any Record Identifying Indicator desired on the Input Specifications and processing may take place as in previous programs.

The entire sample program to sequentially retrieve the indexed sequential file and create the printed report is illustrated in Figure 13-25.

SAMPLE PROGRAM

```
DOS/360*RPG*CL 3-9                    CASHMAN                    09/27/72          PAGE 0001

           01 010 H                                                               PRNTIS
001        01 020 FISIN    IP  F 900  30L06KI    1 DISK14 SYS016S                 PRNTIS
002        01 030 FPRINT   O   F 132 132      OF    PRINTERSYSLST                 PRNTIS
003        01 040 FRAFILE  IR  F  80  30 06      EREAD40 SYSIPT                   PRNTIS
004        01 050 E   RAFILE   ISIN                                              PRNTIS
005        02 010 IISIN    AA  01                                                PRNTIS
006        02 020 I                             1   6 CUSTNO                     PRNTIS
007        02 030 I                             7  26 NAME                       PRNTIS
008        02 040 I                         P  27  302SALES                      PRNTIS
009        03 010 C   01     TOTSAL    ADD SALES     TOTSAL  82                   PRNTIS
010        04 010 OPRINT   H  201    1P                                          PRNTIS
011        04 020 O            OR         OF                                     PRNTIS
012        04 030 O                       UDATE     H ' / / '                    PRNTIS
013        04 040 O                                 27 'CUSTOMER  LISTING'       PRNTIS
014        04 050 O                                 35 'PAGE'                    PRNTIS
015        04 060 O                       PAGE  Z   40                           PRNTIS
016        04 070 O         H  1    1P                                           PRNTIS
017        04 080 O            OR         OF                                     PRNTIS
018        04 090 O                                  5 'CUST'                    PRNTIS
019        04 100 O                                 21 'CUSTOMER'                PRNTIS
020        04 110 O                                 38 'SALES'                   PRNTIS
021        04 120 O         H  2    1P                                           PRNTIS
022        04 130 O            OR         OF                                     PRNTIS
023        04 140 O                                  6 'NUMBER'                  PRNTIS
024        04 150 O                                 19 'NAME'                    PRNTIS
025        05 010 O                                 39 'AMOUNT'                  PRNTIS
026        05 020 O         D  1    01                                           PRNTIS
027        05 030 O                       CUSTNO     6                           PRNTIS
028        05 040 O                       NAME      29                           PRNTIS
029        05 050 O                       SALES     41 '  ,  0. '                PRNTIS
030        05 060 O         T  2    LR                                           PRNTIS
031        05 070 O                                 29 'SALES TOTAL'             PRNTIS
032        05 080 O                       TOTSAL    41 '$  ,  0. '               PRNTIS
```

Figure 13-25 Sample Problem

13.26

ADDITIONS, RANDOM RETRIEVAL AND UPDATING

It was noted previously that an indexed sequential file may be processed sequentially or randomly. In addition, records may be added to the indexed sequential file without reorganizing the entire file as in sequential organization. The third sample program will illustrate a technique to randomly update the indexed sequential file with a card transaction file and to also add records to the indexed sequential file. The input to the program consists of the indexed sequential file created in the first sample program and a file of transaction cards. The format of the transaction cards is illustrated below.

Transaction Cards

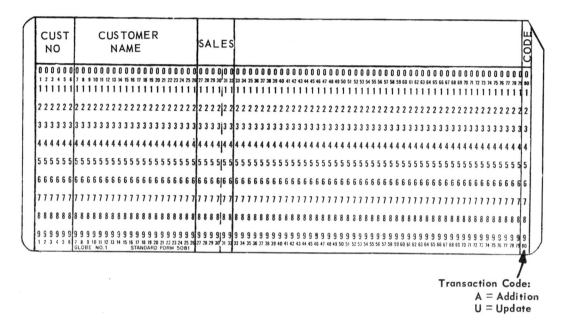

Transaction Code:
A = Addition
U = Update

Figure 13-26 Transaction Card

Note in the example above that the transaction card consists of the Customer Number in columns 1-6, the Customer Name in columns 7-26, the Sales in columns 27-32, and a transaction code in column 80. If the transaction code is equal to the letter "A", then the transaction record is to be added to the indexed sequential file. If the transaction code is equal to the letter "U", the sales amount in the transaction record is to be added to the sales amount in the master record.

There are two errors which may occur when randomly updating and adding records. First, an update transaction may be read for which there is no corresponding master record and second, a transaction record may indicate the addition of a record already on the indexed sequential file. When either of these two errors occur, the transaction record will not be processed and an entry will be made on the Exception Report created in the program. A sample of the Exception Report is illustrated in Figure 13-27.

Exception Report

```
CUST NO        ERROR
012347  DUPLICATE RECORD-NO ADDITION PERFORMED
012348  NO MASTER RECORD-UPDATE NOT PERFORMED
```

Figure 13-27 Exception Report

As can be seen, the Exception Report contains the Customer Number of the transaction in error, so that it may be identified and corrected, and the type of error.

CHAINED RECORDS

In the second sample program in this chapter, it was seen how the Record Address File is used to specify the limits of the file which was to be sequentially retrieved. It should be noted from that example that the only data which is allowable in the RAF is the beginning and ending key values. It is not possible to include sales amounts, for example, to update the retrieved record. Only the key values are allowed in Record Address Files.

In this third sample program, however, data is contained in the transaction record which must be used in processing the record retrieved from the indexed sequential file. A Record Address File, therefore, may not be used in this application. Instead, a process known as CHAINING RECORDS is used. Chaining merely refers to the fact that the data in one input file, in this example, the transaction file, is to contain a "pointer" or key to reference another file, which, in the example, is the indexed sequential file. This concept is illustrated below.

EXAMPLE

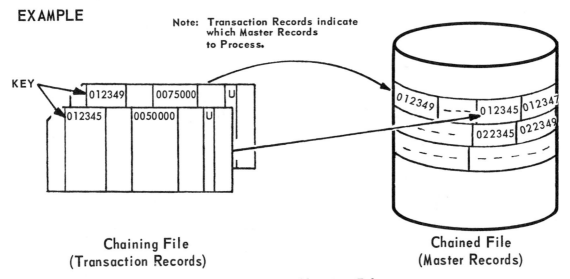

Note: Transaction Records indicate which Master Records to Process.

Chaining File
(Transaction Records)

Chained File
(Master Records)

Figure 13-28 Chaining Files

13.28

Note in Figure 13-28 that the Customer Number which is contained in the Transaction Records is used to supply the "key" which will be used to retrieve the respective master record to be updated. In addition, the transaction record contains data which will be used to update the master file. Thus, the transaction file must act as the chaining file to the master file. The entries on the File Description Specifications, the File Extension Specifications and the Input Specifications to define the Chaining and Chained Files are illustrated below.

EXAMPLE

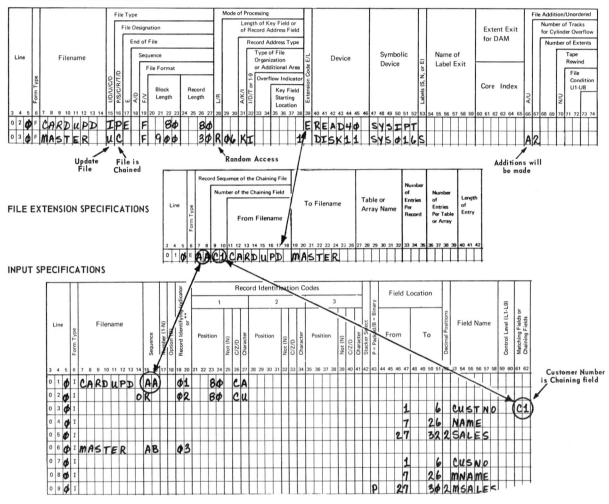

Figure 13-29 Chaining Specifications

As can be seen from the example above, the File Description Specifications, the File Extension Specifications and the Input Specifications are used together to define both the files to be chained together and the field(s) which will be used for the chaining operation. The CARDUPD file, which contains the transaction records, is defined in much the same way as the other card input files have been defined. Two entries, however, are unique in this program. In column 17, it can be seen that the letter "E" is entered for the file. When more than one input file is being processed, such as the transaction file and the indexed sequential file, it is sometimes desirable to consider all processing completed when only one of the files has reached end-of-file. In the sequential update program, it will be recalled, both files had to reach end-of-file before the program was complete. In this example, however, when the transaction file has reached end-of-file, all processing has been completed. When more than one file is to be processed, the value "E" in column 17 indicates that when the corresponding file reaches end-of-file, all processing should be considered complete.

13.29

The letter "E" in column 39 for the CARDUPD file indicates that further entries pertaining to the file will be found on the File Extension Specifications. The definition of the indexed sequential file MASTER must define an indexed sequential file which is to be both randomly updated and is to have records added to it. In order to specify that the file is to be randomly updated, two entries are required. In column 15, note the value "U" is entered for the File Type. The "U" indicates that the file is to be updated, that is, records are to be read from the file, updated in main storage, and rewritten back onto the same file. Note the difference between this processing and the sequential update where the old master file was read and a new master file was created as an output file. With an update file, no new file is created; instead, the records are rewritten back on the same file.

The second entry which is required for a random updating process is the letter of the alphabet "R" in column 28 (Mode of Processing). The letter "R" stands for Random processing and indicates that records are to be retrieved randomly from the file. The value "C" in column 16 (File Designation) specifies that the file is to be a Chained File, that is, another file is to specify the key which will be used to retrieve records from the Random file. The key length (columns 29-30), the "K" and "I" entries, and the Key Field Starting Location must all be specified as in the previous definitions of the indexed sequential file.

In order to allow records to be added to the file, the value "A" must be specified in column 66 of the File Definition Specifications. This entry indicates that new records are to be added to the file. From the definition, then, the following is true about the indexed sequential file — the file is to allow both random updating and the addition of records. The records to be retrieved randomly will be determined by the key values in a chaining file. The key size and location are the same as when the file was loaded.

As was noted, the CARDUPD file, which is the chaining file, must have additional entries on the File Extension Specifications in order to define the field in each record which is to act as the chaining field, that is, the field which will contain the key to be used to randomly retrieve the record from the indexed sequential file. The example in Figure 13-29 illustrates the four entries which are required for the chaining file. The first entry, in columns 7-8, must correspond to the Sequence value which is placed on the Input Specifications for the record which is to be used for the chaining operation. Note that the value "AA" is specified and that this value corresponds to the sequence entry placed on the Input Specifications in columns 15-16 for the record which is to contain the field to be chained to the indexed sequential file. The field which will contain the actual key to be used, the customer number field (CUSTNO), is identified through the use of a Chaining Code. Up to nine different fields may be used to form the key to be used to chain to another file and they are identified by the values C1-C9. These codes act in the same manner as the Matching Field indicators, that is, if more than one field is specified as the Chaining Field, the field with the highest numbered chaining code becomes the high-order field in the key. In the example in Figure 13-22, it can be seen that the CUSTNO field is to be the only field used for the key to be chained to the indexed sequential file, so it is identified by the code C1 in columns 61-62 of the Input Specifications and on the File Extension Specifications in columns 9-10.

The "From Filename" entry on the File Extension Specifications (columns 11-18) must be the name of the file which is to be the chaining file. In this example, it is the card file CARDUPD. The "To File" entry is the name of the file which is to be chained and, in this example, is the name of the indexed sequential master file, MASTER.

ERROR CONDITIONS WHEN RANDOMLY RETRIEVING AND ADDING

As when loading a file, several errors may occur when records in an indexed sequential file are to be randomly retrieved and added. When a record is to be randomly retrieved, the error which may occur is that the key in the chaining record cannot be found in the indexed sequential file, that is, the record which is supposed to be randomly retrieved and updated is not on the file. The other error which normally may occur is that a transaction record is attempted to be added to the file and the record already exists on the file. Obviously, a record may not be added to the file if it already exists on the file.

These errors may be detected through the use of the HO halt indicator and the setting of indicators on the Calculation Specifications. The HO Halt Indicator will be turned "on" whenever a chaining record, that is, a record in the card input file, contains a key which is not found in the indexed sequential file. This is because both the Add records and the Update records will be chained to the master file as specified on the Input Specifications in Figure 13-29. Whether the HO indicator when used in this context means that an error has occurred depends upon the type of transaction to be processed. If the transaction is an addition, there should not be a corresponding master record on the indexed sequential file. Thus, when the record is an addition, if the HO indicator is "on", then the record may be added to the file. The error, in this situation, is when the HO indicator is "off" as a result of the chaining operation, that is, when a record is found on the master file. If a record is found on the master file, then the add record is invalid.

Just the opposite is true if a record is to be randomly retrieved to be updated, that is, if the record is not on the file, then an error has occurred. The entries on the Calculation Specifications to test these conditions and set the appropriate indicators are illustrated below.

EXAMPLE

RPG   CALCULATION SPECIFICATIONS

Line	Form Type	Control Level (L0-L9, LR, SR)	Indicators						Factor 1	Operation	Factor 2	Result Field	Field Length	Decimal Positions	Half Adjust (H)	Resulting Indicators
			And	Not		And	Not	Not								High 54 55 / Low 56 57 / Equal 58 59
0 1	C									SETOF						5Ø 55
0 2	C		NHØ		Ø1					SETON						5Ø
0 3	C		HØ		Ø1					SETOF						HØ
0 4	C		HØ		Ø2					SETON						55
0 5	C		55							SETOF						HØ
0 6	C		Ø2		Ø3				MSALES	ADD	SALES	MSALES				

Figure 13-30 Calculation Specifications

Note in the example above that indicators 50 and 55 are set off as the first step in the Calculation Specifications so that, if an error does not occur, they will not be on from previous errors. The first set of indicators to be checked are NHO and 01. These two indicators would state that an 01 record, that is, an add record, has been read and has been successfully chained to an existing record in the indexed sequential file. The transaction record, therefore, is in error because a record cannot be added to the file if one is already on the file. Thus, if both the 01 indicator is "on" and the HO indicator is "off", indicator 50 will be turned on to indicate the attempted addition of a duplicate record.

If both the HO and 01 indicators are "on", it indicates that when an attempt was made to chain the transaction record to the indexed sequential file, it failed, that is, no record was found in the indexed sequential file which corresponded to the transaction record. This is the desired situation because it means that there is no record in the indexed sequential file which corresponds to the transaction which is to be added to the file. Therefore, the record may be added. Note that when both the 01 and HO indicators are "on", the HO indicator is turned "off" (coding line 030) and that is the only action taken. The reason that the HO indicator is turned "off" is that the program would be cancelled if it were not.

If both the HO and 02 indicators are "on", this indicates an error because the 02 record is used to update the master file (see Figure 13-29). Thus, if no record were found in the indexed sequential file which corresponded to the transaction record and the transaction record is an Update record, then no update may take place and an entry should be made on the Exception Report. This will be indicated by indicator 55, which will be turned "on" if both the HO and the 02 indicators are "on". The HO indicator will then be turned "off" if indicator 55 is "on" so that the program will not be cancelled.

The last line on the Calculation Specifications specifies that when both indicator 02 and indicator 03 are "on", then the sales value in the transaction record is to be added to the sales amount in the master record. This is the updating processing which will occur if an update transaction has a matching master record in the indexed sequential file. It should be noted that indicator 02 is "on" when the transaction input record is read and indicator 03 is "on" when the indexed sequential file is read. This is the only time when the indicators for two different input files will be "on" at the same time, that is, when chaining occurs, both indicators may be "on" at the same time. In all other applications, only one record identifying indicator may be on at one time.

OUTPUT SPECIFICATIONS

The output from the program consists of the Exception Report which lists errors which occur during the processing and the indexed sequential file. Two types of records are placed in the indexed sequential file — updated records which have been retrieved and updated and new records which are added to the file. The output specifications for these two files are illustrated in Figure 13-31.

EXAMPLE

RPG OUTPUT - FORMAT SPECIFICATIONS

Edit Codes						
Commas	Zero Balances to Print	No Sign	CR	–	X =	Remove Plus Sign
Yes	Yes	1	A	J	Y =	Date
Yes	No	2	B	K		Field Edit
No	Yes	3	C	L	Z =	Zero
No	No	4	D	M		Suppress

Line	Form Type	Filename	Type (H/D/T/E)	Stacker Select/Fetch Overflow (F)	Space Before	Space After	Skip Before	Skip After	Not	And Not	And Not	Field Name	Edit Codes	Blank After (B)	End Positon in Output Record	P = Packed/B = Binary	Constant or Edit Word
010	O	ERRORPT	D		1				50								
020	O		OR						55								
030	O											CUSTNO			7		
040	O								50						33		'DUPLICATE RECORD-NO ADDI'
050	O								50						47		'TION PERFORMED'
060	O								55						33		'NO MASTER RECORD-UPDATE'
070	O								55						46		'NOT PERFORMED'
080	O	MASTER	D	ADD					01N50								
090	O											CUSTNO			6		
100	O											NAME			26		
110	O											SALES			30	P	
120	O		D						02	03							
130	O											CUSNO			6		
140	O											MNAME			26		
150	O											MSALES			30	P	

Figure 13 - 31 Output Specifications

In the example above it can be seen that a line will be written on the Exception Report whenever indicators 50 or 55 are "on", that is, whenever an addition of a duplicate record is attempted or whenever an update is to take place but a corresponding master record was not found.

If an addition transaction record is read, that is, if indicator 01 is "on", and a duplicate record is not on the indexed sequential file, that is, if indicator 50 is "off", then the record is to be added to the file. The filename for the output file MASTER is specified as in all other examples. The "D" in column 15 indicates that the record is to be added at detail time. The word "ADD" must be specified in columns 16-18 whenever a record is to be added to the indexed sequential file. Thus, as can be seen on coding line 080 in Figure 13-31, whenever the 01 indicator is "on" and indicator 50 is "off" a record will be added to the indexed sequential file. The individual fields which make up the record to be added to the file are from the transaction record and will be placed in the same format as the other records in the master file, that is, the Customer Number in positions 1-6, the Name in positions 7-26 and the Sales in a packed-decimal format in positions 27-30.

If an update transaction is read and a corresponding master record is randomly retrieved, that is, if indicators 02 and 03 are "on", then the updated record is to be rewritten in the indexed sequential file. This is accomplished on coding lines 120-150 by specifying that the record should be written if both indicators 02 and 03 are "on". The fields to be included in the record are those which are originally in the record (see Figure 13-29). The MSALES field will include the updated sales amount because of the calculation performed in Figure 13-30.

The processing of the transaction file and the indexed sequential file will continue until end-of-file is reached for the transaction file (see Figure 13-29). At that time, the program will be terminated.

13.33

ADDITIONAL INDEXED SEQUENTIAL ENTRIES

The three sample programs in this chapter have illustrated the loading of an indexed sequential file, the sequential retrieval of that file using a Record Address File, and the Random Retrieval and Additions to the file using Chaining. There are other combinations which may be used when processing an indexed sequential file and these are determined both by the entries in columns 15 and 66 of the File Description Specifications and by whether a RAF or chaining is to be used. The following is a summary of the different definitions of the indexed sequential files.

	FILE DESCRIPTION SPECIFICATIONS		PROCESSING
	Column 15	Column 66	
1.	O	blank	Used to load a new indexed sequential file. The input to the program must be in an ascending sequence by key. The Mode of Processing column (column 28) is left blank.
2.	O	A	Add new records to an existing file. The input records may be in any sequence by key. Chaining may be used if a check is to be performed to determine if a record to be added is already on the file. If not, a duplicate record will turn on HO and cancel the program. The word ADD must be specified in columns 16-18 of the Output Specifications for the output file.
3.	I	blank	This specifies that the file is to be processed either sequentially or randomly with no updating or additions to occur. If the entire file is to be processed sequentially, then it is merely defined as a primary input file. If limits are to be used when sequentially retrieving the file, then a RAF must be defined and the value "L" must be placed in column 28. If the file is to be processed randomly, then the value "R" must be placed in column 28 and either a RAF or a Chaining File must be defined.
4.	I	A	This specifies that the file is to be processed either sequentially or randomly but that records may be added to the file. The same processing as in #3 occurs but the record to be added to the file must contain the word ADD in columns 16-18 of the Output Specifications.

	Column 15	Column 66	
5.	U	blank	This specifies that the file is to be processed and records may be updated. If the records are to be processed and updated sequentially, no RAF or Chaining file is required. If processed randomly, one is required. A random processing of the file requires the letter "R" in column 28 of the File Description Specifications.
6.	U	A	This specification will allow processing of the file either sequentially or randomly, will allow records within the file to be retrieved, updated, and rewritten, and will allow records to be added to the file. Either a RAF file or a Chaining file must be defined if Random Processing is to take place.

As can be seen from these previous uses of an indexed sequential file, there are many techniques which may be used to process an indexed sequential file. It is extremely versatile in the type of processing which may be accomplished and as such, finds many uses in business applications.

SAMPLE PROGRAM

The source listing of the third sample program is illustrated below.

```
DOS/360*RPG*CL 3-9              CASHMAN                    10/25/72        PAGE 0001

        01 010 H                                                          ADDISQ
001     01 020 FCARDUPD IPE F  80   80          EREAD40 SYSIPT            ADDISQ
002     01 030 FMASTER  UC  F 900   30R06KI    1 DISK14 SYSO16S      A2   ADDISQ
003     01 040 FERRORPT O   F 132  132     OF    PRINTERSYSLST            ADDISQ
004     01 050 EAAC1CARDUPD MASTER                                        ADDISQ
005     02 010 ICARDUPD AA  01  80 CA                                     ADDISQ
006     02 020 I        OR  02  80 CU                                     ADDISQ
007     02 030 I                             1   6 CUSTNO  C1             ADDISQ
008     02 040 I                             7  26 NAME                   ADDISQ
009     02 050 I                            27  322SALES                  ADDISQ
010     02 060 IMASTER  AB  03                                            ADDISQ
011     02 070 I                             1   6 CUSNO                  ADDISQ
012     02 080 I                             7  26 MNAME                  ADDISQ
013     02 090 I                          P 27  302MSALES                 ADDISQ
014     03 010 C                 SETOF             5055                   ADDISQ
015     03 020 C    NHO 01       SETON             50                     ADDISQ
016     03 030 C    HO  01       SETOF             HO                     ADDISQ
017     03 040 C    HO  02       SETON             55                     ADDISQ
018     03 050 C    55           SETOF             HO                     ADDISQ
019     03 060 C    02 03  MSALES    ADD  SALES    MSALES                 ADDISQ
020     04 010 OERRORPT H   101   1P                                      ADDISQ
021     04 020 O        OR       OF                                       ADDISQ
022     04 030 O                           8 'CUST NO'                    ADDISQ
023     04 040 O                          20 'ERROR'                      ADDISQ
024     04 050 O        D  1      50                                      ADDISQ
025     04 060 O        OR        55                                      ADDISQ
026     04 070 O                   CUSTNO  7                              ADDISQ
027     04 080 O                   50      33 'DUPLICATE RECORD-NO ADDI'  ADDISQ
028     04 090 O                   50      47 'TION PERFORMED'            ADDISQ
029     04 100 O                   55      33 'NO MASTER RECORD-UPDATE '  ADDISQ
030     04 110 O                   55      46 'NOT PERFORMED'             ADDISQ
031     04 120 OMASTER  DADD    01N50                                     ADDISQ
032     04 130 O                   CUSTNO  6                              ADDISQ
033     04 140 O                   NAME    26                             ADDISQ
034     04 150 O                   SALES   30P                            ADDISQ
035     05 010 O        D       02 03                                     ADDISQ
036     05 020 O                   CUSNO   6                              ADDISQ
037     05 030 O                   MNAME   26                             ADDISQ
038     05 040 O                   MSALES  30P                            ADDISQ
```

CHAPTER 13

REVIEW QUESTIONS

1. Explain the use of the Prime Data Area, Cylinder Overflow Area, Independent Overflow Area, Track Index, Cylinder Index and Master Index in an Indexed Sequential file.

2. What is the difference between a Record Address File and a Chaining File?

3. Explain the typical errors which may occur when an indexed sequential file is loaded. When it is randomly retrieved and records are added.

4. Explain the difference between a cylinder on a disk pack and a track on a disk pack.

CHAPTER 13

STUDENT EXERCISES

1. Write the entries on the File Description Specifications, the File Extension Specifications and the Input Specifications to define the following Indexed Sequential File and Transaction File. The transaction file is to randomly update and add records to the indexed sequential file.

Indexed Sequential File:
a) Fixed-length records, 25 characters in length, blocked, 10 records per block.

b) The filename, device, and Symbolic device are to be chosen by the programmer. The file has standard labels.

c) Records: col 1-6 Customer Number — Key for File
col 7-20 Customer Name
col 21-25 Sales (XXX.XX)

Card Transaction File:
a) Fixed-length records, 80 bytes in length, unblocked.

b) The filename, device, and symbolic device are to be chosen by the programmer.

c) Records: col 1-15 Customer Name
col 21-25 Sales (XXX.XX)
col 75-80 Customer Number

File Description Specifications

Line	Form Type	Filename	File Type I/O/U/C/D	File Designation P/S/C/R/T/D	End of File E	Sequence A/D	File Format F/V	Block Length	Record Length	L/R	Record Address Type A/K/I	Type of File Organization or Additional Area I/D/T or 1-9	Overflow Indicator / Key Field Starting Location	Extension Code E/L	Device	Symbolic Device	Labels (S, N, or E)	Name of Label Exit	Extent Exit for DAM / Core Index	A/U	Number of Tracks for Cylinder Over / Number of Ext / Tape Rewind / File Con U1-	N/U
0 2	F																					
0 3	F																					
0 4	F																					
0 5	F																					
0 6	F																					
0 7	F																					

Extension Specifications

Line			Form Type	Record Sequence of the Chaining File		Number of the Chaining Field		From Filename								To Filename								Table or Array Name					
3	4	5	6	7	8	9	10	11	12	13	14	15	16	17	18	19	20	21	22	23	24	25	26	27	28	29	30	31	32
0	1		E																										
0	2		E																										
0	3		E																										

RPG INPUT SPECIFICATIONS

Line			Form Type	Filename								Sequence		Number (1-N)	Option (O)	Record Identifying Indicator or **		Record Identification Codes 1 — Position			Not (N)	C/Z/D	Character	2 — Position			Not (N)	C/Z/D	Character	3 — Position			Not (N)	C/Z/D	Character	Stacker Select	P = Packed/B = Binary	Field Location From				To				Decimal Positions	Field Name						Control Level (L1-L9)		Matching Fields or Chaining Fields		Field Record Relation		Plus		Minus		Zero or Blank	
3	4	5	6	7	8	9	10	11	12	13	14	15	16	17	18	19	20	21	22	23	24	25	26	27	28	29	30	31	32	33	34	35	36	37	38	39	40	41	42	43	44	45	46	47	48	49	50	51	52	53	54	55	56	57	58	59	60	61	62	63	64	65	66	67	68
0	1		I																																																																
0	2		I																																																																
0	3		I																																																																
0	4		I																																																																
0	5		I																																																																
0	6		I																																																																
0	7		I																																																																
0	8		I																																																																
0	9		I																																																																
1	0		I																																																																
1	1		I																																																																
1	2		I																																																																
1	3		I																																																																
1	4		I																																																																
1	5		I																																																																

Debugging RPG Programs

Problem 1

Instructions: The following RPG program contains an error or errors which have occurred during compilation. Circle each error and record the corrected entries directly on the listing. Explain the error and method of correction in the space provided below.

```
DOS/360*RPG*CL 3-9              CASHMAN              10/20/72        PAGE 0001

        01 010 H                                                    ADDISQ
001     01 020 FCARDUPD IPE F  80  80           EREAD40 SYSIPT      ADDISQ
002     01 030 FMASTER   UC  F 900  30R06KI    1 DISK14 SYS016S     ADDISQ
003     01 040 FERRORPT  O   F 132 132     OF    PRINTERSYSLST      ADDISQ
004     01 050 EAAC1CARDUPD MASTER                                  ADDISQ
005     02 010 ICARDUPD AA  01  80 CA                               ADDISQ
006     02 020 I        OR   02  80 CU                              ADDISQ
007     02 030 I                            1    6 CUSTNO  C1       ADDISQ
008     02 040 I                            7   26 NAME            ADDISQ
009     02 050 I                           27  322SALES            ADDISQ
010     02 060 IMASTER  AB  03                                     ADDISQ
011     02 070 I                            1    6 CUSNO           ADDISQ
012     02 080 I                            7   26 MNAME           ADDISQ
013     02 090 I                          P 27  302MSALES          ADDISQ
014     03 010 C                  SETOF              5055          ADDISQ
015     03 020 C  NHO 01          SETON              50            ADDISQ
016     03 030 C  HO  01          SETOF              HO            ADDISQ
017     03 040 C  HO  02          SETON              55            ADDISQ
018     03 050 C  55              SETOF              HO            ADDISQ
019     03 060 C       02 03 MSALES  ADD  SALES  MSALES           ADDISQ
020     04 010 OERRORPT H  101    1P                              ADDISQ
021     04 020 O         OR        OF                             ADDISQ
022     04 030 O                              8 'CUST NO'         ADDISQ
023     04 040 O                             20 'ERROR'           ADDISQ
024     04 050 O         D  1      50                             ADDISQ
025     04 060 O         OR        55                             ADDISQ
026     04 070 O                    CUSTNO    7                    ADDISQ
027     04 080 O                    50         33 'DUPLICATE RECORD-NO ADDI'  ADDISQ
028     04 090 O                    50         47 'TION PERFORMED'   ADDISQ
029     04 100 O                    55         33 'NO MASTER RECORD-UPDATE '  ADDISQ
030     04 110 O                    55         46 'NOT PERFORMED'    ADDISQ
031     04 120 OMASTER  DADD      01N50                           ADDISQ
032     04 130 O                    CUSTNO    6                    ADDISQ
033     04 140 O                    NAME     26                    ADDISQ
034     04 150 O                    SALES    30P                   ADDISQ
035     05 010 O         D      02 03                              ADDISQ
036     05 020 O                    CUSNO     6                    ADDISQ
037     05 030 O                    MNAME    26                    ADDISQ
038     05 040 O                    MSALES   30P                   ADDISQ
```

13.40

SYMBOL TABLES

RESULTING INDICATORS

ADDRESS RI	ADDRESS RI	ADDRESS RI	ADDRESS RI	ADDRESS RI	ADDRESS RI	ADDRESS RI
000011 OF	000014 1P	000015 LR	000016 00	000017 01	000018 02	000019 03
000048 50	00004D 55	00007A L0	000085 H0	000086 H1	000087 H2	000088 H3
000089 H4	00008A H5	00008B H6	00008C H7	00008D H8	00008E H9	

FIELD NAMES

ADDRESS FIELD	ADDRESS FIELD	ADDRESS FIELD	ADDRESS FIELD	ADDRESS FIELD
000123 CUSTNO	000129 NAME	00013D SALES	000141 CUSNO	000147 MNAME
00015B MSALES				

LITERALS

ADDRESS LITERAL	ADDRESS LITERAL	ADDRESS LITERAL
00015F CUST NO	000166 ERROR	00016B DUPLICATE RECORD-NO ADDI
000183 TION PERFORMED	000191 NO MASTER RECORD-UPDATE	0001A9 NOT PERFORMED

     031 MASTER   NOTE 155

NOTE 155 ENTRY IN COLUMNS 16-18 VALID FOR INDEXED SEQUENTIAL ADD ONLY. ENTRY IS IGNORED.

EXPLANATION _____

_____

_____

_____

PROGRAMMING ASSIGNMENT 1

INSTRUCTIONS

An Indexed Sequential File is to be loaded as a master file for parts inventory. The master file will contain the part number, the part description, and the quantity on hand. Write the RPG program to cause the file to be loaded from the input data.

INPUT — Parts Quantity Cards

The parts quantity cards contain the Part Number, the Part Description, and the Quantity of parts currently in stock or "on hand". The format of the card is illustrated below.

OUTPUT — Parts Master File

The format of the Parts Master File may be any desired by the student. The quantity, however, should be stored in the packed-decimal format and the part number will be the key for the records in the file.

An Exception Report should also be created to record any errors, such as duplicate records or out of sequence records. The format of the report should be defined by the student.

TEST DATA — ASSIGNMENT NO. 1

Part Number (col 1 - 5)	Description (col 6 - 25)	Quantity (col 26 - 30)
10051	Handle	10098
19876	Wrench	00987
23154	Saw	00651
23154	Hammer	09877
34529	Level	00056
34499	Pliers	00899
43219	Screwdriver	01231

DOS JOB CONTROL

```
// JOB jobname
// OPTION LINK
// EXEC RPG

  — Source Deck —

/*
// LBLTYP NSD(02)
// EXEC LNKEDT
// ASSGN SYS016,X'192'
// DLBL filename,'PART MASTER',72/001,ISC
// EXTENT SYS016,111111,4,1,1600,2
// EXTENT SYS016,111111,1,2,1610,10
// EXEC

  — Test Data —

/*
/&
```

PROGRAMMING ASSIGNMENT 2

INSTRUCTIONS

Write the RPG program to sequentially retrieve the data stored on the Parts Master File and create a printed report of all of the data on the file. The input to the program is the indexed sequential file and the output is a printed report. The student is to design the format of the printed report.

DOS JOB CONTROL

```
// JOB jobname
// OPTION LINK
// EXEC RPG

  — Source Deck —

/*
// LBLTYP NSD(02)
// EXEC LNKEDT
// ASSGN SYS016,X'192'
// DLBL  filename,'PART MASTER',,ISE
// EXTENT SYS016,111111,4,1,1600,2
// EXTENT SYS016,111111,1,2,1610,10
// EXEC
/&
```

CHAPTER 13

PROGRAMMING ASSIGNMENT 3

INSTRUCTIONS

Write the RPG program to randomly update the Parts Master File and also to add records to the file.

INPUT — Transaction Cards and Parts Master File

The input to the program consists of the Part Master File which was created in Programming Assignment #1 and a file of transaction cards which will cause both random updating to take place and also the additions to the file.

"1" = ADDITION
"2" = UPDATE

OUTPUT

The output from the program will be the updated Parts Master File and an Exception Report of any transactions in error. The update processing of the master file will consist of adding the quantity on the Update card to the quantity already stored in the master file. It should be noted that this quantity in the transaction card may be a positive or a negative value. Also, if an addition is to take place, the description field must be included on the card. If it is not, the transaction is in error.

After the file has been updated, the print program of Assignment #2 should be executed in order to verify that the changes and additions have taken place.

13.45

TEST DATA — ASSIGNMENT NO. 3

Part Number (col 1-5)	Description (col 6-25)	Quantity (col 26-30)	Code (col 80)
10051	Micrometer	00100	2
18972	Pipe Wrench	00050	1
23154	Hack Saw	00980	1
42315		00087	2
42546		99809	1
43219		0005M	2
44289	Nails	00982	1

DOS JOB CONTROL

// JOB jobname
// OPTION LINK
// EXEC RPG

— Source Deck —

/*
// LBLTYP NSD(02)
// EXEC LNKEDT
// ASSGN SYS016,X'192'
// DLBL filename,'PART MASTER',,ISE
// EXTENT SYS016,111111,4,1,1600,2
// EXTENT SYS016,111111,1,2,1610,10
// EXEC

— Test Data —

/*
/&

CHAPTER 14

ADDITIONAL RPG STATEMENTS

INTRODUCTION

The sample programs in the previous chapters have presented most of the statements and processing techniques which may be used with the RPG language in programming business applications. There are, however, several additional statements and techniques which may prove useful in certain applications. These are explained below.

TWO INPUT/OUTPUT AREAS

In all of the previous examples of processing data in the "input area" which is used by RPG, one input area was illustrated. It is possible to specify that two input/output areas should be used for one file. In many applications, this may increase the efficiency of the program by processing records more quickly. The entries on the RPG Control Card and the File Description Specifications for two input/output areas are illustrated below.

EXAMPLE

Control Card Specifications

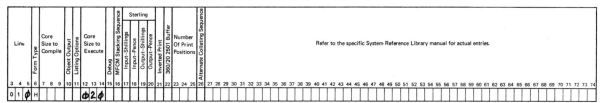

File Description Specifications

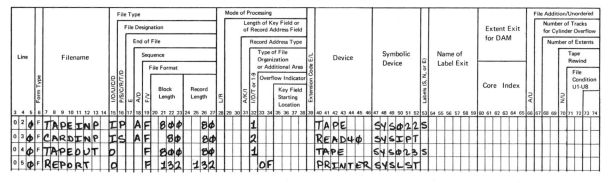

Figure 14-1 Entries for Two Input/Output Areas

Note from the example above that two entries are required in order to specify that more than one input/output area is to be used for a file. First, an entry is required in columns 12-14 of the Control Card to specify the size of main storage available to the object program. This entry must state the number of 1024 byte areas (1K) which are available. In the example, note that the value 020 is specified. This states that 20-1024 byte regions, or a total of 20,480 bytes are available to the object program. The size of core which is to be used by the program must be known by the programmer prior to the compilation process. The example of 20K bytes is used merely to illustrate the use of the entry on the control card.

The entries to indicate which files are to have two I/O areas are made in column 32 of the File Description Specifications. The number placed in this column may be 1-9 and this number is a "priority" for specifying which files will have two I/O areas. When the program is compiled, the compiler will determine how much excess core storage is available. It does this by comparing the size of the object program to the amount of available storage as specified on the Control Card. Any excess core storage will be assigned to two I/O areas for each file based upon the priority specified. The files with the value "1" in column 32 are given first priority. Thus, in the example in Figure 14-1, the TAPEINP and TAPEOUT have first priority on core storage for two I/O areas. The TAPEINP file would have first priority because it is specified first on the File Description Specifications. Thus, after the program is compiled and the size of the object program is known, the compiler will first assign the core storage necessary for another I/O area for the TAPEINP file. If there is sufficient space remaining, it will then assign the core storage for a second I/O area for the TAPEOUT program. Since the CARDINP file has the priority "2", if any core storage space is left, a second I/O area will be assigned for it.

The primary use of a second Input/Output area is to speed up the input/output operation of transferring data to and from main storage. In most cases, the most time will be saved if additional I/O areas are specified for sequential tape and sequential disk files. This is because of the additional speeds of these devices. It should be noted that two I/O areas may only be specified for sequential input, sequential output, and sequential update files. It may not be used for table files, printer files, and nonsequential Direct Access files.

LINE COUNTER SPECIFICATIONS

The Line Counter Specifications provide the facility for having reports stored on an intermediate device such as a tape or sequential disk. These reports can then be printed on the printer from these devices using a common Utility program.

This form is necessary because when the "printer" records are written on tape or disk, the channel 12 control punch in the carriage control tape cannot be sensed. Therefore, the Line Counter Specifications are used to relate the line of the printed page of the report to its corresponding punch in the carriage control tape. The entries in Figure 14-2 illustrate the entries required to cause a printed report to be stored on a tape for subsequent printing on the printer.

File Description Specifications

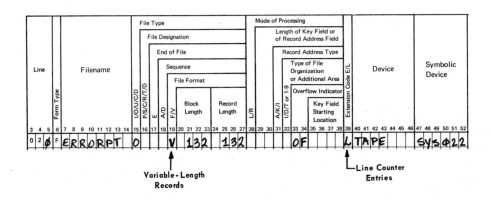

14.2

Line Counter Specifications

Line Counter Specifications

Line	Form Type	Filename	1		2		3		4		5	
			Line Number	FL or Channel Number	Line Number	OL or Channel Number	Line Number	Channel Number	Line Number	Channel Number	Line Number	Channel Number
3 4 5	6	7 8 9 10 11 12 13 14	15 16 17	18 19	20 21 22	23 24	25 26 27	28 29	30 31 32	33 34	35 36 37	38 39
1 1 0	L	ERRORPT	004	01	056	12						

Figure 14-2 Entries for Line Counter Specifications

Note from Figure 14-2 that the ERRORPT file is defined as an output file as when the printed output is to be placed directly on the printer. When using the Line Counter Specifications, the File Format must be defined as Variable-Length Records ("V" in column 19). The block length and record length are 132 characters, the same as in previous examples. The overflow indicator (OF) is also specified in the same manner as used in previous definitions of a printer file. The entry "L" must be included in column 39 of the File Description Specifications to indicate that additional entries concerning the file will be found on the Line Counter Specifications. Even though the data in the file is to eventually be printed on a printer, the Device specified must be type of device to be used to store the file when the program is executed. Thus, in this example, since the data is to be stored temporarily on magnetic tape, the word TAPE is placed in the Device field of the File Definition Specifications. The Symbolic Device SYS022 is specified because this is the programmer logical unit assigned to the tape unit on which the file will be written.

The entries on the Line Counter Specifications are used to simulate the occurrence of the channel punches in the carriage control tape. The filename, which is entered in columns 7-14, must be the same as the filename on the File Description Specifications. Following the Filename entry, there are 12 sets of entries which may be included on the form. Each set contains a three digit Line Number and a two-digit Channel Number entry. These positions are used to relate the line on the output form to a channel punch in the carriage control tape. The line number on the printed page is recorded in the first three positions and the channel number is recorded in the next two positions. Thus, in Figure 14-2, it can be seen that the line number 004 on the printed page is to correspond to channel 1 in the carriage control tape, that is, the fourth line on the printed page is to be considered "head of forms". The 56th line on the printed page (columns 20-22) is to be the last line printed because it is associated with channel 12 (columns 23-24). When the program is executed, the internal line count, which is processed by coding developed as a result of specifying the Line Counter Specifications, is set at 004 because this is the first line on the report as specified in columns 15-17. As each record is written on the output device (tape unit), the line count is increased by one space per record. When the line count equals 56, the overflow indicator (OF) is set on, and overflow output occurs in the same manner as if the channel 12 punch had been sensed in the carriage control tape. The next record is written with a special carriage control character associated with it so that a skip to head of forms will occur when the record is printed on the printer. The line count is then reset to 004 and the process begins again.

The entries on the Output Specifications are the same as if the data were being directly written on the printer instead of on an intermediate device. All space before and space after entries will cause appropriate records to be written on the tape file so that when the data is transferred from the tape to the printer, the spacing takes place properly.

In order to retrieve the data stored on the tape and to print it on the printer the following job stream could be used.

EXAMPLE

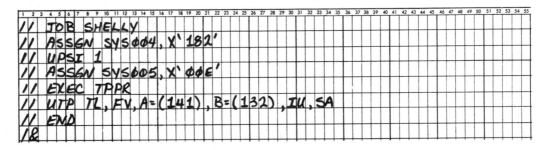

1 2 3 4 5 6	7 8 9 10 11 12 13 14 15 16 17 18 19 20 21 22 23 24 25 26 27 28 29 30 31 32 33 34 35 36 37 38 39 40 41 42 43 44 45 46 47 48 49 50 51 52 53 54 55
//	JOB SHELLY
//	ASSGN SYS004, X'182'
//	UPSI 1
//	ASSGN SYS005, X'00E'
//	EXEC TPPR
//	UTP TL, FV, A=(141), B=(132), IU, SA
//	END
/&	

Figure 14-3 Tape-to-Print Utility Program

In the example above, the DOS Tape-to-Print Utility program is used to read the tape which contains the data from the program and print it on the printer. For a further explanation of the use of the DOS Utility programs, consult the book DOS UTILITIES SORT/MERGE MULTIPROGRAMMING, Anaheim Publishing Co.

CALCULATION SPECIFICATIONS

There are a number of operations which may be specified on the Calculation Specifications and which perform functions which may be useful in a given application. The following sections will deal with the operations which have not been covered previously in the text.

Zero and Add (Z-ADD)

The Zero and Add operation causes the field specified in the Result Field portion of the Calculation Specifications to be set to zeros and then causes the data contained in the numeric literal or the field specified in the Factor 2 portion of the form to be placed in the Result Field. Factor 1 is not used in this operation. The example in Figure 14-4 illustrates the use of the Zero and Add operation.

EXAMPLE

RPG CALCULATION SPECIFICATIONS

Line	Form Type	Control Level (L0-L9, LR, SR)	Indicators And Not	And Not	Not	Factor 1	Operation	Factor 2	Result Field	Field Length	Decimal Positions	Half Adjust (H)	Resulting Indicators Arithmetic Plus Minus Zero / Compare High 1>2 Low 1<2 Equal 1=2 / Lookup Table (Factor 2) is High 54 55 Low 56 57 Equal 58 59
0 1	0	C L2					Z-ADD 0		TOTFLD	72			

Before: After:

0	7	8	4	3	2	5

TOTFLD

0	0	0	0	0	0	0

TOTFLD

Figure 14-4 ADD Operation

14.4

Note in Figure 14-4 that the literal zero is placed in the Factor 2 position on the form. Thus, after the Z-ADD operation is completed, the value in TOTFLD will be set to zero. As noted, the value in the Result field will be the same as the value in the field specified in Factor 2.

Zero and Subtract

This operation causes the negative of the number contained in the literal or the field in Factor 2 to be placed in the result field specified. This operation is performed after the result field has been set to zeros. Factor 1 is not used in this operation. Figure 14-5 contains an example of the Z-SUB operation.

EXAMPLE

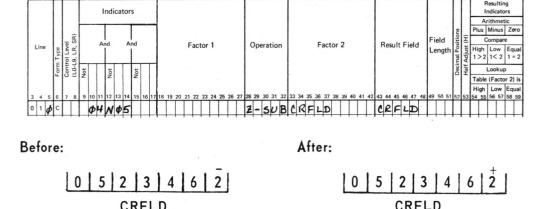

Figure 14-5 Example of Z-SUB Operation

Note in the example above that before the Z-SUB operation takes place, the field CRFLD contains the negative value 0523462. After the execution of the instruction, the field contains the positive value 0523462. Thus, as can be seen, the Z-SUB operation has been used to switch the sign of the field from negative to positive. The same sign switching will take place from a positive field to a negative field. This function of sign switching, which is necessary in some business applications, is the primary function of the Z-SUB instruction.

Move Zone Operations

Alphabetic data or special characters are stored in main storage in the zoned-decimal format. When data is stored in the zoned-decimal format, each byte is said to contain a zone portion and a digit portion. This is illustrated in Figure 14-6.

EXAMPLE

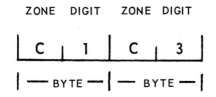

Figure 14-6 Example of Zoned-Decimal Format

Each byte which is in main storage consists of eight bits. The leftmost four bits of data in the zoned decimal format is called the zone and the right-most four bits is called the digit portion of the byte.

Numeric data in an RPG program is stored in the packed-decimal format. Figure 14-7 contains an example of the packed-decimal format.

EXAMPLE

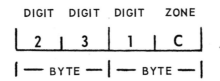

DIGIT DIGIT DIGIT ZONE

| 2 | 3 | 1 | C |

|— BYTE —|— BYTE —|

Figure 14-7 Example of Packed-Decimal Format

Note in the packed-decimal format illustrated above that the zone portion of the field is the low-order four bits in the field. This is the sign of the number, that is, whether it is positive or negative. Every numeric field in an RPG program is stored in the packed-decimal format as illustrated above.

The Move Zone operations are used to move the zone portion of a field or literal to the zone portion of another field. There are four variations of the Move Zone instructions. They are the Move High-To-Low Zone operation (MHLZO), the Move Low-To-Low Zone operation (MLLZO), the Move Low-To-High Zone operation (MLHZO), and the Move High-To-High Zone operation (MHHZO). The "high" in these operations refers to the left-most byte in the field and the "low" refers to the right-most byte in the field. Thus, the Move High-To-Low Zone operation moves the zone portion of the left-most byte in a field to the zone portion of the right-most byte in a field. The Move High-To-Low Zone operation is illustrated in Figure 14-8.

EXAMPLE

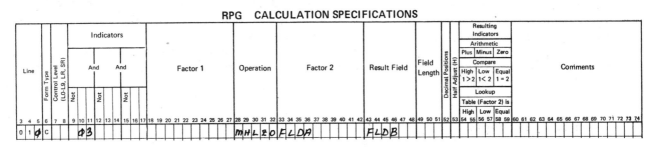

RPG CALCULATION SPECIFICATIONS

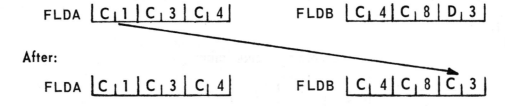

Before:

FLDA | C 1 | C 3 | C 4 | FLDB | C 4 | C 8 | D 3 |

After:

FLDA | C 1 | C 3 | C 4 | FLDB | C 4 | C 8 | C 3 |

Note: Values are illustrated in Hexadecimal Format so the movement of the Zone portion of the byte can be seen.

Figure 14-8 Example of MHLZO

Note in Figure 14-8 that the zone portion of the High-Order byte in the field FLDA is moved to the zone portion of the Low-Order byte in the field FLDB. The operation code, which must be specified in columns 28-32 of the Calculation Specifications, is MHLZO. The Factor 1 portion of the form is not used. The field specified in Factor 2 is the sending field, that is, it contains the zone which is to be moved. The field specified in the Result Field portion of the form is the receiving field. The zone portion of the high-order byte in the Factor 2 field is moved to the zone portion of the low-order byte in the Result Field.

The other Move Zone operations work in a similar manner except that the designation of which zone is to be moved and where it is to be moved is made by the "High-Low" or "Low-High" specification. A summary of the Move Zone instructions and the zones which are moved is contained in Figure 14-9.

Instruction	Factor 2 Field	Result Field	Result of Move
MLLZO	Alphameric	Alphameric	Bits 0-3 of rightmost byte of Factor 2 are moved to bits 0-3 of rightmost byte of Result Field.
MLLZO	Alphameric	Numeric	Bits 0-3 of rightmost byte of Factor 2 are moved to bits 4-7 of the rightmost byte of the Result Field.
MLLZO	Numeric	Alphameric	Bits 4-7 of rightmost byte of Factor 2 are moved to bits 0-3 of rightmost byte of the Result Field.
MLLZO	Numeric	Numeric	Bits 4-7 of rightmost byte of Factor 2 are moved to bits 4-7 of rightmost byte of Result Field.
MHLZO	Alphameric	Numeric	Bits 0-3 of leftmost byte of Factor 2 are moved to bits 4-7 of rightmost byte of Result Field.
MHLZO	Alphameric	Alphameric	Bits 0-3 of leftmost byte of Factor 2 are moved to bits 0-3 of rightmost byte of the Result Field.
MLHZO	Alphameric	Alphameric	Bits 0-3 of rightmost byte of Factor 2 are moved to bits 0-3 of leftmost byte of Result Field.
MLHZO	Numeric	Alphameric	Bits 4-7 of rightmost byte of Factor 2 are moved to bits 0-3 of leftmost byte of the Result Field.
MHHZO	Alphameric	Alphameric	Bits 0-3 of leftmost byte of Factor 2 are moved to bits 0-3 of leftmost byte of Result Field.

Figure 14-9 Summary of Move Zone Instruction

Note from Figure 14-9 that the portion of the byte moved, that is, whether bits 0-3 or 4-7 are moved, is dependent upon the format of the field. If the field is alphameric (zoned-decimal), bits 0-3 are processed in the instruction. If the field is numeric (packed-decimal), then bits 4-7 are processed. Note also that whenever the high-order zone of the sending field is used (MHLZO or MHHZO), the Factor 2 field must be alphameric. It cannot be numeric. In addition, the receiving field (Result Field) for the MLHZO and MHHZO instructions must be alphameric and numeric fields cannot be used with the MHHZO instruction.

Test Zone Instruction

The Test Zone Instruction (TESTZ) is used to test the zone of the leftmost position of the alphameric field that is entered in the result field. This is illustrated in Figure 14-10.

EXAMPLE

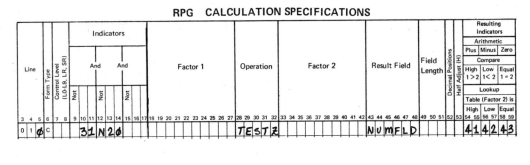

Figure 14-10 Example of TESTZ Instruction

In the example above note that the operation code TESTZ is placed in columns 28-32 to indicate that the zone of the high-order byte in the field specified in columns 43-48 is to be tested. If the zone portion of the high-order byte in the field NUMFLD contains a 12-zone (&, A-I), the indicator specified in columns 54-55 will be turned "on". Thus, as can be seen, since the first example shows the value C3F8F2 in NUMFLD, indicator 41 will be turned on because the hexadecimal value C3 is equivalent to the letter of the alphabet "C". The hexadecimal value D3 (L) turns on indicator 42 which is specified in columns 56-57. An 11-zone (-, J-R) will cause the indicator in column 56-57 to be turned "on". If neither of these conditions is satisfied, then the indicator specified in columns 58-59 is turned "on". Thus, when the value F3 is found in the high-order byte, indicator 43 is turned "on".

EXTERNAL SUBROUTINES

In some business applications, there may be processing routines which are common to more than one program. For example, the routine to calculate the Calendar Date from a given Julian Date may be used in many programs. Thus, instead of writing this routine for each RPG program which requires it, the routine may be written as an Assembler Language SUBROUTINE and may be automatically included in each program in which it is required without rewriting the subroutine each time. A Subroutine of this type, which is included in many different programs, is called a Closed Subroutine. It is a closed subroutine because it is entered from the RPG program, performs its function, and then returns to the RPG program. This is illustrated below.

EXAMPLE

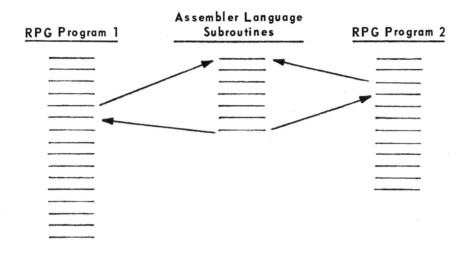

Figure 14-11 Example of Subroutine

Note in the example above that two different RPG programs are to use the same Assembler Language Subroutine. This subroutine may be used to perform any calculations or other processing which is necessary within the program. In order to use a subroutine, several things must occur. First, the RPG program must "Exit" from the program to the subroutine, that is, it must transfer control to the subroutine. Second, when the subroutine has completed processing, it must return control to the RPG program at the point where the exit took place. In addition, it may be desirable for the subroutine to reference data which was defined within the RPG program and it may also be necessary for the RPG program to reference data which is stored in the subroutine. In order to allow this processing to take place, RPG provides three instructions which are specified on the Calculation Specifications — the EXIT instruction, the RLABL instruction, and the ULABL instruction.

EXIT Instruction

The EXIT instruction is used in the RPG program to cause control to be passed to an Assembler Language subroutine. The EXIT instruction which could be used to pass control to the JULCON subroutine is illustrated below.

EXAMPLE

RPG CALCULATION SPECIFICATIONS

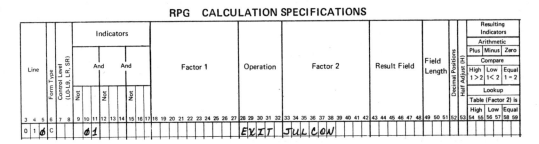

Figure 14-12 Example of EXIT Instruction

In the example above it can be seen that the operation code EXIT is specified in columns 28-31. This operation causes control to be passed to the routine which is named in the Factor 2 portion of the Calculation Specifications. In the example, the subroutine name is JULCON. The subroutine name must be six characters or less and must begin with an alphabetic value. When the EXIT instruction is executed, control is passed to the object coding in the JULCON subroutine. The subroutine will be executed until it has completed its processing at which time it will return control to the instruction immediately following the EXIT operation. Thus, the EXIT instruction provides the Linkage to the subroutine from the RPG program and also provides the address to which the subroutine will return control when it has completed its processing.

As can be seen from the example in Figure 14-12, the EXIT operation may be conditioned by indicators. Thus, the EXIT operation in the example will take place only if indicator 01 is "on". The Factor 1, Result Field, and other fields on the Calculation Specifications are not used for the EXIT instruction.

RLABL Instruction

As was noted previously, it may be necessary for the subroutine to reference data which is defined within the RPG program. In order for this to occur, the RPG program must use the RLABL instruction to identify the fields to be used by the subroutine. The example in Figure 14-13 illustrates the use of the RLABL operation.

EXAMPLE

RPG   CALCULATION SPECIFICATIONS

Line	Form Type	Control Level (L0-L9, LR, SR)	Indicators And Not	And Not	And Not	Factor 1	Operation	Factor 2	Result Field	Field Length	Decimal Positions	Half Adjust (H)	Resulting Indicators Arithmetic Plus Minus Zero / Compare High 1>2 Low 1<2 Equal 1=2 / Lookup Table (Factor 2) is High 54 55 Low 56 57 Equal 58 59
0 1 Ø	C		Ø1				EXIT	JULCON					
0 2 Ø	C						RLABL		JULDTE				

Figure 14-13 Example of RLABL Instruction

In the example in Figure 14-13 it can be seen that the operation code RLABL is specified in columns 28-32. The name placed in the Result Field portion of the form is the name of the field which is to be referenced in the subroutine. Thus, as can be seen, the field JULDTE, which must be defined within the RPG program, either on the Input Specifications or the Calculation Specifications, will be available to the subroutine for use. The subroutine may alter the data in the field or use it in any other way which is necessary. If the field specified has not been previously defined in the RPG program, it must contain entries in the Field Length and, if necessary, the Decimal Positions portions of the Calculation Specifications in the same manner as if an undefined field were to be used in an arithmetic operation.

It should be noted that the RLABL instruction is not an executable instruction, that is, it will cause no processing to occur. It merely identifies a field within the RPG program which is to be referenced within the Assembler Language subroutine. In addition to any fields which may be used with the RLABL instruction, it may also be required that the subroutine reference one or more indicators within the RPG program. Any indicator which is to be referenced within the subroutine must be defined using the RLABL instruction with the value INxx in the Result Field where xx is the number of the indicator. Thus, if indicator 34 were to be referenced in the subroutine, the RLABL instruction, with the name IN34 in the Result Field would be specified.

ULABL Instruction

A field which is defined within the Assembler Language subroutine but which is to be referenced within the RPG program must be identified through the use of the ULABL instruction. This is illustrated in Figure 14-14.

EXAMPLE

RPG   CALCULATION SPECIFICATIONS

Line	Form Type	Control Level (L0-L9, LR, SR)	Indicators						Factor 1	Operation	Factor 2	Result Field	Field Length	Decimal Positions	Half Adjust (H)	Resulting Indicators		
			And		And											Arithmetic		
																Plus	Minus	Zero
																Compare		
			Not		Not		Not									High 1>2	Low 1<2	Equal 1=2
																Lookup		
																Table (Factor 2) is		
																High	Low	Equal
0 1	C		01							EXIT	JULCON							
0 2	C									RLABL		JULDTE						
0 3	C									ULABL		CALDTE	60					

Figure 14-14   Example of ULABL Instruction

The ULABL instruction, like the RLABL instruction, is used to merely identify a field which is to be used within the program. It is not an executable statement. The operation code ULABL must be specified in columns 28-32 of the Calculation Specifications. The name specified in the Result Field portion of the form must be the six character or less name which is used to define the field within the Assembler Subroutine. Note in the example that this name is CALDTE. Again, it must be emphasized that the name is a name which is defined within the subroutine; it is not any name which is previously defined within the RPG program.

Since the field which is defined using the ULABL operation code is not defined within the RPG program, entries are required in the Field Length portion of the Calculation Specifications (columns 49-51) and, if the field is numeric, in the Decimal Positions portion of the form (column 52). These entries are used to specify to the RPG program the attributes of the field so that it may be used in subsequent RPG statements. Note in the example above that the CALDTE field is specified as a field containing 6 digits and that the field is a numeric field with no digits to the right of the decimal point. Whenever a numeric field is defined in the subroutine for use within the RPG program, it must be stored in the packed-decimal format. This is because all numeric fields within an RPG program are stored in the packed-decimal format. If the data which is stored in the subroutine for use within the RPG program is not in a packed-decimal format, erroneous results and sometimes program cancellation will result.

SUMMARY

The RPG programming language as has been explained in the previous chapters is an extremely valuable tool in business application programming. It offers the capabilities to perform most of the types of processing which are required in the business data processing community. It is a very precise language in terms of usage and this leads somewhat to standardization of use which is an asset in writing business programs.

The version of RPG which has been used in this text is designed for use on the System/360 or System/370 operating under the Disk Operating System. There are several other versions of the language available from both IBM and other manufacturers such as NCR and Honeywell. Certain features of the RPG language which are available in the version discussed in the text may not be available in the other versions and, conversely, there may be features in other versions which are not available in the IBM DOS version. It should be noted, however, that all of these different versions are designed to accomplish the same end result, that is, provide for the processing of business application programs and there is really very little difference between the languages offered by different manufacturers and for different operating systems.

A recent addition to the repertoire of RPG programming is the RPG II programming language. Originally designed to be used on the IBM System/3, it is now available for use under both DOS and OS on System/360 and System/370 computers. For the most part, RPG II offers extended capabilities over the original RPG programming language. These extended capabilities are quite helpful in some programming applications but, as can be seen from the previous examples in the text, the majority of business applications can be solved through the use of RPG.

It will be found that the step from using the RPG illustrated in this text to using the RPG languages supplied by other manufacturers or the RPG II programming language is quite small. Thus, if the use of the RPG illustrated in this text is well understood, the use of another RPG will be an interesting but not difficult task.

CASE STUDY

The final programming assignment incorporates many of the concepts studied in the previous chapters. Upon solution of this problem, the student should be able to solve a wide variety of business type programming problems.

INSTRUCTIONS

The invoice for the Data Processing Publishing Company is currently being prepared by hand. A copy of a typical invoice is illustrated below.

DATA PROCESSING PUBLISHERS, INC.
9221 E. HANSEN BLVD.
LINESVILLE, CALIFORNIA

INVOICE

2273

SOLD TO:

Jackson School
365 Dart St.
Utopia, CA 90701

SHIP TO:

Same

DATE RECEIVED	INVOICE	TERMS	DATE SHIPPED		ORDER NUMBER
10-22-72	2273	Net 30 Days	10-30-72		P. O. #66754

ORDERED	SHIPPED	DESCRIPTION	PRICE	AMOUNT
20	20	INTRO TO COMP PROG S/360 ASSEMBLER LANG	7.95	159.00
		20% DISCOUNT		31.80
		NET		127.20

It has been decided to convert the manual preparation of the invoices for the publishing company to the computer and the application is to be written in RPG. The following system has been designed to process the invoices.

CUSTOMER MASTER FILE

The Customer Master File is to be stored on Magnetic Tape or Sequential Disk as a sequential file sorted on the Customer Number. The following information will be contained on the master file.

Col 1-5:   Customer Number — A five digit unique number assigned to every customer.

Col 6-25: Customer Name — The name of the customer ordering the books.

Col 26-45: Street Address — The street address of the customer ordering the books.

Col 46-65: City,State,Zip — The City, State, and Zip Code of the customer ordering the books.

Col 66-67: Discount   — The percentage (XX%) discount allowed the customer, if any. If the customer is not entitled to any discount, this field will contain zeros.

HEADER CARD

The Header Card is a punched card which will be the first card in the card input stream and will contain the following information.

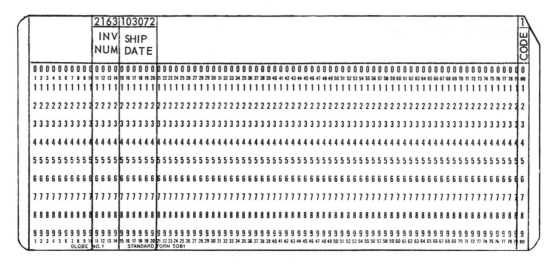

Col 11-14: Beginning Invoice Number — The number with which the invoice numbers will begin. Each new invoice which is written will contain a new invoice number which is calculated by adding "1" to the invoice number just used.

Col 15-20: Shipping Date — This is the date on which all orders being processed in the run have been shipped.

Col 80: Code "1" — The code "1" identifies the card as a Header Card.

There will be one header card for each batch of invoices that are to be processed for the day.

CUSTOMER CARD

The Customer Card is used to identify the customer and to contain information concerning the particular order from the customer. The Customer Card contains the following information.

Col 1-5:   Customer Number — This is the customer number of the customer which is making the purchase.

Col 6-12:   Purchase Order — This field contains the purchase order from the customer. This purchase order number is required before an invoice can be written and if it is omitted from the Customer Card, an invoice should not be written. Instead, an error message should be printed on the body of the invoice.

Col 13-18: Date Received — This field contains the date the order was received from the customer.

Col 20-39: Ship To Name — This field, and the fields to follow, contain the name and address where the books are to be shipped if it is different from the address of the customer who ordered the books. (The address of the customer is contained on the master magnetic tape file.) If these fields contain blanks, then the Ship To portion of the invoice will contain the value "SAME". If they do not contain blanks, then the Name, Address, City, and State should be placed in the Ship To portion of the invoice.

Col 40-59: Ship to Street Address — This is the address which is to be placed in the Ship To portion of the form if there are not blanks in the Ship To Name field.

Col 60-79: Ship To City, State, Zip — This is the City, State, and Zip Code which is to be used for a separate Ship To address.

Col 80:   Code "2" — This field contains the code value "2" to identify the card as a Customer Card.

ORDER CARD

The Order Card contains information relating the type of book which has been ordered and the Quantity ordered. Its format is shown below.

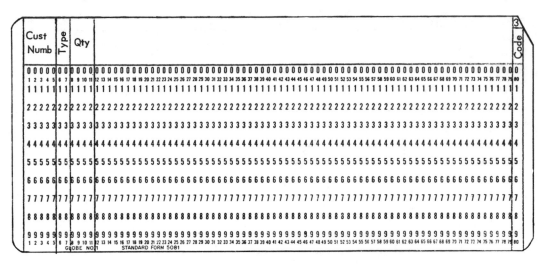

Col 1-5:	Customer Number	– This is the Customer Number of the Customer which is making the purchase.
Col 6-7:	Book Type	– This field contains a code (1-20) which identifies the book which is to be ordered. This code is used to search the Book Table which contains the book name and the book price.
Col 8-11:	Quantity	– This field contains the number of books which have been ordered.
Col 80:	Code	– The code "3" identifies an Order Card.

BOOK TABLE

The "book table" is a table which contains a code identifying the books, the title of the books, and the unit price for each book. The data which is to be stored in the table is illustrated below.

CODE (2 Characters)	BOOK TITLE (50 Characters)	UNIT PRICE (XX.XX)
01	INTRO TO COMP PROG S/360 ASSEMBLER LANG	07.95
02	S/360 ASSEMBLER LANGUAGE PROBLEM TEXT	04.95
03	S/360 ASSEMBLER DISK/TAPE ADV. CON.	08.95
04	REVIEW MANUAL FOR CDP EXAM	08.95
05	INTRO TO COMP PROG S/360 COBOL	08.95
06	S/360 COBOL PROBLEM TEXT	04.95
07	S/360 COBOL DISK/TAPE ADV. CON.	08.95
08	INTRO TO FLOWCHARTING AND COMP LOGIC	04.95
09	INTRO TO COMP PROG BASIC FORTRAN IV	08.95
10	DOS JOB CONTROL FOR ASSEM PROG	06.95
11	DOS JOB CONTROL FOR COBOL PROG	06.95
12	DOS UTILITIES SORT/MERGE MULTIPROG	06.95
13	OS JOB CONTROL	07.95
14	INTRO TO COMP PROG S/360 PL/I	08.95
15	INTRO TO COMP PROG RPG	08.95
16	PRACTICAL PROJECTS IN DATA PROC	04.95
17	BASIC PROJECTS IN DATA PROC	02.45
18	CONTROL PANEL WIRING 407 ACCT MACH	02.95
19	CONTROL PANEL WIRING 402 ACCT MACH	02.95
20	CONTROL PANEL WIRING 548 INTERPRETER	01.45

The data in the table above will be loaded as a table in the program and will be referenced by the codes illustrated above and punched in the Order Card.

PROCESSING

The input to the program will be arranged in a given order as follows: 1) Table Data; 2) Header Card (one only); 3) Customer Card (one per customer); 4) Order Card (one or more per customer). The Customer Card and the Order Card will be sorted in a Customer Number sequence and the customer card will always be the first card for a given customer (ie. the cards will be sorted on Code within Customer Number). A sample input stream is illustrated below.

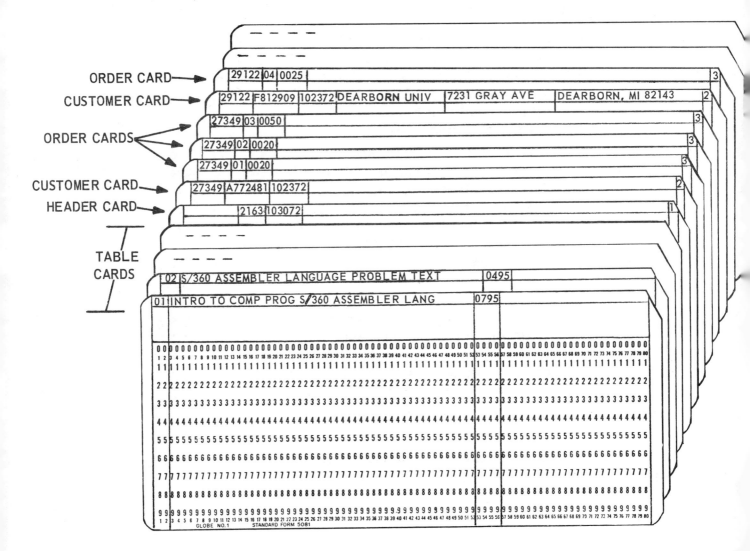

As can be seen from the input stream above, the Book Table cards will be first in the input stream. The data cards consist of a single header card followed by each group of cards for a customer order. These cards consist of one Customer Card and one or more Order Cards.

RULES AND CALCULATIONS

The following processing rules and calculations are to be followed for the Invoicing Program.

1. The first Invoice Number to be used on the printed invoices is to be the number which is contained on the Header Card. Each subsequent invoice is to have an invoice number one greater than the previous invoice number.

2. The Sold To entry is to be the customer which is identified by the Customer Number on the Customer Card.

3. If there is a Name and Address in the Ship To portion of the Customer Card, then this value is to be used on the Ship To portion of the invoice. If not, then the word SAME should be included following the Ship To heading on the invoice.

4. The Date Received is to be retrieved from the Customer Card.

5. The terms on all invoices are "Net 30 Days".

6. The date shipped is found on the Header Card.

7. The purchase order number is found on the Customer Card. If a purchase order number is not found on the Customer Card, that is, if the field is blank, then the word NONE is to be entered on the Invoice in place of the purchase order number and the message "NO PURCHASE ORDER — INVOICE INVALID" is to be printed on the body of the invoice in place of the quantity and description of the book. All subsequent order cards for the customer are not to be processed.

8. The quantity ordered and the quantity shipped are always the same and are found on the Order Card.

9. There will be one line on the invoice for each order card which is read.

10. The description of the book will be found by the appropriate entry in the Book Table which is searched using the Book Type number which is found in the Order Card.

11. The price is also found in the Book Table for each type of book.

12. The amount is determined by multiplying the quantity by the unit price of each book.

13. The total amounts for each of the book orders for a customer are to be totaled. After all of the order cards have been read for a customer, a discount of the total is to be taken if there is to be a discount for the customer. This is determined by the value in the Discount field of the Customer Master File. If the field contains zeros, then there is no discount. If the field does not contain zeros, then the value in the discount field, which is a percentage value, is multiplied by the total which has been accumulated. The answer to this multiplication is subtracted from the total, giving a Net Due Amount. This Net Due is printed on the invoice.

14. After one customer has been processed, the page is to be skipped to a new page prior to beginning the next invoice. Thus, only one invoice per page will be printed. There will never be more than 1 page per customer.

15. If a customer card is found with no matching master record, the customer number and the message "NO MASTER RECORD" should be written in the Sold To portion of the invoice and the invoice should not be printed.

16. All constant information illustrated on the printer spacing chart is to be printed on the invoice.

INVOICE FORMAT

The following is the printer spacing chart for the invoice.

INTERNATIONAL BUSINESS MACHINES CORPORATION
PRINTER SPACING CHART
IBM 407, 408, 409, 1403, 1404, 1443, and 2201

Print span:

FIELD HEADINGS/WORD MARKS — 6 Lines Per Inch

IBM 1403 Models 1 & 4
IBM 407, 408, 409
IBM 1403 Models 2, 3, 5, 140
IBM 1443 Models 1 and N1

```
DATA PROCESSING PUBLISHERS, INC.
           9221 E. HANSEN BLVD.
         LINESVILLE, CALIFORNIA

SOLD TO:
         XXXXXXXXXXXXXXXXXXXXX
         XXXXXXXXXXXXXXXXXXXXX
         XXXXXXXXXXXXXXXXXXX

SHIP TO:
         XXXXXXXXXXXXXXXXXXXX
         XXXXXXXXXXXXXXXXXXXXX
         XXXXXXXXXXXXXXXXXX

DATE            INVOICE                         DATE          PURCHASE
RECEIVED        NUMBER         TERMS            SHIPPED       ORDER NO

XX-XX-XX        XXXX       NET 30 DAYS          XX-XX-XX      XXXXXXX

QTY         QTY                                          UNIT
ORDERED     SHIPPED         DESCRIPTION                  PRICE         AMOUNT

XXØX        XXØX      XXXXXXXXXXXXXXXXXXXXXXXXXXXXXXXXXXX  XØ.XX      XX,XXØ.XX
XXØX        XXØX      XXXXXXXXXXXXXXXXXXXXXXXXXXXXXXXXXXX  XØ.XX      XX,XXØ.XX

                                              TOTAL                  XX,XXØ.XX

                                      XX% DISCOUNT                    X,XXØ.XX

                                              NET                    XX,XXØ.XX
```

14.22

INSTRUCTIONS

Two programs are to be written. The first is to be used to load the Customer Master File from card input. The second is to process the input as described previously and create the Customer Invoices.

The input to the program to load the master file is illustrated below.

The Output from the program is to be a sequential file stored either on tape or a direct-access device. The format of the file is illustrated on page 14.15.

The second program should read the data as previously described and create the customer invoices.

TEST DATA — CASE STUDY

PROGRAM NUMBER 1

Cust Numb (col 1-5)	Name (col 6-25)	Address (col 26-45)	City/State (col 46-65)	Discount (col 66-67)
10054	Jackson School	365 Dart St.	Utopia, CA 90701	20
10061	Claiborn Univ.	8897 Vally St.	Claiborn, NY 90011	10
10098	Georgia College	987 Gore Ave.	Atlanta, GA 88765	20
11886	Harold Johnson	9983 Herrity Blvd.	Yorktown, PA 88231	00
77512	Sutherland Univ.	331 South St.	Boise, ID 77654	20

PROGRAM NUMBER 2

Header Card:

Invoice Number (col 11-14)	Date Shipped (col 15-20)	Code (col 80)
2271	10-30-72	1

Customer Cards:

Cust Numb (col 1-5)	P.O. No. (col 6-12)	Date Received (col 13-18)	Ship To Name (col 20-39)	Ship To Address (col 40-59)	Ship To City/State (col 60-79)	Code (col 80)
10054	A332789	10-22-72				2
10098	F665378	10-25-72				2
11864	G645365	10-26-72				2
77512	6521654	10-27-72	Sutherland U.	556 North St.	Boise, ID 77654	2

Order Cards:

Cust Numb (col 1-5)	Type (col 6-7)	Quantity (col 8-11)	Code (col 80)
10054	05	0050	3
10054	09	0100	3
10054	11	0020	3
10098	01	0150	3
10098	02	0150	3
10098	03	0050	3
10098	14	0100	3
11864	15	0020	3
77512	10	0075	3
77512	13	0100	3
77512	04	0030	3

DOS JOB CONTROL

The following job stream assumes the master file is to be stored on magnetic tape.

```
// JOB jobname
// OPTION LINK
// EXEC RPG

  – Source Deck - Program #1 –

/*
// LBLTYP TAPE
// EXEC LNKEDT
// ASSGN SYS021,X'181'
// TLBL filename,'CUSTOMER MASTER',72/001
// EXEC

  – Test Data - Program #1 –

/*
// OPTION LINK
// EXEC RPG

  – Source Deck - Program #2 –

/*
// LBLTYP TAPE
// ASSGN SYS021,X'181'
// TLBL filename,'CUSTOMER MASTER'
// EXEC

  – Table and Test Data - Program #2 –

/*
/&
```

APPENDICES

A. INTERNAL DATA REPRESENTATION

B. GENERAL LOGIC FLOWCHARTS

C. RPG SOURCE LISTING AND DIAGNOSTICS

D. SUMMARY OF RPG SPECIFICATIONS

E. SUMMARY OF CALCULATION SPECIFICATION ENTRIES

APPENDIX A

INTERNAL DATA REPRESENTATION

INTERNAL DATA REPRESENTATION

Most computer systems currently in use utilize MAGNETIC CORE STORAGE. A magnetic core is a very small ring of ferromagnetic material, a few hundredths of an inch in outside diameter. Cores are placed on a wire and an electrical current is sent through the wire. If enough current passes through, the cores become magnetized. Reversing the direction of the current through the wire changes the magnetic state or polarity of the core. Thus, the direction of the magnetic charge, or polarity of the core, can be used to represent an "on" or "off" condition or a "0" or "1". It is this basic concept that provides the basis for the storing of information in the Central Processing Unit of a computer system.

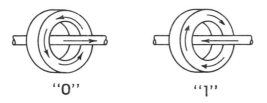

"0"   "1"

Figure A-1 Magnetic Cores

Because computer systems store information by means of magnetic core storage in which there are only two possible states, "0" or "1", the system is said to operate in a binary mode. To understand the logical structure of recording data utilizing this method requires a basic understanding of the binary number system.

DECIMAL NUMBER SYSTEM

A review of the "place value" concept as used with the decimal number system is of value in understanding the structure of the binary number system.

In the decimal number system each place position from right to left is as follows: units, tens, hundreds, thousands, etc. This is obtained by using a base of 10 (as there are ten symbols 0-9 in this decimal system) and raising this base to the next highest power each position to the left.

The following chart illustrates the place values of the first four positions of the decimal number system.

THOUSANDS	HUNDREDS	TENS	UNITS	Place Value
10^3	10^2	10^1	10^0	Base

Figure A-2 Decimal Number System Place Value Chart

Thus, the decimal number 1110 when analyzed means:

1 — One thousand
1 — One hundred
1 — Ten
0 — Units

or one thousand one hundred and ten.

1	1	1	0	
THOUSANDS	HUNDREDS	TENS	UNITS	Place Value
10^3	10^2	10^1	10^0	Base

Figure A - 3 Representation of the Decimal Number 1110

BINARY NUMBER SYSTEM

In the binary number system 0 and 1 are the only digits used. With the use of these two digits any number may be represented by use of the positional notation concept.

The binary number system uses a base of 2 with each place position assigned the following values: one, two, four, eight, sixteen, etc. (values double each place position to the left). The base of 2 is used as there are only two symbols in the binary number system (0-1). The place value is established by raising the base of 2 to the next highest power each place position to the left.

The following chart illustrates the place values of the first four positions in a binary number system.

EIGHT	FOUR	TWO	ONE	Place Value
2^3	2^2	2^1	2^0	Base

Figure A - 4 Binary Number System Place Value Chart

Thus, the binary number 10 is equal to the decimal number 2.

1 - two
0 - units or ones

0	0	1	0	
EIGHT	FOUR	TWO	ONE	Place Value
2^3	2^2	2^1	2^0	Base

Figure A - 5 Representation of the Binary Number 10

The number three in binary would be:

0	0	1	1	
EIGHT	FOUR	TWO	ONE	Place Value
2^3	2^2	2^1	2^0	Base

Figure A-6 Representation of the Binary Number 0011

Thus, 11 in binary is equal to the number three.

The following is a summary of the binary equivalents of the decimal numbers 0-9.

Decimal	Binary
0	0000
1	0001
2	0010
3	0011
4	0100
5	0101
6	0110
7	0111
8	1000
9	1001

Figure A-7 Decimal and Binary Numbers 0-9

In most computer systems magnetic core storage is designed to utilize a binary coding structure. In this type of storage organization cores are assigned the values of 1, 2, 4, and 8. Cores are placed on a matrix of wires. At the point where two impulsed wires intersect, the current is great enough to change the polarity of a core and thus alter the information stored.

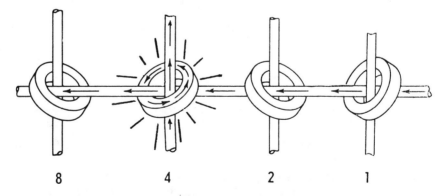

8   4   2   1

Figure A-8 Magnetic Core Storage

Thus, using magnetic cores as a form of storage with each core capable of representing either a "0" or a "1", and combining this concept with the place values of the binary number system it is possible to develop a mathematically logical method of representing numerical values in magnetic core storage. For example, by the use of four magnetic cores operating as one unit of information, it is possible to represent the digits 0 through 9 by turning "ON" the proper combination of cores.

The following diagram illustrates how the digits 0-9 could be represented in core storage using a binary type of coding structure.

```
0= ○○○○        5= ○●○●
1= ○○○●        6= ○●●○
2= ○○●○        7= ○●●●
3= ○○●●        8= ●○○○
4= ○●○○        9= ●○○●
   8 4 2 1        8 4 2 1
```

● = Core "On"
○ = Core "Off"

Figure A-9 Representation of the Decimal Values 0-9 in Core Storage

Information entered into the storage unit of the central processing unit of a computer system is recorded in specific core storage locations which are "addressable". The data placed in these addressable locations can thus be processed or moved internally in storage as required. It should be noted that the series of instructions used to process the data are also stored in the storage unit through the use of magnetic cores.

EXTENDED BINARY CODED DECIMAL INTERCHANGE CODE

A variety of coding methods have been used in computer systems to represent numbers, letters of the alphabet and special characters. The coding structure used on the System/360 is known as the Extended Binary Coded Decimal Interchange Code or EBCDIC. This coding technique provides a means of storing letters of the alphabet, numbers, or special characters internally in a series of 8 magnetic cores or "bits" which totally are referred to as a byte.

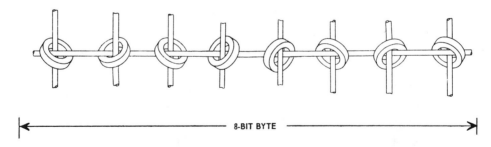

8-BIT BYTE

Figure A-10 Core Representation of the Eight-Bit Byte

Each byte of storage has a unique address associated with it so that the programmer can selectively locate or retrieve a unit of information placed in storage. The "storage locations" are numbered from zero up to the size of storage available for a particular system. The System/360 provides for a storage capacity of from 8,192 bytes of storage to 6,291,456 bytes of storage. The storage capacity of models are normally referred to as 8K, 32K, 64K, etc., meaning 8 thousand, 32 thousand, 64 thousand, etc., bytes of storage. "Typical" systems range from 8K to 512K bytes of storage.

Zoned Decimal Format

When one character is represented in storage by one addressable byte it is said to be stored in the Zoned Decimal Format. For purposes of referencing the individual cores or bits in a byte, each bit position is numbered as follows:

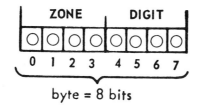

Figure A-11 Schematic Representation of Eight-Bit Byte

Thus, it is possible to refer to bits 0-3 when referencing the four leftmost bit positions of the byte, or bits 4-7 when referencing the four rightmost bit positions of the byte.

When a character is stored in the byte, a particular binary value is placed in each of the four bits of the byte and together these eight bits of the byte determine the character stored. Bit positions 0-3 of the byte are used to express the ZONE portion of a character and bit positions 4-7 are used to express the DIGIT portion. It should be noted that bit positions 0-3 and 4-7 have a place value of 8, 4, 2, 1 respectively. (Note the relationship to the binary number system.)

The letters of the alphabet A-I have a bit configuration of 1100 (decimal 12) in the zone portion of the byte. The digit position would contain the decimal values of 1-9 for A-I respectively. Thus, the letter of the alphabet A would be represented in the byte as:

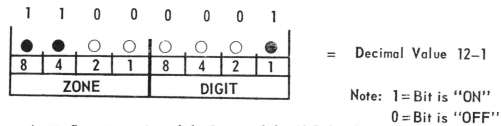

Figure A-12 Representation of the Letter of the Alphabet A

The letters of the alphabet J-R have a bit configuration of 1101 (decimal 13) in the zone portion of the byte. The digit portion of the byte would contain the decimal values 1-9 for J-R respectively. Thus, the letter of the alphabet J would appear as follows:

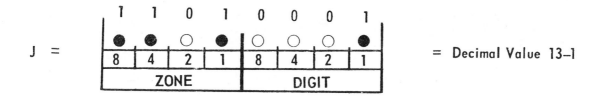

Figure A-13 Representative of the Letter of the Alphabet J

The letters of the alphabet S-Z have a bit configuration of 1110 (decimal 14) in the zone portion of the byte. The digit portion of the byte would contain the decimal values 2-9 for S-Z respectively. Thus, the letter of the alphabet S would appear as follows:

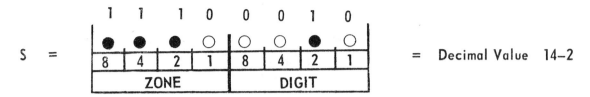

Figure A-14 Representation of the Letter of the Alphabet S

The following diagram illustrates the bit configurations for the letters of the alphabet A-Z.

Figure A-15 Letters of the Alphabet A-Z in the Byte

Special characters also may be represented using the zoned decimal format. The following illustrates the representation of the "$" and "?".

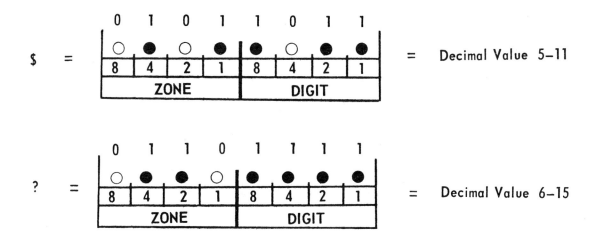

Figure A-16 Representation of Special Characters

The following chart illustrates the bit configuration for the letters of the alphabet and frequently used special characters.

EBCDIC Code	EBCDIC Graphic	EBCDIC Code	EBCDIC Graphic
1100 0001	A	1101 1001	R
1100 0010	B	1110 0010	S
1100 0011	C	1110 0011	T
1100 0100	D	1110 0100	U
1100 0101	E	1110 0101	V
1100 0110	F	1110 0110	W
1100 0111	G	1110 0111	X
1100 1000	H	1110 1000	Y
1100 1001	I	1110 1001	Z
1101 0001	J	0101 1011	$ (dollar sign)
1101 0010	K	0101 1100	* (asterisk)
1101 0011	L	0110 1111	? (question mark)
1101 0100	M	0111 1010	: (colon)
1101 0101	N	0111 1011	# (number sign)
1101 0110	O	0111 1100	@ (at the rate of)
1101 0111	P	0111 1101	' (apostrophe)
1101 1000	Q		

Figure A-17 Summary of Representation of Letters and Special Characters

Parity Check

It should be noted that there is also an internal hardware check bit associated with each byte. When data is read into the system, a PARITY CHECK BIT will automatically go on, if required, to maintain an odd number of bits "on". Thus, the System/360 is called an odd parity check machine.

In the following examples, note that the use of the parity bit.

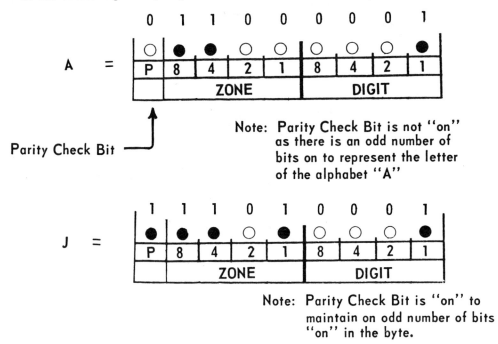

Figure A-18 Use of the Parity Check Bit

When data is moved internally or other operations occur, the machine automatically checks each position for odd parity. If odd parity does not exist (the machine "drops a bit"), an error condition is indicated to the operator. (Future diagrams of the byte will not illustrate the use of the parity bit but it should be noted that each byte of storage contains a check bit.)

NUMERIC REPRESENTATION

The general form of data stored in the zoned decimal format is as follows:

General Format

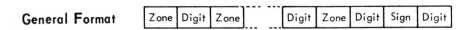

Figure A-19 General Form - Zoned Decimal Format

Note that bits 0-3 of the rightmost byte of a field are used for sign control.

When positive numbers are read into core, the zone portion of the byte (including the rightmost byte) is filled with 1's. This technique makes numbers higher than letters of the alphabet in a collating sequence.

The following examples illustrate the representation of the numbers 1-9 in the zoned decimal format.

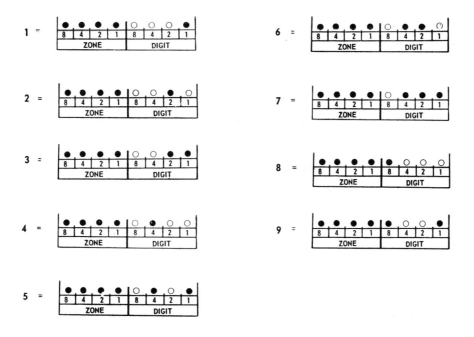

Figure A - 20 Representation of the Numbers 1 - 9 in the Byte

In a binary type notation the numbers 1-9 could be illustrated as follows:

Decimal	EBCDIC[*] CODE
1	1111 0001
2	1111 0010
3	1111 0011
4	1111 0100
5	1111 0101
6	1111 0110
7	1111 0111
8	1111 1000
9	1111 1001

[*]Extended Binary-Coded-Decimal Interchange Code.

Sign Control

A "Quantity" field in card columns 79-80 read from a card could be stored in bytes 10000 and 10001 as follows: (It should be noted bytes 10000 and 10001 were selected arbitrarily to illustrate the concept of an addressable byte.)

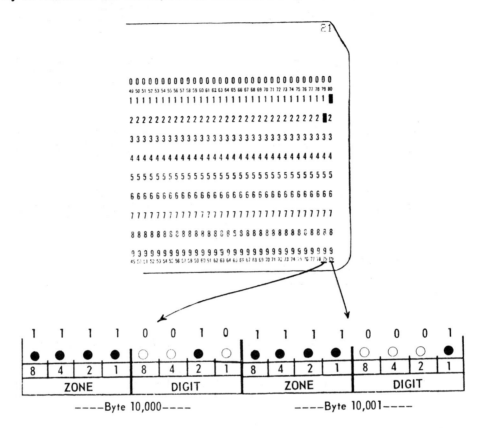

Figure A-21 Representation of a Positive Quantity Field

Note that bits 0-3 of the rightmost byte contains 1111. The bit configuration of 1111 is used as a + sign. Thus, the Quantity Field in bytes 10000 and 10001 is represented as a positive value.

On a punched card, an 11 zone punch in the low-order position of the field is used to indicate a minus or negative amount. The following example illustrates how a negative amount would appear in storage in bytes 10000 and 10001.

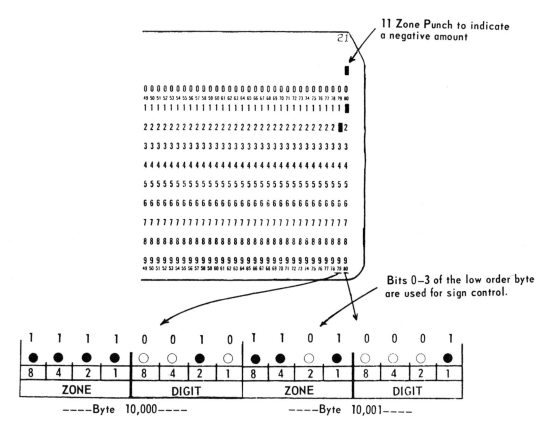

Figure A-22 Representation of a Negative Quantity Field

Note that the sign in bits 0-3 of the low-order byte contains the bit configuration 1101. A 1101 in bits 0-3 represents a minus sign. Thus, the Quantity Field 21 stored in bytes 10000 and 10001 is considered to be a negative amount.

PACKED DECIMAL FORMAT

When performing arithmetic operations data must be converted from the Zoned Decimal Format to a PACKED DECIMAL form. The general form of the packed decimal format is below:

Figure A - 23 General Form — Packed Decimal Format

As can be seen from the above illustration, two decimal digits are stored in a single byte with the sign in bits 4-7 of the low-order byte.

The following diagram illustrates a card read into core and stored in the zoned decimal format and the same field after it has been "packed".

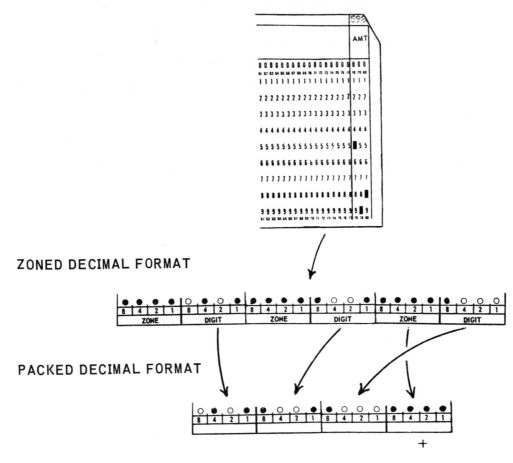

Figure A - 24 Steps in Packing a Field

A.12

After arithmetic operations have been performed on data, a positive number will contain a sign bit configuration of 1100. The following example illustrates the number +598 in the packed decimal format with a sign bit configuration of 1100.

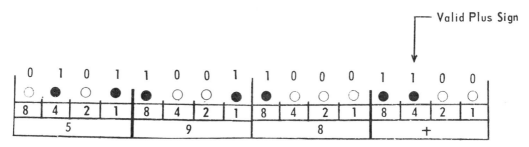

Figure A - 25 Representation of Positive Amount After a Calculation

Thus, valid + signs include the bit configuration of 1111 and also 1100. Before data can be printed out the bit configuration 1100 must be changed back to 1111 however.

When data is recorded in packed decimal format, one-half of a byte cannot be used; therefore, when a number such as +22 is recorded, bits 0-3 of the leftmost byte contain zeroes.

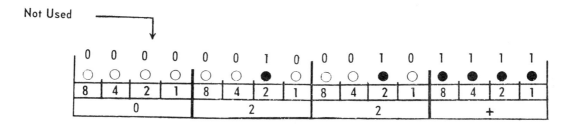

Figure A - 26 Representation of the storage of a Field with an Even Number of Digits

It must again be emphasized that when data is read into a system from a punched card, it is recorded in the Zoned Decimal Format; however, before arithmetic operation can be performed the data must be converted to a packed form.

HEXADECIMAL NUMBER SYSTEM

As explained previously, data is recorded by means of a series of magnetic cores being "Off" or "On" which may be represented by "0's" or "1's". Data recorded in this form is difficult to work with, however. A "core dump" in this binary form in which the contents of each of the four bits in the byte is printed out might appear as follows:

111110011111010111110011 . . . . . etc.

To facilitate the reading of data in a binary form using EBCDIC, hexadecimal notation is used.

The hexadecimal system represents the decimal values 0 - 15 by means of 16 individual symbols. The representation of the digits 0 - 9 are the same in the hexadecimal number system as in the decimal number system; however, to represent the decimal quantities 10 - 15, the hexadecimal system uses the letters of the alphabet A - F. Thus, the decimal quantity 10 is represented in a hexadecimal as "A". The decimal quantity 11, as hexadecimal "B" etc.

DECIMAL VALUE	HEXADECIMAL NOTATION
0	0
1	1
2	2
3	3
4	4
5	5
6	6
7	7
8	8
9	9
10	A
11	B
12	C
13	D
14	E
15	F

Figure A - 27 Decimal and Hexadecimal Representation of Numbers 0 - 15

As previously illustrated, a core dump in binary form would appear as a series of 0's and 1's.

1111010111110110111101111111011

This type of notation is difficult for programmers to read; therefore, the System/360 uses the hexadecimal notation. With hexadecimal notation every four bits represent a hexadecimal number. Thus, if the binary notation (0's and 1's) is separated into 4 bits and converted to hexadecimal notation, it would appear as illustrated.

Binary	1111 0101	1111 0110	1111 0111	1111 0011
Hex	F 5	F 6	F 7	F 3
Decimal	5	6	7	3

Figure A - 28 Binary, Hexadecimal, and Decimal Representation of Numeric Values

It can be seen that the original binary representation converted to hexadecimal notation is F5F6F7F3. Thus, the F's (1111) imply numeric data is recorded in the zoned decimal format. The data in decimal form is thus +5673.

An example of alphabetic data in storage is as follows:

110000011100001011000011

Again it can be seen that pure binary notation is difficult to read. By converting this string of 0's and 1's to a hexadecimal notation the form becomes:

Binary	1100 0001	1100 0010	1100 0011
Hex	C 1	C 2	C 3
Alpha	A	B	C

Figure A - 29 Binary, Hexadecimal, and Alphabetic Representation of Data

By noting that the hexadecimal C is used as the zone portion of the letters of the alphabet A-I it can be determined that C1C2C3 in hexadecimal is actually the alphabetic data ABC represented internally in the byte.

The following chart summarizes the representation of the numbers 0 - 9 and the letters of the alphabet A - Z in a binary and a hexadecimal form.

Graphics	Binary	Hexadecimal
0	1111 0000	F0
1	1111 0001	F1
2	1111 0010	F2
3	1111 0011	F3
4	1111 0100	F4
5	1111 0101	F5
6	1111 0110	F6
7	1111 0111	F7
8	1111 1000	F8
9	1111 1001	F9
A	1100 0001	C1
B	1100 0010	C2
C	1100 0011	C3
D	1100 0100	C4
E	1100 0101	C5
F	1100 0110	C6
G	1100 0111	C7
H	1100 1000	C8
I	1100 1001	C9
J	1101 0001	D1
K	1101 0010	D2
L	1101 0011	D3
M	1101 0100	D4
N	1101 0101	D5
O	1101 0110	D6
P	1101 0111	D7
Q	1101 1000	D8
R	1101 1001	D9
S	1110 0010	E2
T	1110 0011	E3
U	1110 0100	E4
V	1110 0101	E5
W	1110 0110	E6
X	1110 0111	E7
Y	1110 1000	E8
Z	1110 1001	E9

Figure A - 30 Summary of Data Representation in Hexadecimal Form

Hexadecimal Number System — Place Value

A hexadecimal number system is comprised of 16 symbols representing the decimal digits 0-15. The hexadecimal system uses the decimal value of 16 as its base. By raising a base of 16 to the next highest power moving to the left, the place values of 1, 16, 256, 4096, etc. are established. The following diagram illustrates a place value chart for the first four positions of a hexadecimal number system.

4096	256	16	1	Place Value
16^3	16^2	16^1	16^0	Base

Figure A-31   Place Value Chart For the Hexadecimal Number System

The decimal value 16 is represented in hexadecimal as 10; that is, there is "1" sixteen, and "0" ones. See Figure A-32 below.

		1	0	
4096	256	16	1	Place Value
16^3	16^2	16^1	16^0	Base

Figure A-32   Representation of Hexadecimal 16

Thus, 10 in hexadecimal represents the decimal value 16.

The hexadecimal number 110 represents the decimal value 272. Using the place value chart it can be seen that there is "1" two hundred and fifty six, "1" sixteen, and "0" ones, for a total of 272.

	1	1	0	
4096	256	16	1	Place Value
16^3	16^2	16^1	16^0	Base

Figure A-33   Representation of Hexadecimal 110

The chart below illustrates the representation of the decimal numbers 0 -54 in hexadecimal form.

Decimal	Hexadecimal
0	0
1	1
2	2
3	3
4	4
5	5
6	6
7	7
8	8
9	9
10	A
11	B
12	C
13	D
14	E
15	F
16	10
17	11
18	12
19	13
20	14
21	15
22	16
23	17
24	18
25	19
26	1A
27	1B
28	1C
29	1D
30	1E
31	1F
32	20
33	21
34	22
35	23
36	24
37	25
38	26
39	27
40	28
41	29
42	2A
43	2B
44	2C
45	2D
46	2E
47	2F
48	30
49	31
50	32
51	33
52	34
53	35
54	36

Figure A - 34 Summary of Decimal and Hexadecimal Numbers

All machine language instructions, storage locations, and data stored in core are printed out for use by the programmer in a hexadecimal form; therefore, an understanding of the structure of the hexadecimal number system is important for the programmer.

The following is an illustration of "print-out" of storage. Note how data is printed in hexadecimal form.

```
0027E0   D5D640D5  C1D4C540  FF150007  FA00292E      0A0407F1  6A0028C2  00002868  000036E8
002810   00002890  0Q006FFF  00002800  00006FCC      FFFFFF34  00002858  000027F0  00004140
002840   00000000  00000000  00000000  00000000      C0000000  00000000  00008000  08000000
002870   00002974  00002938  02002974  20000050      47000000  47000000  00000000  00000000
0028A0   00002B48  08900909  000029C4  00000000      07004700  00000000  090029C4  20000050
0028D0   00002890  0A02D24F  A102A152  5810A20E      58F10010  45EF000C  5810A212  58F10010
002900   A103A0B2  D213A115  A0B7D203  A133A0CB      D204A145  A0D45810  A20E58F1  001045EF
002930   A1A6A216  47F0A026  D24FA102  A1A8F321      A123A1A6  96F0A125  F363A143  A1A296F0
002960   4110A206  4500A0AE  00002858  00002890      0A020A0E  F1F2F3F5  F6C2D6D3  E3404040
002990   F6404040  4040F5F2  52187F40  40404040      40404040  40404040  40404040  40404040
0029C0   40404040  40F1F2F3  F5F64040  40404040      40404040  404040C2  D6D3E340  40404040
0029F0   40404040  40F2F1F5  F6404040  40404040      40404040  404040F5  F2F1F8F7  40404040
002A20   40404040  40404040  40404040  C4C5E2C3      D9C9D7E3  C9D6D540  40404040  40404040
002A50   40404040  404040C1  D4D6E4D5  E3404040      40404040  0000000C  000CE3C8  C540D5E4
002A80   D6C3C5E2  E2C5C440  C9E24040  40404040      40404040  E3C8C540  E3D6E3C1  D340C1D4
002AB0   40404040  40404040  404007FE  615C0000      5B5BC2D6  D7C5D540  5B5BC2C3  D3D6E2C5
002AE0   0A320000  0A320000  47F0F01A  0A320000      C9D1C3C6  E9C9E9F3  F3F20A00  91801002
002B10   10044780  F04858E0  F0609140  10024780      F01A58E0  101C07FE  D501F05C  E0004770
002B40   BA0028F4  0A320000  0A320000  0A32C000      0A320000  47F0F01A  C9D1C4C6  E9E9E9E9
002B70   00000000  00000000  00000000  00000000      00000000  00000000  00000000  00000000

006FE0   00000000  00000000  00000000  00000000      00000000  00000000  00000000  00000000
```

Figure A-35 Hexadecimal Core Dump

SUMMARY

The following chart summarizes the representation of digits, letters of the alphabet and special characters with EBCDIC.

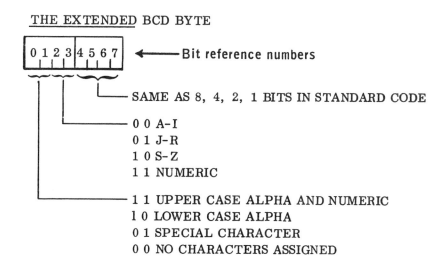

THE EXTENDED BCD BYTE

`0 1 2 3 4 5 6 7` ← Bit reference numbers

— SAME AS 8, 4, 2, 1 BITS IN STANDARD CODE

0 0 A-I
0 1 J-R
1 0 S-Z
1 1 NUMERIC

1 1 UPPER CASE ALPHA AND NUMERIC
1 0 LOWER CASE ALPHA
0 1 SPECIAL CHARACTER
0 0 NO CHARACTERS ASSIGNED

SUMMARY

- A hexadecimal F (1111) in the zone portion of the byte indicates numeric data is stored in the byte in the zoned decimal format.

- A hexadecimal C (1100) is used in the zone portion of the byte when representing the letters of the alphabet A–I.

- A hexadecimal D (1101) is used in the zone portion of the byte when representing the letters of the alphabet J–R.

- A hexadecimal E (1110) is used in the zone portion of the byte when representing the letters of the alphabet S – Z.

GENERAL LOGIC FLOWCHARTS

This appendix contains the general logic flowcharts for every RPG object program which is compiled. The flowchart consists of two parts — the general logic for every program and the general logic for the Matching Records selection of the next record to be processed.

GENERAL LOGIC

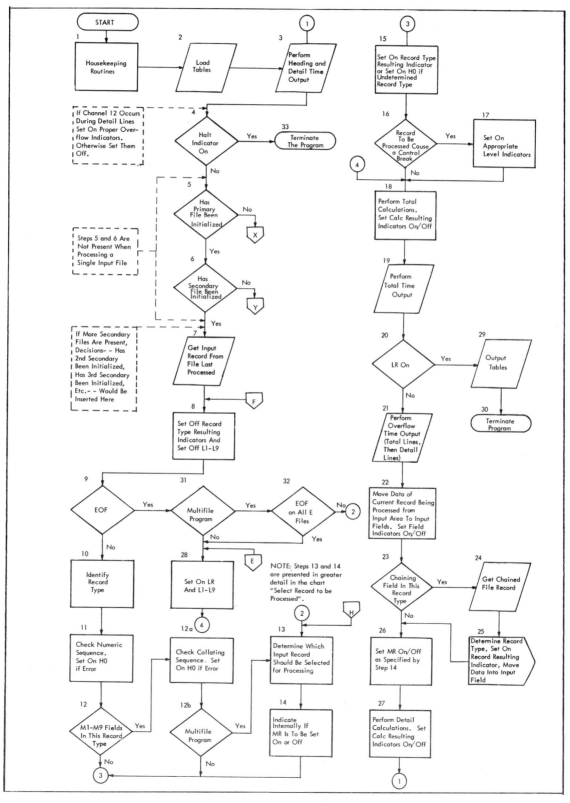

Matching Records Logic

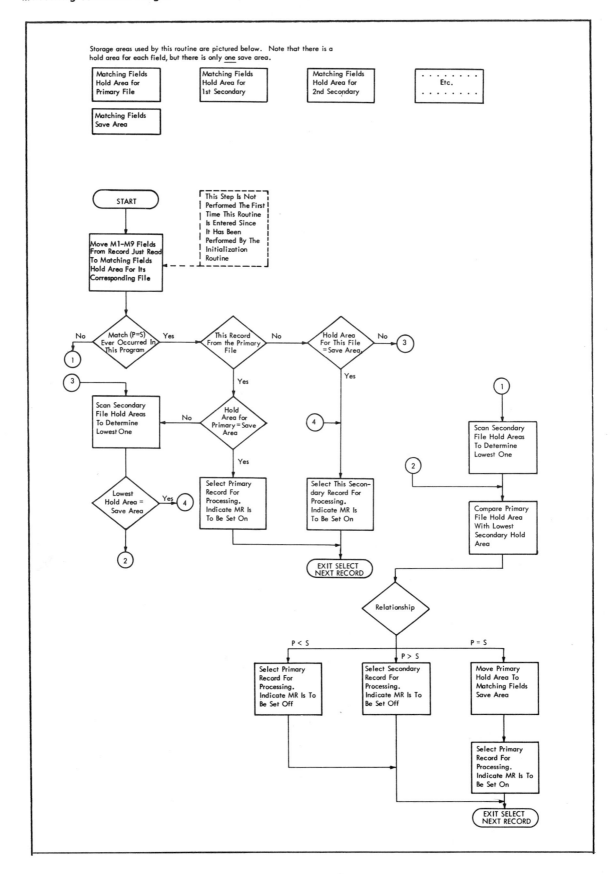

Storage areas used by this routine are pictured below. Note that there is a hold area for each field, but there is only one save area.

| Matching Fields Hold Area for Primary File | Matching Fields Hold Area for 1st Secondary | Matching Fields Hold Area for 2nd Secondary | . . . . Etc. . . . . |

Matching Fields Save Area

START

Move M1-M9 Fields From Record Just Read To Matching Fields Hold Area For Its Corresponding File

This Step Is Not Performed The First Time This Routine Is Entered Since It Has Been Performed By The Initialization Routine

Match (P=S) Ever Occurred In This Program — No → (1)   Yes →

This Record From the Primary File — No → Hold Area For This File = Save Area — No → (3)

(3) → Scan Secondary File Hold Areas To Determine Lowest One ← No — Hold Area for Primary = Save Area

Yes ↓ (from This Record From Primary File)

Yes → Hold Area For This File = Save Area ↓ (4)

Lowest Hold Area = Save Area — Yes → (4)

↓ (2)

Select Primary Record For Processing. Indicate MR Is To Be Set On

Select This Secondary Record For Processing. Indicate MR Is To Be Set On

EXIT SELECT NEXT RECORD

(1) → Scan Secondary File Hold Areas To Determine Lowest One

(2) →

Compare Primary File Hold Area With Lowest Secondary Hold Area

Relationship

P < S → Select Primary Record For Processing. Indicate MR Is To Be Set Off

P > S → Select Secondary Record For Processing. Indicate MR Is To Be Set Off

P = S → Move Primary Hold Area To Matching Fields Save Area → Select Primary Record For Processing. Indicate MR Is To Be Set On

EXIT SELECT NEXT RECORD

APPENDIX C

RPG SOURCE LISTING AND DIAGNOSTICS

When an RPG program is compiled, the RPG compiler normally will print a source listing of the source program and also the Symbol Tables and any diagnostics which are found in the source statements. An explanation of the listings printed by the compiler is contained below.

```
DOS/360*RPG*CL 3-9                CASHMAN                09/15/72        PAGE 0001

        01 010 H                                                        PAYRPT
001     01 020 FPAYCARD IP  F  80  80              READ40 SYSIPT        PAYRPT
002     01 030 F REPORT   O  F 132 132     OF      PRINTERSYSLST        PAYRPT
003     02 010 I YCARD AA    01  80 C1                                  PAYRPT
004     02 020 I        OR   02  80 C2                                  PAYRPT
005     02 030 I        OR   03  80 C3                                  PAYRPT
006     02 040 I        OR   04  80NC1  80NC2  80NC3                    PAYRPT
007     02 050 I                            1    40EMPNO                PAYRPT
008     02 060 I                            5    24 NAME                PAYRPT
009     02 070 I                           25    292REGERN              PAYRPT
010     02 080 I                           30    342OVTERN              PAYRPT
011     03 010 C     N04    REGERN    ADD  OVTERN   TOTERN  52          PAYRPT
012     03 020 C     02     TOTTERN   ADD  5.00     TOTERN              PAYRPT
                                                                NOTE 098
013     03 030       03     TOTERN    ADD  10.00    TOTERN              PAYRPT
014     04 010 OREPORT  H  201   1P                                     PAYRPT
015     04 020 O        OR      OF                                      PAYRPT
016     04 030 O                       UDATE      9 ' / / '             PAYRPT
017     04 040 O                                 45 'P A Y R O L L '    PAYRPT
018     04 050 O                                 57 'R E P O R T'       PAYRPT
019     04 060 O                                 73 'PAGE'              PAYRPT
020     04 070 O                       PAGE      78 '  0 '              PAYRPT
021     04 080 O        H   1   1P                                      PAYRPT
022     04 090 O        OR      OF                                      PAYRPT
023     04 100 O                                  9 'EMP'               PAYRPT
024     04 110 O                                 53 'REGULAR'           PAYRPT
025     04 120 O                                 65 'OVERTIME'          PAYRPT
026     04 130 O                                 85 'TOTAL'             PAYRPT
027     04 140 O        H   2   1P                                      PAYRPT
028     04 150 O        OR      OF                                      PAYRPT
029     05 010 O                                  8 'NO'                PAYRPT
030     05 020 O                                 22 'NAME'              PAYRPT
031     05 030 O                                 41 'SHIFT'             PAYRPT
032     05 040 O                                 54 'EARNINGS'          PAYRPT
033     05 050 O                                 65 'EARNINGS'          PAYRPT
034     05 060 O                                 74 'BONUS'             PAYRPT
035     05 070 O                                 86 'EARNINGS'          PAYRPT
036     05 080 O        D   1   01                                      PAYRPT
037     05 090 O        OR      02                                      PAYRPT
038     05 100 O        OR      03                                      PAYRPT
039     05 110 O        OR      04                                      PAYRPT
040     05 120 O                       EMPNO Z    9                     PAYRPT
041     05 130 O                       NAME      33                     PAYRPT
042     05 140 O                 01              41 'FIRST'             PAYRPT
043     05 150 O                 02              42 'SECOND'            PAYRPT
044     06 010 O                 03              41 'THIRD'             PAYRPT
045     06 020 O                 04              45 'INVALID SHIFT'     PAYRPT
046     06 030 O                 N04   REGERN    53 '   $0. '           PAYRPT
047     06 040 O                 N04   OVTERN    64 '   $0. '           PAYRPT
048     06 050 O                 01              74 '   $.00'           PAYRPT
049     06 060 O                 02              74 '   $5.00'          PAYRPT
050     06 070 O                 03              74 '$10.00'            PAYRPT
051     06 080 O                 N04   TOTERN    85 '   $0. '           PAYRPT
052     06 090 O        T   2   LR                                      PAYRPT
053     06 100 O                                 21 'END OF PAYROLL REPORT'  PAYRPT
```

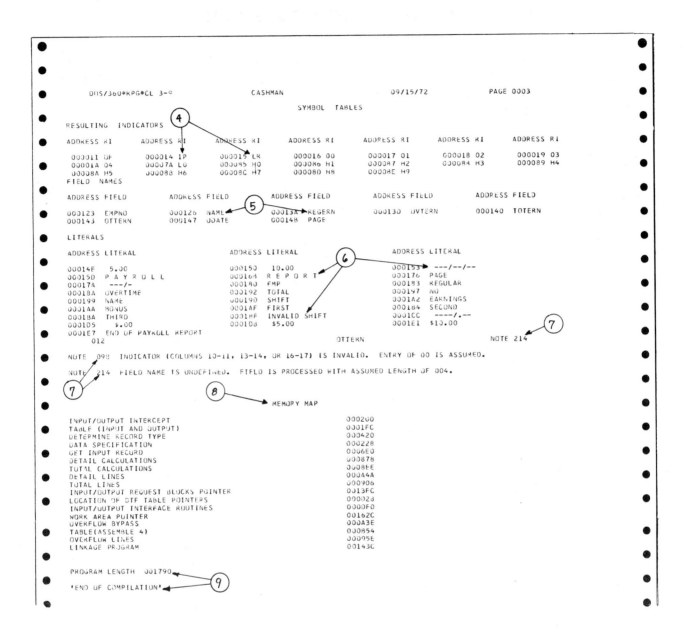

```
    DOS/360*RPG*CL 3-9              CASHMAN                    09/15/72          PAGE 0003
                                       SYMBOL   TABLES

RESULTING  INDICATORS

ADDRESS RI         ADDRESS RI         ADDRESS RI         ADDRESS RI         ADDRESS RI         ADDRESS RI         ADDRESS RI

 000011 OF          000014 1P          000015 LR          000016 00          000017 01          000018 02          000019 03
 00001A 04          00007A L0          000085 H0          000086 H1          000087 H2          000088 H3          000089 H4
 00008A H5          000088 H6          00008C H7          00008D H8          00008E H9
FIELD  NAMES

ADDRESS FIELD        ADDRESS FIELD        ADDRESS FIELD        ADDRESS FIELD        ADDRESS FIELD

 000123 EMPNO         000126 NAME          00013A REGERN        00013D OVTERN        000140 TOTERN
 000143 OTTERN        000147 ODATE         00014B PAGE

LITERALS

ADDRESS LITERAL                  ADDRESS LITERAL                  ADDRESS LITERAL

00014E   5.00                    000150   10.00                   000153   ---/--/--
00015D   P A Y R O L L           000168   R E P O R T             000176   PAGE
00017A   ---/-                   000180   FMP                     000183   REGULAR
00018A   OVERTIME                000192   TOTAL                   000197   NO
000199   NAME                    000190   SHIFT                   0001A2   EARNINGS
0001AA   BONUS                   0001AF   FIRST                   0001B4   SECOND
0001BA   THIRD                   0001BF   INVALID SHIFT           0001CC   ----/.--
0001D5   5.00                    0001D8   $5.00                   0001E1   $10.00
0001E7   END OF PAYROLL REPORT
   012                                               OTTERN                           NOTE 214

NOTE  098  INDICATOR (COLUMNS 10-11, 13-14, OR 16-17) IS INVALID.  ENTRY OF 00 IS ASSUMED.

NOTE  214  FIELD NAME IS UNDEFINED.  FIELD IS PROCESSED WITH ASSUMED LENGTH OF 004.


                                  MEMORY MAP


    INPUT/OUTPUT INTERCEPT                        000200
    TABLE (INPUT AND OUTPUT)                      0001FC
    DETERMINE RECORD TYPE                         000420
    DATA SPECIFICATION                            000228
    GET INPUT RECORD                              0006E0
    DETAIL CALCULATIONS                           000878
    TOTAL CALCULATIONS                            0008EE
    DETAIL LINES                                  000A4A
    TOTAL LINES                                   000906
    INPUT/OUTPUT REQUEST BLOCKS POINTER           0013FC
    LOCATION OF DTF TABLE POINTERS                000028
    INPUT/OUTPUT INTERFACE ROUTINES               0000F0
    WORK AREA POINTER                             00162C
    OVERFLOW BYPASS                               000A3E
    TABLE(ASSEMBLE 4)                             000854
    OVERFLOW LINES                                00095E
    LINKAGE PROGRAM                               00143C


    PROGRAM LENGTH  001790

    'END OF COMPILATION'
```

The following is an explanation of the numbered portions of the listings.

1. Line Numbers — These numbers are generated by the RPG compiler to reference each line of source coding. Diagnostics which are found as a result of errors in the source coding may reference these line numbers.

2. Page/Line Numbers — These page and line numbers are the values which are included in columns 1-5 of the source cards. They are not used in the diagnostics but should be included in each source program.

3. Form Identification — The form identification, which is also punched on the source card, is listed on the source listing so that each form may be identified. The remainder of the source listing is a listing of each source statement which is processed by the compiler.

4. Resulting Indicators — The Symbol Tables listing is produced after the source listing. The first portion of the Resulting Indicators table specifies the relative addresses of the indicators which may be used in the program. The "Address" portion of the listing specifies the relative address of the indicator within the program. Thus, the 1P indicator is X'14' bytes from the beginning of the program, that is, if the hexadecimal value '14' is added to the address where the program is loaded in main storage, the address of the 1P indicator will be found. It will be noted that each of the possible indicators which may be used within the program are listed here.

5. Field Names — The Field Names which are utilized within the program are listed next together with the relative address of each field within the program. Thus, the NAME field is located X'126' bytes from the beginning of the program.

6. Literals — The literals which are used within the program are listed next. Note that the term literal means both values which are used as literals on the Calculation Specifications and also any constant values which are specified on the Output Specifications. Note also that any edit words which are specified on the Output Specifications are included in this list. Thus, the edit word at relative location '17A', for example, is for the page number which is specified on line 020 of the source listing. Note that the character dash (—) is used to indicate the blank areas within the edit word which will be used for data and the slash (/) is used to specify where zero suppression is to stop.

7. Diagnostics — As was noted previously, whenever the RPG compiler finds an error within the source program, it will make a note of the error in the diagnostics portion of the listing. It should be noted that the error is not an error in logic or program design but an error in the syntax which is required by the compiler. In the example, there are two diagnostic messages. These messages are identified by the "Note" statements (Note 098 and Note 214). The identification of the line of coding to which the note applies may be found in one of two places — the source listing or immediately above the Notes themselves. Note 098 is found on the source listing (coding line 012). Note 214 is found on the right side of the listing immediately above the actual note statements. The coding line which is specified by Note 214 is found on the left side of the page (012) and the fieldname in question is found in the middle of the page (OTTERN). The meanings of the diagnostic messages is normally clear from the message on the listing. For example, Note 214 states that the fieldname OTTERN is unreferenced in the program. This is because the fieldname is misspelled in the source program.

8. Completion Messages — The total number of bytes which are used by the program are given as a hexadecimal value (in the example, X'1790), and the message 'END OF COMPILATION' is always printed to signal the end of the compilation listing.

APPENDIX D

SUMMARY OF RPG SPECIFICATIONS

The following is a summary of all of the entries which can be made in the various RPG Specifications forms. The common fields of all of the forms and the individual fields on each form are summarized.

This summary contains a brief position-by-positions description of each of the five RPG specification forms. The purpose of the summary is to provide the user with a concise reference guide.

The first five items are common to all five specification forms.

Page 1-2

Enter number of specification page. Assign ascending numbers to the pages of each program specification set to collate in the following sequence:

> Control Card Specifications
> File Description Specifications
> Extension Specifications
> Line Counter Specifications
> Input Specifications
> Calculation Specifications
> Output-Format Specifications

Line 3-5

First two digits of line number are preprinted. Use third position (5) to identify additional lines to be inserted between two preprinted lines.

Form Type 6

Contains a pre-printed code (H, F, E, L, I, C, or O) which must be punched into all RPG specification cards.

Comments 7

Enter an asterisk (*) in each line to be used exclusively as a comments line.

Program Identification 75-80

Insert any information to identify certain cards or portions of an RPG source program.

CONTROL CARD SPECIFICATIONS

Positions 7-11

Not used by DOS/TOS RPG.

Positions 12-14

For the assignment of two I/O areas, specify the length of the partition in which the object program is to be run. Valid entries are 1 through 512.

Positions 15-16

Not used by DOS/TOS RPG.

Sterling 17-20

Blank entries in these positions indicate that sterling currency is not being used.

Input-Shillings (17)
 1 = Input shilling field is in IBM format.
 2 = Input shilling field is in BSI format.

Input-Pence (18)
 1 = Input shilling field is in IBM format.
 2 = Input shilling field is in BSI format.

Output-Shillings (19)
 0 or blank = The output shilling field is to be printed
  only.
 1 = The output shilling field is to be in IBM format.
 2 = The output shilling field is to be in BSI format.

Output-Pence (20)
 0 or blank = The output pence field is to be printed only.
 1 = The output pence field is to be in the IBM format.
 2 = The output pence field is to be in the BSI format.

Inverted Print 21

For DOS RPG: Leave blank for domestic format of month/day/year of UDATE and decimal point notation of numeric fields.

Enter D for United Kingdom format of day/month/year and decimal point notation.

Enter I for European format of day/month/year and decimal comma notation.

For TOS RPG: Blank is the only valid entry.

Positions 22-25

Not used by DOS/TOS RPG.

Alternate Collating Sequence 26

Enter A if an external subroutine is used to translate the sequence of a matching field to the collating sequence of System/360. Otherwise, leave blank.

Positions 27-74

Not used by DOS/TOS RPG.

FILE DESCRIPTION SPECIFICATIONS

Filename 7-14

Enter a name for each file used in the program. Names must begin in position 7 and can be eight characters or fewer. However, only the first seven characters of an eight-character name are used.

File Type 15

Enter one of the letters I, O, U, or C to identify Input, Output, Update, or Combined file.

File Designation 16

P for primary, S for secondary input or combined files. Enter P if only one input file or combined file is used. C for chained file, R for RA file or ADDROUT file, or T for table file. Leave blank for output files.

End of File 17

Enter E for each input file or combined file that is to be checked to determine when the last record has been read and processed (LR indicator on). Leave blank if LR is to be turned on when the last record of all input and combined files has been read.

Sequence 18

Required when Matching Fields is used. A if the input file or combined file is in ascending sequence, D if it is in descending sequence. Leave blank for output files, or for input or combined files without Matching Fields.

File Format 19

F: Fixed length records.
V: Variable length records.

Block Length 20-23

Unblocked

If the records are unblocked, enter the length of a record. If variable length records are used, enter the length of the longest record.

Blocked

If the records are blocked, enter the length of the largest block.

Record Length 24-27

Used to enter the length of the logical records contained in the file. If the file contains records that are variable in length, enter the length of the largest record.

Mode of Processing 28

Used to indicate the method or mode by which the file is processed. Enter an L in this position if a segment of the file is to be processed. Enter an R in this position if the records are to be processed randomly. If no entry is made in this position for the file, the entire file will be processed sequentially.

Length of Key Field or of Record Address Field 29-30

If an input, output, or update file identifies records by key, enter the number of positions in the key. If the file is a record address file, enter the number of positions that each entry in the RA file occupies.

Record Address Type 31

If the records from the file are retrieved by using record keys, enter a K in this position. If record ID is used to retrieve records, enter I in this position.

Type of File Organization or Additional Area for Dual I/O 32

If the file is an input, output, or update file and is organized sequentially, enter the priority for two I/O areas. Valid entries are the numbers 1 through 9. Enter an I if the file has indexed sequential organization. Enter a D if the file has direct organization. Enter a T if the file is the output from the ADDROUT (Address Output) option of the Disk Sort Program.

Overflow Indicator 33-34

If overflow indicators are used, enter the overflow indicator associated with the file. A maximum of eight overflow indicators is allowed: OA, OB, OC, OD, OE, OF, OG, and OV.

Key Field Starting Location 35-38

Indicates the location of the key field within the data record. Enter the starting position of the key field for indexed sequential files. If a key area, separate from the data area, is to be defined for unblocked indexed sequential files on either the Input or Output-Format Specifications, this entry must be omitted.

Extension Code 39

Indicates that additional information about the file is coded on the Extension Specifications form or Line Counter Specifications form.

Enter an E if the file defined on the line is a:

> Chaining file
> Table file
> Record Address (RA) file
> Tag (Address) file (from the ADDROUT option)

Enter an L if the Line Counter Specifications form is used for the output file described on this line.

Device 40-46

Relates a file to a specific type of input or output unit.

If the output file is a printer, enter PRINTER.

If the file is an I/O file and it is associated with a card reader or card punch unit, enter:

READ01	IBM 2501 Card Reader
READ20	IBM 2520 Card Read-Punch
READ40	IBM 2540 Card Read-Punch
READ42	IBM 1442 Card Read-Punch

If the file is an I/O file and it is associated with a tape unit enter TAPE.

If the file is associated with a direct access storage device, enter one of the following:

DISK11	IBM 2311 Disk Storage Drive
DISK14	IBM 2314 Direct Access Storage Facility
CEL01	IBM 2321 Data Cell Drive with master and and cylinder indices (MI/CI) on the same device.
CEL0111	IBM 2321 Data Cell Drive with MI/CI on an IBM 2311 Disk Storage Drive
CEL0114	IBM 2321 Data Cell Drive with MI/CI on an IBM 2314 Direct Access Storage Facility

Symbolic Device 47-52

Valid entries are:

SYSRDR	System Card Reader
SYSLST	System Printer
SYSIPT	System Input Unit
SYSPCH	System Punch Unit
SYS000-SYS244	Any input or output unit

Note 1: Input units containing files organized in indexed sequential or direct organization must be assigned Symbolic Device codes of SYS000-SYS244.

Note 2: If the logical file extends over more than one physical unit, the device codes must be adjoining.

Labels 53

S	Standard Labels.
E	Standard Labels followed by User-Standard Labels.
N	Non-Standard Labels.
b	No Labels.
M	Multi-Volume Unlabeled Tape

Name of Label Exit 54-59

Enter the name of the routine to process nonstandard lables. If the entry is shorter than six characters, it must be left justified.

Extent Exit for DAM/Core Index 60-65

Enter the name of the routine written to receive information regarding the extent of the file.

The name can be either alphabetic or numeric, but the first character must be alphabetic. If shorter than six characters, it must be left justified.

File Addition/Unordered 66

Entries in this column are used in combination with those in position 15 to determine indexed sequential functions. To add records to a file, enter an A:

Position 15	Position 66	Function
O	blank	Create new file or extend existing file (LOAD)
O	A	Add new records to existing file (ADD)
I	blank	Process file
I	A	Process file and add new records
U	blank	Process file and update records
U	A	Process file, update records, and add new records (ADDRTR)

Number of Tracks for Cylinder Overflow 67

For indexed sequential LOAD or ADD functions, enter the number of tracks (between 0 and 8 for 2311, 0 and 9 for 2314/2321) per data cylinder that are to be used for overflow records.

Number of Extents 68-69

Not used by DOS/TOS RPG.

Tape Rewind 70

This position is used only by DOS RPG. If the file is a tape file, enter an R, U, N, K, L, or M to specify the rewind option to be performed at OPEN and CLOSE.

Positions 71-74

Not used by DOS/TOS RPG.

EXTENSION SPECIFICATIONS

Record Sequence of the Chaining File 7-8

Used only for chaining files. Enter the same entry that is made for the chaining file in Sequence on the Input Specifications Form.

Number of the Chaining Field 9-10

Used only for chaining files. Enter the identifying number of the chaining field. This number is entered in Chaining Field of the Input Specifications Form.

From Filename 11-18

Used in conjunction with To Filename to identify — for the RPG program — the relationship between two files. For example, they provide the name of a chaining file and the name of the file that is chained to it.

To Filename 19-26

(See description above)

Table or Array Name 27-32

Enter name of table:
    for alternating input format,
    enter name of table to which
    the first entry in each input
    record belongs;
    for non-alternating input format,
    enter name of single table.

For an RA File or chaining file, specify the label of the address conversion routine. Table name must consist of 6 characters, the first 3 must be TAB, the remaining 3 may be any alphabetic or numeric characters.

Number of Entries per Record 33-35

Enter the maximum number of table entries (arguments or functions) that are contained in each input record. The entry must be right justified.

Number o. Entries per Table or Array 36-39

Enter the exact numbe. of table entries (arguments or functions) contained in the table. The entry must be right-justified.

Length of Entry 40-42

Enter the length of each table entry. The maximum size of a numeric entry is 15 characters, of an alphameric entry 256 characters. The entry must be right-justified.

P = Packed/B = Binary 43

If the data for the table is in the packed-decimal format, enter P in this position. Otherwise, leave this position blank.

Decimal Positions 44

If the data contained in the table is numeric, enter the number of decimal positions (1-9). Enter a zero if there are no decimal positions. If the field is alphameric, leave this position blank.

Sequence 45

If the data contained in the table is in ascending sequence, enter an A; in descending sequence, enter a D. Leave blank if the data is not in ascending or descending sequence or if this specification is not required.

Table or Array Name (Alternating Format) 46-51

If alternating arguments and function tables are used, enter the second table name. It must be of the form TABnnn. The entry must be left justified.

Length of Entry 52-54

Enter the length of each table entry. The maximum size of a numeric entry is 15 characters; of an alphameric entry 256 characters. The entry must be right-justified.

P = Packed/B = Binary 55

Enter a P if the data for the table is in the packed-decimal format. Otherwise, leave this position blank.

Decimal Positions 56

If the data contained in the table is numeric, enter the number of decimal positions (1-9). Enter a zero if there are no decimal positions. If the field is alphameric, leave blank.

Sequence 57

If the data contained in the table is in ascending sequence, enter an A; in descending sequence, enter a D. Leave blank if the data is not in ascending or descending sequence or if this specification is not required.

Comments 58-74

Leave positions 58-74 blank, unless comments are entered in these positions.

LINE COUNTER SPECIFICATIONS

Filename 7-14

Enter the name of the output file.

Line Number (1) 15-17

Enter the number of the first line controlled by the carriage tape in these positions.

The remaining specifications (items 2-12) perform the same function.

FL or Channel Number (1) 15-19

Enter the channel number corresponding to the line number in positions 15-17. The remaining specifications (items 2-12) perform the same function.

INPUT SPECIFICATIONS

Filename 7-14

Enter a file name for each input or combined file, one entry per file. Must be left justified; it may have up to 8 characters (only the first 7 characters are used); first character must be alphabetic; remaining characters may be alphabetic or numeric; special characters or embedded blanks may not be used.

AND/OR Relationship 14-16

Enter AND to indicate that the AND relationship of Record Identification Codes in the preceding line is to be continued. Enter OR (positions 14 and 15) to indicate that the entries in Record Identification Codes of this line are to be in an OR relationship to the entries in the preceding line.

Sequence 15-16

Enter a number, beginning with 01 for each file and continuing in consecutive sequence to 99, to specify sequence checking of record types. Enter leading zeros. Enter any two alphabetic characters to indicate that sequence-checking is not required. Lines with alphabetic entries in Sequence must precede lines with numeric entries.

Any numeric entry in Sequence requires an entry in Number.

Number 17

1 indicates that one and only one record of a specific record type should be present in each group.

N indicates that one or more records of a specific record type may be present in each group. (Used only with numeric entry in positions 15-16.)

Option 18

O indicates that a record of a specific control group used need not be present. Leave blank if a record must be present, or if records are non sequential. (Used only with numeric entry in positions 15-16.)

Record Identifying Indicator 19-20

Enter any indicator from 01 through 99 to establish a two-digit code for the input-record type defined in Record Identification Codes. This sets special condition(s) in the object program each time the input record is read.

Record Identification Codes 21-41

This field is divided into three identical sub-fields: positions 21-27, 28-34, and 35-41. An AND relationship exists between these three sub-fields.

Position. Enter the number of input record containing the identifying code. Must be right-justified.

Not. Enter N if the code described must not be present in the identifying code. Must be right-justified.

C/Z/D. Enter D if only the digit portion of the specified position is to be checked. Enter Z if only the zone portion is to be checked. Enter C if both portions are to be checked.

Character. If C/Z/D contains C or D, enter any one of the 256 EBCDIC characters.

If C/Z/D contains Z, enter: &, A through I, or $\overset{+}{0}$ to check for a 12-zone; −, J through R, or $\tilde{0}$ to check for an 11-zone; S-Z for 0-zone; 0 through 9, or blank to check for the absence of zones.

Note: Record Identification Codes may be continued in the subsequent specification line by means of an AND entry for AND relationships or an OR entry for OR relationships.

Stacker Select 42

Enter number of stacker to which input cards are to be selected. Leave blank for single-stacker devices and for combined files.

Note: Stacker select cannot be specified for files that request dual I/O areas.

P=Packed/B=Binary 43

P if input data is in packed decimal format. Blank if input data is in standard format.

Field Location 44-51

This specification describes the location of fields in input records.

From (44-47). Enter the number of input record position containing the first position of the field specified in Field Name. To define a field within the key area for each data record in an unblocked indexed sequential file (with key not part of the data), enter a K to the immediate left of the high-order digit.

To (48-51). Enter the number of the input record position containing the last position of the field defined in Field Name. Entries must be right justified; leading zeros may be omitted. To define a field within the key area for each data record in an unblocked indexed sequential file (with key not part of the data), enter a K to the immediate left of the high order digit. If a K was specified in the From entry, then it must also be specified in the To entry, and vice versa.

Decimal Positions 52

Used only for numeric fields. Enter a digit 0 through 9 to indicate number of decimal positions in input field. Leave blank for alphameric fields.

Note: Each input field that is to be used in arithmetic operations must have an entry in Decimal Positions. Also use this specification for fields that are to be edited or zero-suppressed.

Field Name 53-58

Enter the name of each field defined in Field Location. Field names may be up to 6 characters in length; left justified. First character must be alphabetic; remaining characters may be alphabetic or numeric. Special characters or embedded blanks may not be used.

Control Level 59-60

Enter any one of the control-level indicators L1 through L9 to identify control fields. (L1 for lowest level, L9 for highest level of control.)

Matching Fields or Chaining Fields 61-62

Enter any one of the codes M1, M2, or M3 for TOS RPG, or M1, M2, M3, M4, M5, M6, M7, M8, or M9, for DOS RPG to specify record-matching for two input files, or to specify sequence-checking for the fields of the single input file.

Enter the codes C1 through C9 to specify a chaining field.

Field-Record Relation 63-64

Enter any one of the indicators defined in positions 19-20 of the Input Specifications to provide field record relation for identical fields contained in different locations (OR-relationships), or for selective processing of chaining fields.

Field Indicators 65-70

If the field is alphameric, i.e., if position 52 is blank, only the Zero or Blank specification may be used. Enter any one of the indicators 01 through 99 or H0 through H9, as required, in each of the fields. Indicator in Plus (positions 65 and 66) is set on, if the field specified in positions 53-58 contains a positive value, except +0. Indicator in *Minus* (positions 67 and 68) is set on if the field contains a negative value, except -0. Indicator in Zero or Blank (positions 69 and 70) is set on if the field contains no other character than zero or blank. It is also set on if the field is numeric and contains no other character than +0 or -0, or when a Blank After output specification is executed.

Sterling Sign Position 71-74

Used only for programs processing sterling currency amounts. If sign of Sterling field is in normal position, enter S in position 74. If sign is not in normal position, enter the position in the record that contains the sign. Leave blank in all other RPG programs.

CALCULATION SPECIFICATIONS

Control Level 7-8

Enter one of control level indicators L1 through L9, L0, or LR to specify that the calculation contained in this line is to be performed at total time. Leave blank if calculation is to be performed at detail time.

Indicators 9-17

Enter one to three indicators to establish conditions controlling calculation specified in the line. Any of the indicators 01 through 99, L1 through L9, L0, LR, MR, or any halt or overflow indicator may be used. Positions 9, 12, and 15 may contain blank or N.

Note: If there is more than one indicator in a line, RPG assumes an AND-relationship between the individual indicators.

Factor 1 18-27

Field name — left-justified, maximum length 6 characters. Do not use special characters or embedded blanks. First character must be alphabetic. Must be defined in Input Specifications or as a result field in another calculation specification.

Literal   — *numeric:* left-justified, maximum length ten characters, characters must be numeric (0 through 9), one decimal symbol and/or one sign (plus or minus) allowed. If a sign is present, it must be in the first position of the field.

alphameric: left-justified must be enclosed in apostrophe symbols ('), maximum length 8 characters, any one of the 256 EBCDIC characters may be used.

Apostrophe symbols required within constants must be represented as two consecutive apostrophe symbols.

Operation 28-32

Enter one of the RPG operation codes. An entry in this specification is required in each line, except in a comments line defined by an asterisk in position 7. Entries must be left-justified.

Factor 2 33-42

Enter field name or literal to be used in the specified operation. (For a definition of field name and literal, see Factor 1.) Entries must be left justified.

Result Field 43-48

Enter field name to designate location in storage into which result of pertinent operation is to be placed, First character of field name must be alphabetic; remaining characters may be alphabetic or numeric, cannot contain special characters or embedded blanks. Must be left justified.

Field Length 49-51

Enter number of storage positions to be reserved for result field on this line. Maximum length of numeric result fields is 15 digits. Maximum length of alphameric result fields is 256 characters. Must be right justified. May be left blank, if length of result field specified in this line is defined in a previous line of calculation specifications, or in input specifications.

Decimal Positions 52

Enter number of decimal positions (0 through 9) to be reserved in result field. Required for all numeric result fields

used with arithmetic operations. Must be blank if the result field is alphameric.

Note: The number of decimal positions is included in Field Length specification in positions 49-51. E.g., if a number of decimal positions specified is 7, the maximum number of positions to the left of the decimal symbol is $15 - 7 = 8$. (The maximum length of a numeric field is 15.)

Half Adjust 53

Enter H to specify half adjustment of result field. Must be blank if result field is alphameric.

Resulting Indicators 54-59

Any one of the indicators 01 through 99, H0 through H9 and L1 through L9 may be used for this specification.

Arithmetic Operations: enter up to 3 indicators to be set on whenever the result of an arithmetic operation is positive (*Plus*, positions 54 and 55), or negative (*Minus*, positions 56 and 57), or zero (Zero, positions 58 and 59).

Compare Operations: enter up to 3 indicators to be set on whenever result of COMP operation is Factor 1 > Factor 2 (High, positions 54 and 55), or Factor 1 < Factor 2 (Low, positions 56 and 57), or Factor 1 = Factor 2 (Equal, positions 58 and 59).

LOKUP Operations: enter one or two indicators in High, or Low, or Equal, or High and Equal, or Low and Equal. (This defines type of entry to be located by means of LOKUP operation.)

TESTZ Operations: enter up to 3 indicators to be set on whenever a 12-zone (High, positions 54 and 55), or an 11-zone (Low, positions 56 and 57), or any other zone or no zone (Equal, positions 58 and 59) is detected in the field specified in *Result Field* of this line.

SETOF, SETON Operations: enter up to 3 indicators to be set on (SETON) or off (SETOF). If more than 3 indicators are to be set on (or off), specify another SETON (SETOF) statement in subsequent line. Any RPG indicator can be used, except L0 and 00.

Note: Headings High, Low, Equal do not apply to indicators specified in conjunction with SETOF or SETON operations.

Comments 60-74

Enter any desired comments. An asterisk in position 7 must not be used if this type of comment is in a line containing specifications.

OUTPUT-FORMAT SPECIFICATIONS

Filename 7-14

Enter name of each output file. Names must be left justified.

AND/OR Relationships 14-16

Enter AND for records in an AND relationship. Enter OR for records in an OR relationship (positions 14-15).

Type 15

> H — identifies heading line
> D — identifies detail time output
> T — identifies total time output

Stacker Select 16

Enter number of stacker to which cards are to be selected. Leave blank for single-stacker devices.

Note: Stacker select cannot be specified for files that request dual I/O areas.

Space 17-18

Note: At least one entry is required in positions 17-22 if the line is to be printed.

Before Enter 0, 1, 2, or 3 to specify 0, 1, 2, or 3 lines spacing before printing. Leave blank if no space before printing is required.

After Enter 0, 1, 2, or 3 to specify 0, 1, 2, or 3 lines spacing after printing. Enter zero to specify no space after printing.

Indexed Sequential ADD 16-18

The entry ADD should be made in these positions on the specification line that identifies the type of output record

(H, D, or T in position 15) if the output record is being added to an indexed-sequential file.

Skip 19-22

Before. Enter any number from 01 through 12 to specify skipping before printing to channel 01 through 12 of the carriage control tape. Leave blank for no skip before printing.

After. Enter any number from 01 through 12 to specify skipping after printing 01 through 12 of the carriage control tape.

Output Indicators 23-31

Enter up to three RPG indicators to identify files or to describe fields. Positions 23, 26, 29 must contain blank or the letter N.

Field Name 32-37

Enter any field name defined in either Input Specifications or Calculation Specifications. Leave blank for constants specified in Constant or Edit Word. Use field name PAGE to cause automatic page numbering.

Edit Codes 38

Enter Z if leading zeros of a numeric field are to be suppressed and the sign is to be stripped from the rightmost position. Leave blank if leading zeros are not suppressed, or if field specified in Field Name is alphameric or if line contains a constant or an edit word.

Blank After 39

Enter B to reset alphameric output fields to blanks or numeric output fields to zeros. Reset occurs after execution of the specified output operation.

End Position in Output Record 40-43

Enter position in output record to contain rightmost character of output field. To define a field within the key area for each data record in an unblocked indexed sequential file (with key not part of the data), enter a *K* to the immediate left of the high-order digit.

P=Packed/B=Binary 44

Enter P if output data in packed-decimal format. Leave blank if data in standard format.

Constant or Edit Word 45-70

Constant. Enter any required constant. Must be enclosed in apostrophe symbols. May consist of any of the 256 EBCDIC characters. Maximum length is 24 characters.

Apostrophe symbols required within constants must be represented as two consecutive apostrophe symbols.

Edit Word. Enter any edit word to specify editing with respect to punctuation, printing of dollar symbols, sign status, zero suppression, etc. Edit words must be enclosed in apostrophe symbols.

Sterling Sign Position 71-74.

Provided for programs processing sterling currency amounts. Leave blank for all other RPG programs.

APPENDIX E

SUMMARY OF CALCULATION SPECIFICATION OPERATIONS

Add (ADD)

This operation causes the contents of the field or the literal in Factor 2 to be added, algebraically, to the contents of the field or literal in Factor 1. The result field is specified in the Result Field portion of the form.

Zero and Add (Z-ADD)

This operation causes the field specified in the Result Field to be set to zeros and then causes the data contained in the numeric literal or the field in Factor 2 to be placed in the Result Field. Factor 1 is not used in this operation.

Subtract (SUB)

This operation causes the contents of the field or literal in Factor 2 to be subtracted, algebraically, from the contents of the field or literal in Factor 1. The result of this operation is placed in the Result Field specified.

Zero and Subtract (Z-SUB)

This operation causes the negative of the number contained in the literal or the field in Factor 2 to be placed in the Result Field specified.

Multiply (MULT)

This operation causes the contents of the field or literal in Factor 1 to be multiplied algebraically by the contents of the field or the literal in Factor 2. The result of this operation is placed in the Result Field specified.

Divide (DIV)

This operation causes the contents of the field or literal in Factor 1 to be divided by the contents of the field or literal in Factor 2. The result of this operation (quotient) is placed in the specified Result Field. The contents of the field or literal in Factor 2 cannot be zero.

Move Remainder (MVR)

This operation is used to move the remainder from a divide operation to a separate field. If MVR is used, it must immediately follow the divide operation. The divide may not be half-adjusted. The result of the MVR operation may not be half-adjusted.

Move (MOVE)

This operation code causes data characters (starting at the rightmost position) to be moved from the field or literal contained in Factor 2 to the rightmost positions of the result field. If Factor 2 is longer than the result field, the excess leftmost positions of Factor 2 are not moved. If the result field is longer than the field specified by Factor 2, the positions to the left of the data that is moved remains undisturbed.

Move Left (MOVEL)

This operation code causes data characters (starting at the leftmost position) to be moved from the field or literal contained in Factor 2 to the leftmost positions of the Result Field. Factor 1 is not used. If Factor 2 is longer than the result field, the excess rightmost positions of Factor 2 are not moved. If the result field is longer than the field specified by Factor 2, positions to the right of the data that is moved remain undisturbed. When moving data to a numeric field, the sign of the result field is retained except when Factor 2 is as long or longer than the Result Field. In this case, the sign of Factor is assumed.

Move High-To-Low (MHLZO)

This operation moves the zone at the leftmost position of Factor 2 to the rightmost position in the result field. Factor 2 can only be alphameric. The result field can be numeric or alphanumeric.

Move Low-To-High Zone (MLHZO)

This operation moves the zone at the rightmost position of Factor 2 to the leftmost position of the result field. Factor 2 can be numeric or alphameric, but the result field must be alphameric.

Move High-To-High Zone (MHHZO)

This operation moves the zone at the leftmost position of Factor 2 to the leftmost position of the Result Field. Factor 2 and the Result Field must be alphameric.

Move Low-To-Low Zone (MLLZO)

This operation moves the zone at the rightmost position of Factor 2 to the rightmost position of the Result Field. Factor 2 and the Result Field are alphameric or numeric.

Compare (COMP)

This operation causes the contents of the field or literal in Factor 2 to be compared against the content of the field or literal in Factor 2. The outcome of the operation can be used to set on an indicator that has been specified in the Resulting Indicators portion of the form. No result field is specified.

Test Zone (TESTZ)

This operation is used to test the zone of the leftmost position of the alphameric field that is entered in the result field. If the result of the test is a 12-zone, the indicator in positions 54-55 is set "on". If the result is an 11-zone, indicator specified in columns 56-57 is set on. Any other zone sets the indicator in columns 58-59 on.

Exit To A Subroutine (EXIT)

This operation code enables the programmer to transfer control from the RPG program to a user subroutine. Factor 2 contains the name of the subroutine. The name of the subroutine cannot be greater than six alphameric characters; the first character must be alphabetic. Factor 1 and the Result Field are not used.

RPG Label (RLABL)

This operation provides the facility for a subroutine, external to the RPG program, to reference a field in the RPG program. The name of the field to be referenced is entered in the Result Field.

User's Label (ULABL)

This operation enables the RPG program to reference a field contained in a user subroutine. The name of the field to be referenced is entered in the Result Field. This name may be from one to six alphameric characters and the first character must be alphabetic. A ULABL field can be specified on the Calculation or Output Specifications, but cannot be specified on Input Specifications.

Branching or Go To (GOTO)

The operation code GOTO enables branching to occur in the object program. This means leaving one point in the program and beginning operations at some other location in the program. The location of the other routine is identified by a name. This name is entered in Factor 2 and the code GOTO is entered in the Operation portion of the form.

Providing a Label for GOTO (TAG)

The operation TAG provides a name to which the program can branch. Enter this name in Factor 1 and the code TAG in the Operation portion of the form. The name will be used as Factor 2 of the operation code GOTO.

Set Indicators On (SETON)

This operation code causes the indicators specified in positions 54-55, 56-57 or 58-59 to be set on.

Set Indicators Off (SETOF)

This operation causes the indicators specified in positions 54-55, 56-57, or 58-59 to be set off.

Table Lookup (LOKUP)

The LOKUP operation code causes the contents of the field or literal contained in Factor 1 to be used as the search argument. Factor 2 contains the name of the argument table to be searched, and the Result Field contains the table name from which the associated function will be obtained. At least one indicator must be specified in positions 54-59. If an indicator is specified in either the high or low positions, either ascending or descending sequence must be specified for the table on the Extension Specifications.

INDEX